Access for Windows® 95

The Visual Learning Guide

Other Prima Visual Learning Guides

Internet for Windows: America Online 2.5 Edition
Windows 95: The Visual Learning Guide
Word for Windows 95: The Visual Learning Guide
Excel for Windows 95: The Visual Learning Guide
PowerPoint for Windows 95: The Visual Learning Guide
WinComm PRO: The Visual Learning Guide
PROCOMM PLUS for Windows: The Visual Learning Guide
WordPerfect 6.1 for Windows: The Visual Learning Guide
Word 6 for the Mac: The Visual Learning Guide
Cruising America Online
Quicken for Windows: The Visual Learning Guide
1-2-3 for Windows: The Visual Learning Guide
ACT! 2.0 for Windows: The Visual Learning Guide
Excel for the Mac: The Visual Learning Guide
Windows 3.1: The Visual Learning Guide
Excel 5 for Windows: The Visual Learning Guide
PowerPoint: The Visual Learning Guide
Word for Windows 6: The Visual Learning Guide
WordPerfect 6 for Windows: The Visual Learning Guide
WinFax PRO: The Visual Learning Guide

Upcoming Books!

Cruising America Online 2.5
Internet for Windows, Microsoft Network Edition
Sidekick 95: The Visual Learning Guide
Quicken 5 for Windows: The Visual Learning Guide

How to Order:

Individual orders and quantity discounts are available from the publisher, Prima Publishing, P.O. Box 1260BK, Rocklin, CA 95677-1260; (916) 632-4400. For quantity orders, include information on your letterhead concerning the intended use of the books and the number of books you wish to purchase.

Access for Windows® 95

The Visual Learning Guide

Grace Joely Beatty, Ph.D.

David C. Gardner, Ph.D.

David A. Sauer, M.S.

PRIMA PUBLISHING

P™, Visual Learning Guides™, and "The Fastest, Easiest Way to Learn"™ are trademarks of Prima Publishing, a division of Prima Communications, Inc. Prima Publishing™ is a trademark of Prima Communications.

Project Editor: Susan Silva

If you have problems installing or running Access for Windows® 95 (version 7) contact Microsoft at (206) 882-8080. Prima Publishing cannot provide software support.

Prima Publishing and the authors have attempted throughout this book to distinguish proprietary trademarks from descriptive terms by following the capitalization style used by the manufacturer.

Information contained in this book has been obtained by Prima Publishing from sources believed to be reliable. However, because of the possibility of human or mechanical error by our sources, Prima Publishing, or others, the Publisher does not guarantee the accuracy, adequacy, or completeness of any information and is not responsible for any errors or omissions or the results obtained from use of such information.

ISBN: 0-7615-0238-6
Library of Congress Catalog Card Number: 95-70666
95 96 97 98 AA 10 9 8 7 6 5 4 3 2 1
Printed in the United States of America

Acknowledgments

We are deeply indebted to reviewers around the country who gave generously of their time to test every step in the manuscript. Mark Allen, Linda Beatty, Carolyn Holder, Tina Terhark and Dan Terhark cannot be thanked enough!

Linda Beatty and Carolyn Holder performed minor miracles and wrote chapters under extreme time pressures. Once again, Linda and Carolyn, you saved our collective necks!

We are personally and professionally delighted to work with everyone at Prima Publishing.

Linda Miles, technical editor; Suzanne Stone, copy editor; Danielle Foster and Shawn Morningstar, interior layout; Katherine Stimson, indexer; and Paul Page, cover design, contributed immensely to the final product.

Bill Gladstone and Matt Wagner of Waterside Productions created the idea for this series. Their faith in us has never wavered.

Joseph and Shirley Beatty made this series possible. We can never repay them.

Asher Schapiro has always been there when we needed him.

Paula Gardner Capaldo and David Capaldo have been terrific. Thanks, Joshua and Jessica, for being such wonderful kids!

Thanks to Cyrus and Jemmie for their continued support.

We could not have met the deadlines without the technical support of Ray Holder, our electrical genius, Diana M. Balelo, Frank E. Straw, Daniel W. Terhark and Martin J. O'Keefe of Computer Service & Maintenance, our computer wizards. Thank you all!

Contents at a Glance

Customize Your Learning

Prima Visual Learning Guides are not like any other computer books you have ever seen. They are based on our years in the classroom, our corporate consulting, and our research at Boston University on the best ways to teach technical information to non-technical learners. Most important, this series is based on the feedback of a panel of reviewers from across the country who range in computer knowledge from "panicked at the thought" to sophisticated.

Each chapter is illustrated with color screens to guide you through every task. The combination of screens, step-by-step instructions, and pointers makes it impossible for you to get lost or confused as you follow along on your own computer.

LET US KNOW...

We truly hope you'll enjoy using the book and Access for Windows® 95. Let us know how you feel about our book and whether there are any changes or improvements we can make. You can contact us through Prima Publishing at the address on the title page or send us an e-mail letter. Our Internet address is write.bks@aol.com. Thanks for buying the book. Have fun!

Joely Beatty, David Gardner, and David Sauer

ACCESS FOR WINDOWS 95

Part I: Creating and Using a Predesigned Database

CHAPTER 1

Creating a Database Using the Database Wizard

Database programs have had the well-deserved reputation of being difficult to use and almost impossible to learn. Access has changed all that. The Access Wizard asks you to make a few simple decisions, then the Wizard does all the work for you. Gone are the tedious hours of dealing with nitpicking details and trying to figure out arcane technobabble commands. Gone are the unfriendly screens filled with a jumble of ugly blanks. If it's your job to clean up an information mess in your office, using Access will make you look like a miracle worker. (Don't let on that it's easy; act like it took weeks of working overtime!) In this chapter, you will do the following:

✔ Create a database using the Access Database Wizard

OPENING ACCESS

1. **Click** on the **Start button**. The Start Menu will appear.

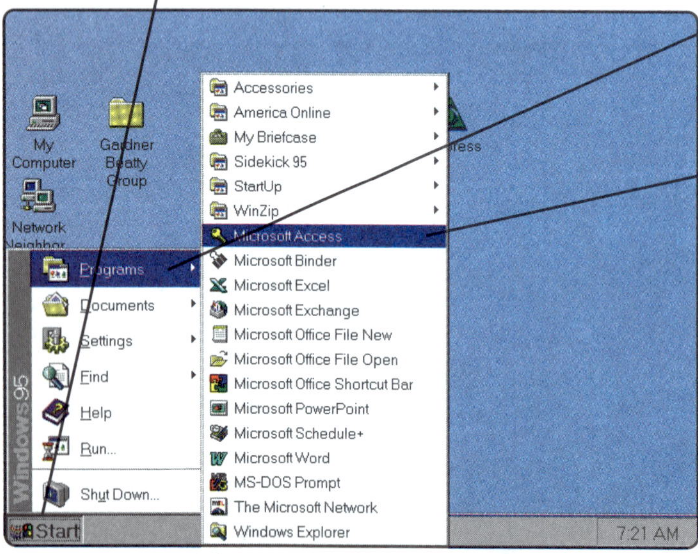

2. **Move** the **cursor** over **Programs**. The Programs menu will appear.

3. **Click** on **Microsoft Access**. (It may be named Access on your menu.) Access will open. Because of the many ways in which Windows 95 can be customized, your menu will contain different items than you see here.

The Access logo screen will display for a moment, then the Microsoft Access dialog box shown in the example below will appear.

STARTING THE WIZARD

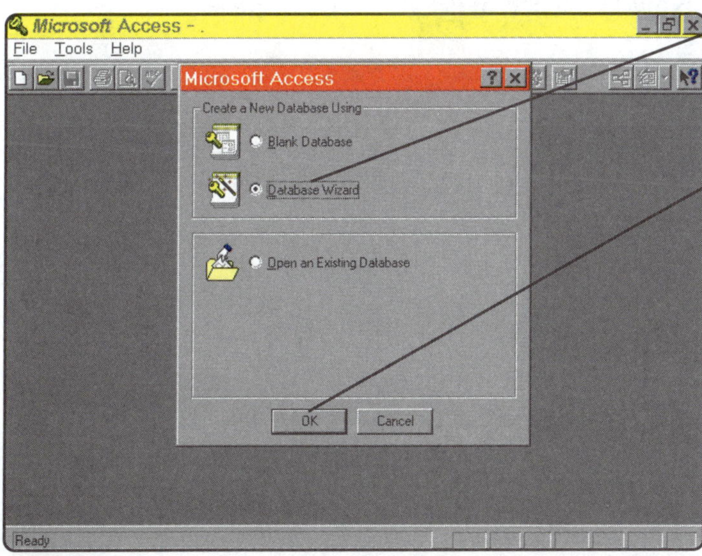

1. **Click** on **Database Wizard** to place a dot in the circle.

2. **Click** on **OK**. The New dialog box will appear.

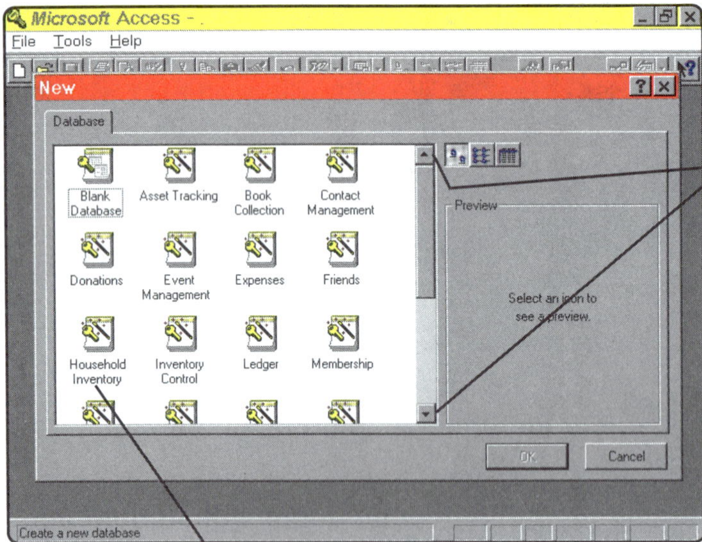

The New dialog box lists types of databases that the Wizard can create for you.

3. **Click** on the ▼ or ▲ to scroll up and down and view all of the choices.

4. **Click** on a **choice** and notice that a preview appears on the right.

You're not limited to exactly what is shown for a given database. You can add and delete elements from the model. You can also rename the model to be more descriptive of your database.

For our example, we're going to use the Household Inventory model and customize it.

5. **Click twice** on **Household Inventory**. The File New Database dialog box will appear.

Access is set up to save the database in the My Documents folder (directory) on the C drive.

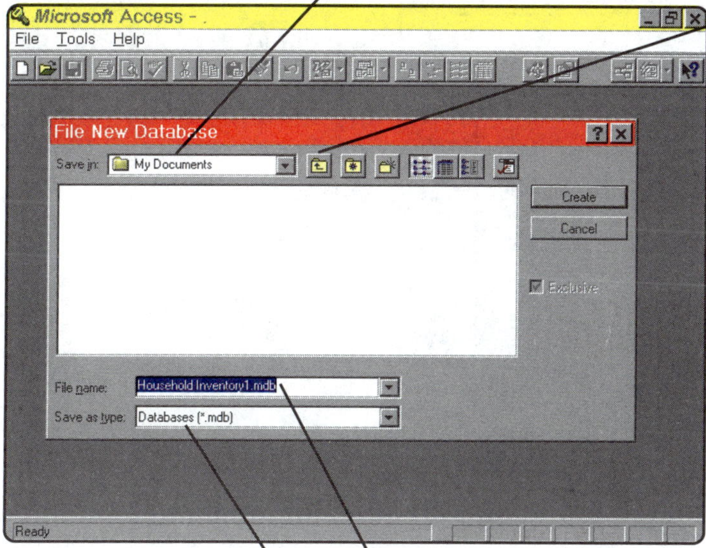

If you want to save the database in another folder, click on the Up One Level button to the right of My Documents to go back to (C:). A list of all folders on the C drive will appear in the box below (not shown here). Click twice on the appropriate folder.

For our example, we'll accept the "My Documents" folder that is set up by Access as the default folder.

6. **Type** a **name** for the database if you want to change the one that comes with the Wizard. For our example we're going to keep the name you see here.

7. **Confirm** that the Save as type text box shows "Databases (*.mdb)." This means that Access will automatically add the .mdb extension to the filename. Your screen may not show the .mdb extension. Either way is correct.

8. **Click** on **Create**. The file will be stored on your computer with the name and in the folder you selected.

CREATING THE DATABASE

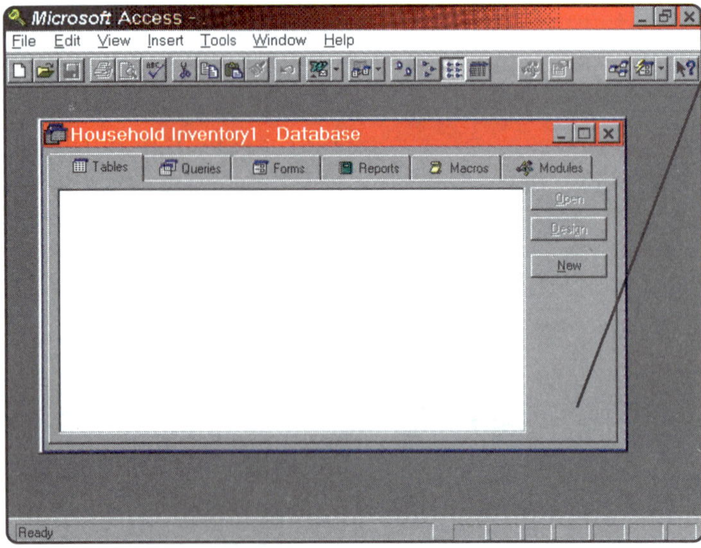

As Access starts to create the database, this dialog box will display on your screen for a few moments. Next, the Database Wizard dialog box you see below will appear.

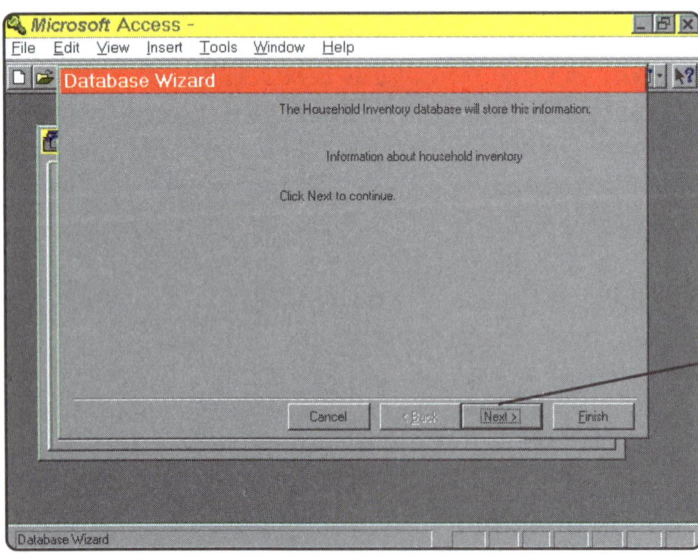

This dialog box lists the components of the database that the Wizard will create. If you find that you need others later, you can add them. You can also delete any that you do not need later.

1. **Click** on **Next >**. Another Database Wizard dialog box will appear.

Adding Fields to the Tables

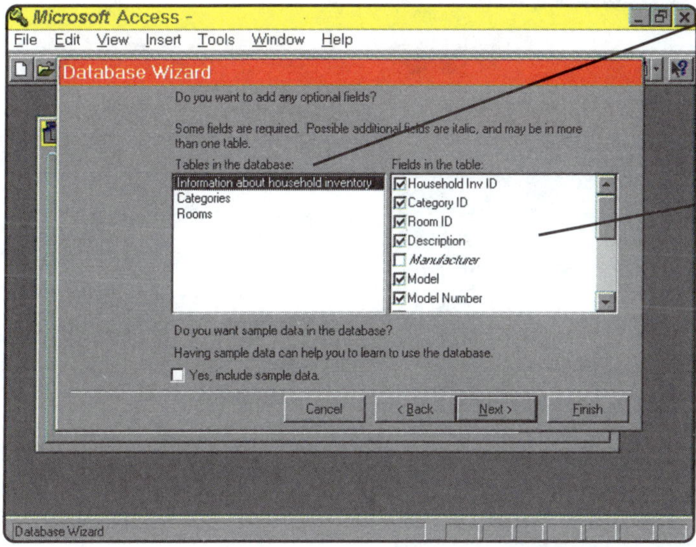

The left side of this dialog box lists the tables that come with the Household Inventory database.

The right side shows the fields that are in the highlighted table. In this example, the fields on the right are in the Information About Household Inventory table. In this section, you'll add fields to the high-lighted table.

1. **Click** on the ▼ to scroll through all of the fields in the Household Inventory Table.

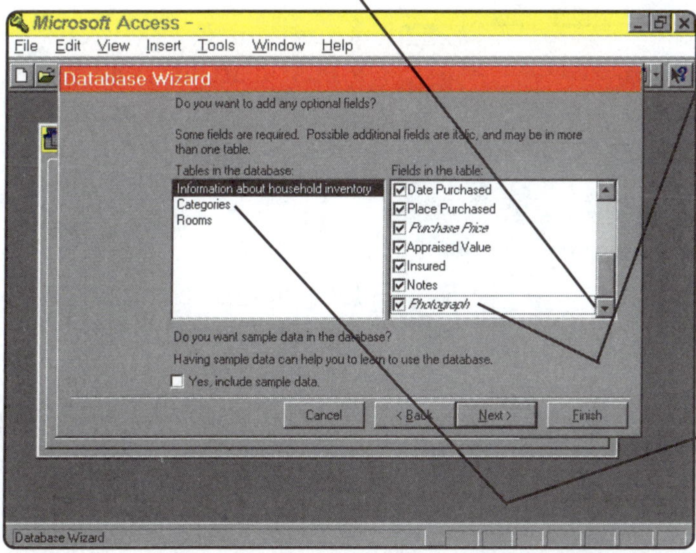

2. In our example, we **clicked** on ***Manufacturer***, ***Purchase Price***, and ***Photograph*** to put a ✔ in each box.

You can click on any field to *remove* the ✔ if you do not want to include the field in the table.

3. **Click** on **Categories** and **scroll** through the **fields** on the right to see what information will be in your database.

Including Sample Data in the Database

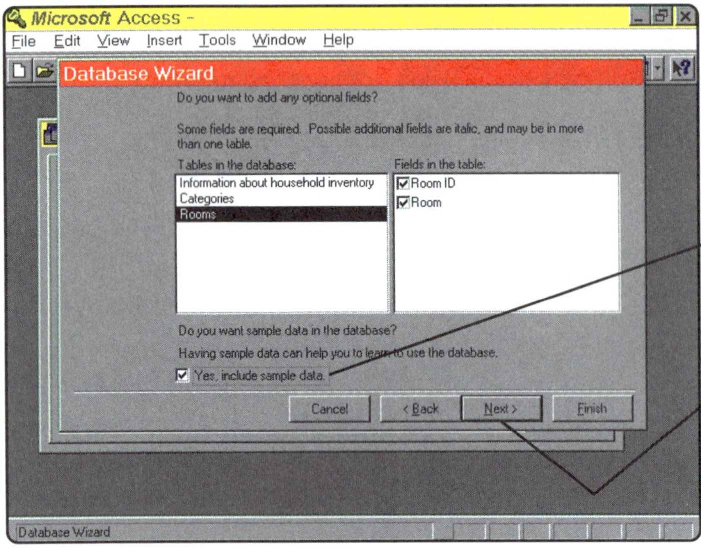

Access can include sample data in the tables you create. This is very useful if you're just learning how to work with a database.

1. **Click** on **Yes, include sample data** to place a ✔ in the box.

2. **Click** on **Next >**. Another Database Wizard dialog box will appear.

Choosing a Display Style

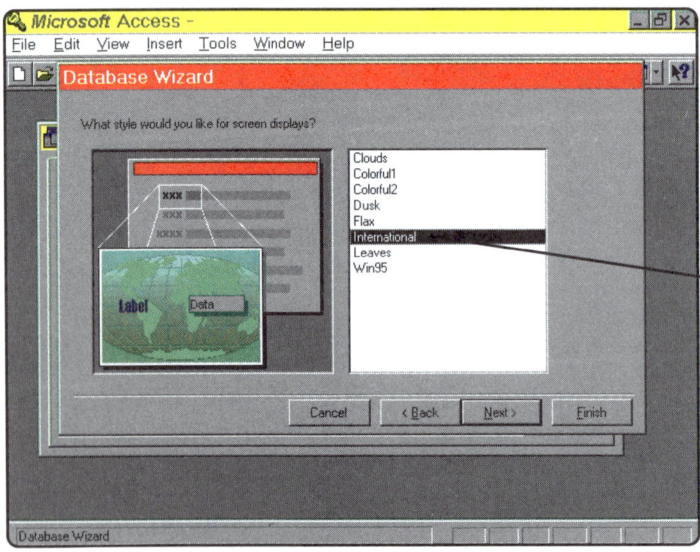

Access can display your forms on artistic backgrounds. This dialog box shows samples of the screen display styles for the forms that the Wizard will create.

1. **Click** on each of the **style names** to see what they all look like. A sample will appear in the left half of the dialog box. This is an example of the "International" style design.

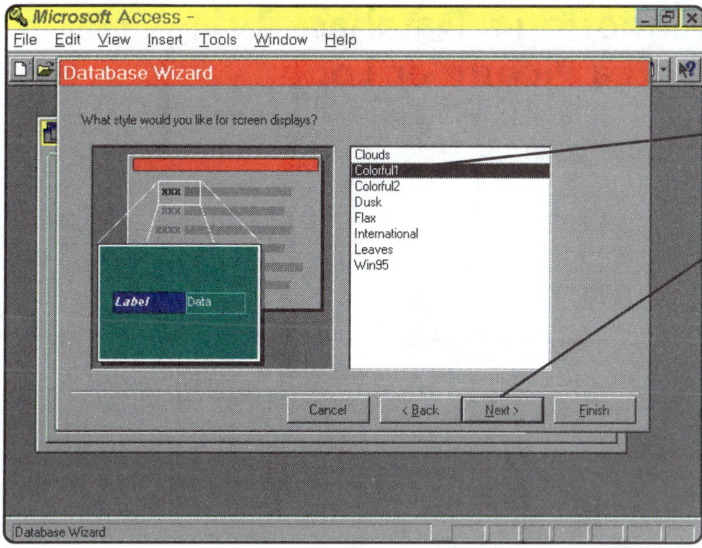

For our example, we'll choose "Colorful1."

2. **Click** on **Colorful1** to select that style.

3. **Click** on **Next >**. Another Database Wizard dialog box will appear.

Don't worry if all of these choices don't make much sense to you at this time. After the database is created by the Wizard, we'll explore and refine it. During that process you'll see how it all fits together.

Choosing a Report Style

This dialog box lets you select from several styles for reports, printouts, and letters that the database will produce.

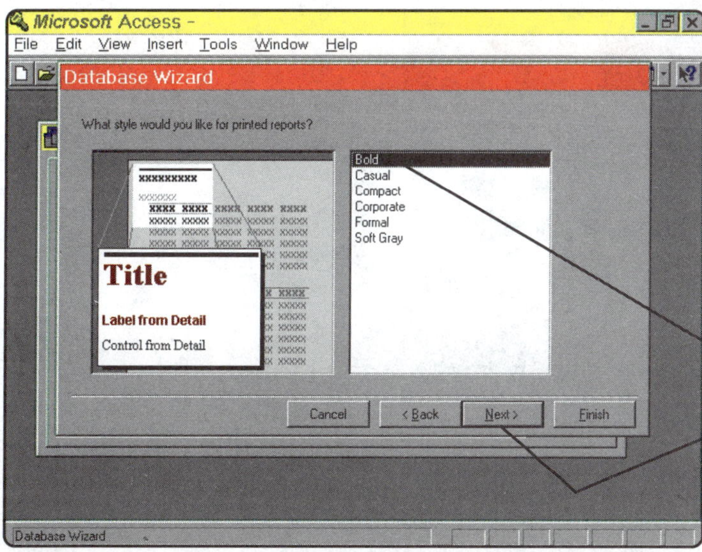

1. **Click** on each of the **style names** to see what they look like. A sample will appear in the left half of the dialog box.

For our example, we'll select the one called "Bold."

2. **Click** on **Bold**.

3. **Click** on **Next >**. Another Database Wizard dialog box will appear.

Choosing a Database Title and a Picture or Logo

You can give your database any name you want. In this dialog box, Access also lets you put a picture or logo on screens and reports.

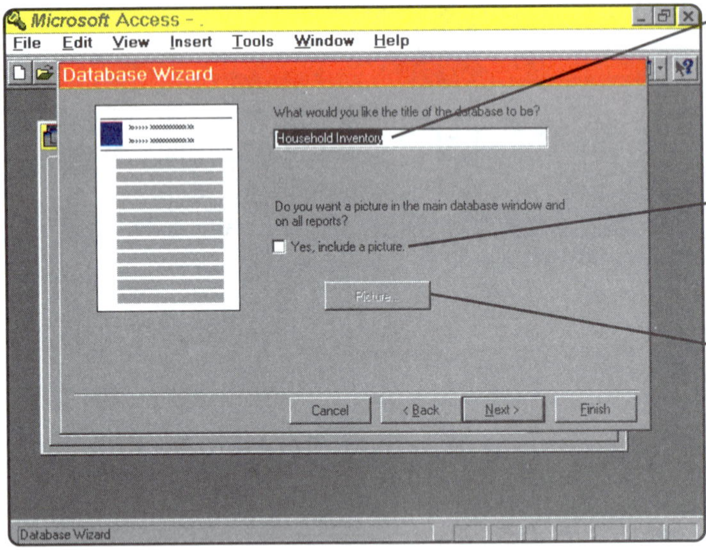

1. **Type** the **database name** in this box. For our example, we're using the name you see here.

2. **Click** on **Yes, include a picture** to put a dot in the circle.

3. **Click** on **Picture** to add your logo (or a graphic) to reports. The Select Picture dialog box will appear.

Before we started, we copied a picture to the "My Documents" directory for this example. Access lets you use several graphic file formats. We'll show you how to add a graphic to other screens later.

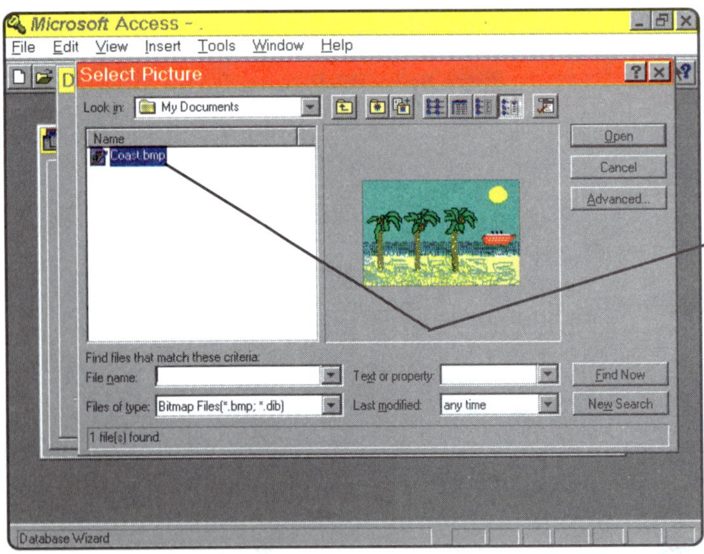

4. **Click twice** on the **file name**. The Select Picture dialog box will close.

If you are not selecting a picture file at this time, click on Cancel. The Database Wizard dialog box will reappear.

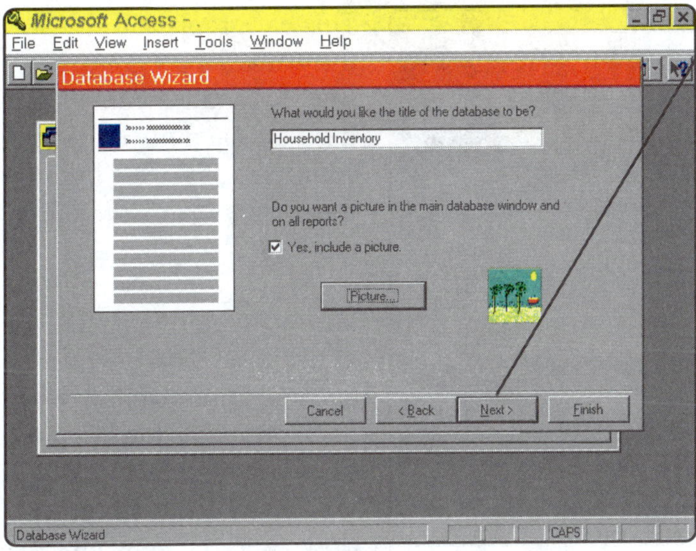

5. **Click** on **Next >**. Another Database Wizard dialog box will appear.

Finishing Up

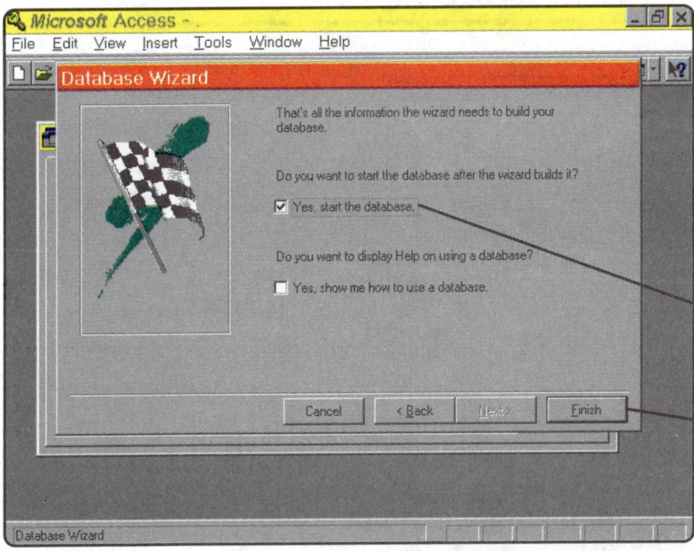

Though our book will be showing you how to use the database, we'll ask the Wizard to include help. We'll also ask it to start (open) the database after it has created it.

1. **Click** on **Yes, start the database**.
2. **Click** on **Finish**.

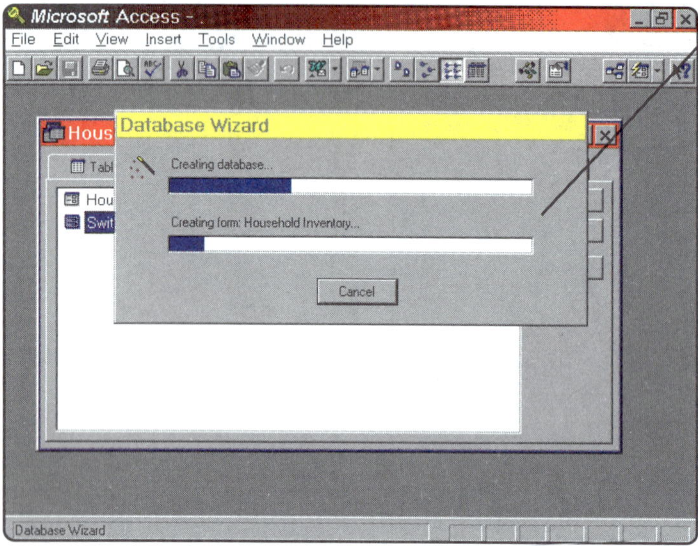

This bar graph will show the Wizard's progress. For several minutes you'll hear hard disk activity on your computer as Access builds the database and all of its associated files.

Various windows will appear and disappear or become minimized in the background as the Wizard does its work. Eventually, your hard disk will settle down and the new database will open.

EXITING THE DATABASE AND CLOSING ACCESS

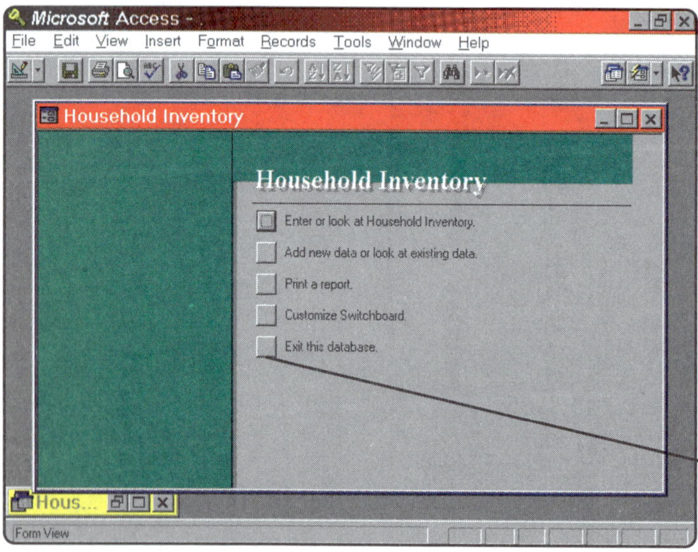

This screen, called the *Switchboard* form, acts as a central point from which to work with the database. We'll show you more about it in later chapters. Right now, we'll have you close this database and reopen Access so you can see what it looks like when you open a saved database.

1. **Click** on **Exit this database**. The database will close.

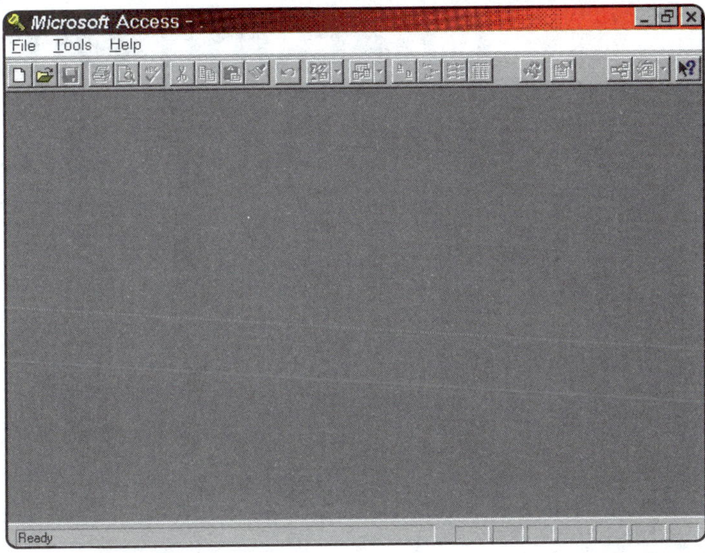

2. **Click** on the **Close Button** (X) in the Microsoft Access title bar. Access will close.

OPENING AN EXISTING DATABASE

Access lists the most recently opened databases in the opening dialog box.

1. **Repeat steps 1 to 3** at the beginning of this chapter to open Access. The Microsoft Access dialog box will appear.

It's all done! Your new database appears on the list of "Existing Databases." All your tables are set up, their fields are defined, and reports, forms, etc. are all ready for use. If you've struggled with other database programs in the past, you're probably not convinced. We'll explore everything that the Database Wizard did for us in subsequent chapters.

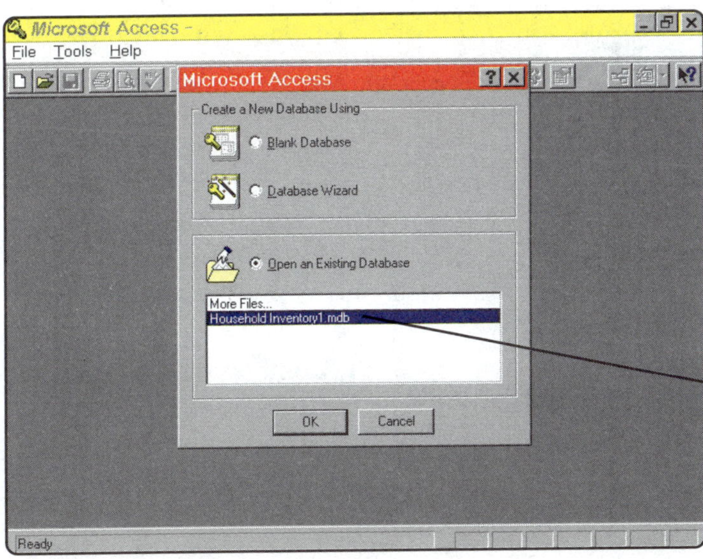

2. **Click twice** on **Household Inventory.mdb** (or the name of your database). Remember, the name of your database may not show the .mdb extension.

CHAPTER 2

Checking Out the Database

If you told the Wizard to include sample data in the database, you can use the samples to check out the way this database is set up and see how the information is organized. You can then decide how you want to customize the design of the database. In this chapter you will do the following:

- ✔ Switch to the Database view
- ✔ View and print the tables that show how the information is organized
- ✔ Learn how to move around in tables
- ✔ Learn how to use the Switchboard

OPENING THE DATABASE WINDOW

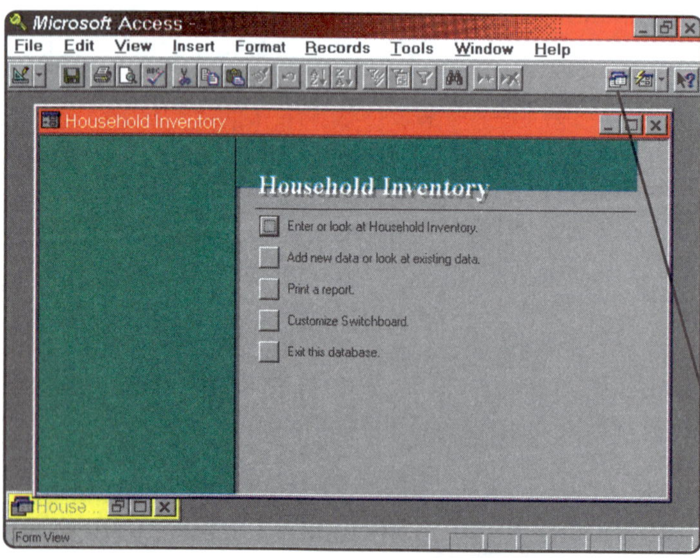

The opening screen in Access shows the Switchboard and a minimized Database window. The Switchboard is created by the Wizard and gives you access to all functions in the database. You'll learn about the Switchboard later in this chapter. Right now, you'll go to the Database window.

1. **Click** on the **Database button** on the toolbar. The database will be opened to window size.

VIEWING A TABLE

If you chose to include sample data in your database, you can see it in the Database tables. In this example, you'll view the Categories Table.

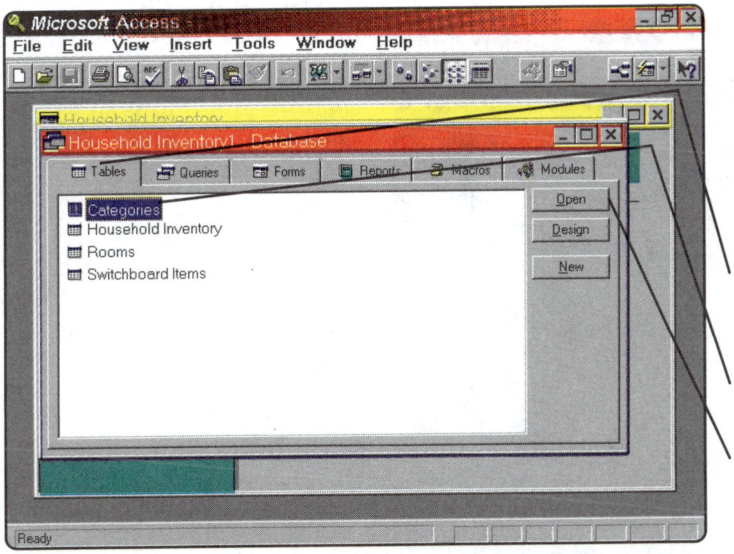

Note: These are the tables that come with the Household Inventory database. If you chose another type of database, you'll have other tables listed here.

1. **Click** on the **Tables tab** to bring it to the front.
2. **Click** on **Categories**.
3. **Click** on **Open**. The Categories: Table window will open.

Printing a Table

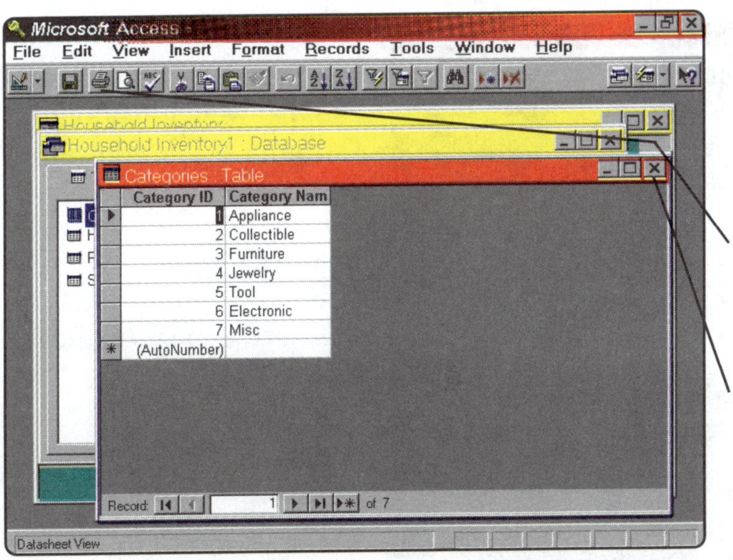

This list shows the categories that the Wizard set up. You can print the list and use it as a basis for customizing your own categories.

1. **Click** on the **Print icon** in the toolbar to print a copy of the Categories table.
2. **Click** on the **Close button** (X) to close this window.
3. **Repeat** the **steps** on this page to view and print other categories.

SEEING RELATIONSHIPS BETWEEN TABLES

The point of a database is that the tables (and the data they contain) are related. One or more pieces of information from any given table should be on one or more other tables. In this section, you'll look at some of the relationships in the Household Inventory database.

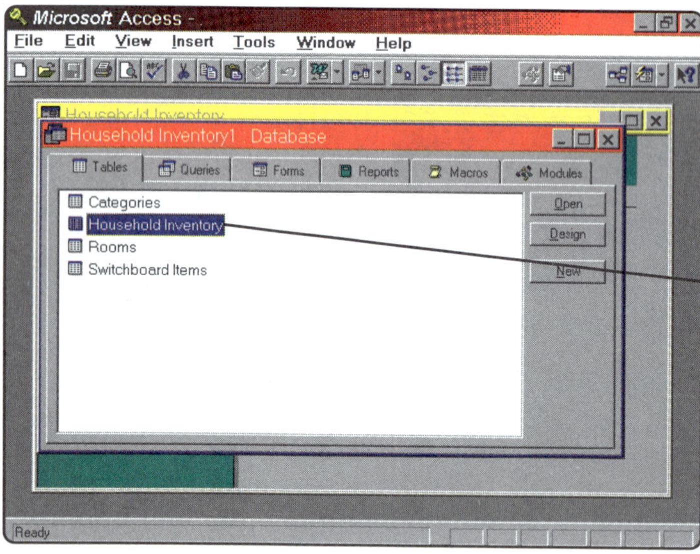

1. In the Database window you see here, **click twice** on **Household Inventory**. (Clicking twice is the same thing as clicking once and then clicking on Open.)

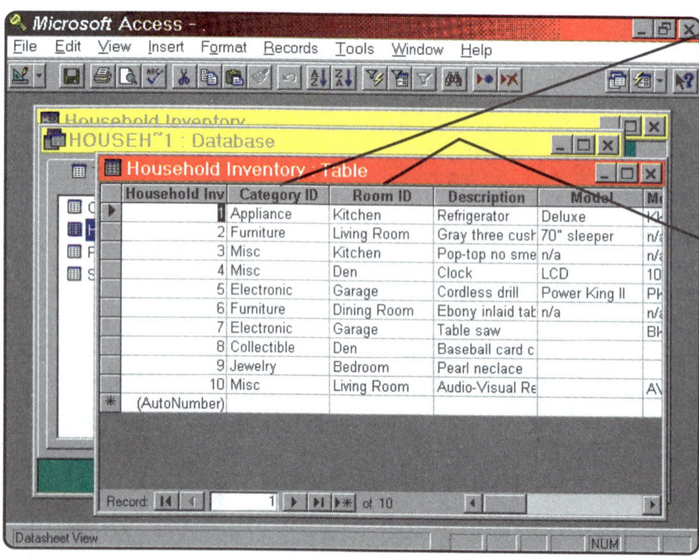

Notice that the Category ID column contains the categories that were listed in the Categories table you viewed on the previous page.

Notice the entries in the Room ID column. You'll see these same rooms in the Rooms table.

MOVING AROUND IN A TABLE

The Household Inventory table contains quite a bit of data.

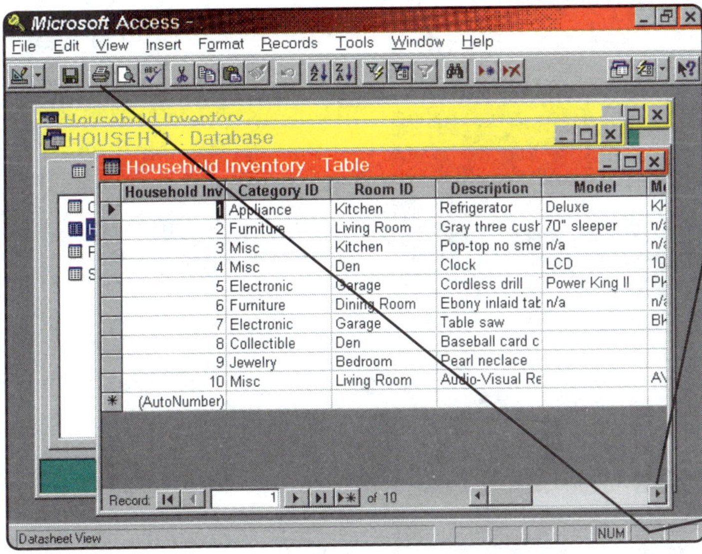

Scrolling Through a Table

1. **Click repeatedly** on the ▸ on the scroll bar to scroll through the table to see the type of data included in this table. You'll learn how to use the other buttons on the scroll bar in Chapter 3, "Adding and Editing Data in a Table."

2. **Click** on the **Print icon** to print this table. This table will take three pages to print.

In Chapter 5, you'll learn how to use the Print Preview feature and how to print so that the long edge of the paper is at the top (called printing in Landscape).

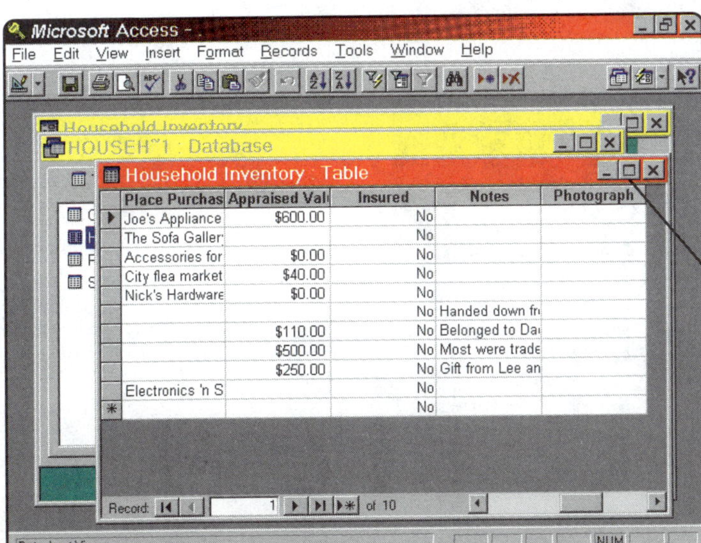

Enlarging the View

When a table contains a lot of data, it's helpful to maximize the view.

1. **Click** on the **Maximize button** (□) on the title bar. The table will fill the screen. Maximizing this table, by the way, maximizes the Database window and everything included in it.

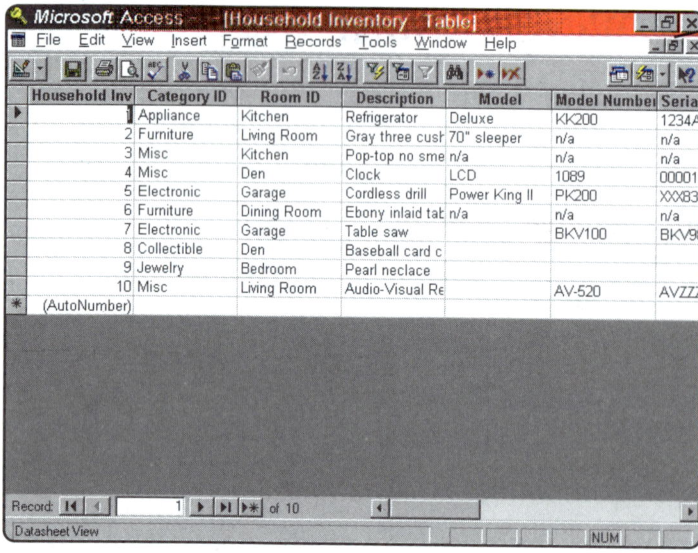

2. **Click** on the **Restore button** (🗗) on the right side of the menu bar. The table will be restored to its previous size. Be careful not to click on the top Restore button on the right side of the Access title bar. This will make the entire program smaller. If this happens, click on the Maximize button (☐) to maximize the program window.

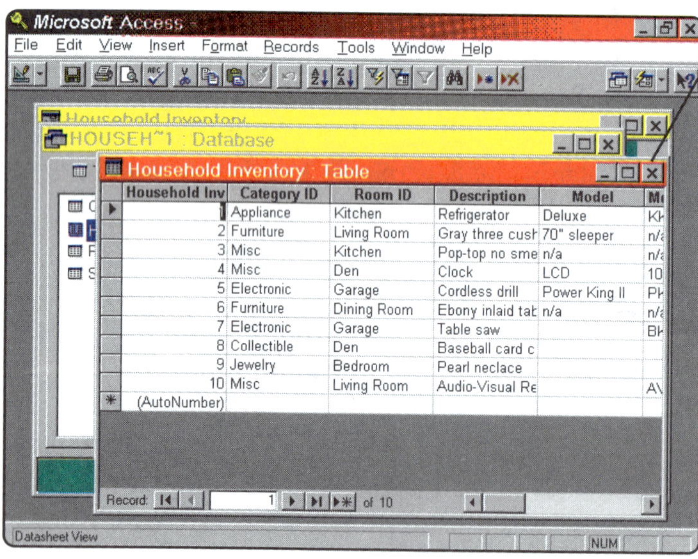

3. **Click** on the **Close button** (☒) on the right side of the table's title bar to close the table.

VIEWING OTHER TABLES

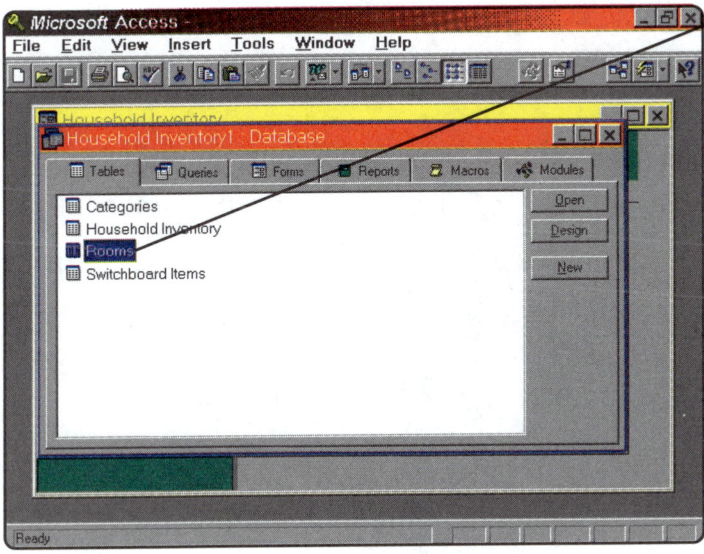

1. **Repeat** the **steps** previously described in this chapter to view, print and close the Rooms table.

When you view the Switchboard Items table, you'll notice that it is different from the other tables. This is a table that was created by the Wizard. It contains the commands necessary to create the Switchboard window. You can print this table if you want, but don't let it intimidate you. You don't need to know anything about how this table was created in order to work with the Switchboard.

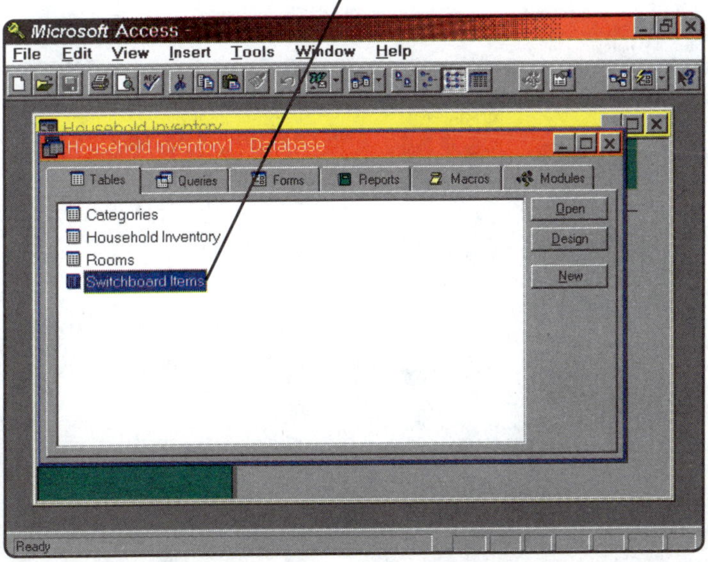

VIEWING FORMS

1. If the Database window you see here is not already on your screen, **repeat step 1** at the beginning of this chapter to open it.

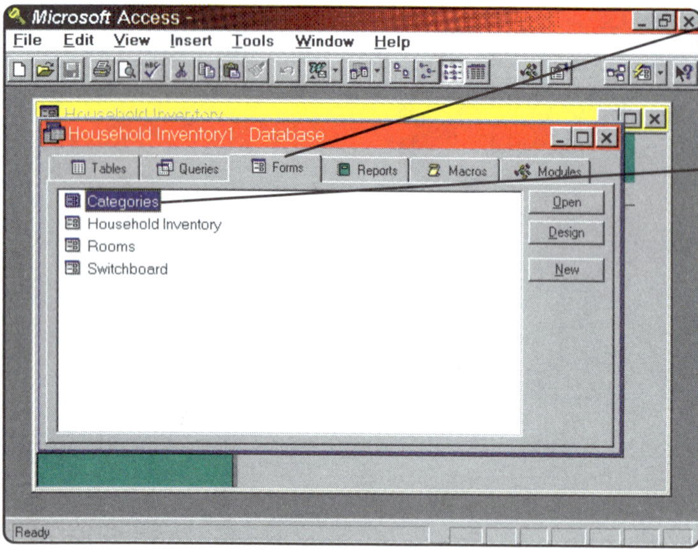

2. **Click** on the **Forms tab** to bring it to the front of the window.

3. **Click twice** on **Categories**. A Categories window will appear.

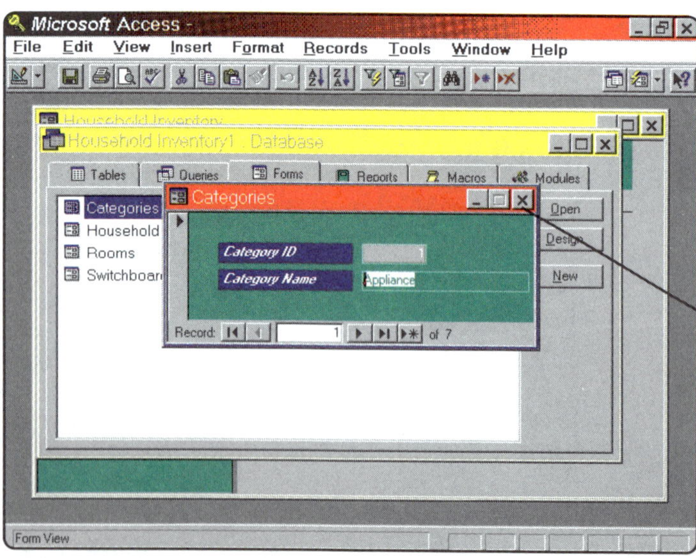

This is the form in which you enter and create categories. You can also enter and create categories in the Table view. You'll learn how to use this form in Chapter 3.

4. **Click** on the **Close button** (X) to close this window.

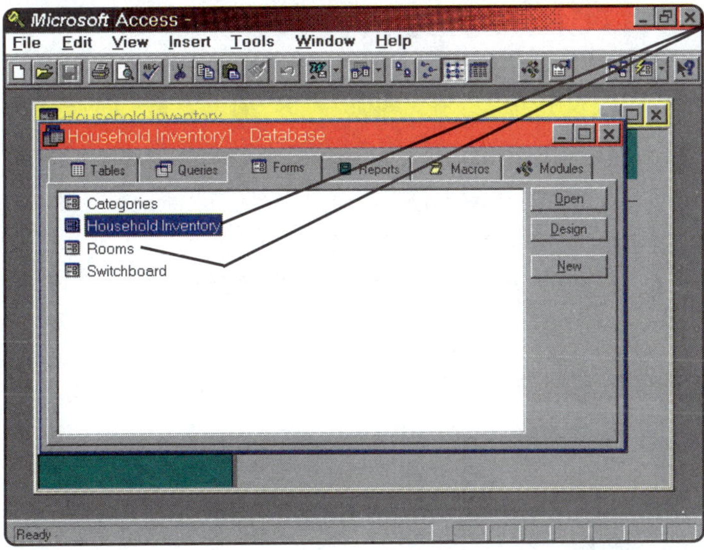

5. **Repeat steps 3 and 4** to view the Household Inventory and the Rooms forms.

6. **Click twice** on **Switchboard**. This will take you to the Switchboard form.

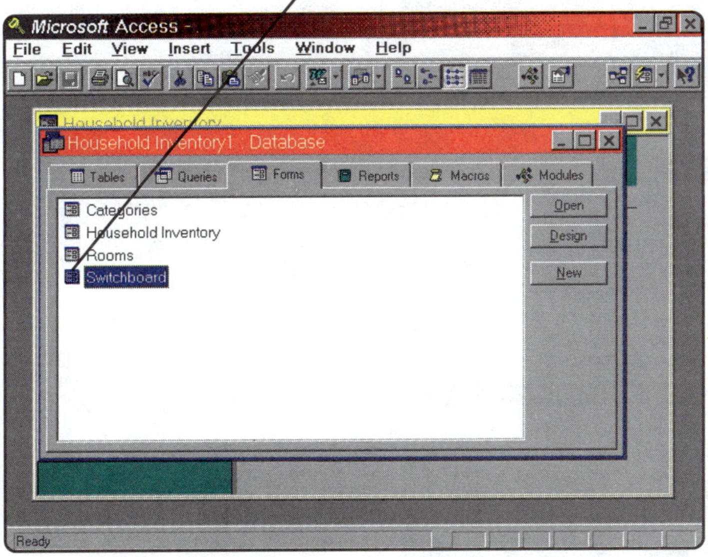

SWITCHING BETWEEN OPEN WINDOWS

If you've been following along with this chapter, you just moved to the Switchboard. The Database window is still open, even though you may not be able to see it. There are two ways to get back to the Database window.

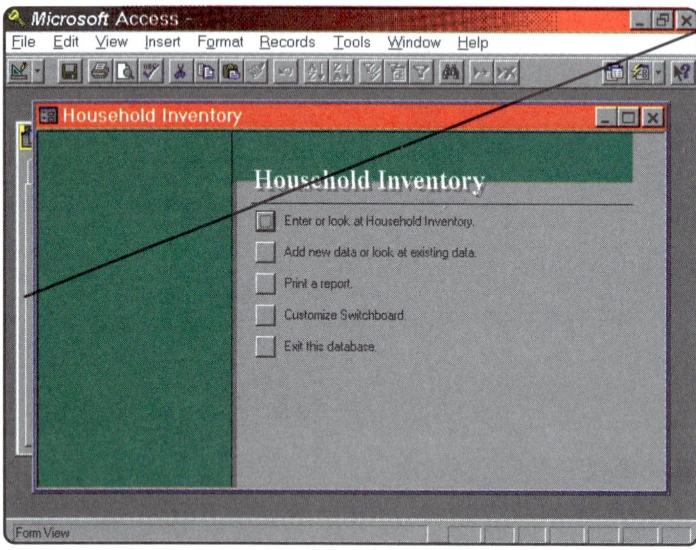

1. If you can see any part of the Database window, **click** on the **part** you can see to bring it to the foreground.

Or, if no part of the Database window is showing:

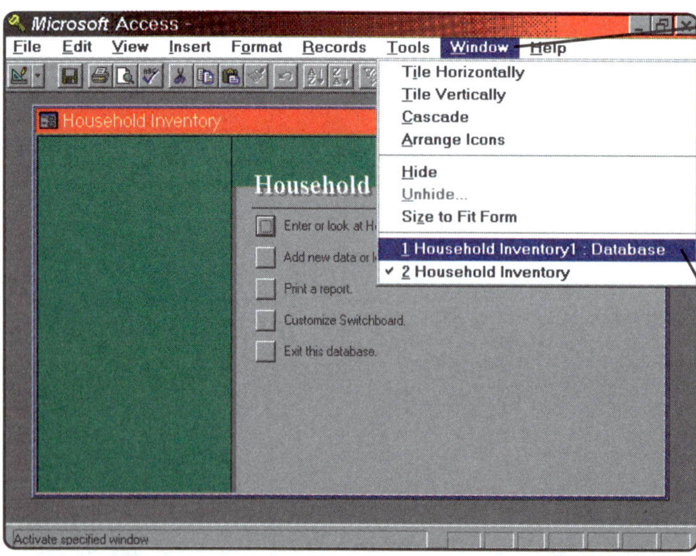

2. **Click** on **Window** in the menu bar. The Window menu will appear.

All open windows will be listed at the bottom of this menu.

3. **Click** on **Household Inventory1: Database**. That window will come to the foreground.

EXPLORING REPORTS

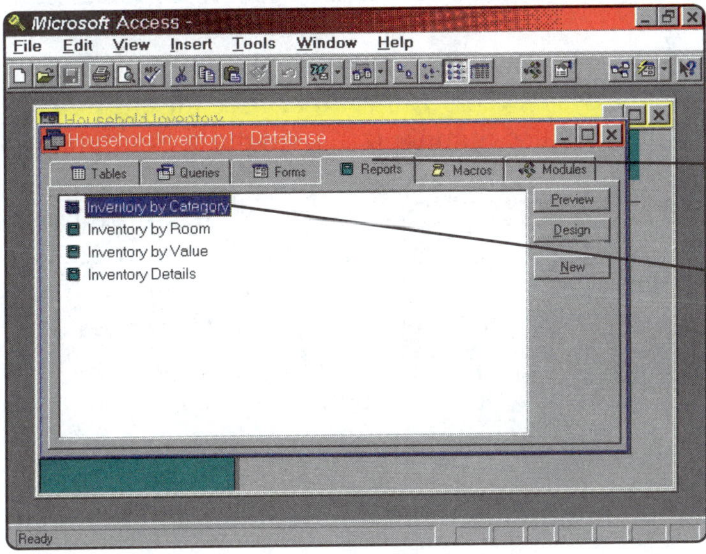

There are four reports that come with the Household Inventory database.

1. **Click** on the **Reports tab** to bring it to the front.

2. **Click twice** on **Inventory by Category** to open the report.

This report has a graphic because we added it in Chapter 1.

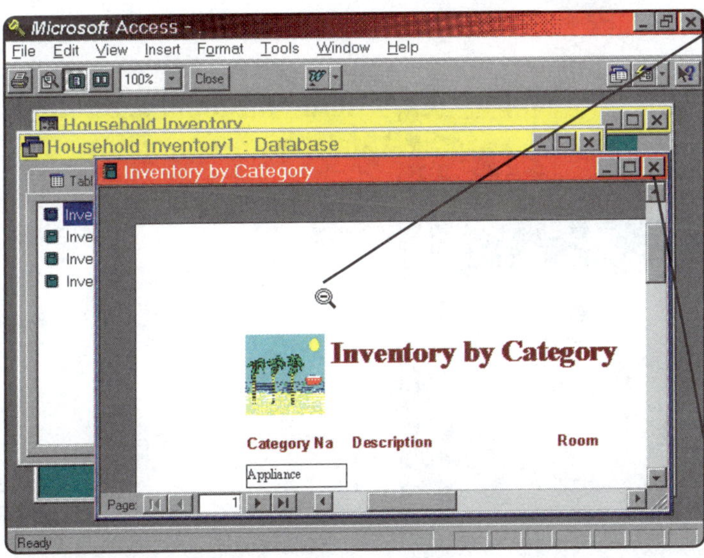

3. **Place** the **mouse pointer**, which has changed into the shape of a magnifying glass with a minus sign in the center, **on the report**.

4. **Click** the **mouse button**. The report will appear in Print Preview view (not shown here).

5. **Click** the **mouse button** on the report once again. It will be restored to full view.

6. **Click** on the **Close button** (X) to close the report.

MINIMIZING THE DATABASE WINDOW

The Database window is, in fact, the database. So don't close it unless you want to close the entire database. Keep it minimized or in the background.

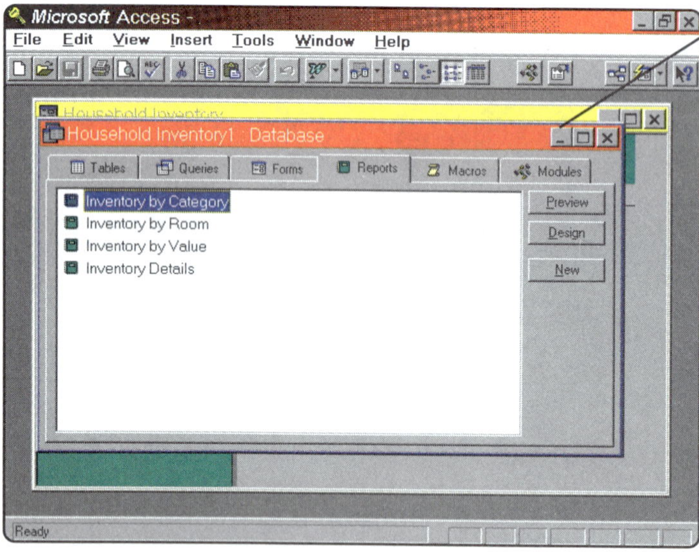

1. **Click** on the **Minimize button** (▁) on the right of the Database window. The window will become a small rectangle at the bottom of your screen.

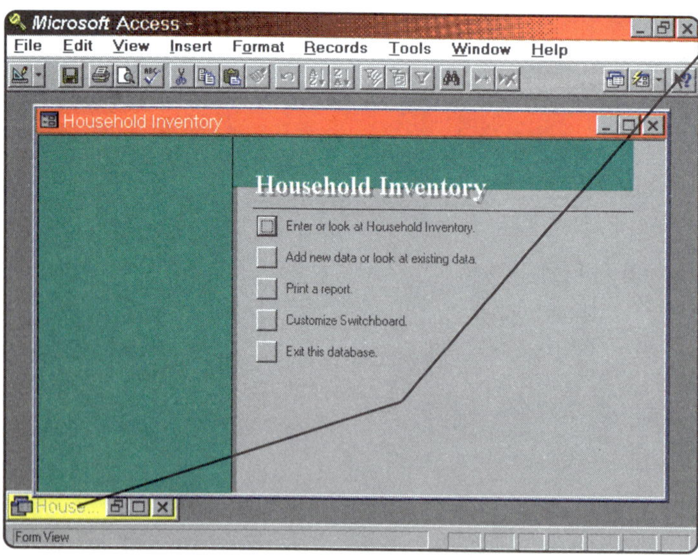

Here's the minimized database.

USING THE SWITCHBOARD TO GET AROUND

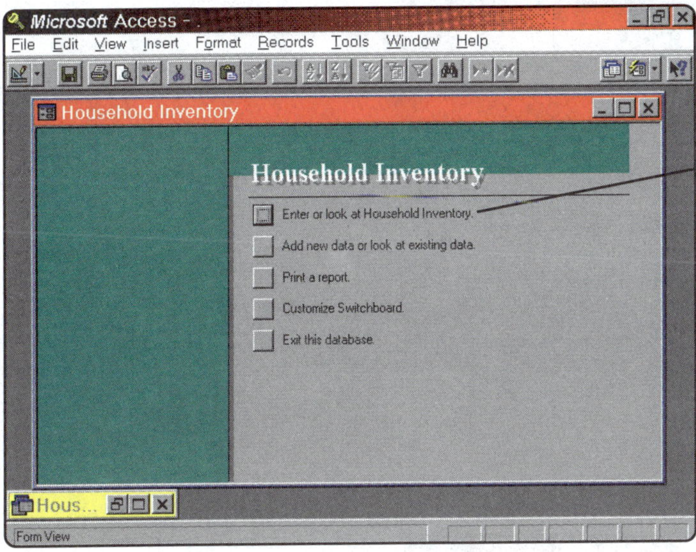

The Switchboard will take you all through the database.

1. **Click** on **Enter or look at Household Inventory**. You'll go to the Household Inventory form.

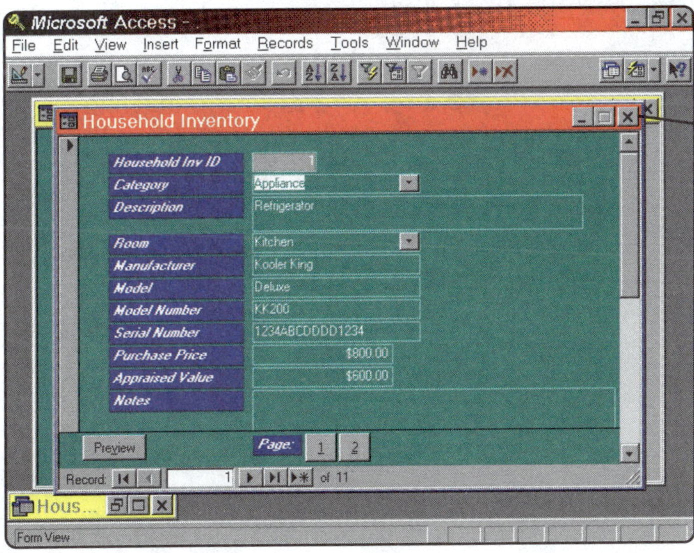

This is the Form view of the Household Inventory.

2. **Click** on the **Close button** ([X]) to close it. You'll go back to the Switchboard.

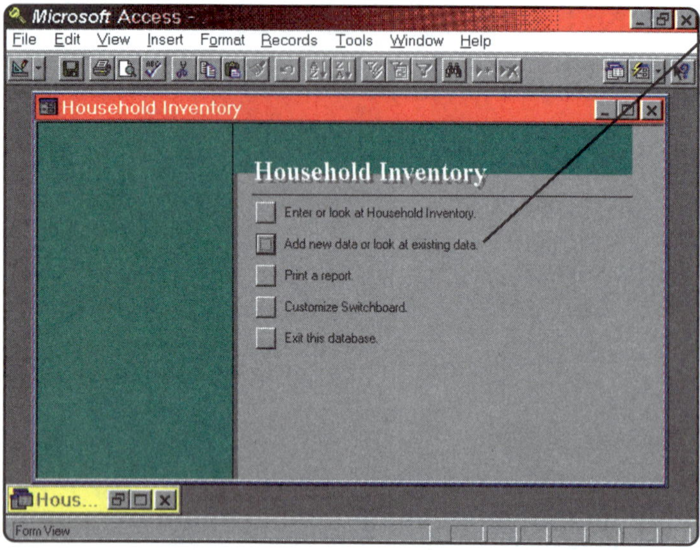

3. **Click** on **Add new data or look at existing data**. This will take you to another list of choices in the Switchboard.

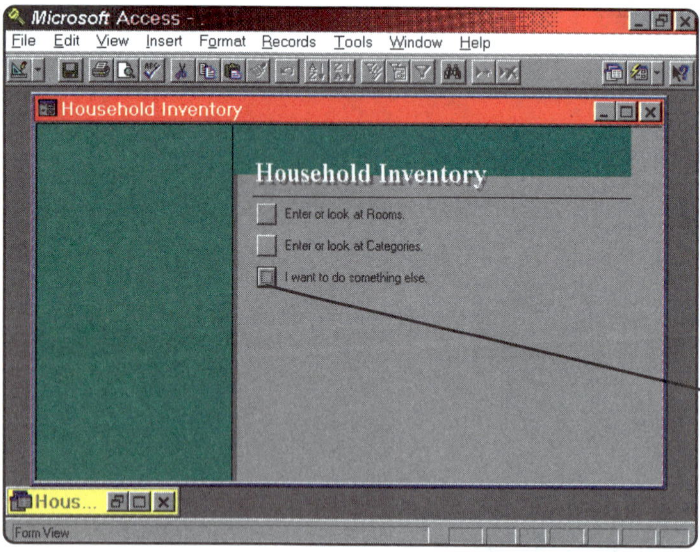

Clicking on the first choice will take you to a form that shows Rooms. Try it on your own.

The second choice will take you to a form that shows Categories. Try it on your own.

4. **Click** on **I want to do something else** to go back to the original Switchboard screen.

EXITING THE DATABASE

You can close the Household Inventory database and stay in Access.

1. **Click** on **Exit this database**. The Household Inventory database will close.

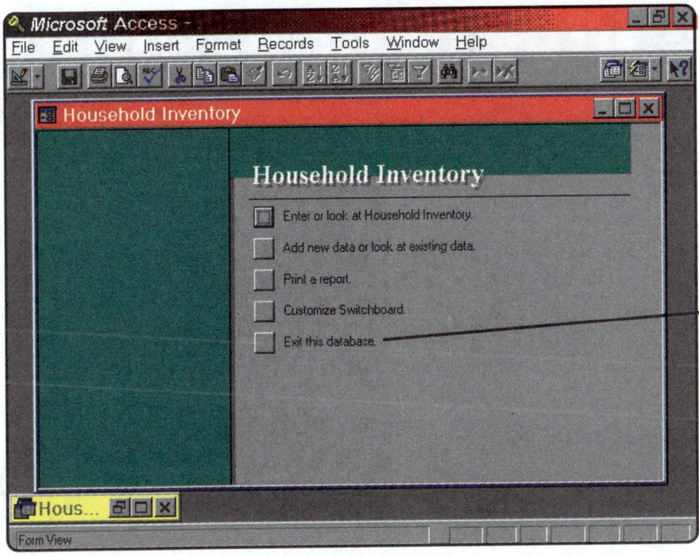

Opening the Database from Within Access

1. **Click** on the **Open tool** in the toolbar. It's the second tool from the left. The Open dialog box you see here will appear.

This dialog box lists databases that have been saved to the folder shown in the Look in box.

2. **Click twice** on the **name** of your database to open it.

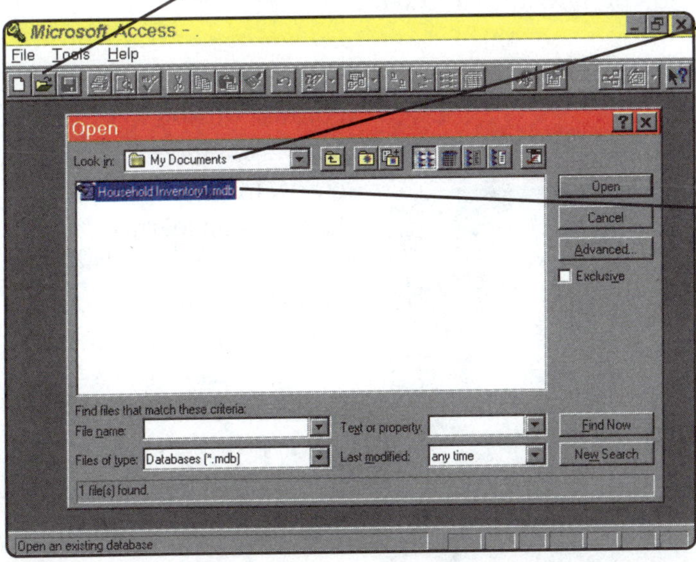

CHAPTER 3

Adding and Editing Data in a Table

The examples in this chapter are based on the Household Inventory database. If you selected another database in Chapter 1, you will have different tables. In this chapter, you will do the following:

- ✔ Review the relationship between tables
- ✔ Add a new category to the Category table
- ✔ Add a new item to the Household Inventory table
- ✔ Change a room on the Rooms table
- ✔ Sort data in a table

OPENING THE DATABASE WINDOW

When you open the database, you'll see the Switchboard window and a minimized Database window. In the next section you'll use the Database window, so you'll restore it to window size first.

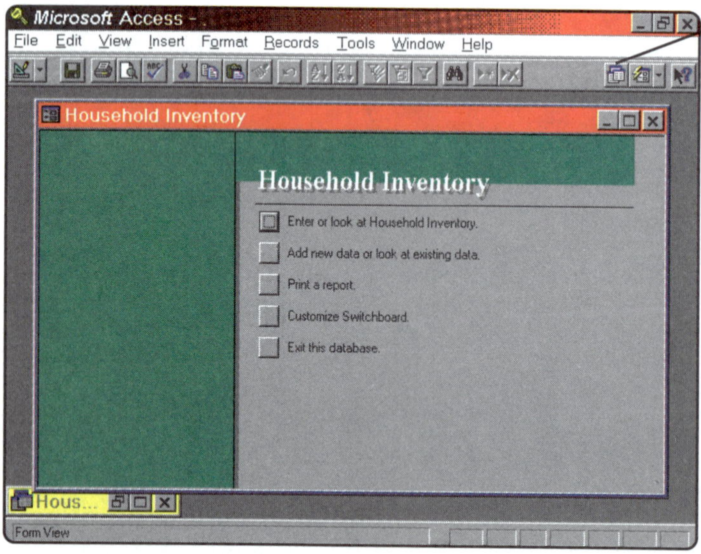

1. **Click** on the **Database window button** to bring the Database window to your screen. In the previous chapter, you learned how to open the minimized Database window and how to use the Window menu to switch between open windows. The Database Window button is another way to open the Database window.

UNDERSTANDING THE RELATIONSHIP BETWEEN TABLES

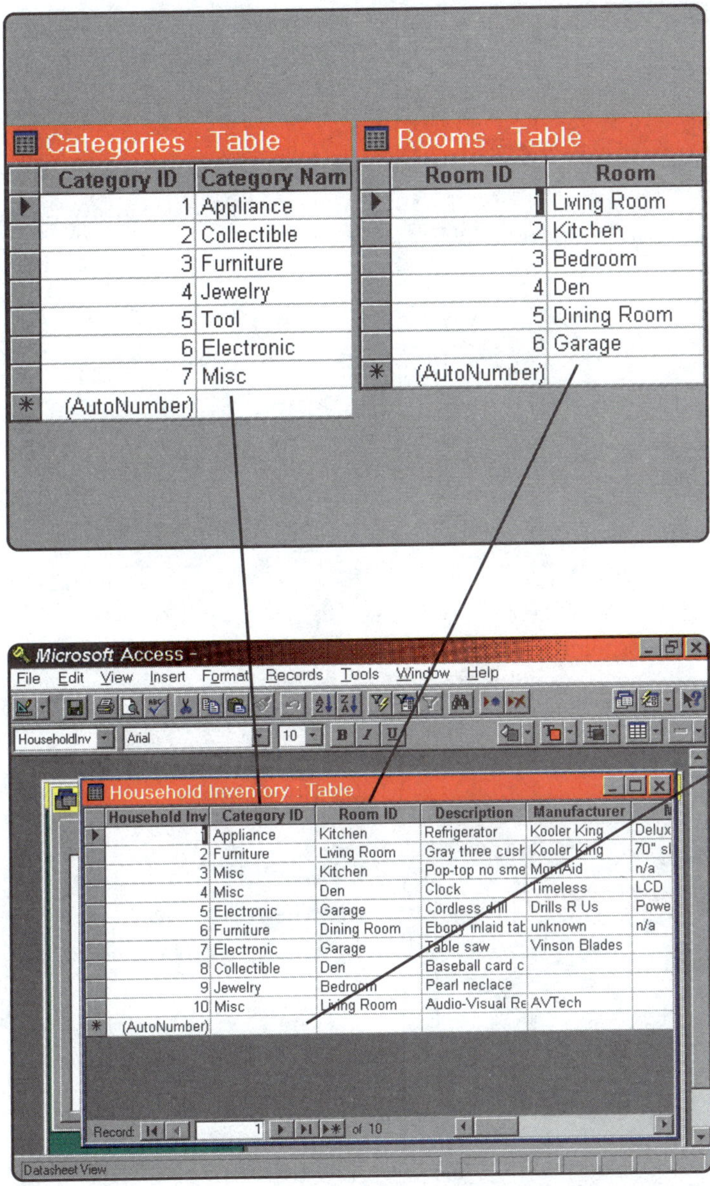

Regardless of what type of database you chose to create in Chapter 1, you will have tables that work the same way the tables in these examples work. Tables like the Categories table and the Rooms table that you see here are called *primary* tables.

Primary tables control what information you can enter into fields (columns) that are related to them. (You can change the level of control, but that's an advanced procedure we won't discuss here.)

If, for example, you try to type "Office Equipment" in the Category ID field on the Household Inventory table you see here, Access is set up to block the entry because there is no "Office Equipment" listing in the Categories table shown above. In order to enter an item that you want to categorize as office equipment, you must first add "Office Equipment" to the Categories table.

ADDING CATEGORY NAMES TO THE CATEGORIES TABLE

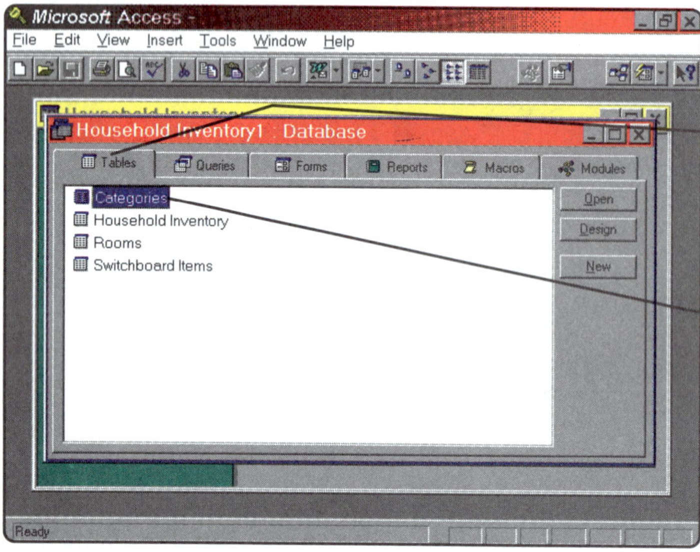

The actual process of adding data to a table is easy.

1. In the Database table you see here, **click** on the **Tables tab** to bring it to the front of the window.

2. **Click twice** on **Categories**. The Categories: Table will appear.

3. **Click** on the **New Record button** (▸✳) on the bottom scroll bar. You'll go to the next available record row as you see here.

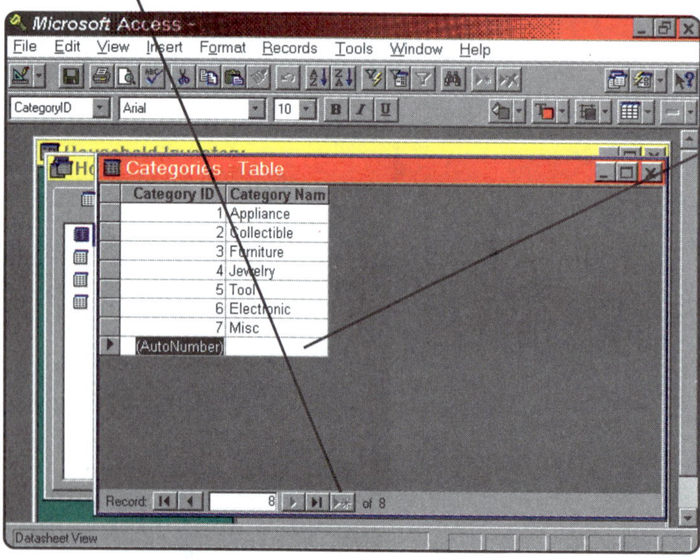

(AutoNumber) will be highlighted.

4. **Press** the **Tab key** on your keyboard to move to the Category Name field.

5. **Type Office Equipment**. The row will automatically be given the next available number and "(AutoNumber)" will move to the next row. The new record 8 is saved automatically.

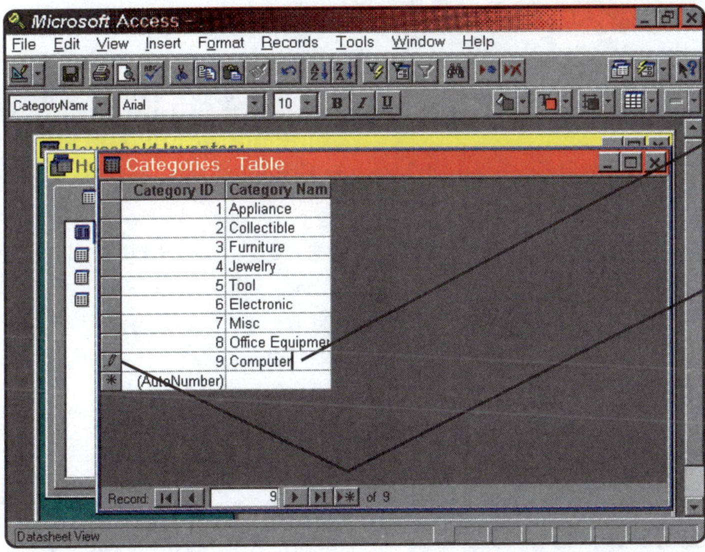

6. **Press** the **Tab key** to go to the next line.

7. **Press** the **Tab key** to move to the Category Name field. **Type Computer**.

Notice the pencil icon to the left of line 9. This indicates that you are in edit mode.

MOVING AROUND IN A TABLE

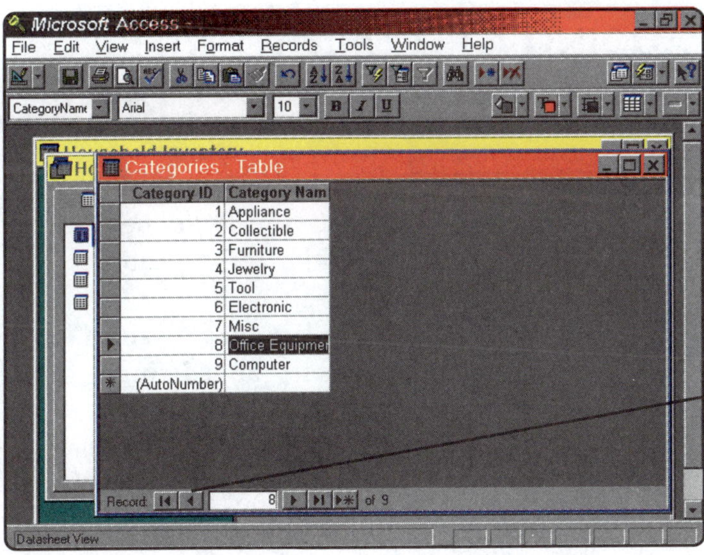

The table in this example is small, which means that you can move around simply by clicking on the line you want to go to. If, however, the table were larger, the buttons on the bottom scroll bar would be very helpful.

1. **Click** on the **Back One Record button** (◂) on the scroll bar. "Office Equipment" will be highlighted in the previous record line as you see here. Because record 8 is now the current record, you'll see a ▸ to the left of the record.

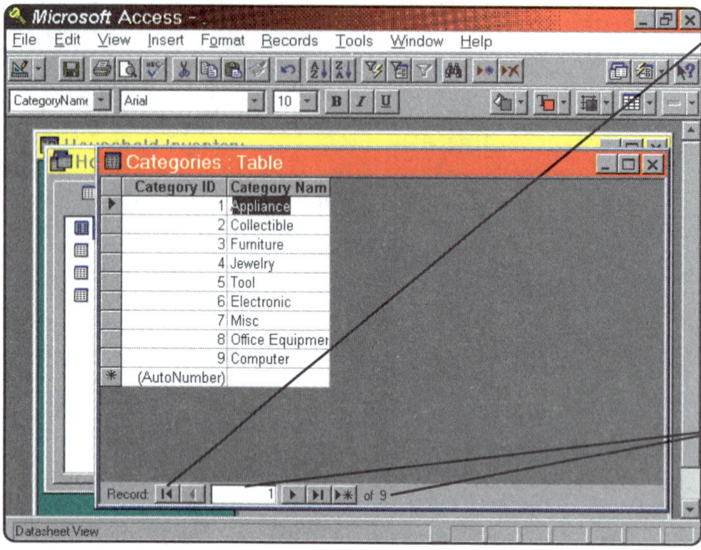

2. **Click** on the **First Record button** (|◀) on the scroll bar. "Appliance" in the first line will be highlighted as you see here.

Note: The Last Record button (▶|) and the Forward One Record button (▶) work the same way.

The current record (the record where the cursor is located) is shown here. The total number of records is shown to the right.

3. **Click** on the **Close button** (☒) on the right of the Categories: Table title bar to close this table.

ADDING A RECORD TO THE HOUSEHOLD INVENTORY TABLE

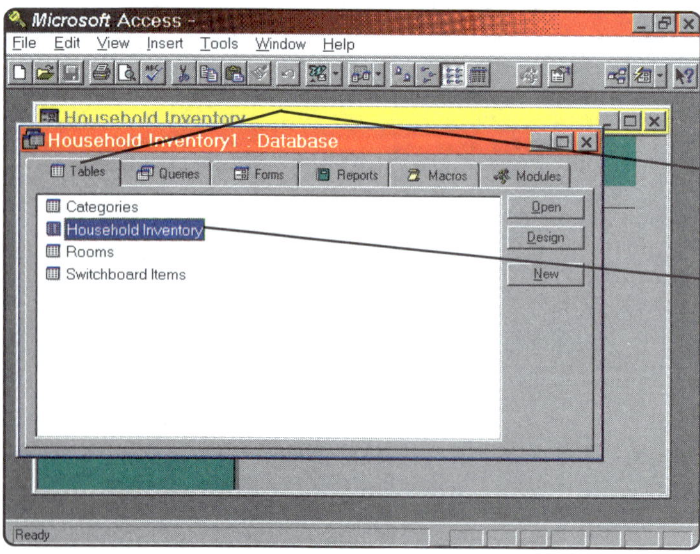

In this section you'll add data directly to the Household Inventory table.

1. **Click** on the **Tables tab** if it is not already in the front.

2. **Click twice** on **Household Inventory**. The Household Inventory: Table will appear.

3. **Click** on the **New Record button** on the bottom scroll bar to go to the next available line.

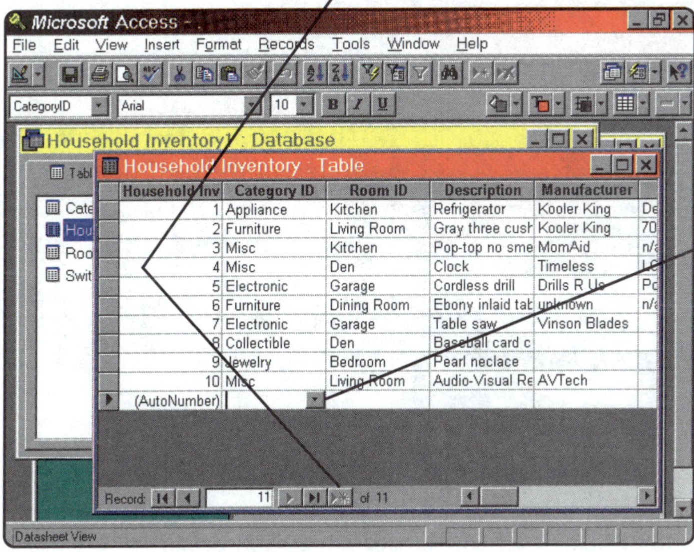

4. **Press** the **Tab key** to move to the Category ID field. (You can also press the Enter key to move between fields.)

Notice that a List button (▼) appears when you tab into or click on this field.

5. **Click** on the **List button** (▼). A list of the categories on the Categories table will appear.

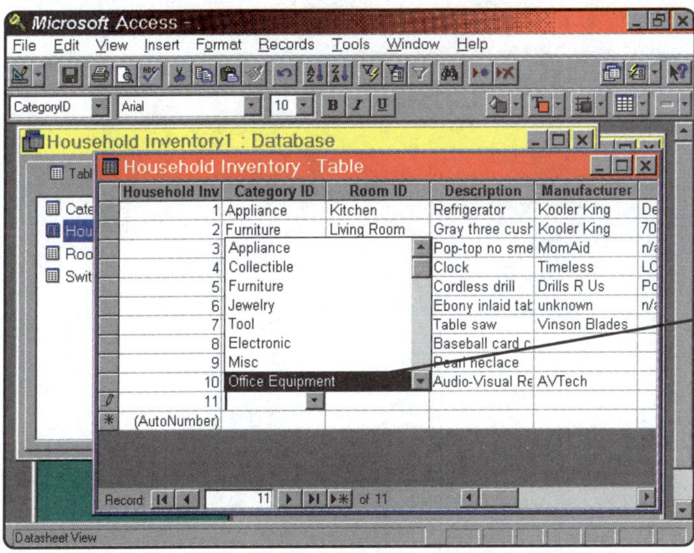

Notice that the categories you added to the Categories table appear on this list. (Actually, "Computer" is not immediately noticeable because you have to scroll down to see it.)

6. **Click** on **Office Equipment**. It will be entered into the field. (You can also type the first couple of letters of the category and it will be filled in.)

7. **Press** the **Tab key** to move to the next field.

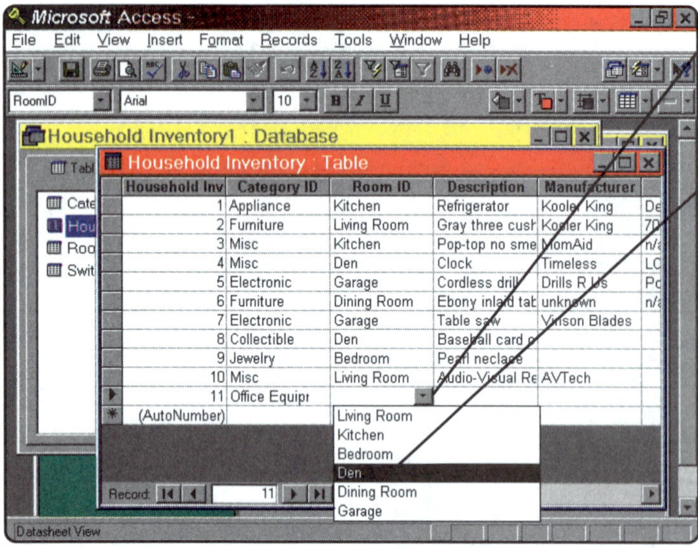

8. **Click** on ▼ in the Room ID field. A list of rooms will appear.

9. **Click** on **Den.**

10. **Press** the **Tab key** to move to the next field.

11. **Continue** to enter data in each field as appropriate and click on the Tab key to move to the next field.

Note: If you're following along with the chapters in this book, the Household Inventory table contains a field for a photo. Tab past that field. You'll learn how to enter a photo in a form in Chapter 4.

When you are in the last field for this record (row) and you press the Tab key, this new record will be recorded in the database.

UNDOING A SAVE

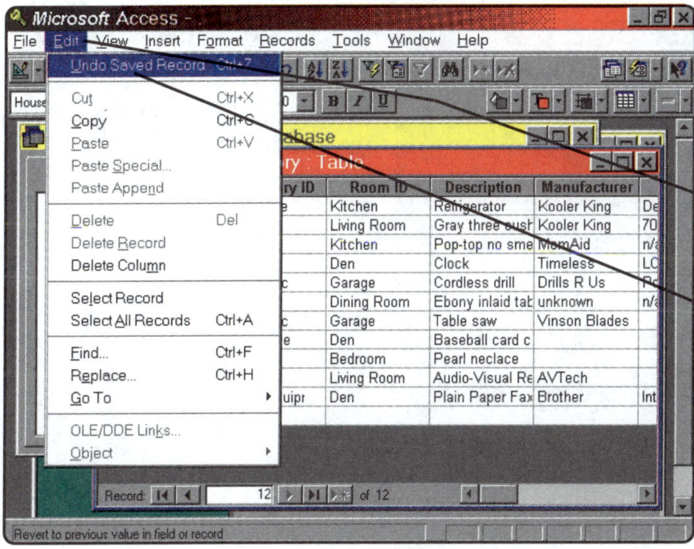

You can undo a save *if* you do it immediately after you enter the record and *before* you do anything else.

1. **Click** on **Edit** in the menu bar to open the Edit menu.

2. **Click** on **Undo Saved Record**. The record will be unsaved.

3. A message box, not shown here, will ask if you want to delete the record. **Click** on **Yes**. The record will be removed.

DELETING A RECORD

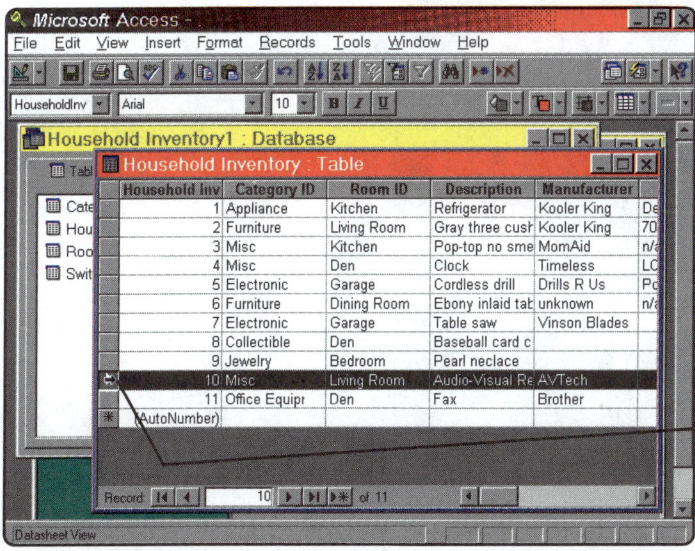

Once a record has been created, its number is carved in stone. If you delete record 10, for example, you cannot assign its number to another record. In your files, you will have records for numbers 1 through 9, record 10 will not be there, and the numbering will begin again at 11.

1. **Click** on the gray **record button** to the left of record 10. The entire line will be highlighted.

2. **Click** on **Edit** in the menu bar. The Edit menu will appear.

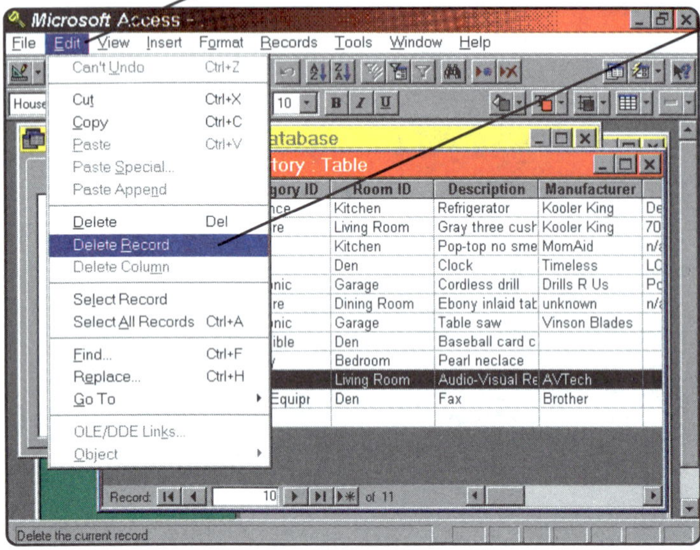

3. **Click** on **Delete Record**. The row will be deleted, and a Microsoft Access message box will appear.

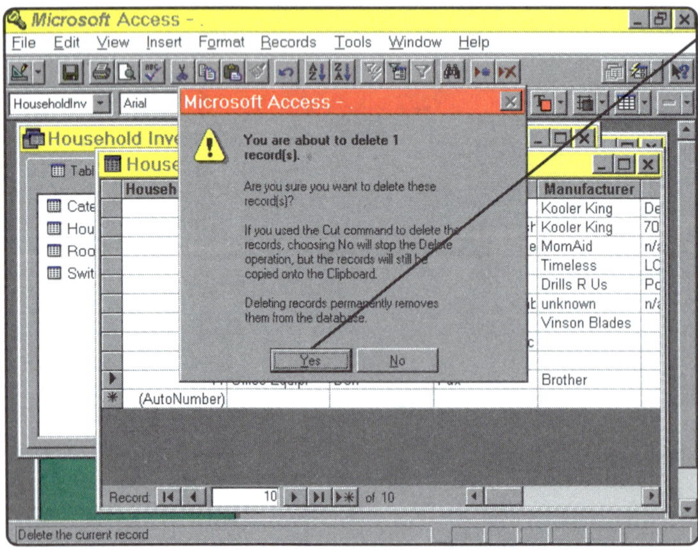

4. **Click** on **Yes** to permanently delete the record.

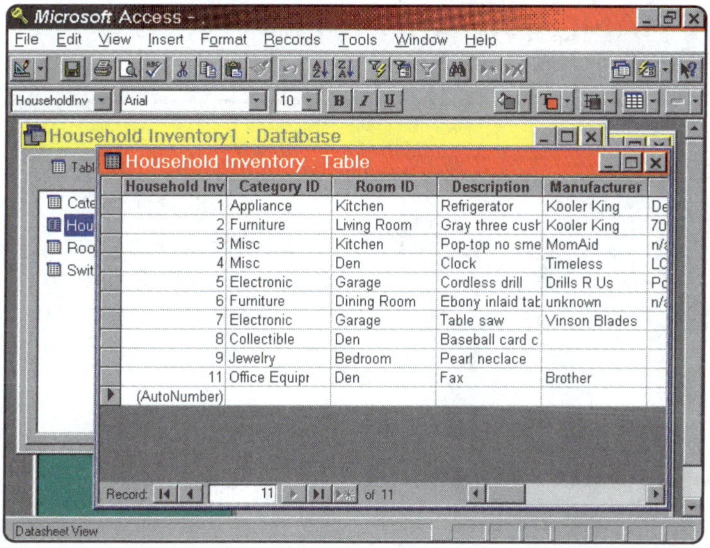

Notice that the record number for 10 has been deleted. This record number is now unavailable in this database.

DELETING THE SAMPLE DATA

If you want to delete the sample data (and the associated record numbers), you can delete them all at once.

1. **Click** on the **record button** on the left of record 1. The entire row will be highlighted.

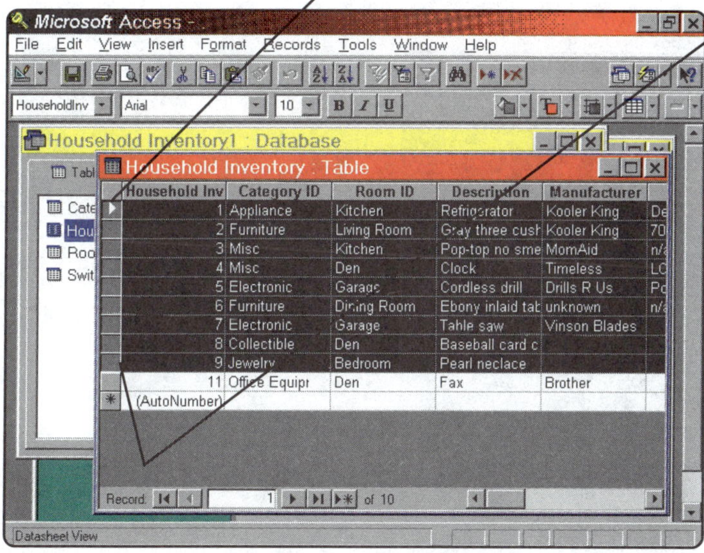

2. **Press and hold** the **mouse button** and **drag** the highlight bar down the record buttons to row 9. Rows 1 through 9 will be highlighted.

3. **Repeat** the **steps** shown above to delete the records. In this example, we won't delete these records.

4. **Click** on the **Close button** (☒) to close the Household Inventory window.

CHANGING AN ENTRY ON A PRIMARY TABLE

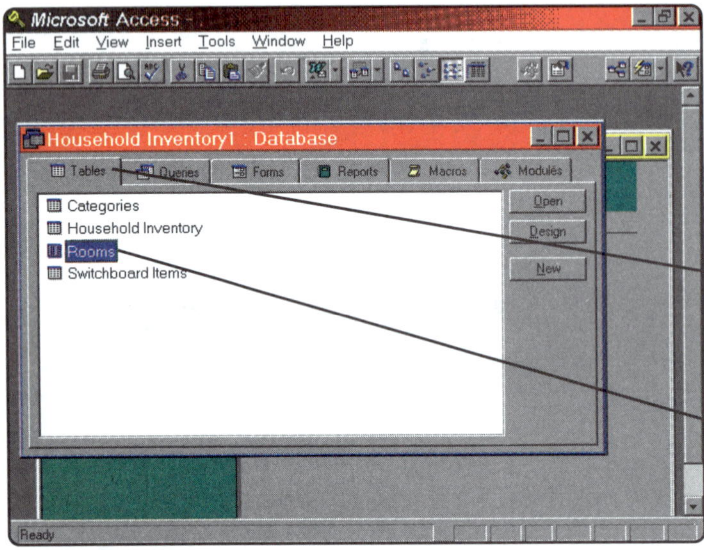

In this example, you'll change an entry on the Rooms table and see how that change is reflected in the Household Inventory table.

1. **Click** on the **Tables tab** if it is not already in the front of the Database window.

2. **Click twice** on **Rooms**. The Rooms table will appear.

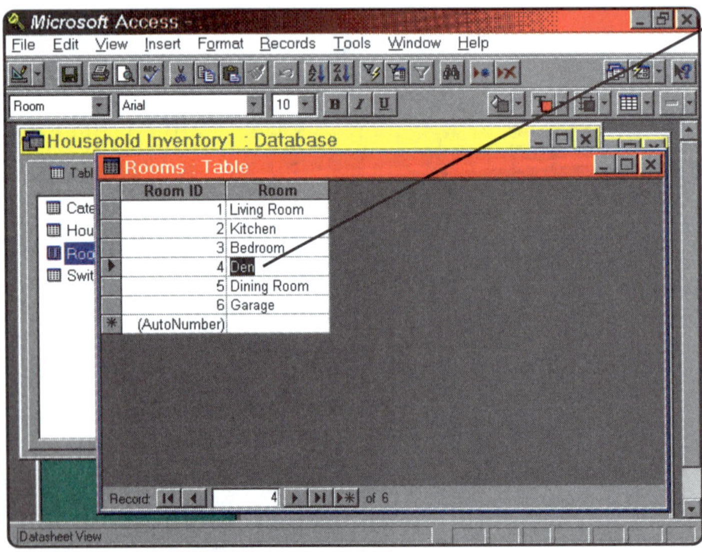

3. **Click twice** on **Den** in record 4. Den will be highlighted.

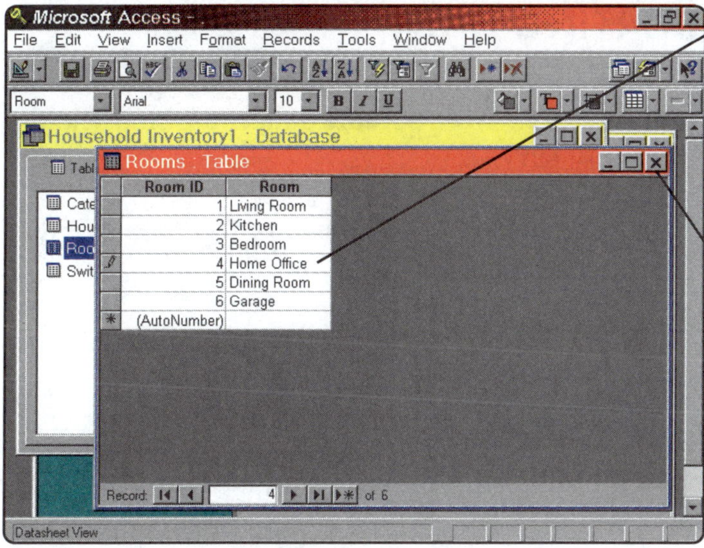

4. **Type Home Office**. It will replace the highlighted text.

In order for this change to register, close the Rooms table.

5. **Click** on the **Close button** (☒) on the Rooms table title bar. The change will now be registered in this table and in any table connected to it, such as the Household Inventory table.

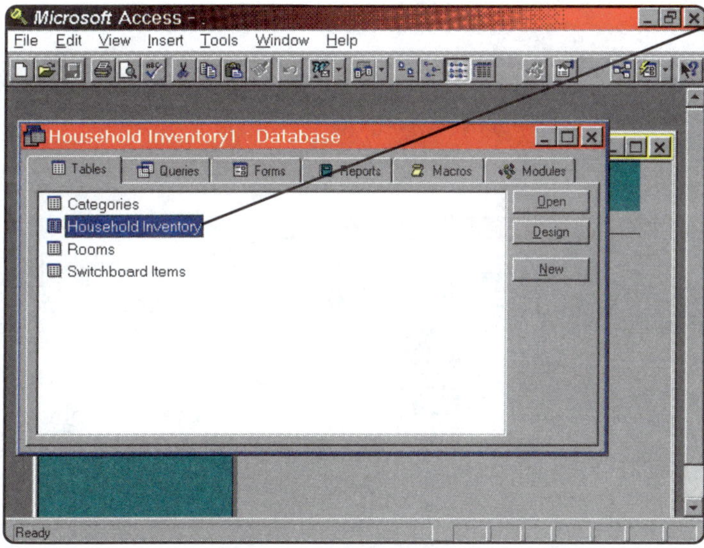

6. **Click twice** on **Household Inventory** to open the table. Notice that "Den" has been changed to "Home Office" in records 4, 8, and 11. (Shown on the next page.)

SORTING DATA

In this section, you'll sort the data in the Household Inventory table.

1. **Click anywhere** in the **Category ID column** of the Household Inventory table.

2. **Click** on the **Sort Ascending button** (the AtoZ button). The data will be rearranged alphabetically according to the data in the Category ID column.

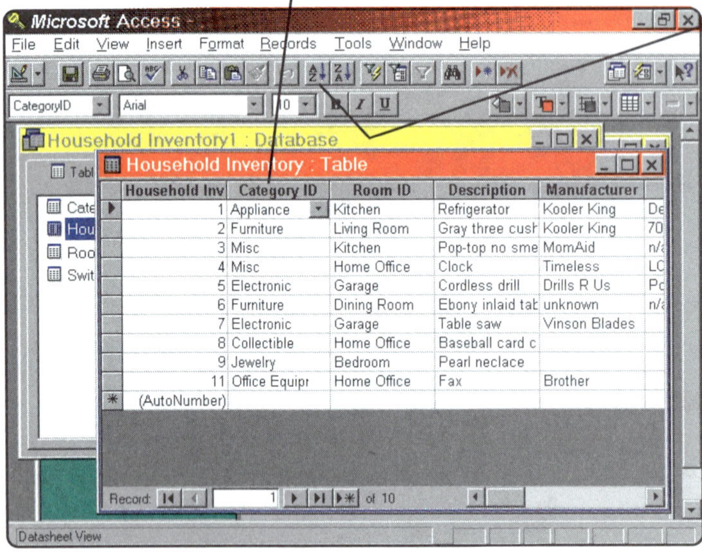

You can print this rearranged version of the table or sort on another column.

3. **Click** on the **Close button** (☒) to close the Household Inventory table. You'll be asked if you want to save the changes to the table (dialog box not shown here). Even if you click on Yes, the sorting change will not be saved. The next time you open this table, it will be sorted numerically by record as it was originally.

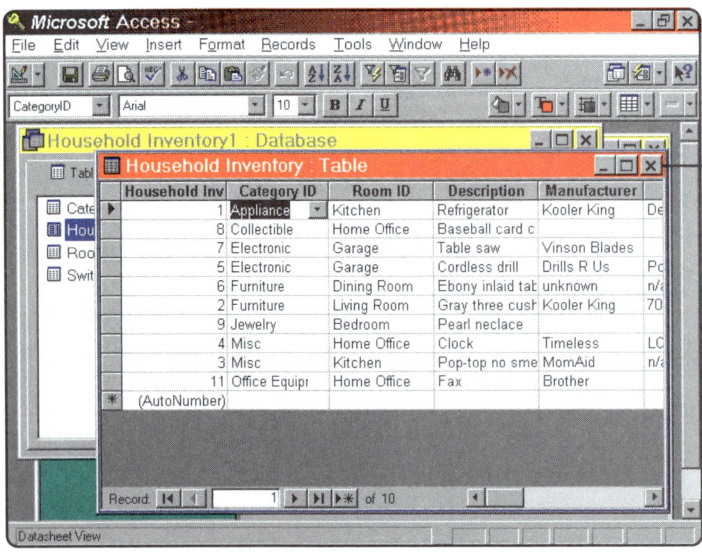

CHAPTER 4

Entering Data and Photos on a Form

In Chapter 3, you entered and changed data directly in the tables. You can also enter and change data using forms. If, in Chapter 1, you told the Wizard to include a photo on the Household Inventory form you'll be able to add a photo to the form. In this chapter, you will do the following:

- ✔ Change data in a form
- ✔ Add data with a form
- ✔ Add a photo to a form

USING A FORM TO CHANGE DATA

In this section, you'll change a listing for one of the rooms.

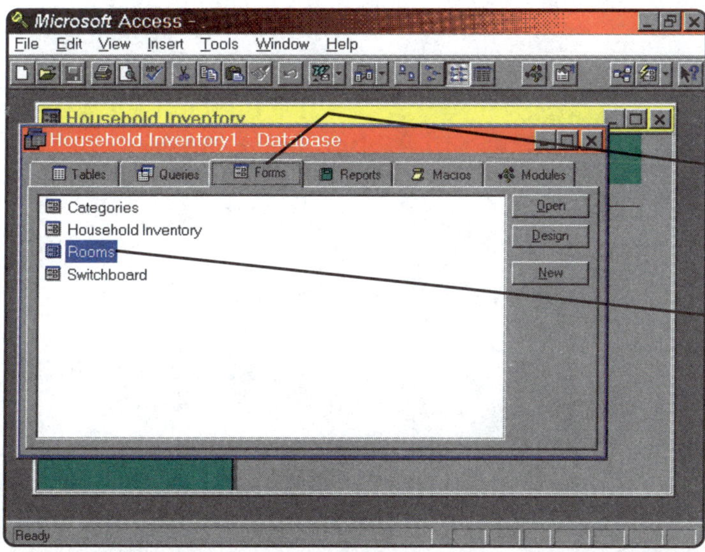

1. **Open** the **Household Inventory1: Database** if it is not already on your screen.
2. **Click** on the **Forms tab** to bring it to the front of the window.
3. **Click twice** on **Rooms**. The Rooms form will appear.

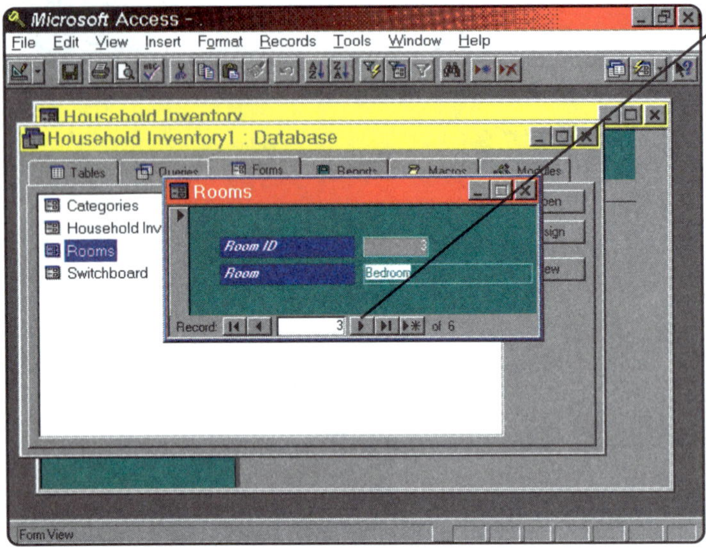

4. **Click repeatedly** on the **Next Record button** (▸) to go to record 3. "Bedroom" will be highlighted in the Room field.

5. **Type Mstr Bedroom**. It will replace the highlighted text.

This change will be recorded when you go to a new record in the section below.

USING THE ROOMS FORM TO ADD A NEW ROOM

In this section, you'll add a new room to the Rooms list.

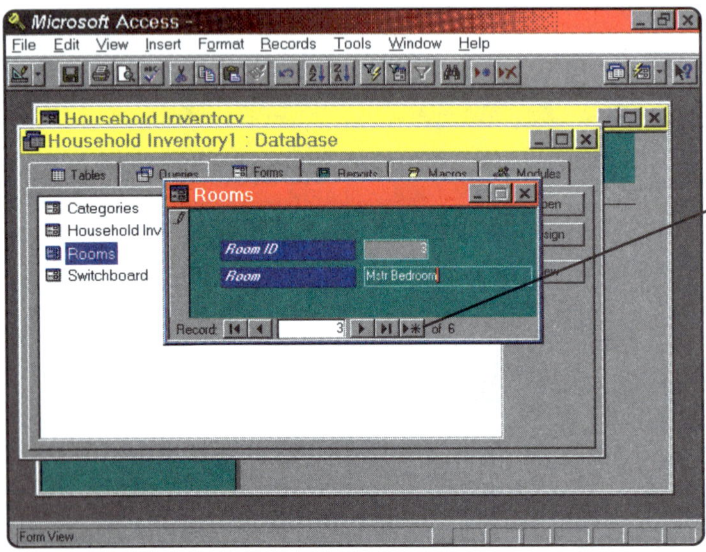

1. **Repeat steps 1 to 3** at the beginning of this chapter to open the Rooms form if it is not already on your screen.

2. **Click** on the **New Record button** (▸✳) to go to the next available record number.

3. **Type Jessica's Bdrm** in the Room field. A new number will be given to this entry in the Room ID field.

4. **Click** on the **Close button** (☒) to close this form.

ADDING A RECORD USING THE HOUSEHOLD INVENTORY FORM

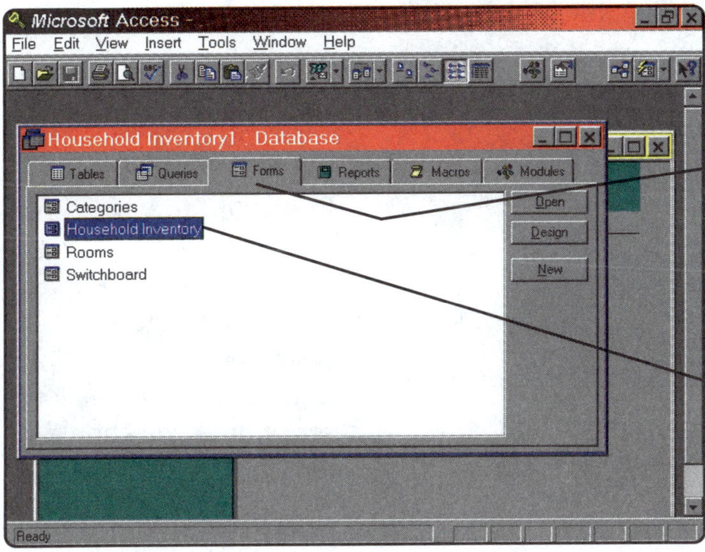

In this section, you'll add a record using the Household Inventory form.

1. In the Household Inventory Database window you see here, **click** on the **Forms tab** if it is not already at the front of the window.

2. **Click twice** on **Household Inventory**. The Household Inventory form will appear.

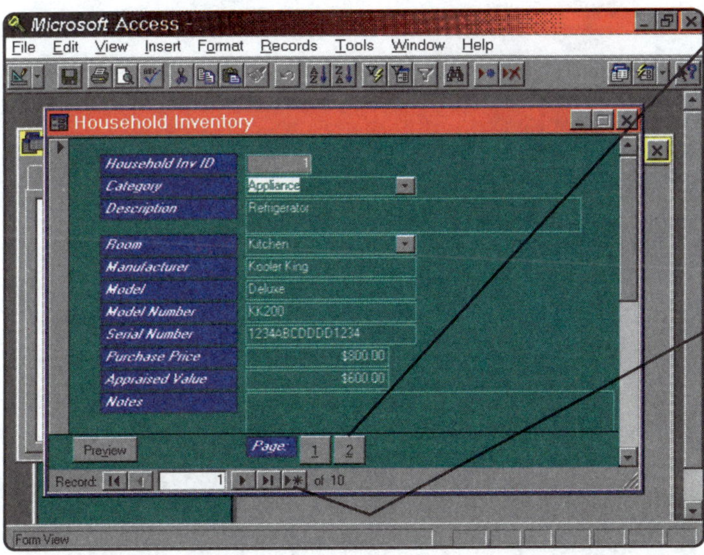

Notice that this form has two pages. You can get to the second page by clicking on the Page 2 button or by scrolling down the form. Try it for yourself, then come back to this view.

3. **Click** on the **New Record button** (▸✳) to go to the next available record number.

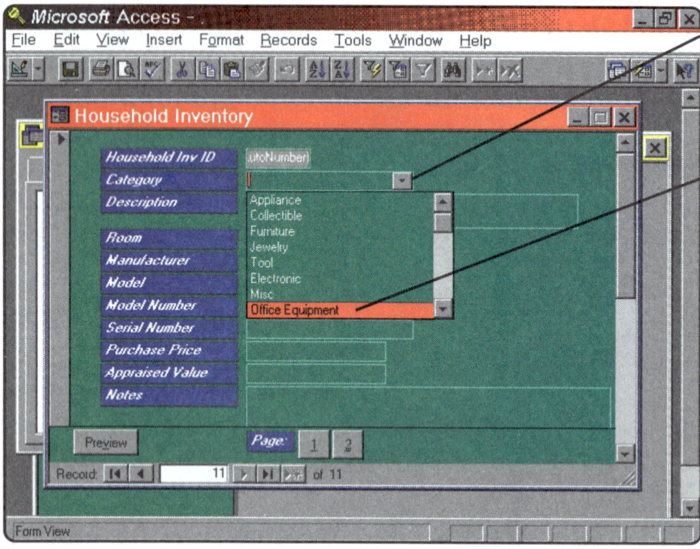

4. **Click** on the ▼ to the right of the Category box. A pull-down list will appear.

5. **Click** on **Office Equipment**. (This category was added to the list of categories back in Chapter 3.

6. **Press** the **Tab key** to go to the Description box. When you go to the Description box, ▲ and ▼ arrows appear. These arrows allow you to scroll through a long description if you should enter one.

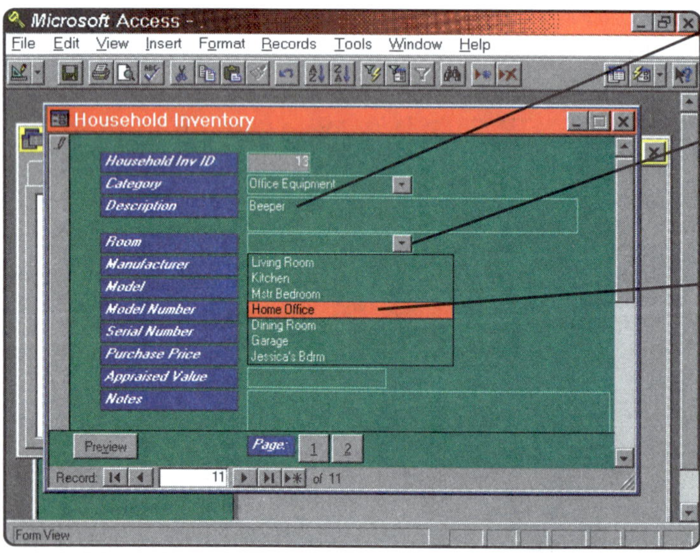

7. **Type Beeper**, then tab to the Room field.

8. **Click** on the ▼ in the Room field to open a list of possible rooms.

9. **Click** on the **room**.

You'll learn how to create a field containing a pull-down list in Chapter 9, "Customizing Table." The purpose of this kind of field is to restrict entries to specific choices. This keeps all entries uniform and allows you to create accurate reports. If one person calls a room the "den" while another calls it the "family room," you won't be able to get an accurate reading on items contained in the room.

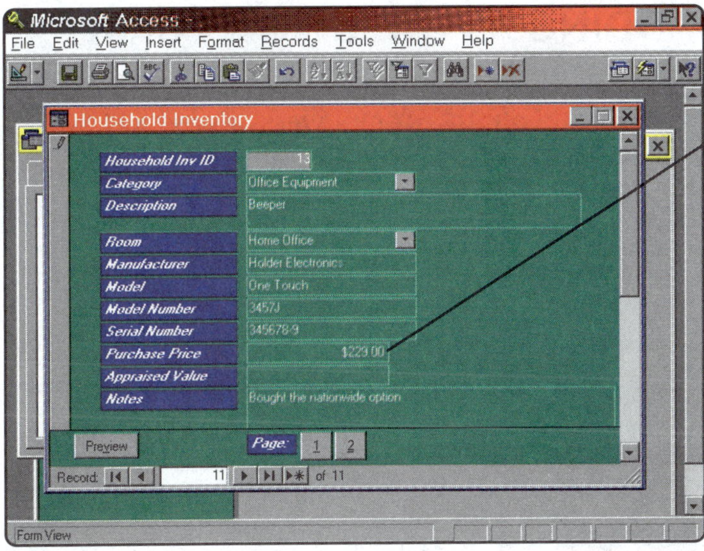

10. Continue to fill in the appropriate information.

Note: When you tab into the Purchase Price field, it may look like the cursor is not there. That's because it is on the extreme right of the box. This field has been coded to align on the right for decimals. It will add the ".00" when you tab to the next field.

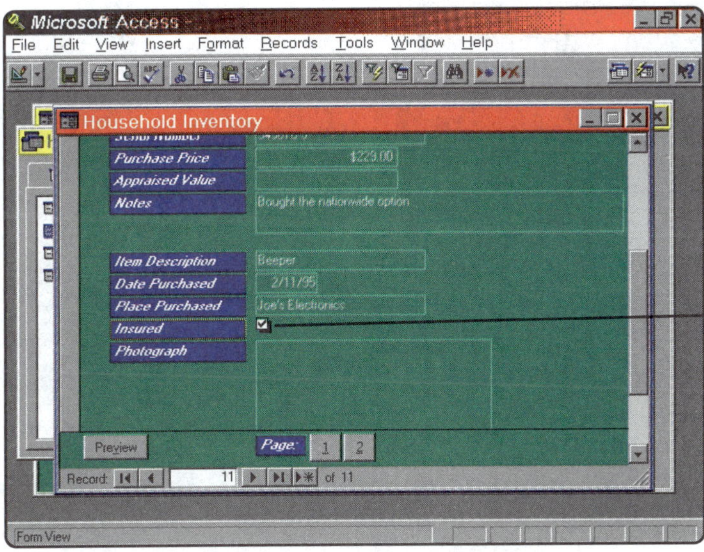

In this example, the Insured field was set up by the Wizard to be a yes/no field. You'll learn how to change the properties of a field in Chapter 9, "Customizing Table."

11. Click on the **Insured box** to add a ✔ to show that the item is insured.

ADDING A PHOTO TO A FORM

You can add photos of employees or products to forms. In this example, you'll add a photo of a household item for insurance purposes.

Note: Your photos must be converted into electronic graphic images before you can add them to a file in Access. If you don't know how to do that or don't have someone on your staff who can do it, look for a professional copy shop or photo shop that will scan your photos and convert them to a format that can be read by the computer. Prices in our area are *well under* $10 per photo. If you have lots of photos, consider investing in a scanner and a program such as Photoshop.

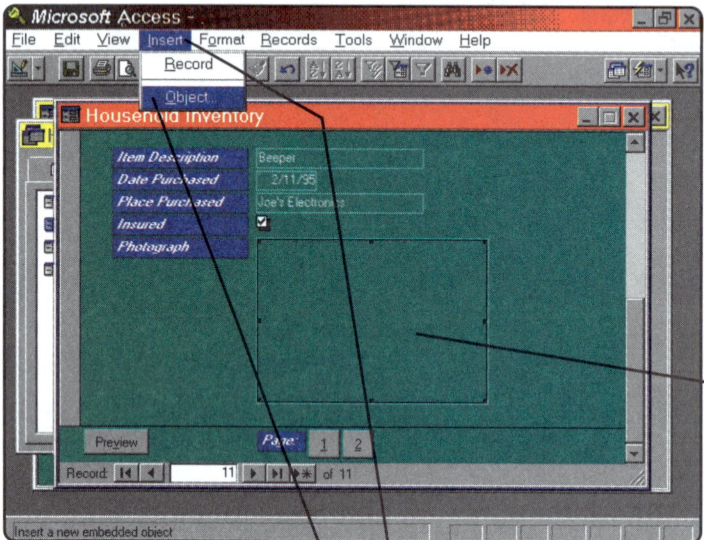

1. **Click anywhere** in the Photograph box. The box will be surrounded by eight small black squares.

2. While the box is surrounded by the black squares, **click** on **Insert** in the menu bar. The Insert menu will appear.

3. **Click** on **Object**. The Insert Object dialog box will appear.

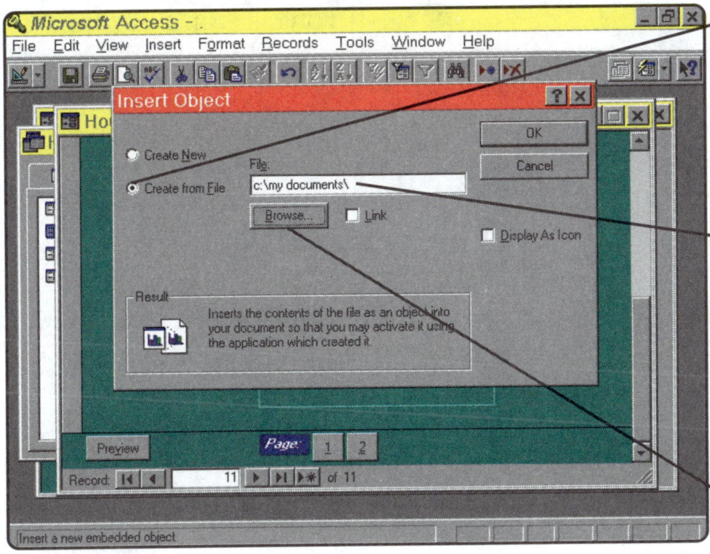

4. **Click** on **Create from File** to put a dot in the circle. The dialog box will change to look like the one you see here.

If you used the Wizard to add a logo or photo to reports back in Chapter 1, the directory (or folder) you went to will still be listed here.

5. **Click** on **Browse**. The Browse dialog box will appear.

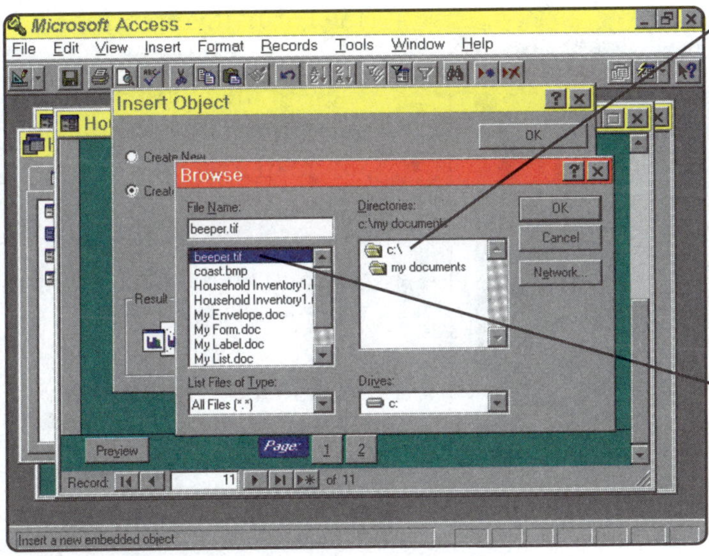

6. If the folder you want does not show in the Directories box, **click twice** on the **c:\ folder** to bring up a list of all folders on your C drive. Next, scroll through the list and click twice on the folder where your image is located.

7. **Click twice** on the **graphic image** you want to insert.

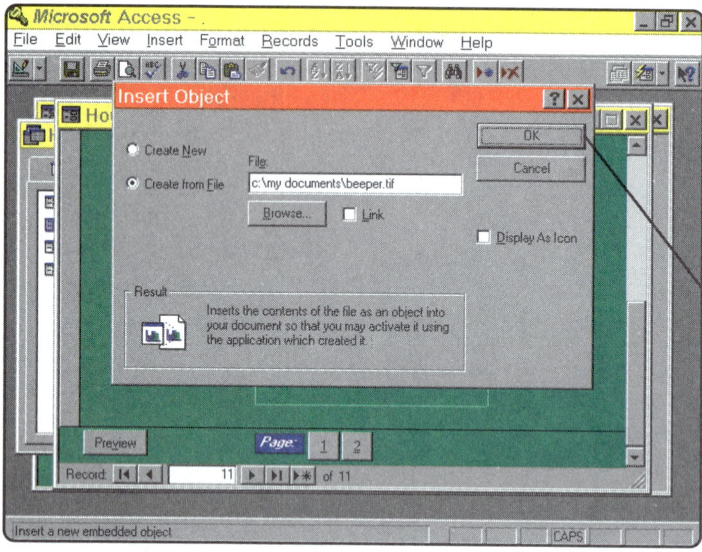

If you click on Link, the image will be linked into Access. If the photo should change, the change will show in the photo displayed in Access. We won't do that here.

8. **Click** on **OK**. The photo will be inserted into the form.

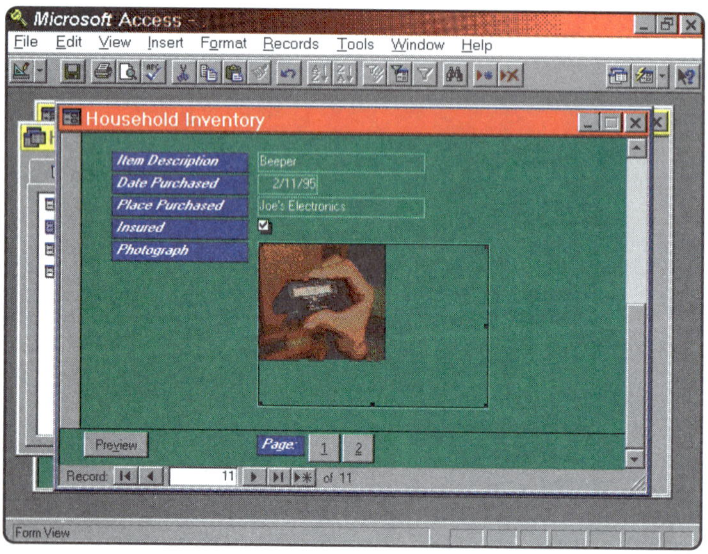

Photos can be seen only on the Form. If you include a photo on a form, the Table view of the Household Inventory will say only "Bitmap image" in the Photo column.

9. **Click** on the **Close button** (☒) to close this form.

10. **Click** on the **Minimize button** (▁) on the Database window to minimize it.

CHAPTER 5

Using Predesigned Reports

The Access Wizards create reports based on the database design you chose in Chapter 1. As with any Windows program, you can view the report in Print Preview to get a bird's eye view. You can also print a report in Landscape, which puts the long edge of the paper at the top. In this chapter, you will do the following:

- ✔ Switch to Print Preview view
- ✔ Print in Landscape

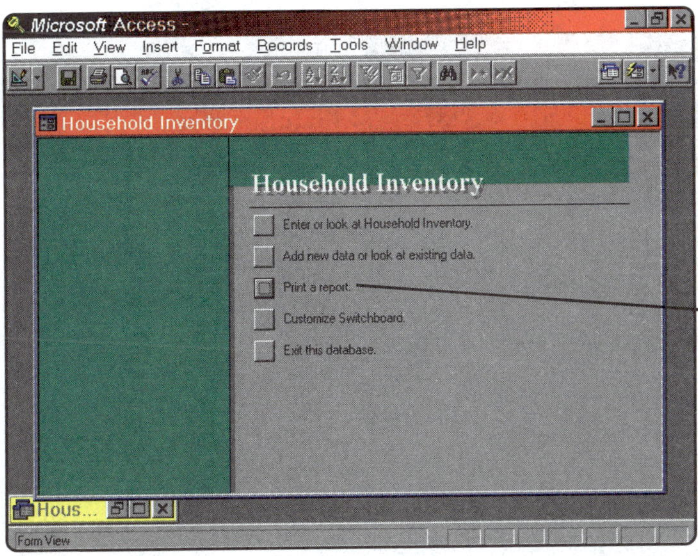

PRINTING A REPORT

This section will use the Switchboard to go to Reports.

1. **Click** on **Print a report**. A list of the predesigned reports will appear.

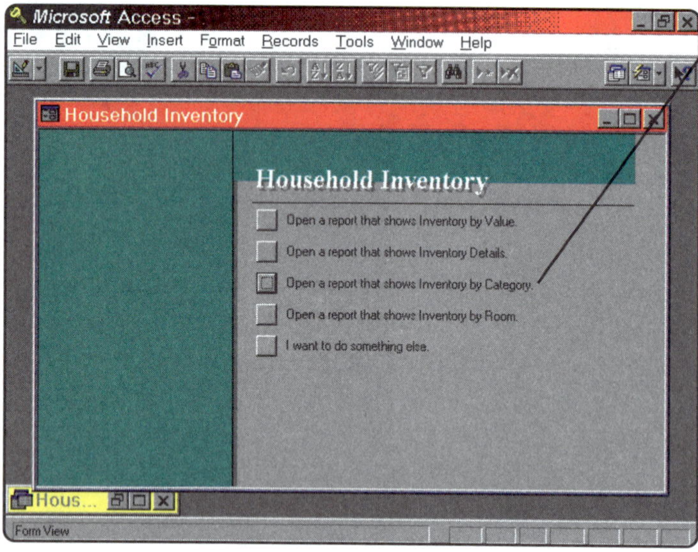

2. **Click** on **Open a report that shows Inventory by Category**.

3. If your window is not maximized, **click** onthe **Maximize button** (□) on the right of the Report window to make the Report fill the screen.

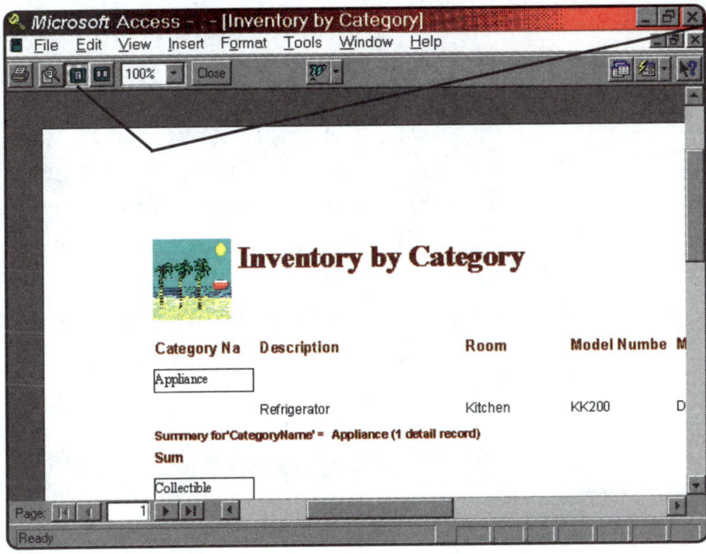

4. **Click** on the **One Page button** to show the first page of the report in Print Preview mode. The button looks like it is already selected because it looks depressed. However, clicking on it will take you to a different view.

5. **Click** on the **Two Page button** to show both pages of the report on your screen.

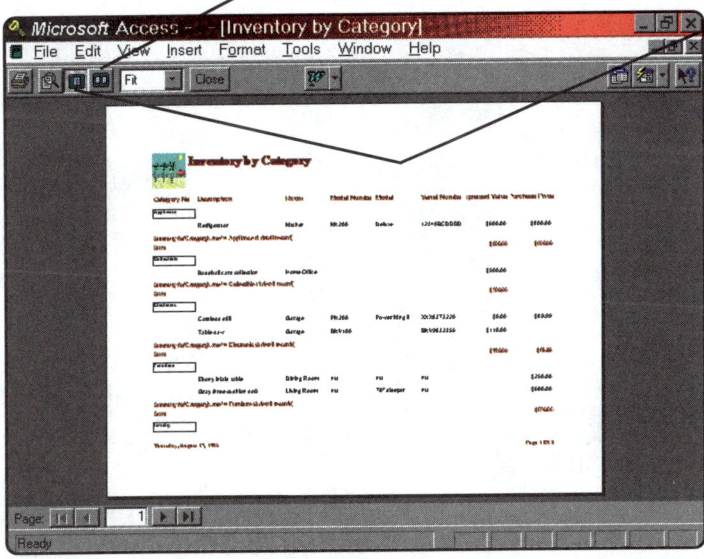

6. **Click** on the **One Page button** again to go back to the first page of the report.

CHANGING THE PAGE SETUP

You can change the margins and the page orientation in the Page Setup dialog box.

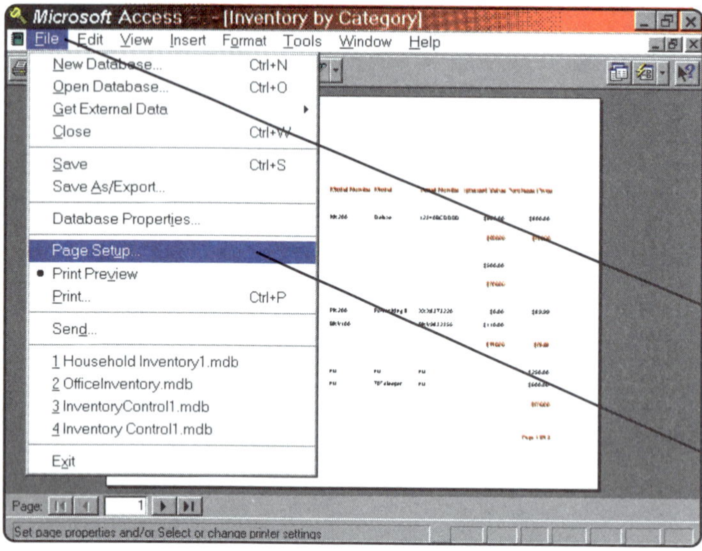

1. **Click** on **File** in the menu bar. The File menu will appear.

2. **Click** on **Page Setup**. The Page Setup dialog box will appear.

3. **Click** on the **Page tab** to bring it to the front of the window.

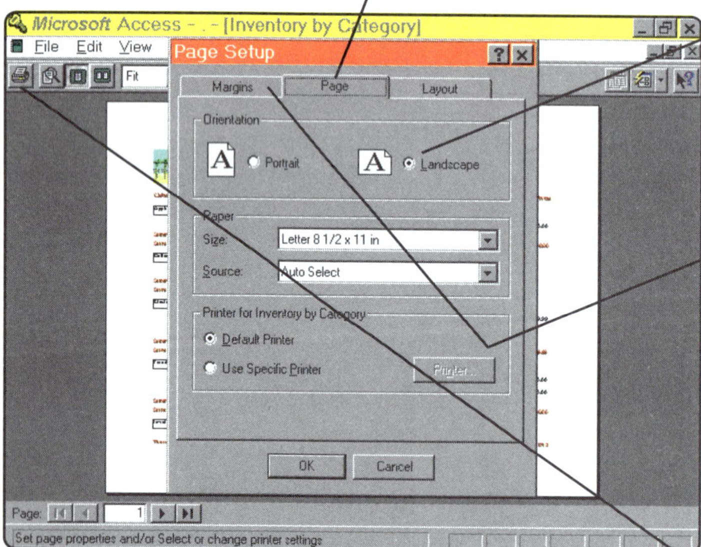

4. **Click** on the **orientation** you want for the printed report. This particular report is already set up to print in Landscape.

5. **Click** on the **Margins tab** if you want to change margins. We won't change margins in this example.

6. When you've made all the changes you want, **click** on **OK** to close this box.

7. **Click** on the **Print button** to print the report.

8. **Click** on the **Close button** (X) to close the report. You may also want to click on the Restore button (🗗) if you don't want all your screens maximized.

CHAPTER

6

Finding Information in the Database

The whole point of having a database program is to make getting at your information and using it easier. Once you've made the database and entered information into it, you'll want to be able to look at it in different ways and analyze it. The forms for entering and editing data let you look at information one record at a time, but it's likely that you'll want to see selected information for several records at once. Reports (see Chapters 5 and 12) give you data formatted and printed, but more often you'll just want to take a look at the data and not print it out. For this, Access provides you with the ability to sort and filter your information, and to ask the database a query. In this chapter, you will do the following:

- ✔ Sort information in a table
- ✔ Use the Query Wizard to find information
- ✔ Filter information from a table
- ✔ Make a query by yourself

OPENING THE DATABASE

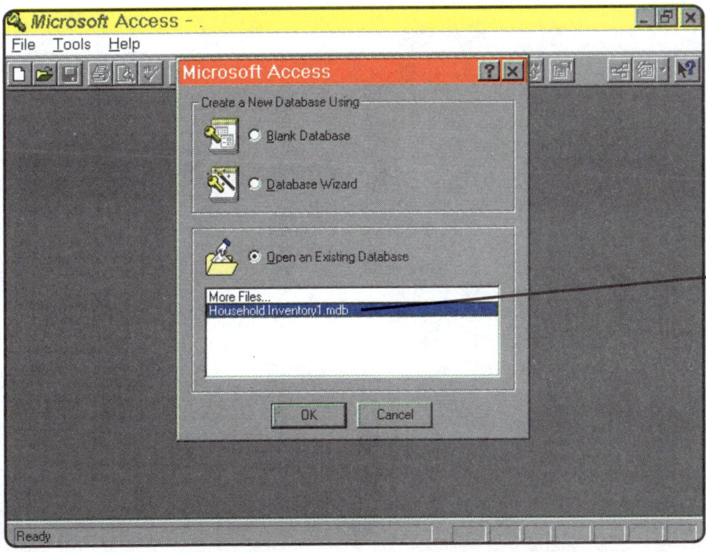

We'll start by using a simple sort to get the data we want from a table.

1. **Open Access** if you have not already done so.

2. **Click twice** on **Household Inventory1** to open the database. After a few moments, the Household Inventory Switchboard will appear.

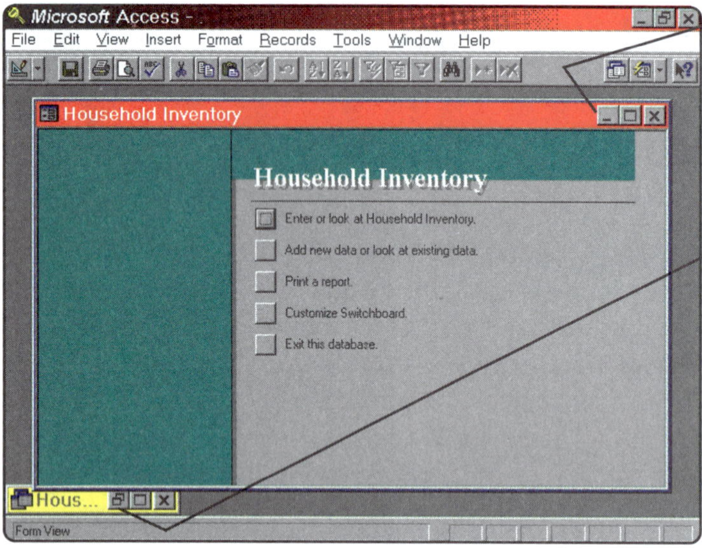

3. **Click** on the **Minimize button** ( ).The Household Inventory Switchboard will become minimized at the bottom of the screen.

4. **Click** on the **Restore button** ( ) on the other minimized item. The Household Inventory1: Database dialog box will appear.

SORTING A FIELD IN A TABLE

Sorting lets you group similar records. In the screens shown in this section, you will see additional "Appliance" records that we added for our example

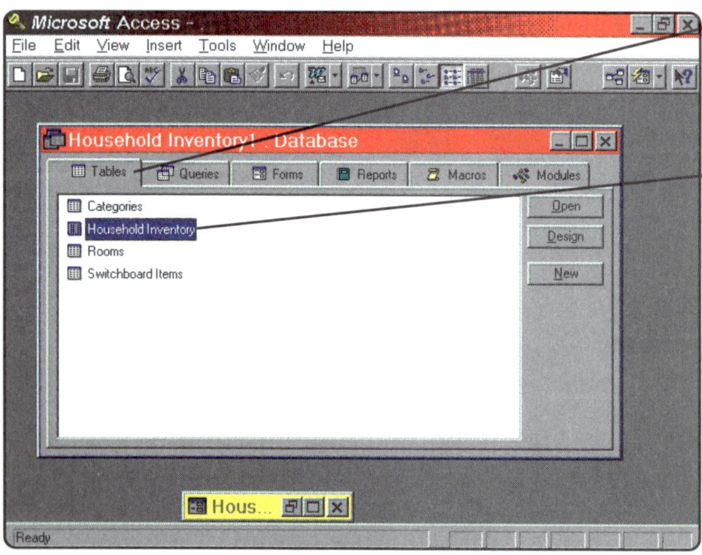

1. **Click** on the **Tables tab**. The list of tables will appear.

2. **Click twice** on **Household Inventory**. The Household Inventory table will appear.

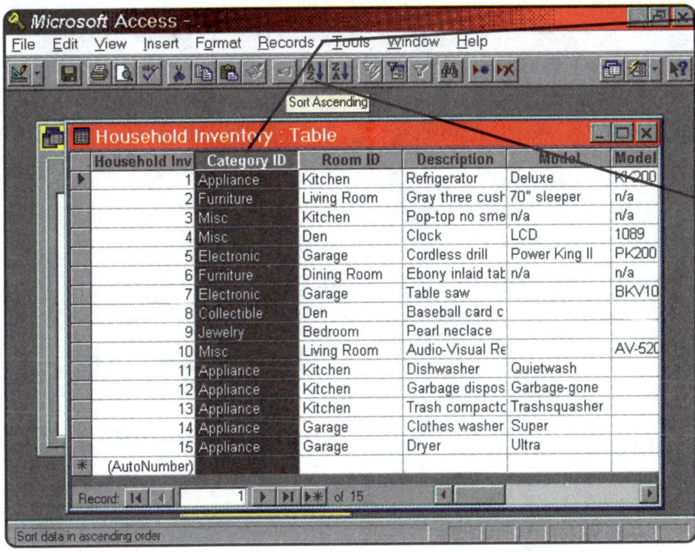

3. Click on the **Category ID heading**. The entire field (column) will become highlighted.

4. Click on the **Sort Ascending icon** in the toolbar. It's the icon with an A above a Z. (If you rest your pointer arrow over the icons one at a time, a "tip" label with the icon's name will appear, as shown in this screen.) The records will be sorted alphabetically according to their category.

In this example, all of the records for appliances (several of which won't appear on your screen) are together, allowing you to compare them easily. You can sort any field in this way to group records with identical information in that field together. As mentioned before, this works fine if you don't have a lot of records. However, if you were doing an apartment building inventory, for example, instead of a household inventory, and had hundreds of appliance records, this method wouldn't work as well. In such a case, you'd have several screens of data to sift through. For large numbers of records, you would want to use a query or a filter (both shown later in this chapter) and print out the results.

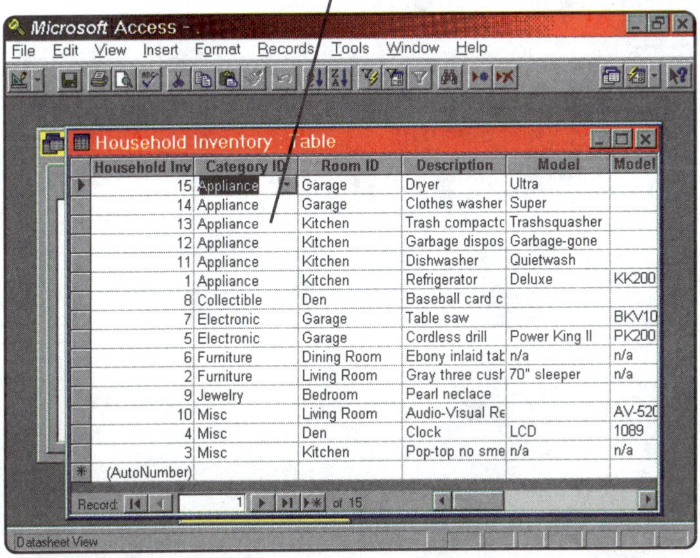

Unsorting a field

It's very easy to undo the sort.

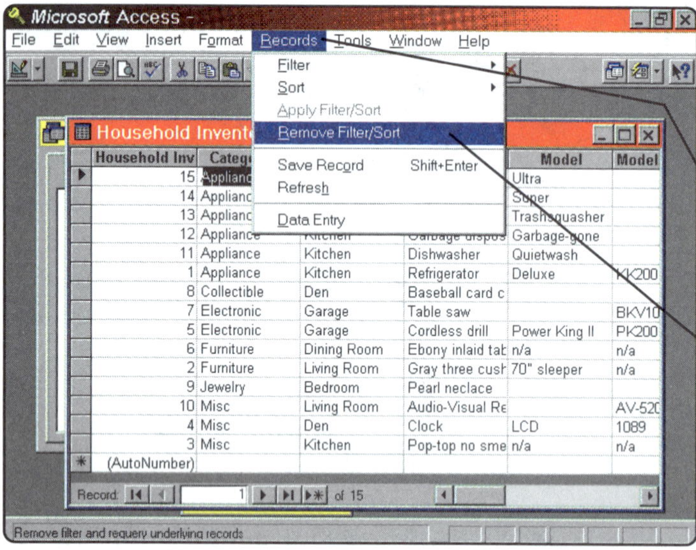

1. **Click** on **Records** in the menu bar. The Records menu will appear.

2. **Click** on **Remove Filter/ Sort**. The records will return to their original order.

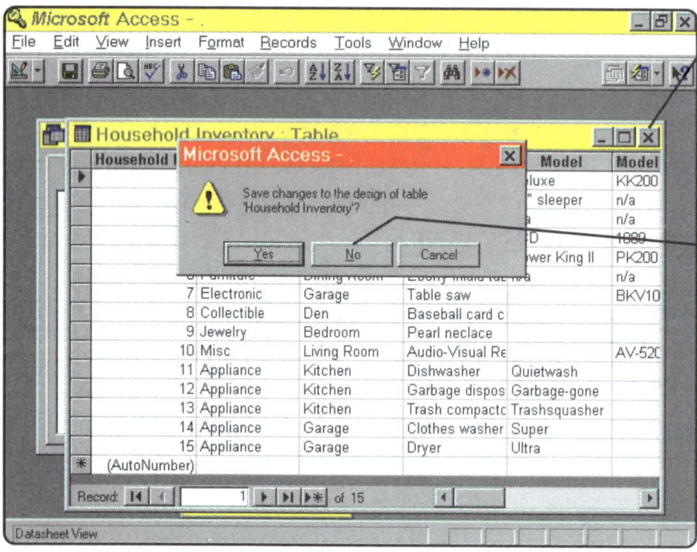

3. **Click** on the **Close button** (☒) in the Household Inventory: Table title bar. A Microsoft Access message box will appear.

4. **Click** on **No**. The message box will disappear, and the table will close.

If you want to sort a field and leave it sorted, do not remove the sort (skip steps 1 and 2 above), and click on Yes in step 4 to save the sorted format.

Now we'll move on to using a query.

USING THE QUERY WIZARD TO FIND INFORMATION

You can ask Access to show you information that you want from your database using what is called a *query*, and save the query so that you can ask for the same information again. If you add new records later, they will show up in the results the next time you make the query.

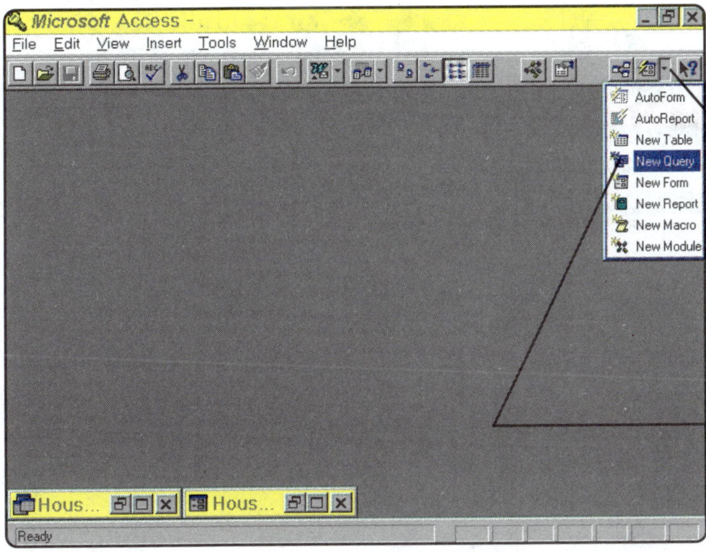

1. **Click** on the **Minimize button** (▁) in the Household Inventory1: Database title bar. The database will become minimized at the bottom of the screen.

2. **Click** on the tiny ▼ next to the New Object icon. A list will appear.

3. **Click** on **New Query**. The New Query dialog box will appear.

You can make many types of queries, with or without the Query Wizard's assistance. We'll demonstrate a simple query in this section, and show you how to design a query yourself in a later section. We won't demonstrate some of the types shown in this screen:

- "Crosstab Query" shows its results in rows and columns, like a spreadsheet. This is useful, for example, for displaying lots of numerical or "yes/no" data that shows well in this form.

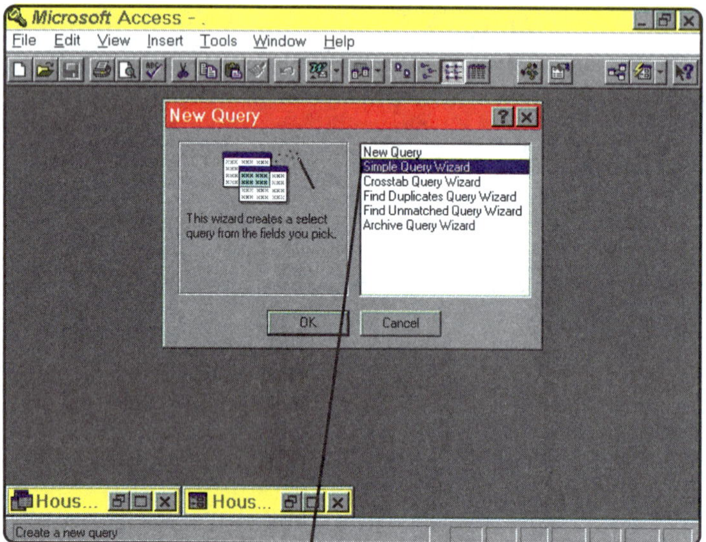

- "Find Duplicates Query" locates records with identical *field values* in your database. A field value is whatever text or number appears where the field (column) and record (row) in a table intersect. This would be another way to find all of the records with, for example, "Appliance" for a field value, as we did using the sort feature a few pages back.

- "Find Unmatched Query" locates records in one table that have no related records in another table. In our sample database, for example, you could locate records in the Household Inventory table that did not have a category or room listed.

- "Archive Query" copies selected records from a table to a new table. The copy will have all of the same fields (columns) that the original one had.

4. **Click twice** on **Simple Query Wizard**. The Simple Query Wizard dialog box will appear.

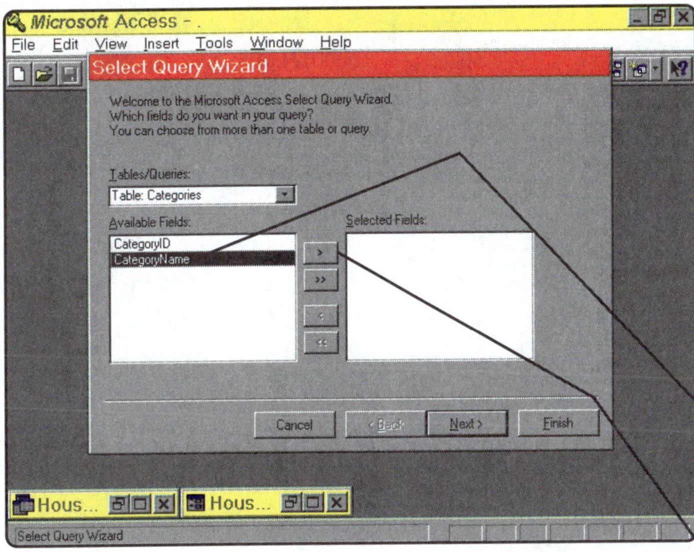

Selecting Fields

In this dialog box you'll tell the Wizard which fields from the different tables to include in the query. For this example, you'll look at the category, date of purchase, and appraised value of items in the inventory.

1. **Click** on **CategoryName** in the Available Fields box to highlight it.

2. **Click** on the **>**. Category Name will appear in the Selected Fields box.

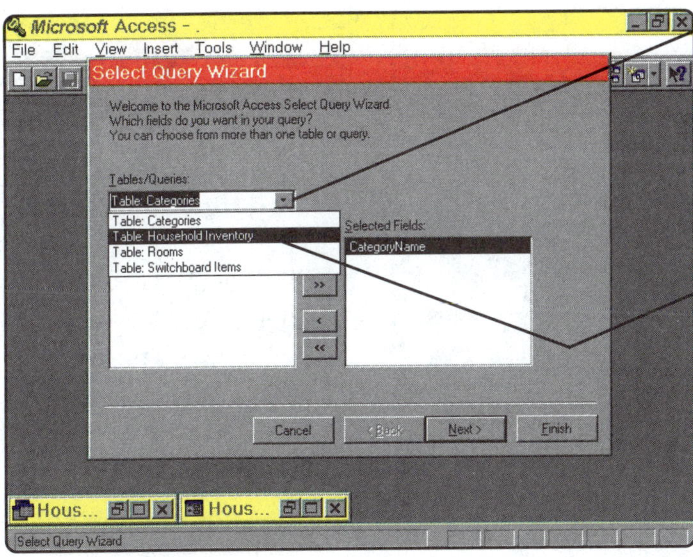

3. **Click** on the ▼ next to the Tables/Queries box. A list of tables will appear. (If you had already created a query, it would show up in this list, too.)

4. **Click** on **Table: Household Inventory**. The list of fields in that table will appear in the box below.

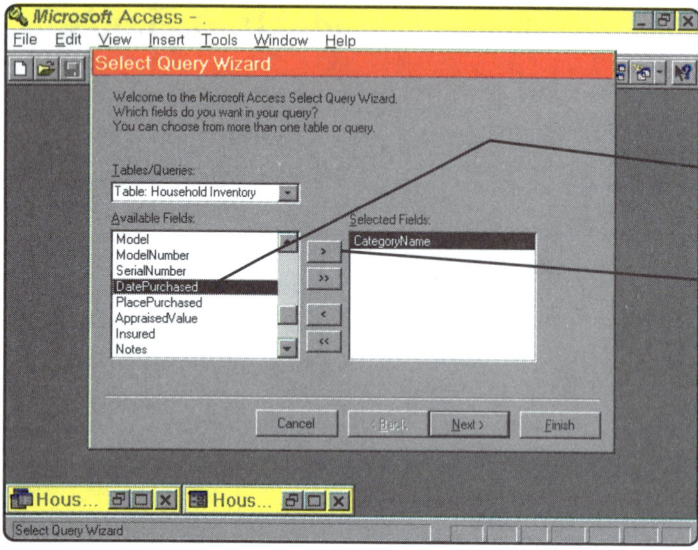

5. **Click** on the ▼ on the scroll bar to scroll through the list of choices.

6. **Click** on **DatePurchased** to highlight it.

7. **Click** on the **>** to add it to the Selected Fields box.

8. **Click repeatedly** on the ▼ to scroll down the list of fields until you see AppraisedValue.

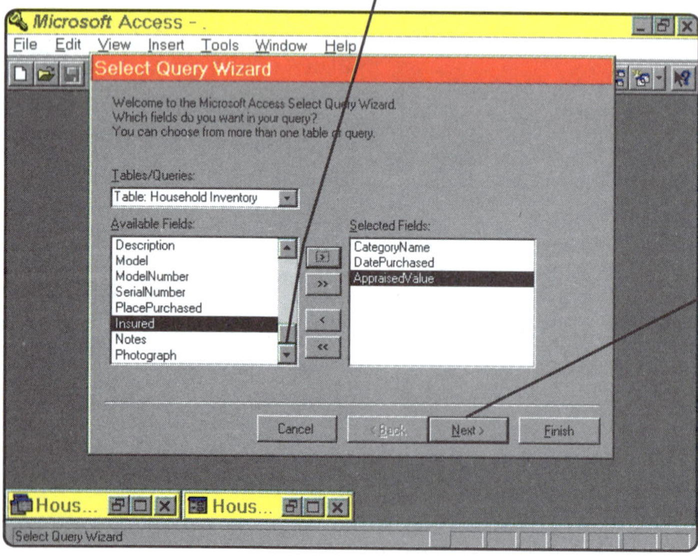

9. **Click twice** on **Appraised Value** in the Available Fields box to add it to the list of Selected Fields. (This is the same as clicking once and then clicking on the ▸.)

10. **Click** on **Next >**. Another Query Wizard dialog box will appear.

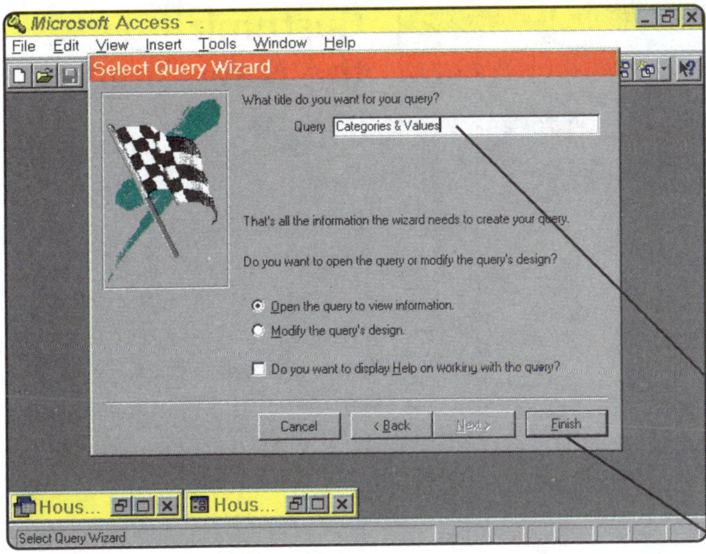

Finishing the Query

At this point you name the query and then have the Wizard create it. A default name, selected by the Wizard, will be highlighted in the Name box.

1. **Type** a **name** for the query. In this example it is Categories & Values.

2. **Click** on **Finish**. After a few moments the finished query will appear.

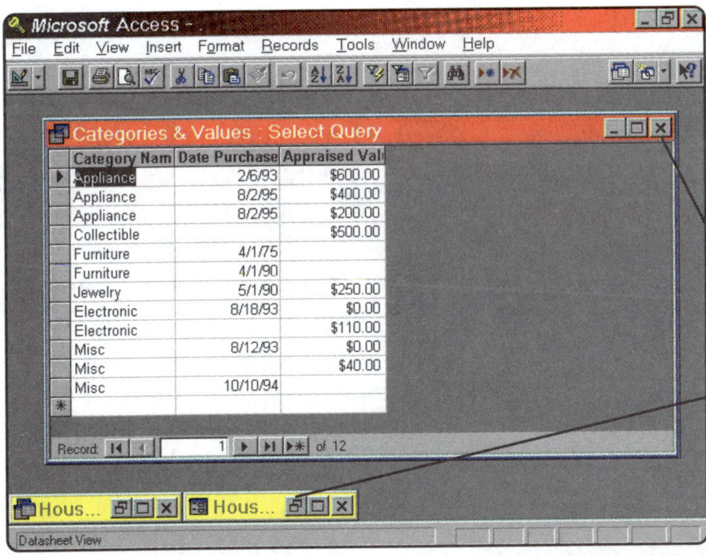

This finished query looks just like the tables that were created for the database, and can be sorted or modified in the same ways as a table.

3. **Click** on the **Close button** ([X]) to close the query.

4. **Click** on the **Restore button** () on the minimized Household Inventory1: Database. The Household Inventory1: Database dialog box will appear.

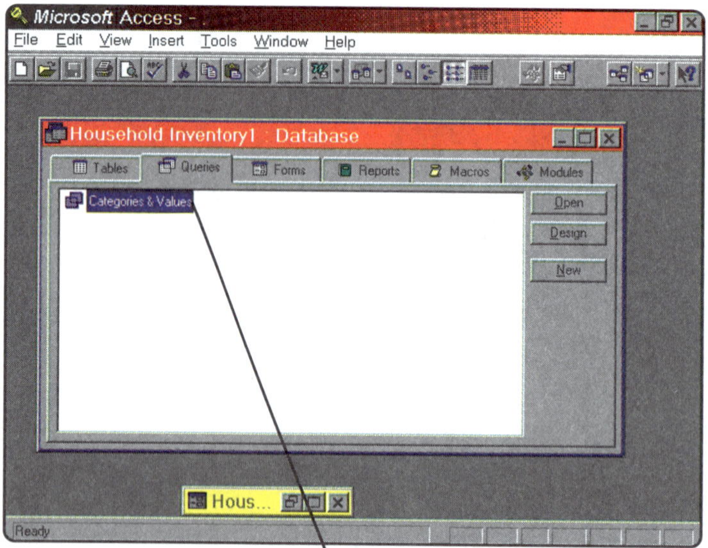

Customizing the New Query

The new query is listed on the Queries tab in the Household Inventory1: Database dialog box. New records can be added to the inventory through the Household Inventory table or form, and they will show up on a new query the next time you look at it. For this example, several more appliance records were added.

1. **Click** on the **Queries tab** if it is not already in front.

2. **Click twice** on **Categories & Values**. Categories & Values: Select Query will open, showing the added records.

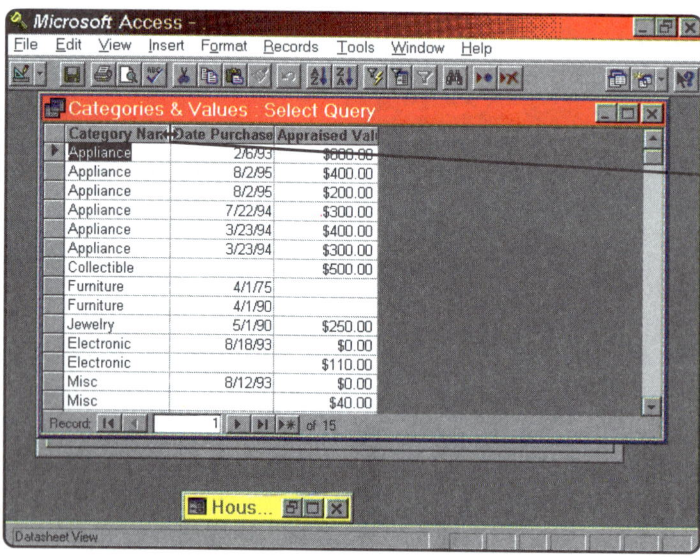

The columns in the query can be adjusted so that their complete headings show.

3. **Move** your **mouse arrow** over the line dividing the first and second column heading. As you do, it will turn into a double-headed arrow.

4. **Press and hold** the **mouse button** and **drag** the column divider to the right. As you do, the column will become wider.

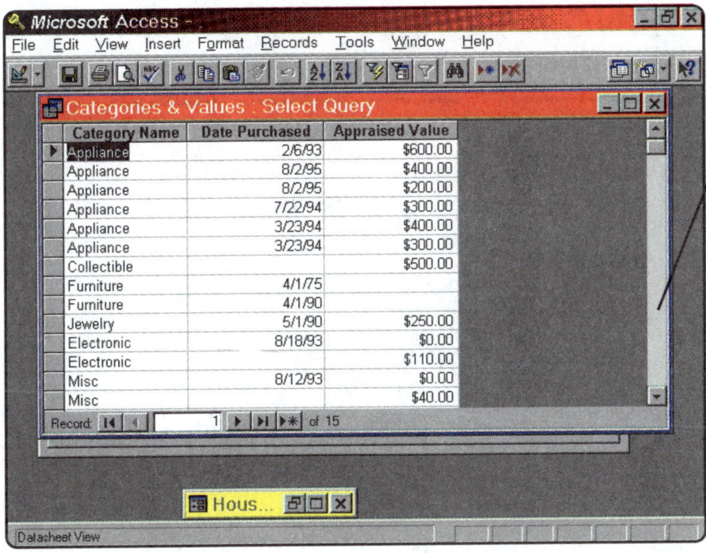

5. Repeat steps 2 and 3 to widen the other columns.

You can scroll down to view the records that don't show.

The query functions just like a table. Records can be added to it, and they will be reflected in the Household Inventory1: Table.

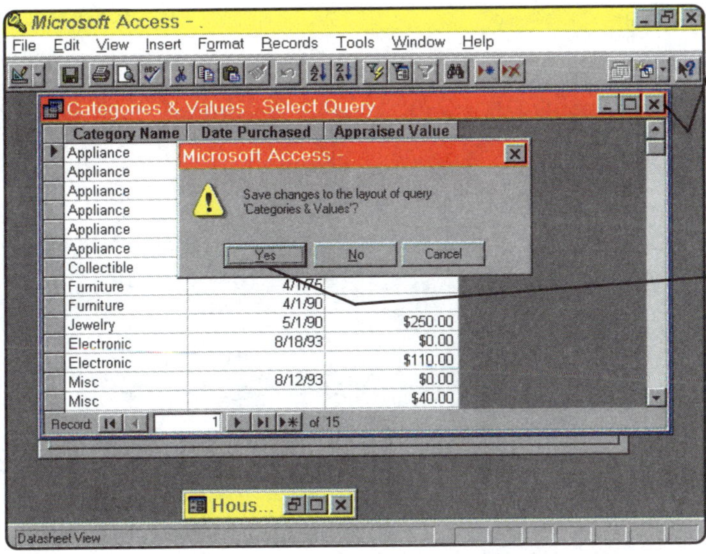

6. Click on the **Close button** ([X]) to close the query. A message box will appear, asking if you want to save the new layout (with the wider columns).

7. Click on **Yes**. The message box will disappear, and the query will close.

Now you'll move on to using filters.

USING A FILTER FOR FINDING INFORMATION

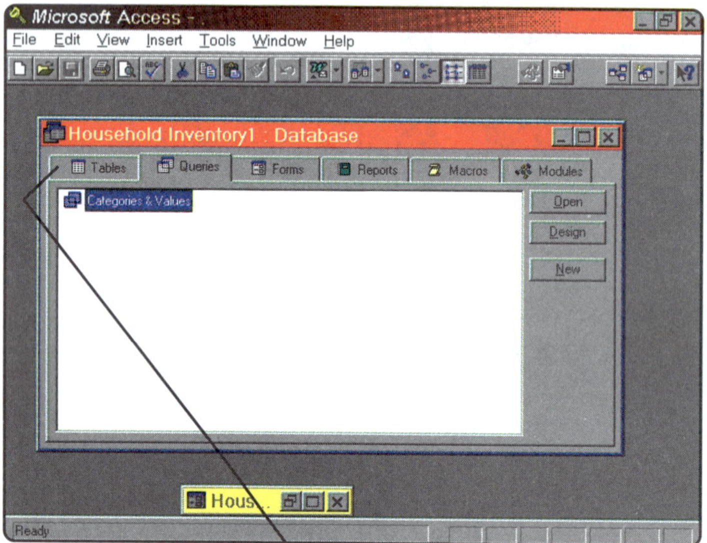

The Simple Query Wizard lets you pick entire fields. If you want to include only certain records in the fields, you'll have to use the filter function, or make a query without the Wizard's help. You'll do both, starting with the filter.

In this example, you'll be looking for records in only one category: appliances. First, you'll want to check the Categories table to get the Category ID for appliances.

1. **Click** on the **Tables tab**. The list of tables will appear.

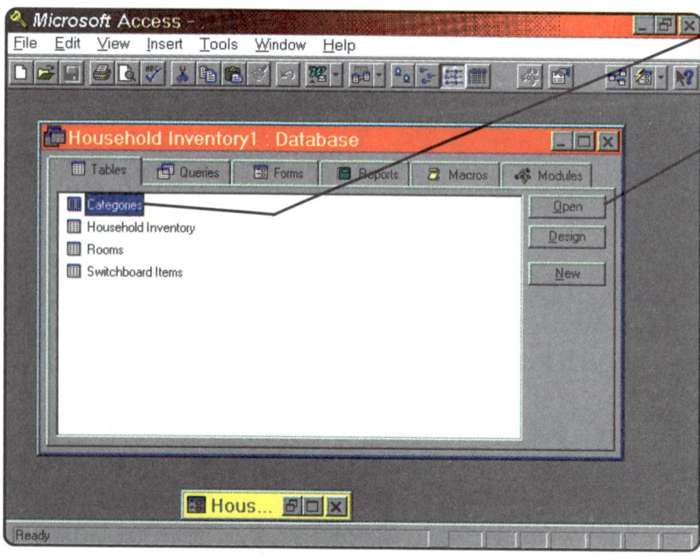

2. **Click** on **Categories**, if needed, to highlight it.

3. **Click** on **Open**. The Categories: Table will appear.

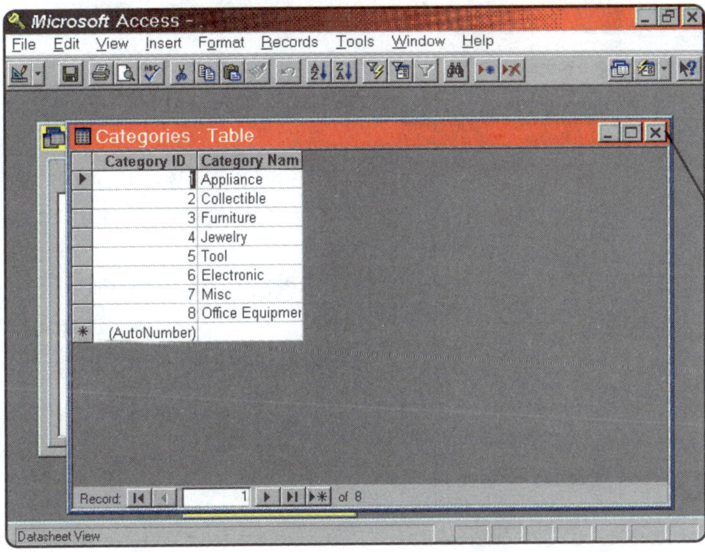

The Categories: Table shows that each category has a unique record number, the Category ID. The ID for Appliance is 1.

4. **Click** on the **Close button** ([X]) to close the Categories: Table.

Selecting the Data to Filter

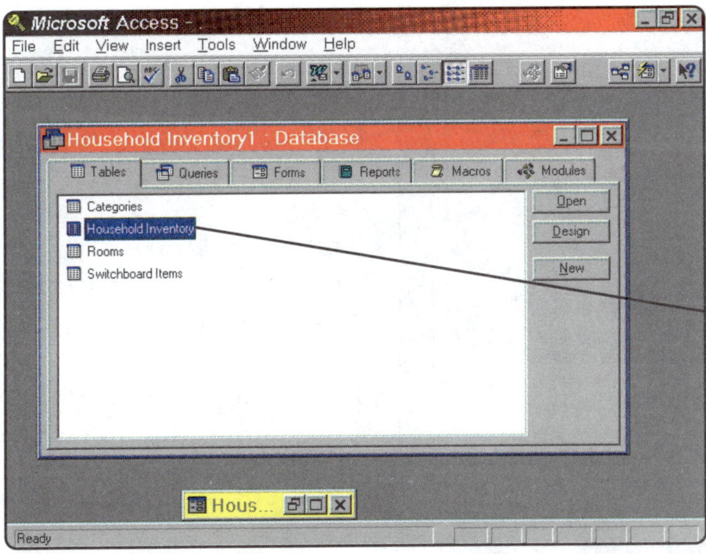

Like a coffee filter, the record filter only lets what you want get through the process.

1. **Click** on the **Tables tab** if it is not already in front.

2. **Click twice** on **Household Inventory**. The Household Inventory: Table will open.

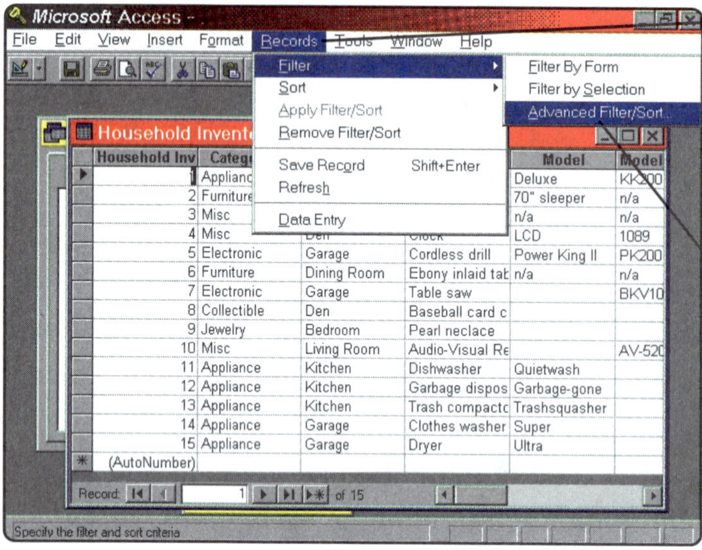

3. **Click** on **Records** in the menu bar. The Records menu will appear.

4. **Click** on **Filter**. Another menu will appear.

5. **Click** on **Advanced Filter/Sort**. The Household InventoryFilter1: Filter dialog box will appear.

Selecting Filter Criteria

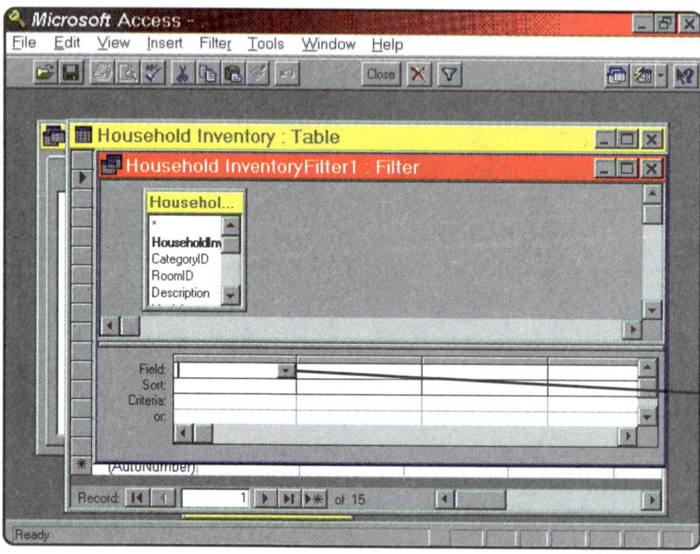

First you indicate which field you want to filter, then you tell it how you want it filtered. The cursor will be flashing in the first column.

If CategoryID does not already appear in the table, do steps 1 and 2.

1. **Click** on the ▼ in the first column. A list will appear.

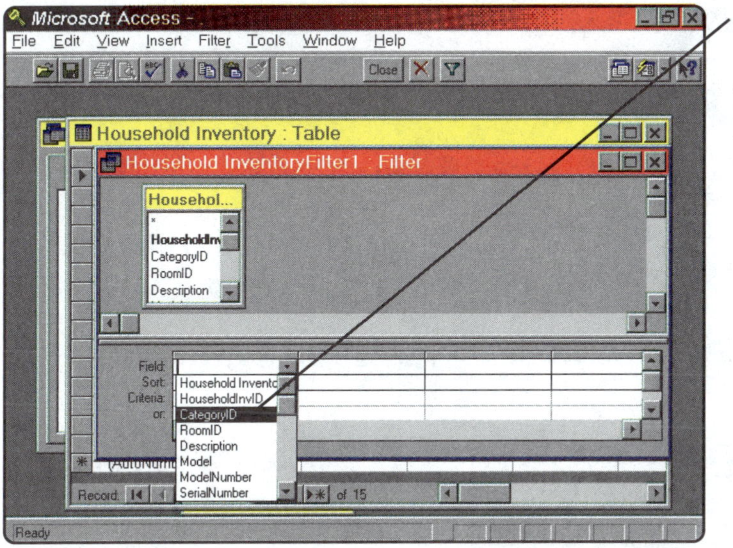

2. Click on **CategoryID.** The list will close, and CategoryID will appear in the Field line of the first column.

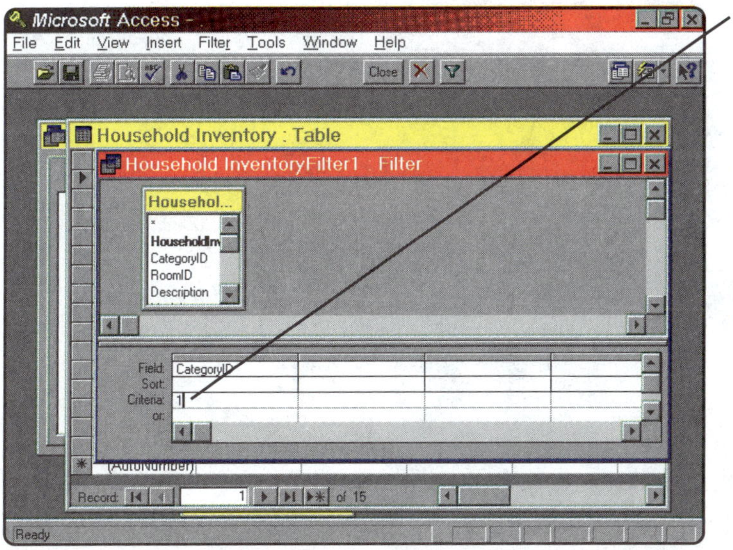

3. Click in the **Criteria line** of the first column to place the cursor. This is where you specify what you want CategoryID to match in the records that get through our filter.

4. Type 1 (the CategoryID for appliances).

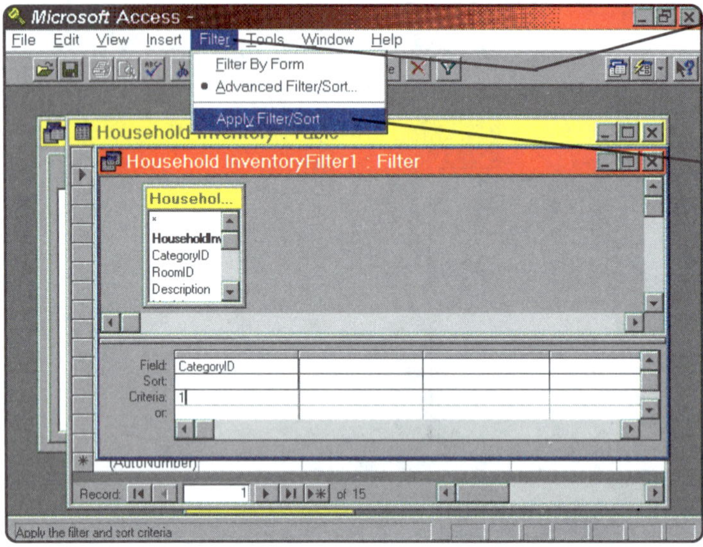

5. **Click** on **Filter** in the menu bar. The Filter menu will appear.

6. **Click** on **Apply Filter/ Sort**. The filter dialog box will close, and the Household Inventory: Table will reappear, with only the appliance records showing.

Saving the Filtered Data as a Query

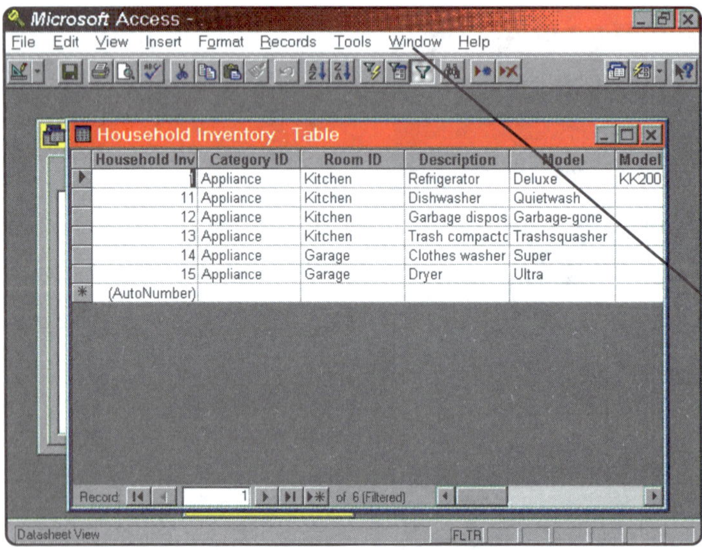

After going to all this trouble, you'll want to save your results. If you try to save this window, however, you run the risk of writing over our original Household Inventory1: Table.

1. **Click** on **Window** in the menu bar. The Window menu will appear.

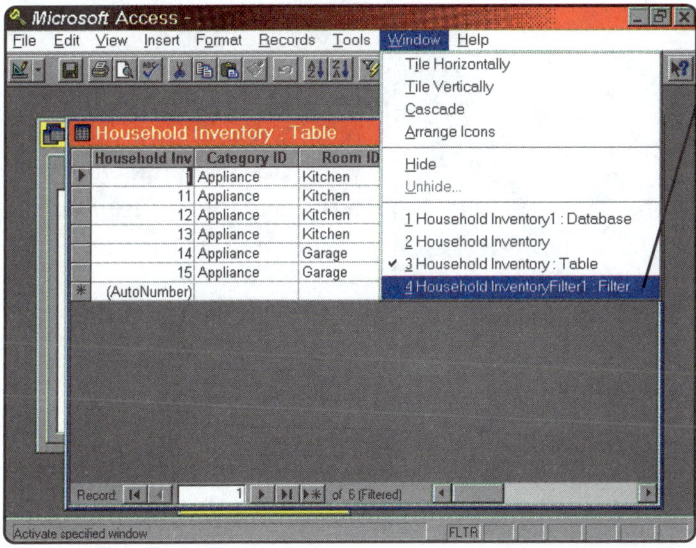

2. **Click** on **Household InventoryFilter1: Filter.** The filter dialog box will reappear.

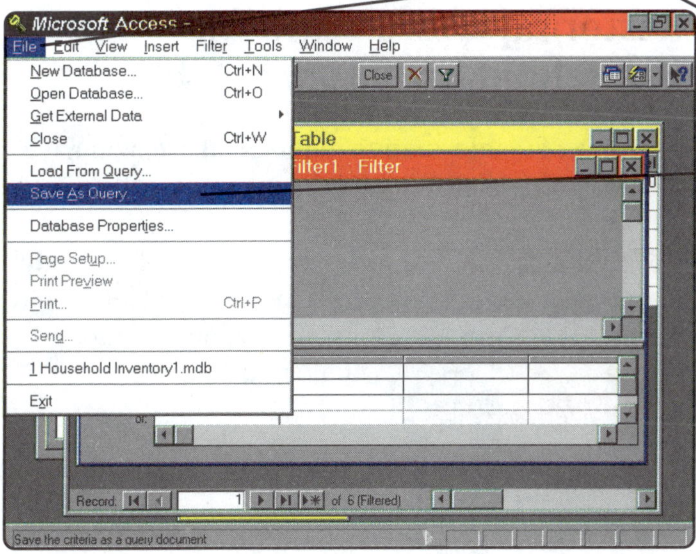

3. **Click** on **File** in the menu bar. The File menu will appear.

4. **Click** on **Save As Query.** A Save As Query dialog box will appear.

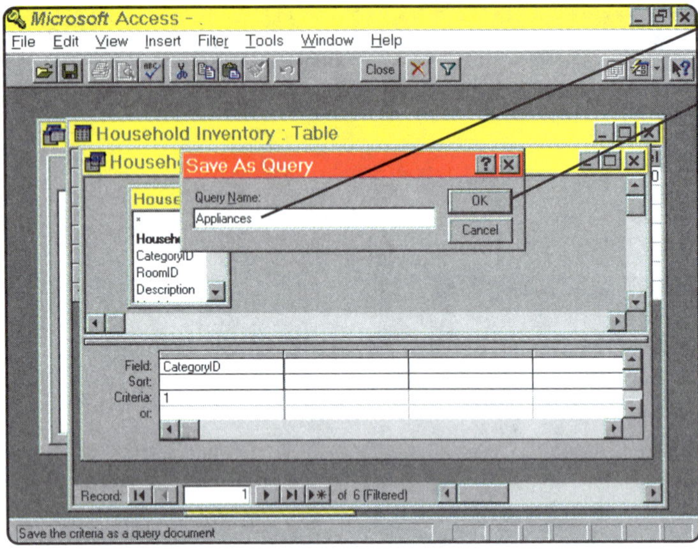

5. **Type Appliances**.

6. **Click** on **OK**. The filter results will be saved, and will appear on the Query tab list of the Household Inventory1: Database.

Restoring and Closing the Household Inventory1: Table

To protect the information in the database, you have to restore the table to its original state and close it.

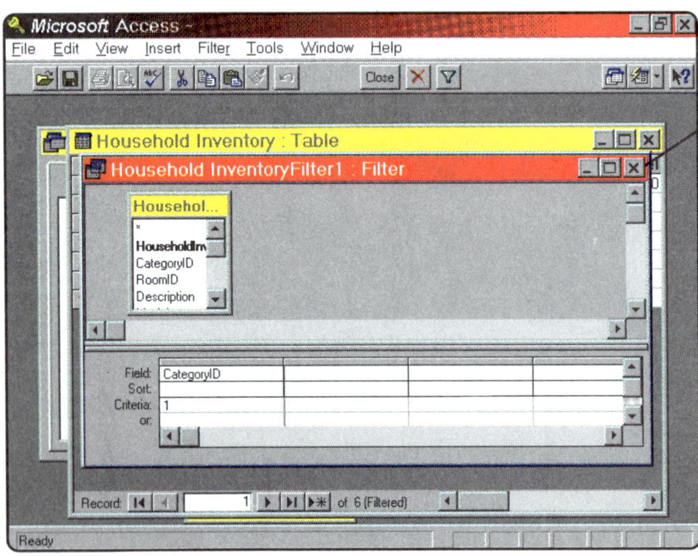

1. **Click** on the **Close button** (X) to close the Household InventoryFilter1: Filter dialog box.

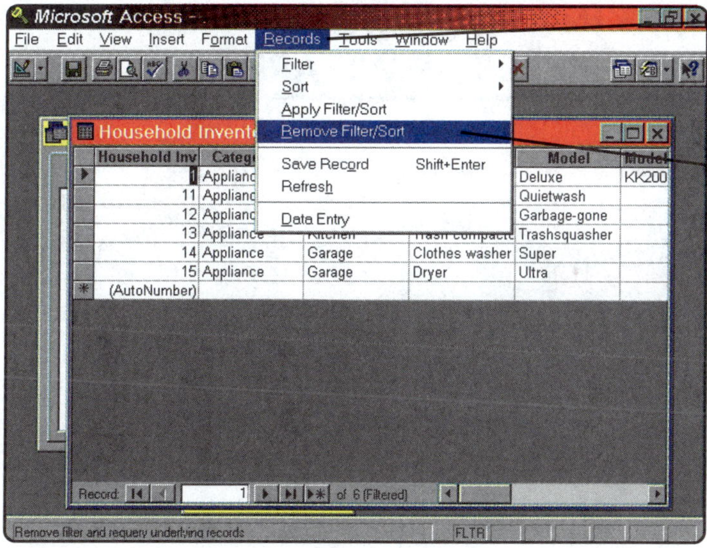

2. **Click** on **Records** in the menu bar. The Records menu will appear.

3. **Click** on **Remove Filter/ Sort**. The table will return to its original condition.

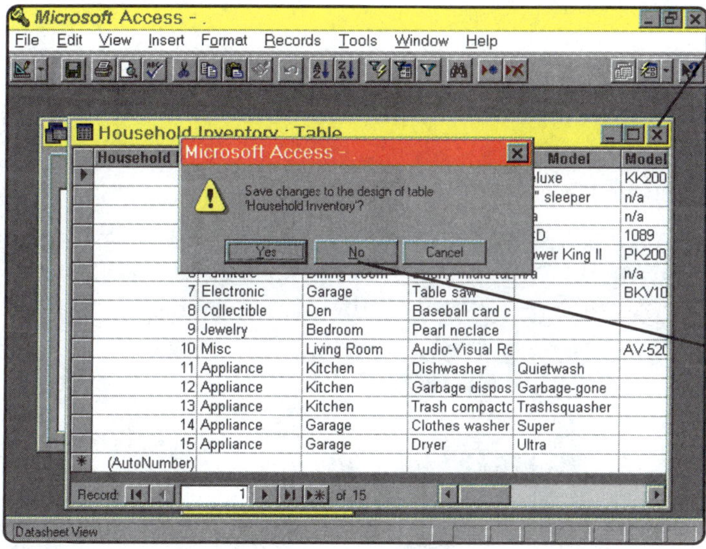

4. **Click** on the **Close button** on the Household Inventory: Table title bar. A message box will appear.

Since you want to keep the table as it was before you started the filter, choose No.

5. **Click** on **No.** The message box and table will close.

MAKING A QUERY WITHOUT THE WIZARD

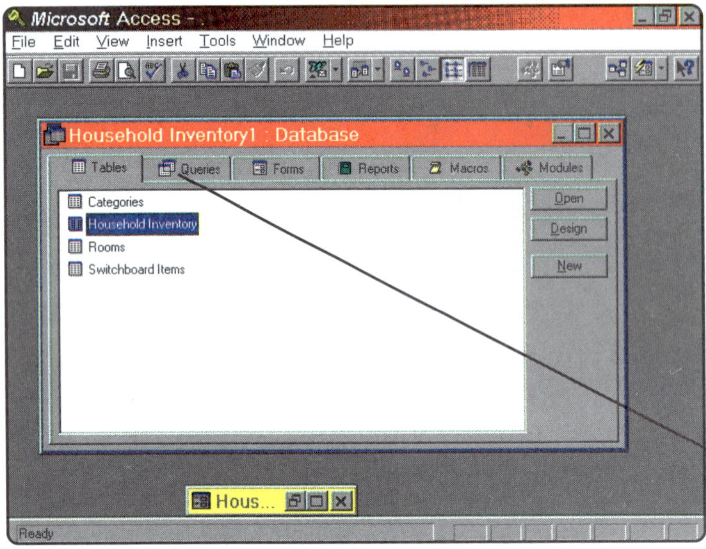

The Simple Query Wizard is great for getting data from particular fields in a couple of tables. To get this data and filter it at the same time, you need to make a query without the Wizard's help. For this example, you'll get the purchase date and appraised value of the appliances.

1. **Click** on the **Queries tab**. The list of queries will appear.

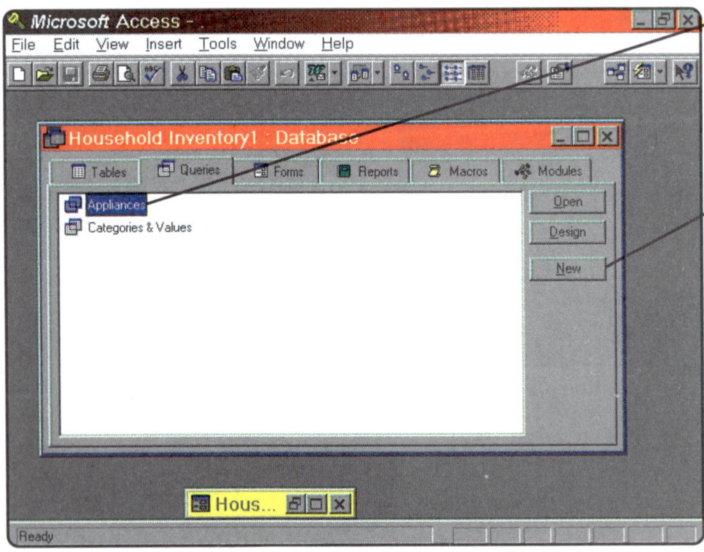

Notice that the "Appliances" query that you made from records filtered out of the Inventory table is here.

2. **Click** on **New**. The New Query dialog box will appear.

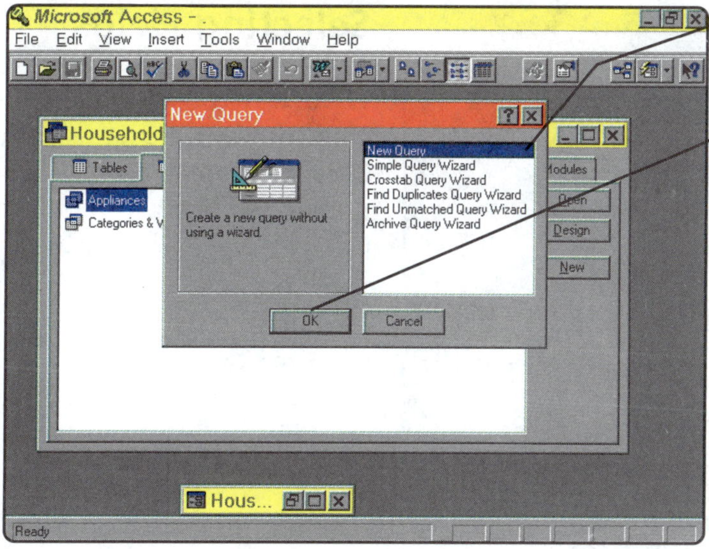

New Query, the choice you want, will be highlighted.

3. **Click** on **OK**. The Show Table dialog box will appear.

The Show Table dialog box lets you pick the tables you want to get information from. For our example, you'll first want to limit your records to those having to do with appliances, much as you did with the filter.

4. **Click** on **Categories** to highlight it.

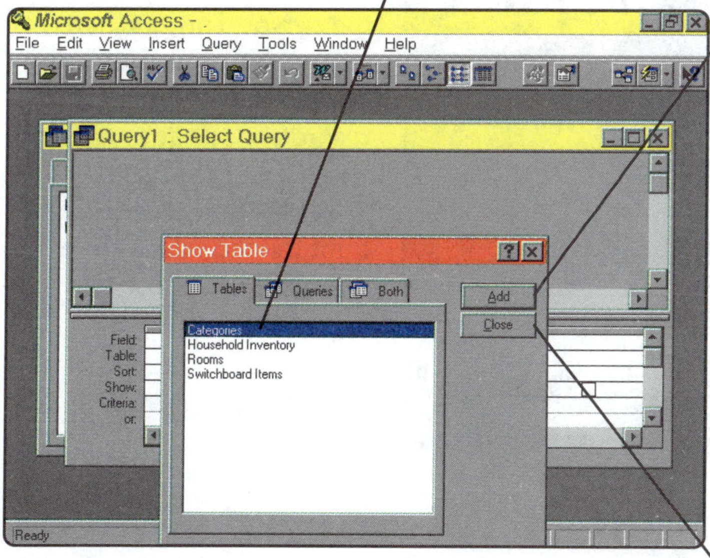

5. **Click** on **Add**. A box for the Categories table will appear in the Query1: Select Query dialog box in the background.

6. **Click** on **Household Inventory** to highlight it.

7. **Click** on **Add**. A box for the Household Inventory table will appear in the dialog box in the background.

8. **Click** on **Close**. The Show Table dialog box will disappear.

Selecting Fields

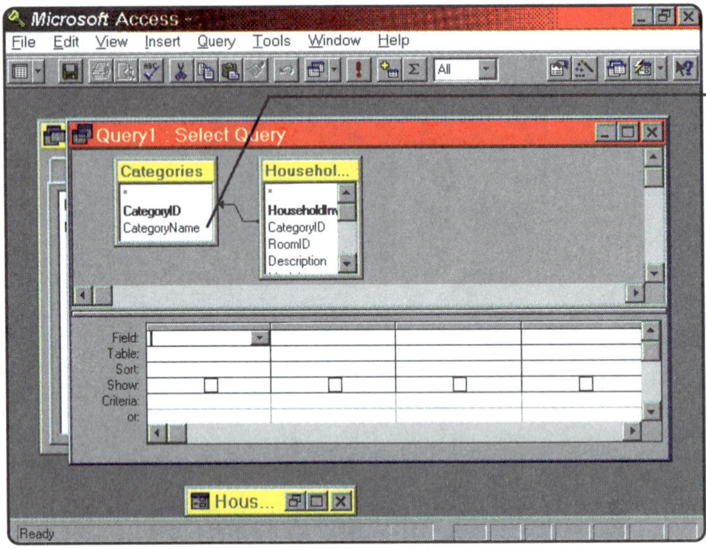

1. **Click twice** on **Category Name** in the Categories box. CategoryName will appear in the Field line, and Categories will appear in the Table line of the first column.

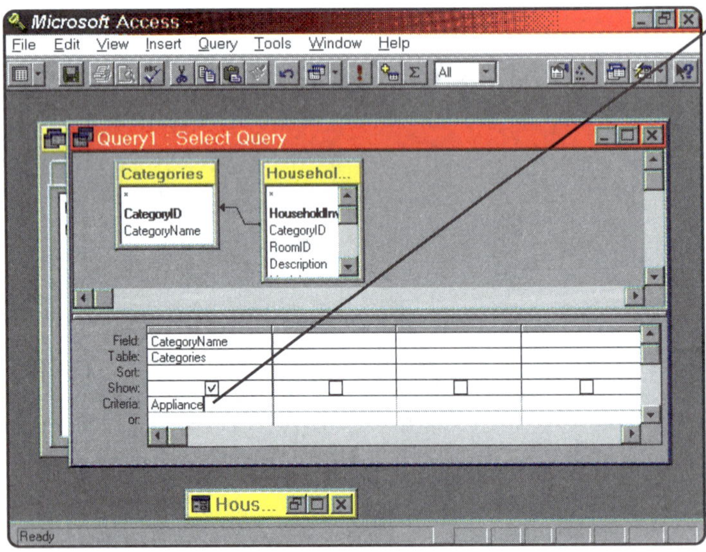

2. **Click** in the **Criteria line** of the first column to place the cursor. This is where you specify what you want the category name for the records in our query to be.

3. **Type Appliance**. This will limit the records in the query to only those for appliances.

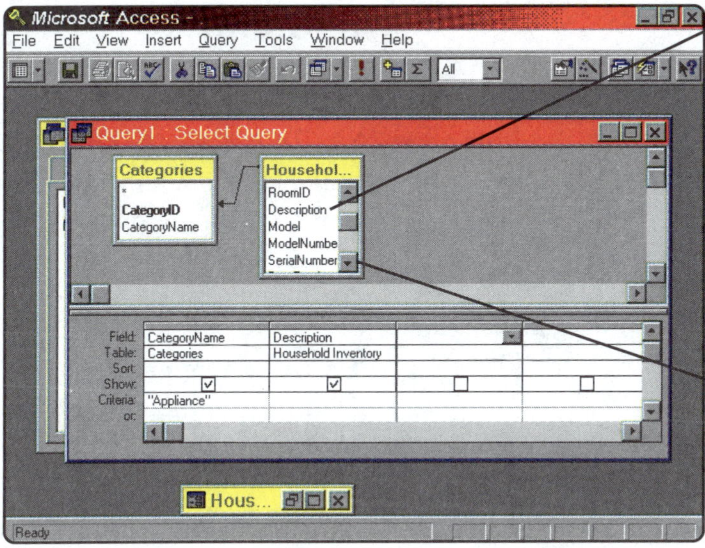

4. **Click twice** on **Description** in the Household box. Description and Household Inventory will appear, respectively, in the Field and Table lines of the second column. This will add the description to the appliance records.

5. **Click repeatedly** on the ▼ to scroll down the list of fields.

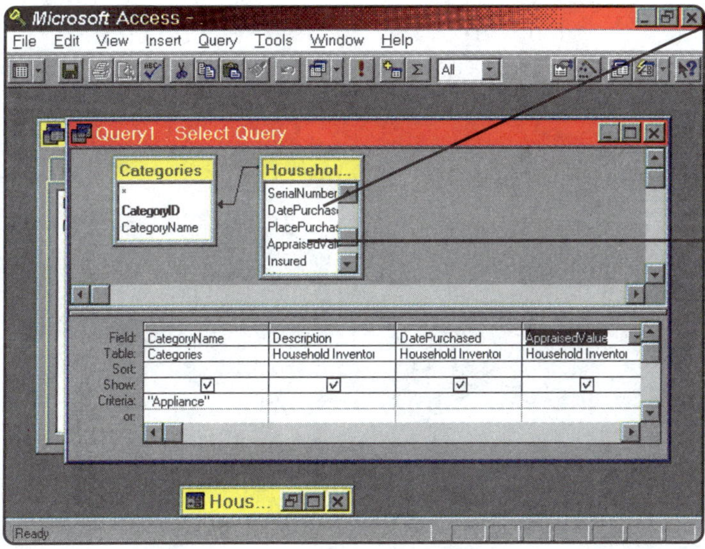

6. **Click twice** on **DatePurchased** in the Household Inventory box to add that field to the third column.

7. **Click twice** on **Appraised Value** to add that field to the fourth column.

If you wanted to, you could limit these fields, too. For example, to find only those appliances that are appraised at over $1000, you'd enter ">1000" (> means "greater than") in the criteria line for Appraised Value.

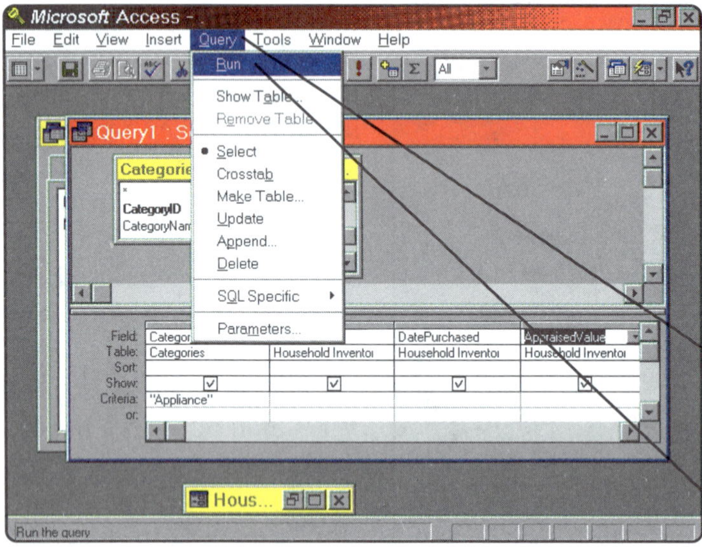

Running the Query

Now that we've specified the fields we want, and limited those fields to certain criteria, we can create the query.

1. **Click** on **Query** in the menu bar. A menu will appear.

2. **Click** on **Run**. The finished query will appear.

Your query contains only the records for appliances, and shows how old they are, and how much they're appraised for. By making a query yourself, you can be extremely specific as to which records you want to view.

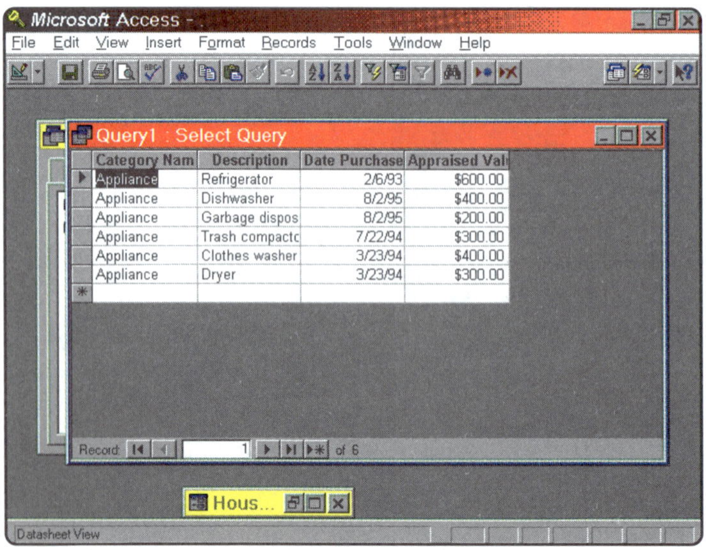

The query can be saved and checked again at any time. You can use the Form Wizard (see Chapter 10) to make a form for viewing the data online. You can also use the Report Wizard (see Chapter 12) to make a formatted printout of the information in your query, or print the query as it is.

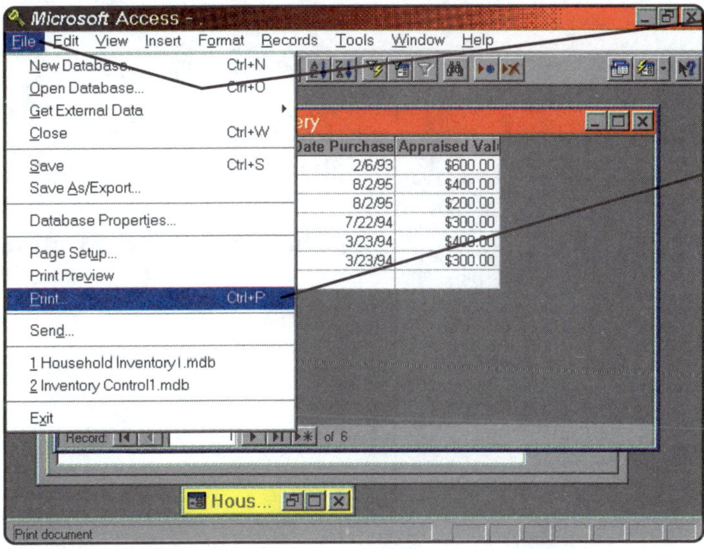

3. Click on **File** in the menu bar. The File menu will appear.

4. Click on **Print**. The query will print.

(You can see what it will look like before printing by clicking on "Print Preview.")

In any event, don't forget to save it.

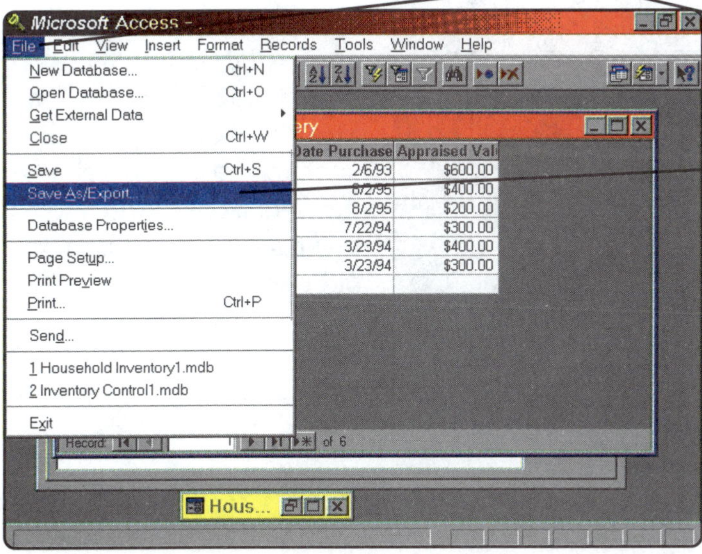

5. Click on **File** in the menu bar. The File menu will appear.

6. Click on **Save As/Export**. A Save As dialog box will appear.

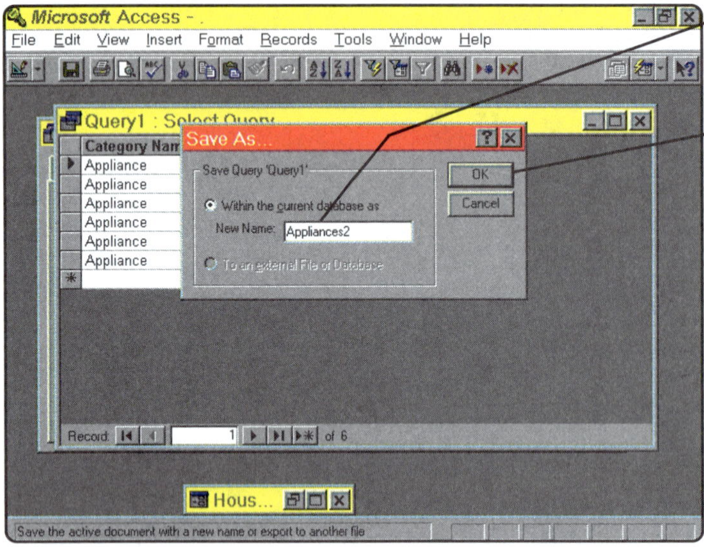

7. **Type** a **name** for the query.

8. **Click** on **OK**. The query will be saved.

9. **Click** on the **Close button** (☒) to close the Query 1 window.

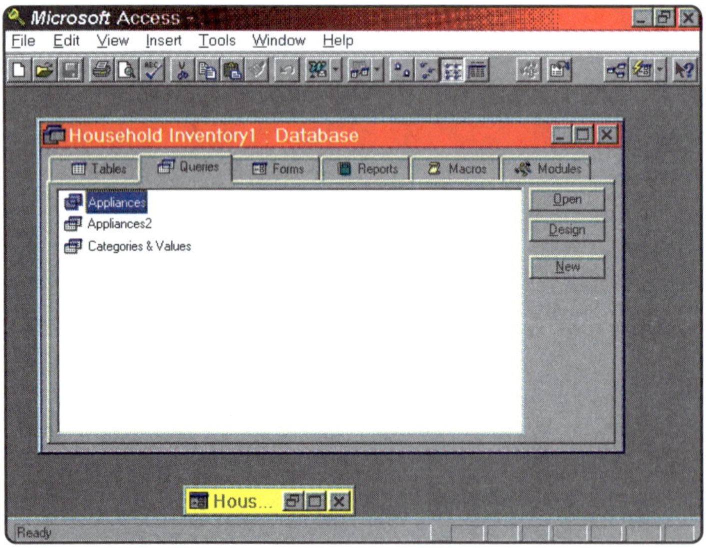

The query appears in the list under the Queries tab. If you want to change the query, highlight it, then click on the Design button. The query dialog box will appear, and you can change the fields, criteria, etc. to make a new query from the old one.

ACCESS FOR WINDOWS 95

Part II: Creating and Customizing Tables, Forms, and Reports

CHAPTER 7

Changing the Look of Your Forms

You can customize the forms design that you chose in Chapter 1. By changing colors, adding or deleting text, changing the font formatting, or importing a logo, you can transform any Wizard template into your own creation. In this chapter, you will do the following:

- ✔ Change background colors
- ✔ Resize background elements
- ✔ Delete, move, and enlarge text
- ✔ Add a logo

OPENING THE FORM DESIGN VIEW

The Form Design view contains special toolbars that allow you to customize a form.

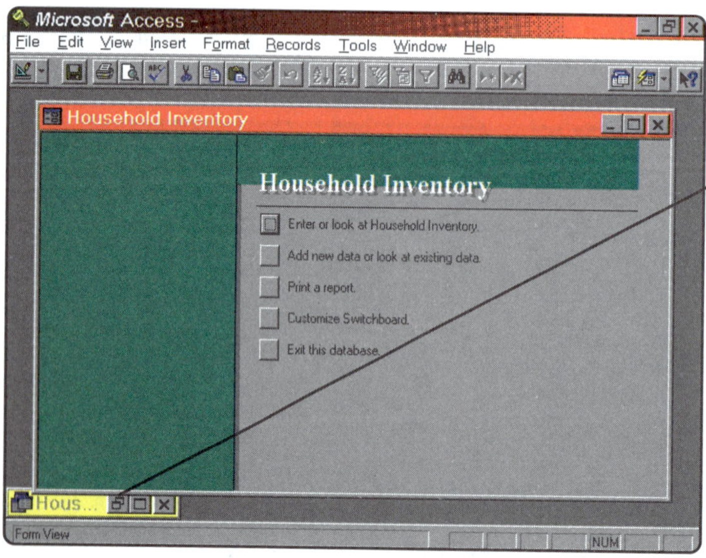

Have the opening window in Access on your screen as you see in this example.

1. **Click** on the **Restore button** on the minimized Database window. The database will open to window size.

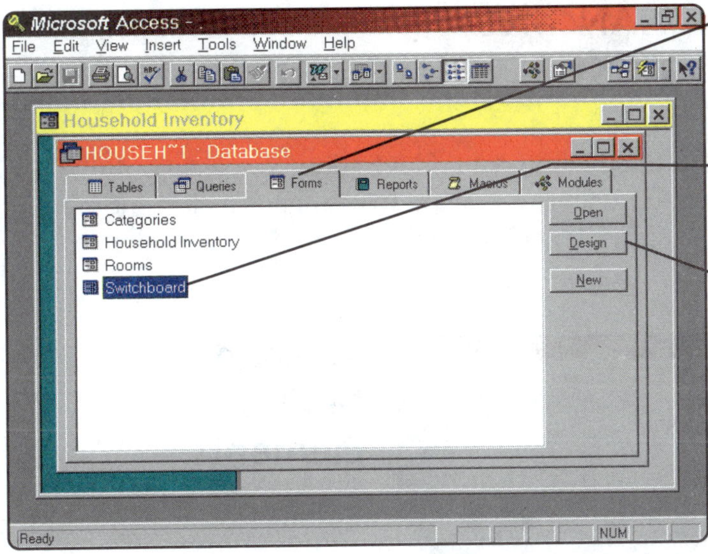

2. **Click** on the **Forms tab** to bring it to the front, if necessary.

3. **Click** on **Switchboard** to highlight it, if necessary.

4. **Click** on **Design**. The Design view window for Switchboard: Form will appear.

WORKING IN DESIGN VIEW

Maximizing the window is a way to give yourself more workspace.

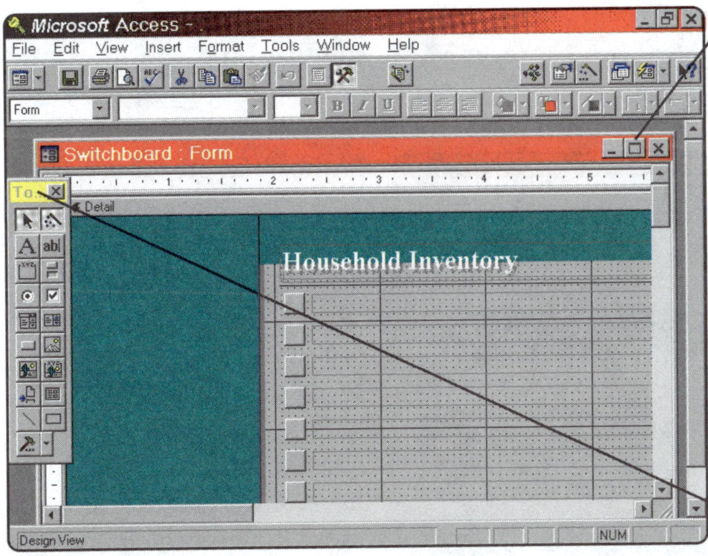

1. **Click** on the **Maximize window** (□) on the right of the Switchboard: Form title bar. The window will enlarge.

Moving a Floating Toolbar

If the design toolbox is at the extreme left of your screen, you can move it.

1. **Place** the **mouse arrow** on the toolbox's title bar. **Press and hold** the **mouse button** and **drag** the toolbox onto the color background as you see in the next example.

CHANGING BACKGROUND COLORS

In this section, you'll learn how to select, or highlight the elements you want to change. An element is any graphic, text block, line, shape, etc. that makes up your form.

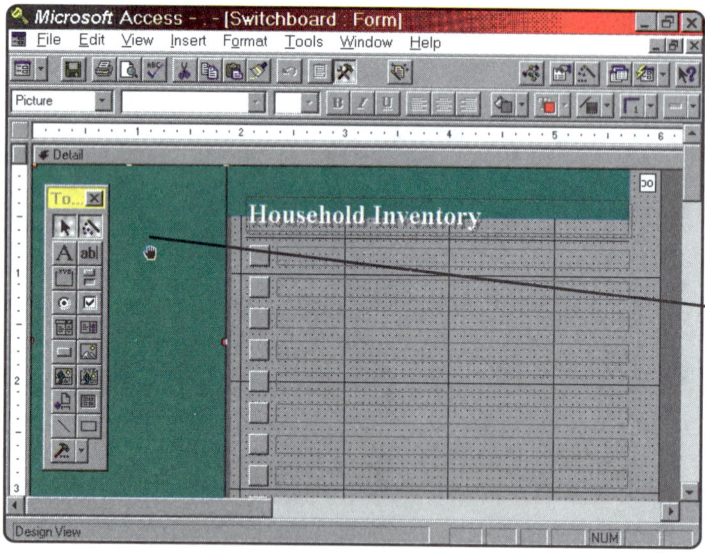

Selecting Multiple Elements

You can change more than one element at a time.

1. **Press and hold** the **Shift key** as you **click** on the large background color rectangle on the left. It will be surrounded by a line with small solid squares, or handles on it.

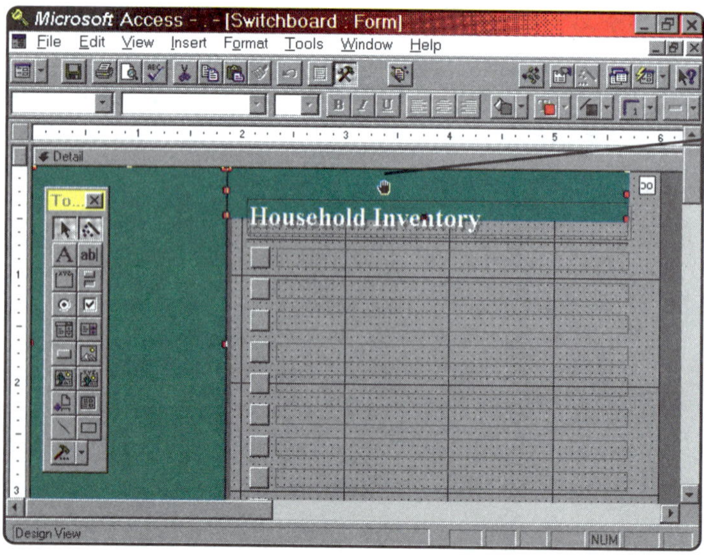

Notice that the mouse arrow becomes a hand.

2. **Continue** to **hold** the **Shift key** as you **click** on the small background color rectangle at the top. It will also be surrounded by handles. Holding the Shift key allows you to select more than one element at a time.

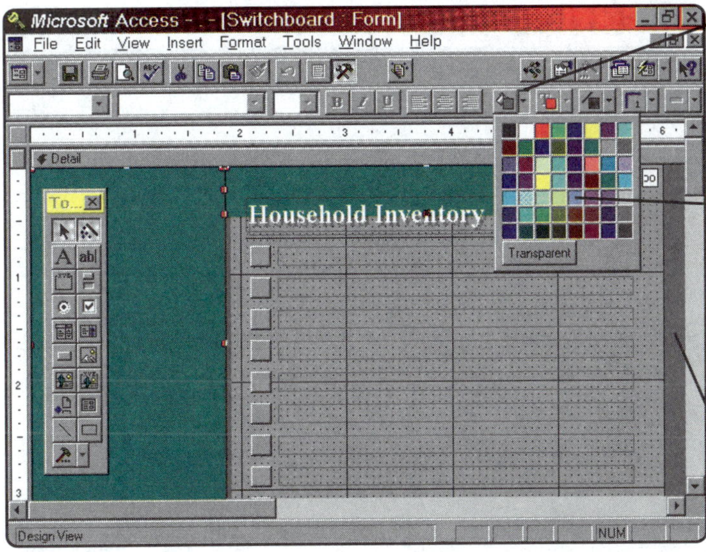

3. **Click** on the ▼ to the right of the Background Color button. A pop-down color palette will appear.

4. **Click** on the **medium blue color square**. It's in the fifth column, fifth row. Both rectangles will change to blue, and the palette will disappear.

5. **Click** on the **dark gray background** to remove the handles from both rectangles.

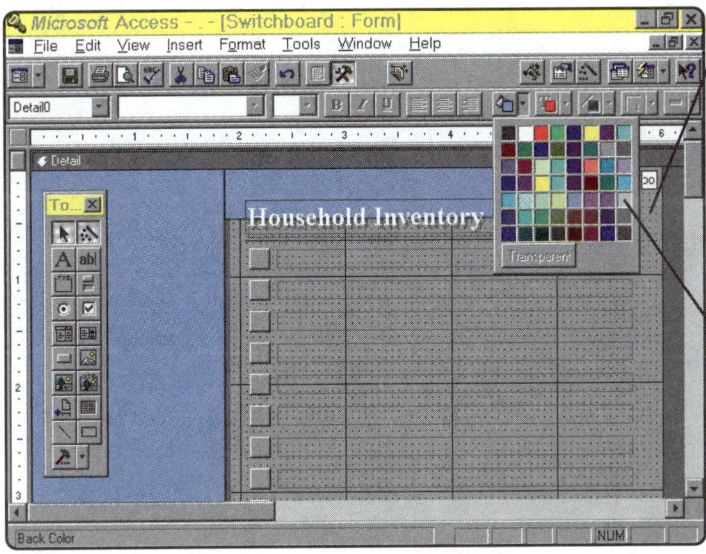

6. **Click** on the **medium gray background** that has the grid pattern.

7. **Repeat steps 3 and 4 above** to see the Background Color palette as you see in this example.

8. **Click** on the **light gray color square**. It's in the last column, fifth row. The background will change to light gray, and the palette will disappear.

DELETING ELEMENTS

In this example, you'll remove the shadow text behind "Household Inventory."

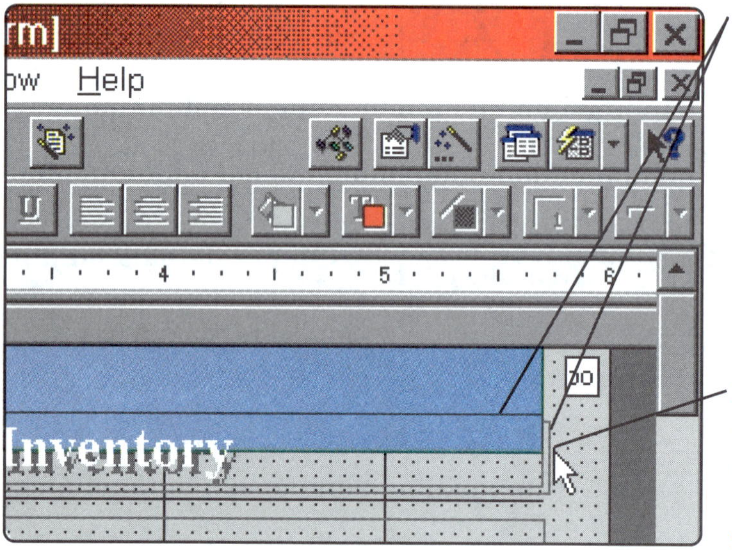

Notice that there are two separate text boxes. The text box on top contains the white "Household Inventory" text. The text box on the bottom contains the gray "Household Inventory" text that is the shadow.

1. **Place** your **mouse arrow** close to, but not touching the bottom text box.

2. **Click** to see the **handles** around the bottom text box as you see in the example below.

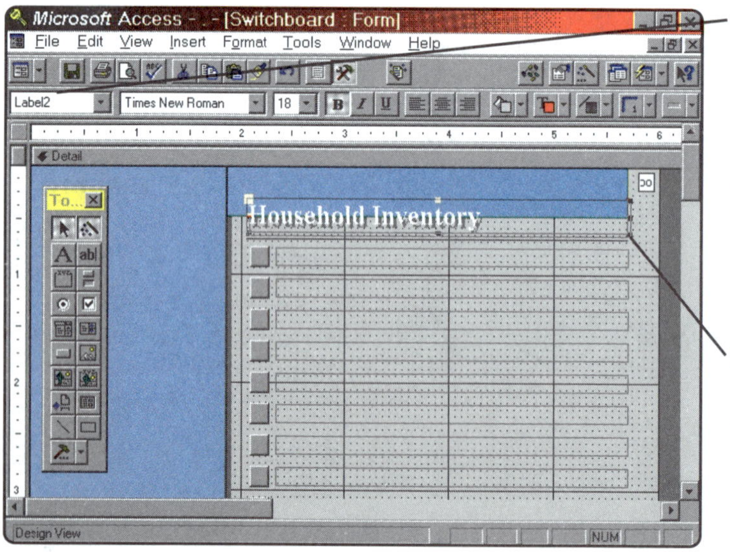

Notice that the box on the far left of the toolbar says "Label2." If the box says "Label1," click on the dark gray background to remove the handles and try again. Don't get discouraged, this can be a bit tricky.

3. When the "Label2" text box is selected, **press** the **Delete key** on your keyboard. The shadow text box will disappear.

RESIZING ELEMENTS

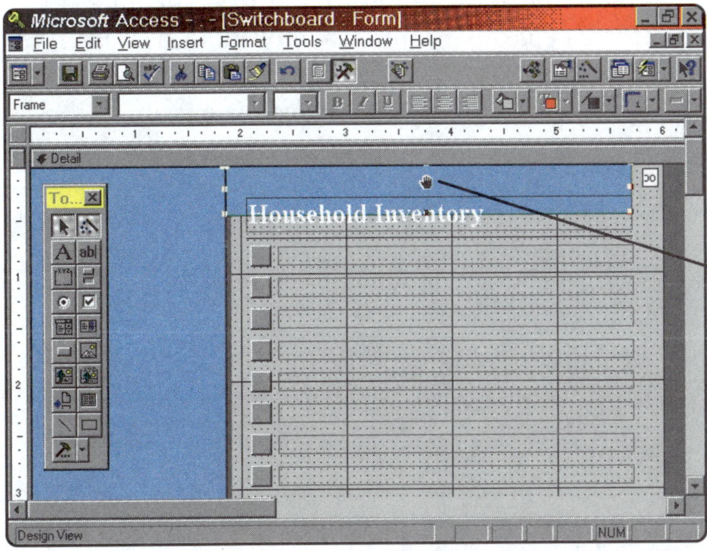

An element is any of the components that make up your form. In this section, you'll resize a background rectangle, and move a text block.

1. **Click** on the **small colored rectangle above Household Inventory** to select it. The selection handles will surround it as you see in this example. The cursor will become a hand.

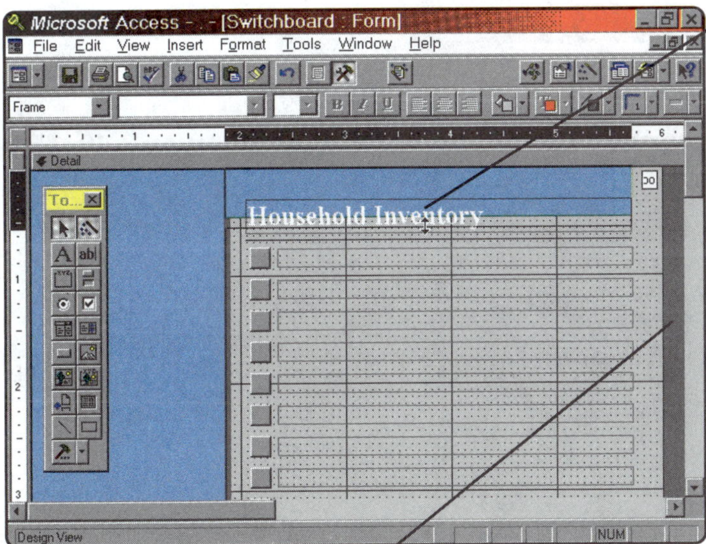

2. **Place** the hand on the **middle handle** at the bottom of the block. The cursor will change to a two-headed arrow.

3. **Press and hold** the **mouse button** as you **drag** the cursor down to below the "y" in Inventory.

Notice that as you drag, black highlighting appears in the rulers at the top and left sides of the window. This shows you the size of the element you have selected. The highlighting changes to reflect the new size as you drag.

4. **Release** the **mouse button,** and **click** on the dark gray background to remove the handles.

Moving an Element

1. **Click** in the **"Household Inventory"** text block to select it. The mouse pointer will become an I-beam.

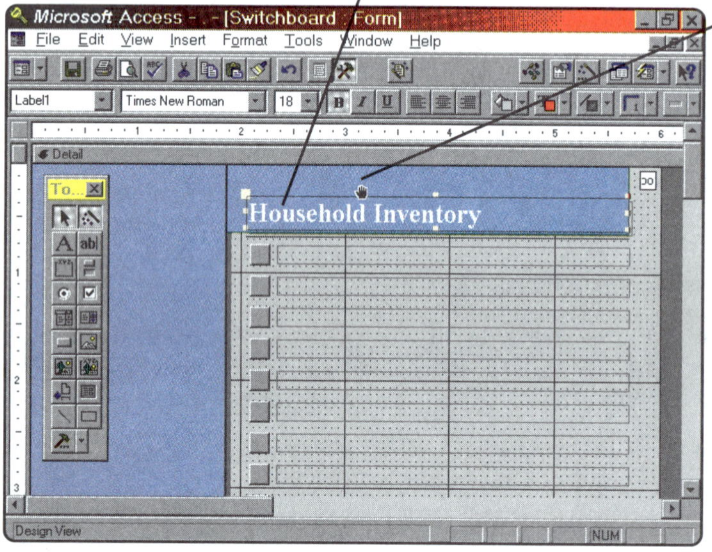

2. **Place** the **cursor** on the **border** of the text block. The cursor will become a hand. Be careful *not* to place the cursor on a square handle.

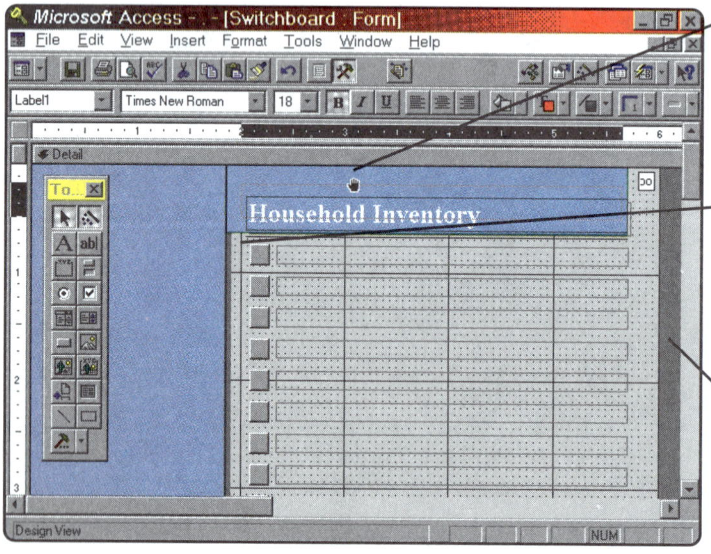

3. **Press and hold** the **mouse button** as you **drag** the text block up and slightly to the left.

Try to align the left edge of the text block with the black line to the left of the gray buttons.

4. **Release** the **mouse button** and **click** in the dark gray background to remove the selection handles.

CHANGING THE FONT SIZE

You change the text, or font size just as you do in word processing.

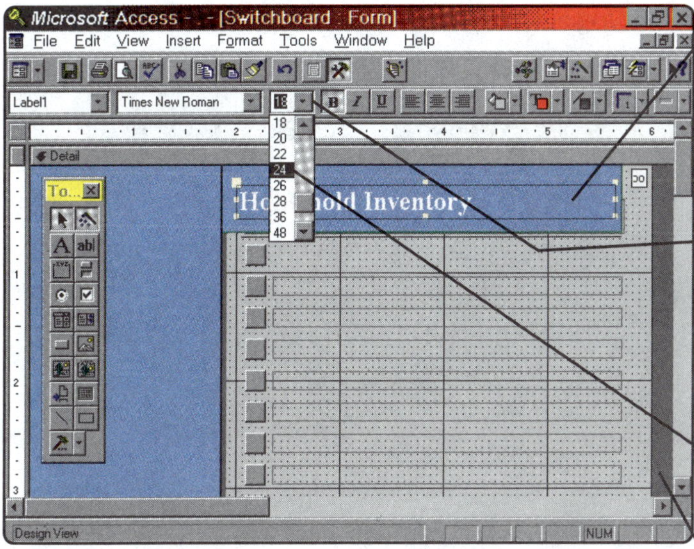

1. **Click anywhere** in the "Household Inventory" text block to select it. The mouse pointer will become an I-beam.
2. **Click** on the ▼ to the right of the Font Size box. A pull-down menu will appear as you see in this example.
3. **Click** on **24**. The text will be resized to 24 points.
4. **Click** on the **dark gray background** to deselect the text block and remove the handles.

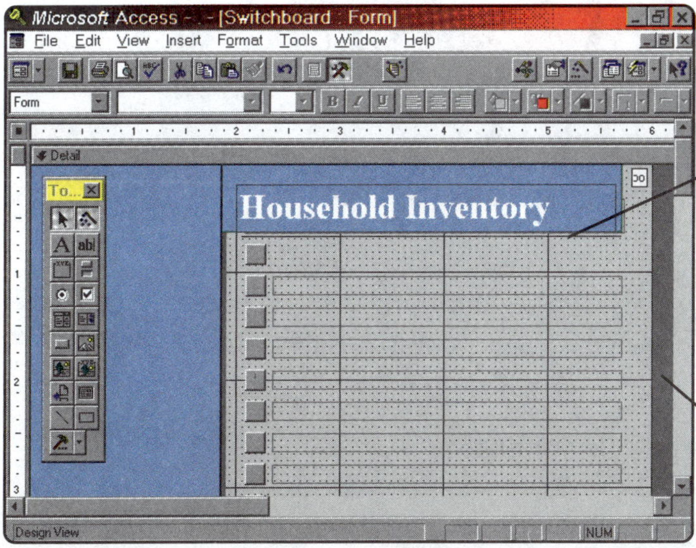

Notice that on your screen the letter "y" gets cut off at the bottom.

5. **Repeat steps 1 to 4** in the previous section entitled "Resizing Elements" to expand the bottom of the text block and show the complete letter "y."
6. **Click** on the **dark gray background** to remove the handles.

CHANGING TEXT COLOR

There is a special color palette for text.

1. **Click anywhere** in the "Household Inventory" text block to select it. The mouse pointer will become an I-beam.

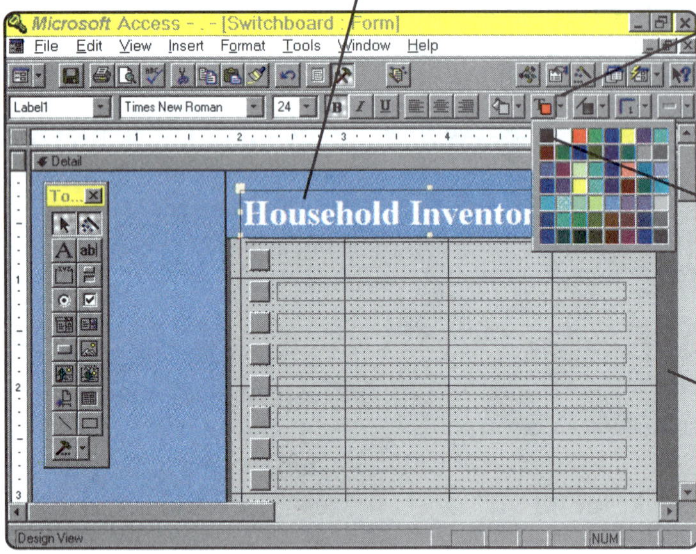

2. **Click** on the ▼ to the right of the Foreground Color button (the one with the T). A color palette will appear.

3. **Click** on the **black square**. It's the first square on the palette. The text will change to black.

4. **Click** on the **dark gray background** to remove the handles.

CHANGING TEXT

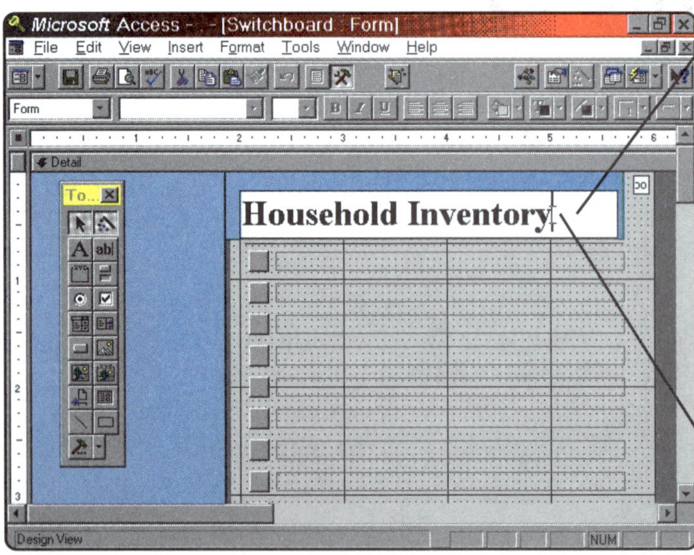

1. **Click anywhere** in the "Household Inventory" text block to select it. The mouse pointer will become an I-beam.

Note: If your text disappears, it's because you have white text on a white background. Try changing the text color.

2. **Click** to place the cursor at the end of the text you want to change.

3. **Press and hold** the **mouse button** as you **drag** the cursor to the left to highlight the words.

4. **Type** the **new text**. In this example, we won't change "Household Inventory."

5. **Click** on the **dark gray background** to remove the selection handles.

ADDING A LOGO

If you have a graphics file that contains your logo, you can add it to your form.

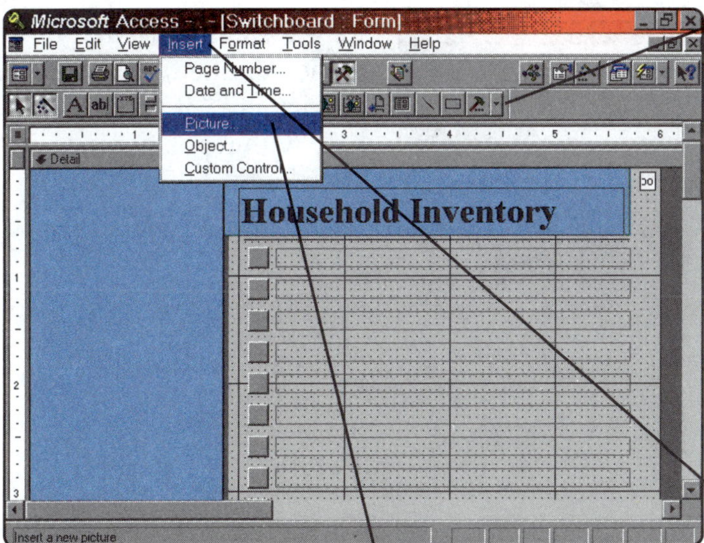

Notice that the Controls toolbar has been moved from the side of the form to the top. You can move the toolbar to another place on the screen with the process described in "Moving a Floating Toolbar" on page 81 of this chapter. You can also "dock" it, as you see here. See Chapter 13 for directions on docking.

1. **Click** on **Insert** in the menu bar. The Insert menu will appear.

2. **Click** on **Picture**. The Insert Picture dialog box will appear.

3. **Click** on the **directory** that contains your file. A list of all files in that dictory will appear.

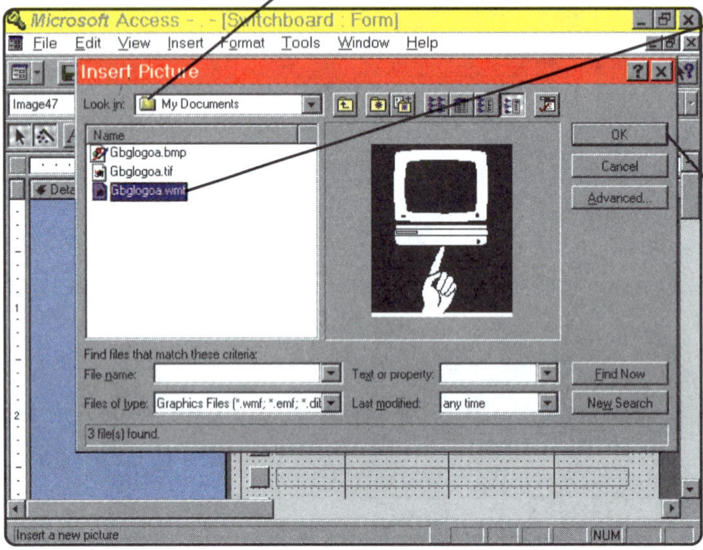

4. **Click** on the **file** you want to place. A picture of the file will appear in the Preview box.

5. **Click** on **OK**. The dialog box will disappear, and the picture will appear on your form.

Repeat steps 1 to 4 in the section entitled, "Moving an Element," if you need help with repositioning your logo.

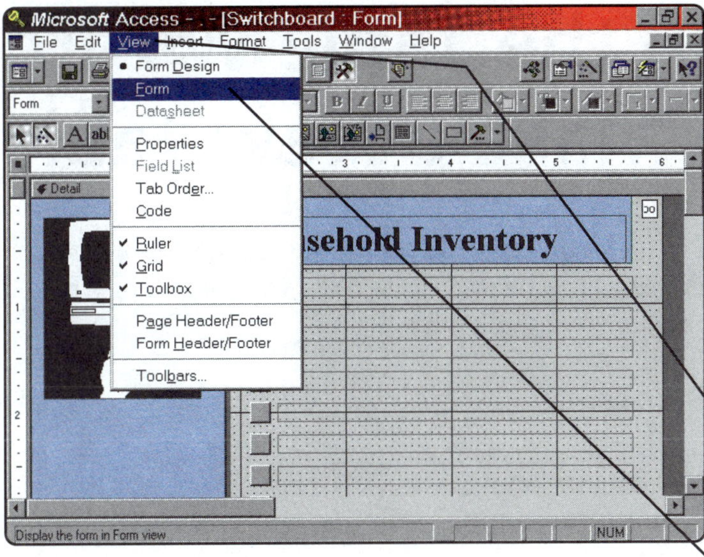

VIEWING AND SAVING YOUR FORM

As you work, you can switch back and forth from Design view to regular view to see what your changes really look like.

1. **Click** on **View** in the menu bar. The View menu will appear.

2. **Click** on **Form**. The Form view will appear.

You can switch between Design view and Form view by repeating steps 1 and 2 above.

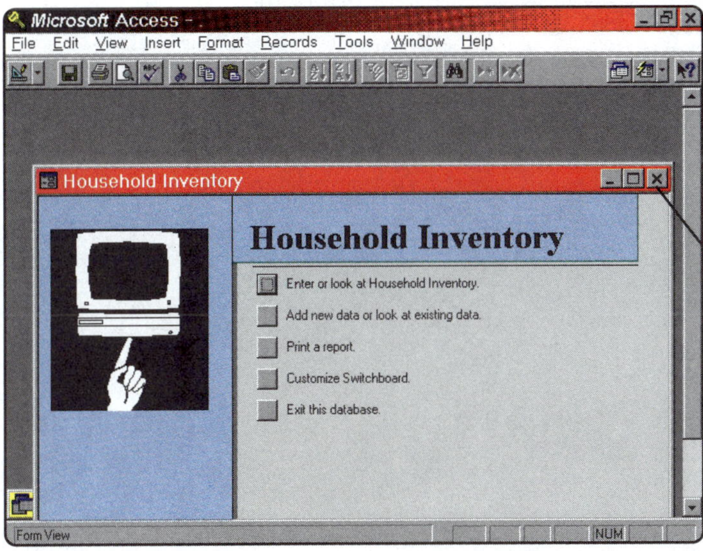

3. If you're satisfied with your new look, **press and hold** the **Control key** as you **type** the letter **s** (ctrl + s). This saves the changes to the form.

4. If you don't like the changes, **click** on the **Close button** (X) on the form. You'll be asked if you want to save the changes. **Click** on **No**.

The good news is that you've created a personalized look for your form. The bad news is that these changes aren't universal. You'll have to change every other form as well.

CHAPTER 8

Using the Table Wizard to Make a New Table

Once again the Wizard is going to make life easy for you! Making a new table to add to your database is quick and easy, and the Wizard has a large variety of tables to choose from. In this chapter, you will do the following:

- ✔ Make a new table using the Table Wizard
- ✔ Rename field names
- ✔ Establish a relationship with a table

STARTING THE TABLE WIZARD

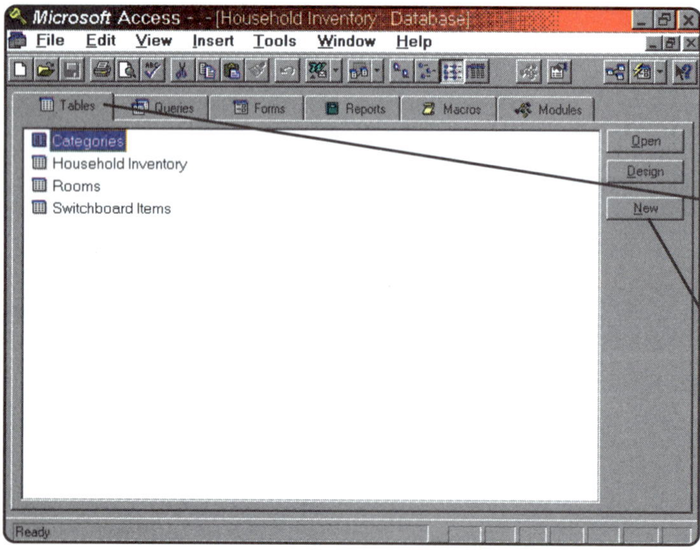

1. **Open** the **Database window**, if it isn't already open. In this example, we maximized the screen.
2. **Click** on the **Tables tab** to bring it to the front of the window.
3. **Click** on the **New button**. The New Table dialog box will appear.

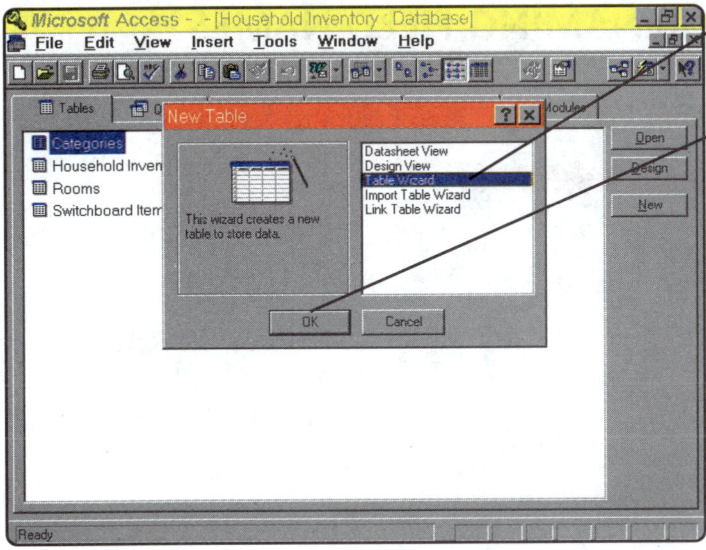

4. **Click** on **Table Wizard** to highlight it.

5. **Click** on **OK**. An hourglass will appear briefly while the Wizard begins to do its thing!

Next the Table Wizard window will appear.

CHOOSING THE TYPE OF TABLE

In this section, we'll make a table to list information about insurance companies and policy numbers.

1. **Use** the **scroll button** to view the different types of tables. By clicking on Personal to place a dot in the circle you can view another list of tables.

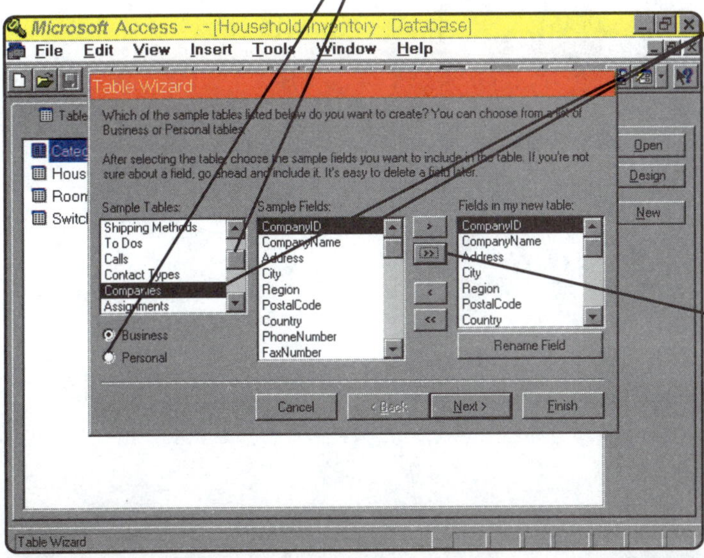

2. **Click** on a **table type.** In this example, it is Companies in the business category. Notice that the field names associated with the table type appear in the Sample Fields dialog box.

3. **Click** on the **>> button** to choose all of the fields associated with this table. We will modify two of those fields in the next section.

RENAMING FIELD NAMES

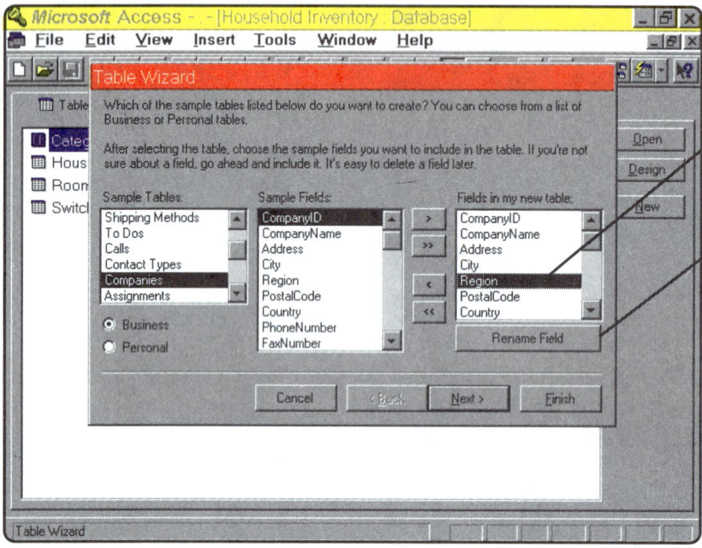

In this section, you will rename two field names.

1. **Click** on **Region** to highlight it.

2. **Click** on the **Rename Field button**. The Rename field dialog box will appear.

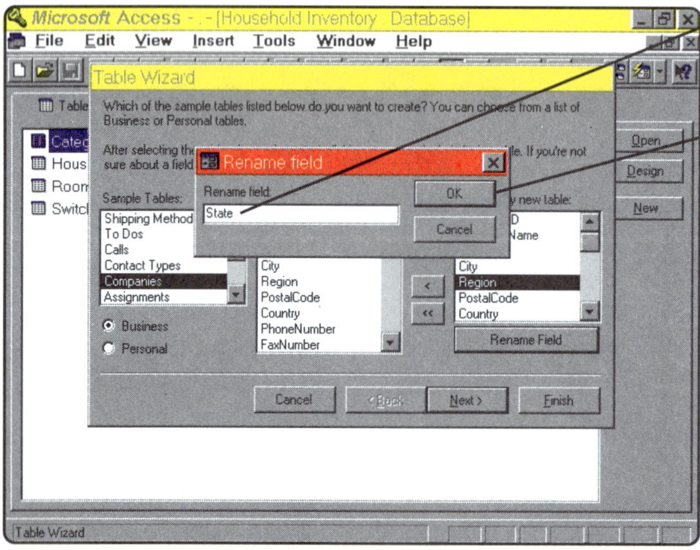

3. **Type** the **new field name**. In this example, it is State.

4. **Click** on **OK**. The dialog box will close.

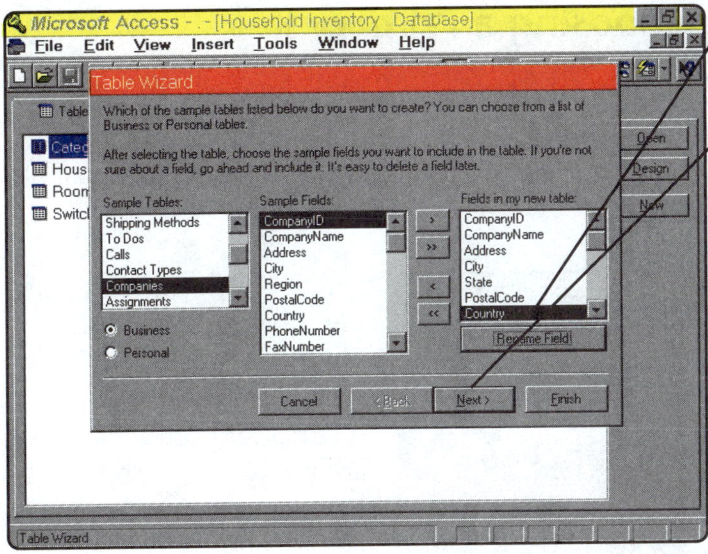

5. **Repeat steps 2 to 4** to change Country to Policy#.

6. **Click** on **Next >**. Another Table Wizard dialog box will appear.

NAMING THE TABLE

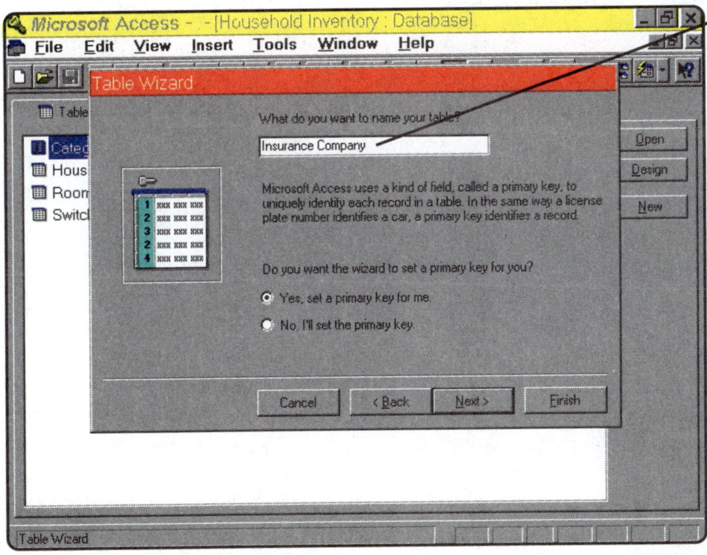

1. **Type** the **name** of the table. We called our table Insurance Company.

Choosing a Primary Key

To get the most from Access, each table should be set up to have at least one primary key field. The Wizard will set up the first column with AutoNumber as the primary key.

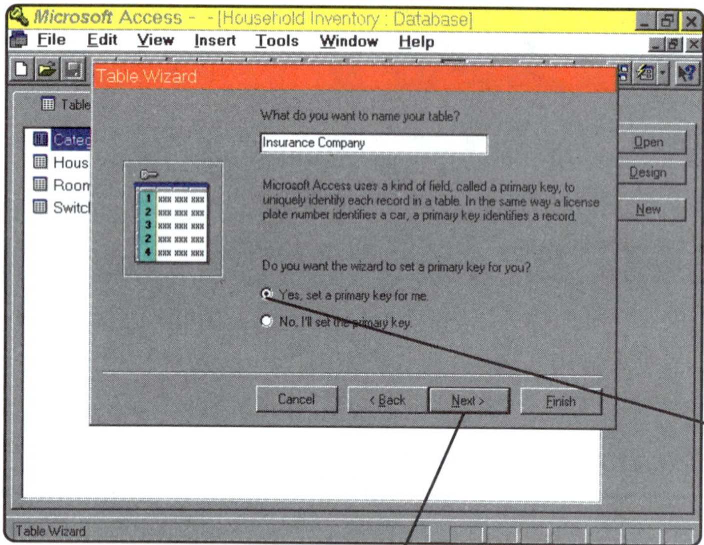

A primary key is a unique identifier for each record. Numbers, such as the AutoNumber or a social security, or product number, are unique. A person's name is not a good primary key because more than one person can have the same name.

1. **Click** on **Yes,** if it doesn't already have a dot in the circle. The Wizard will add AutoNumber to the first column.

2. **Click** on **Next >**. Another Wizard dialog box will appear.

DEFINING RELATIONSHIPS

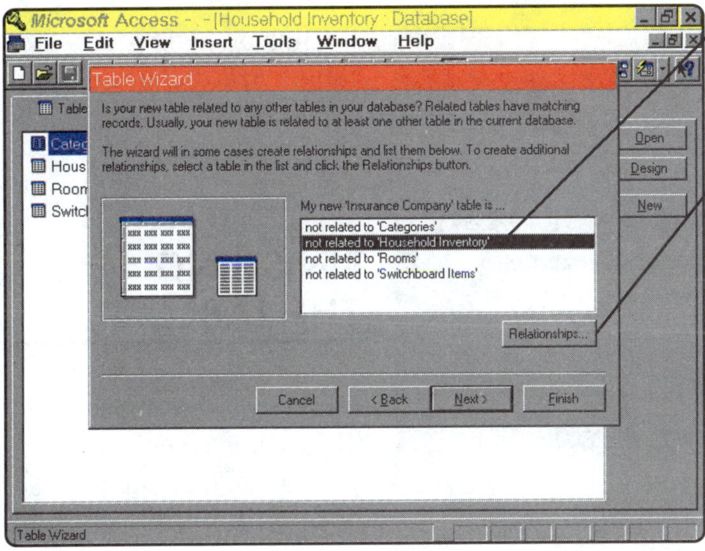

1. **Click** on **not related to 'Household Inventory'** to highlight it.

2. **Click** on the **Relationships button**. The Relationships dialog box will appear.

3. **Click** on the **middle option** to place a dot in the circle.

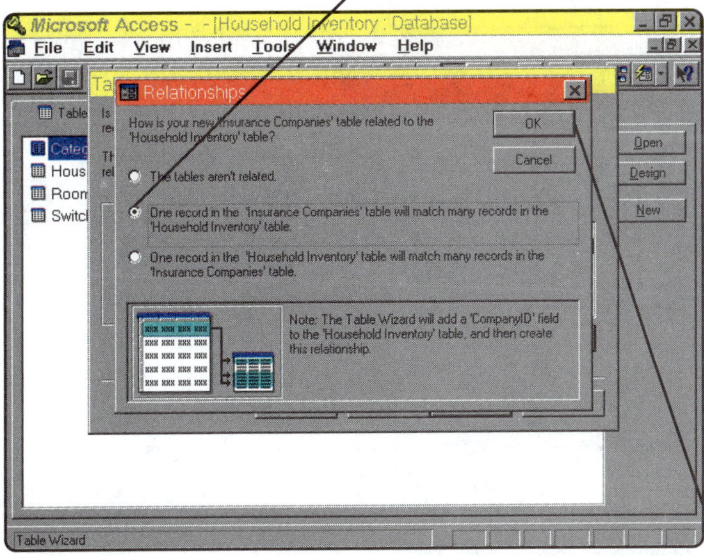

This is called a "one to many" relationship. It means that a particular entry can appear on the Insurance Company table only once, but that the same entry can appear many times on the Household Inventory. For example, Coburn Insurance will be listed on the Insurance Company table only once, but many items on the Household Inventory can be insured by Coburn Insurance.

4. **Click** on **OK**. The dialog box will close.

Notice now that the relationship between this new table and 'Household Inventory' has changed.

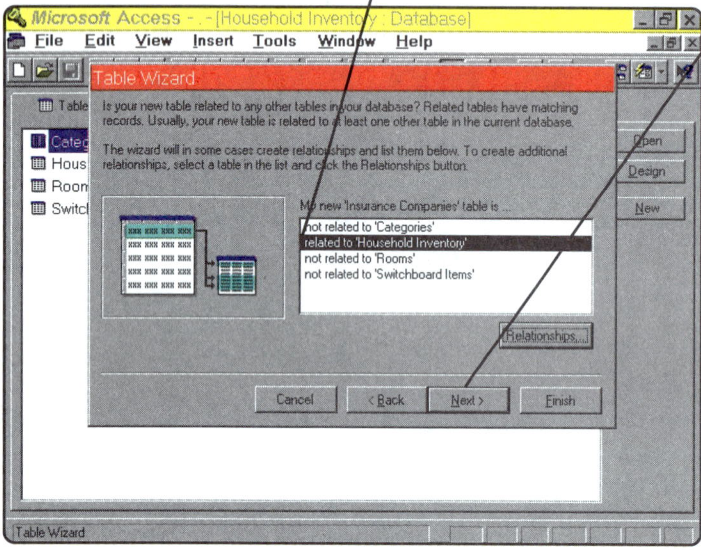

5. **Click** on **Next >**. Another Table Wizard dialog box will appear.

FINISHING THE TABLE

The Wizard has the last dialog box of choices for you to make before your table is complete.

If you want to make any changes to the design of the table, click on the circle to choose this option.

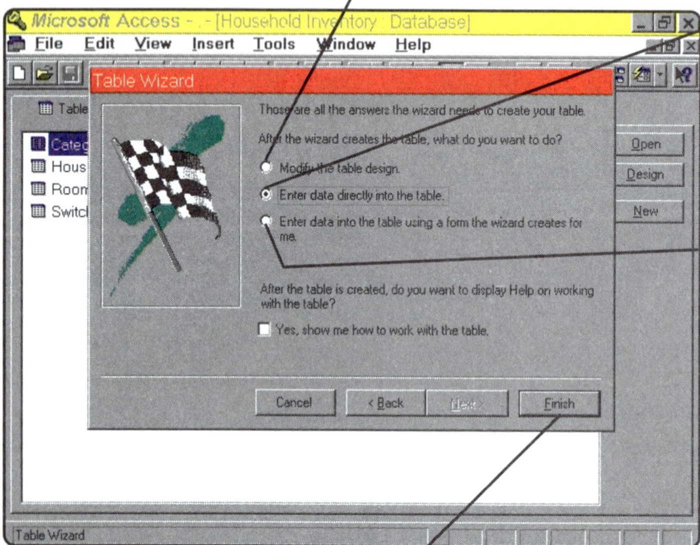

The second option allows you to enter data directly into the table. In this example, we will choose this option.

You can choose to have the Wizard create a data entry form for this table by clicking on the third option. We won't choose this option right now because we want to show you how to create a form independently of a table in Chapter 10.

1. **Click** on **Finish**. The Insurance Company Table will appear.

ENTERING DATA

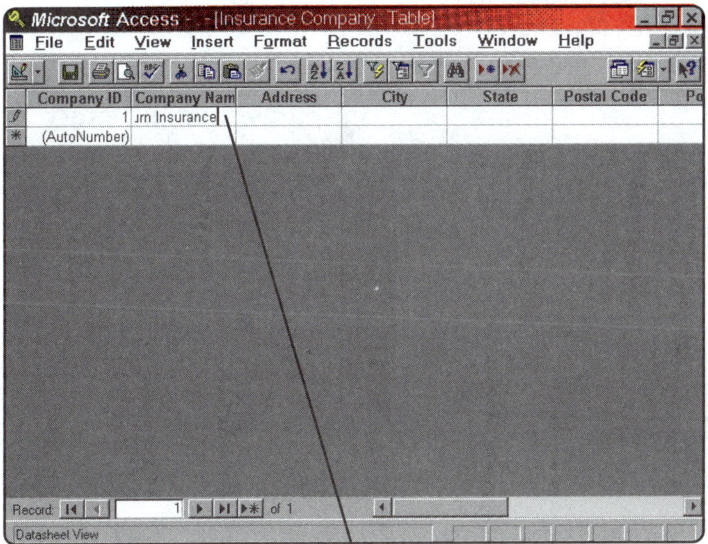

The table is now ready for data entry. You can make your data entries directly onto this table, or you can skip to Chapter 10 "Using the Forms Wizard to Make a New Form" to make a Company Insurance form.

In this example, we will enter information for three Insurance companies. This information will be used in Chapter 9, as the Household Inventory table is customized and a relationship between the two tables is defined.

1. **Click** on **Company Name** to set the cursor and **type** the **name**. The Company ID will automatically appear as you begin typing.

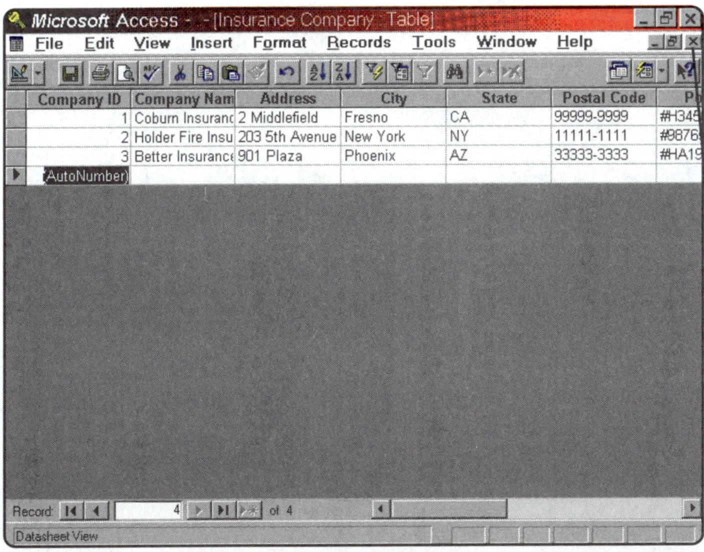

2. **Press** the **Tab key** to move to the next field.

3. **Continue** to **enter** your data using the tab key to move between fields.

CLOSING THE TABLE

1. **Click** on the **Close button** (☒) in the Microsoft Access menu bar. The [Household Inventory: Database] window will appear.

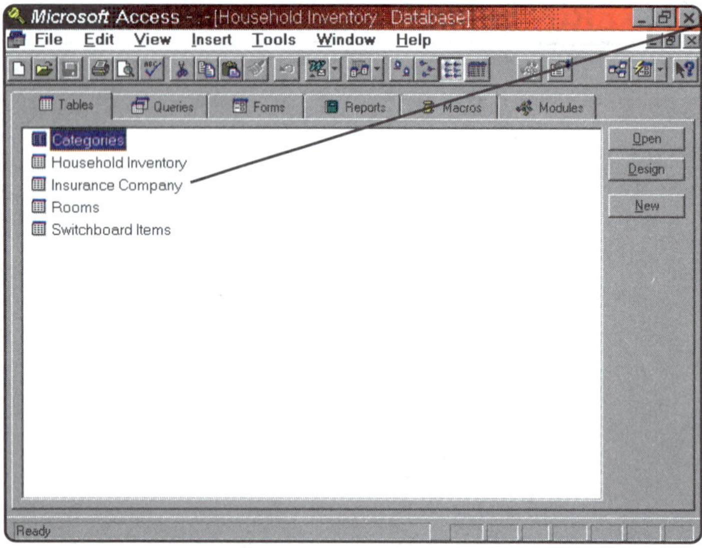

Notice that Insurance Company has been added to your list of Tables.

Note: You now have to go to the Household Inventory table and make a formal connection between it and this new table. See Chapter 9, "Customizing a Table," for details.

CHAPTER 9

Customizing a Table

There are many ways to customize Access tables. Some of the basic options are illustrated in this chapter. Once you are familiar with Access, you can explore the others on your own. This chapter will also show you how to make a combo box, which is one way to access information from another table. You can freeze columns to make it easier to work with large tables. In this chapter, you will do the following:

- ✔ Rename a column and change column width
- ✔ Delete, move, and hide a column
- ✔ Change the properties of a column
- ✔ Add a pull-down list box (combo box)
- ✔ Search and replace text in a column
- ✔ Freeze and unfreeze columns

OPENING A TABLE

In this chapter, you'll customize the Household Inventory table.

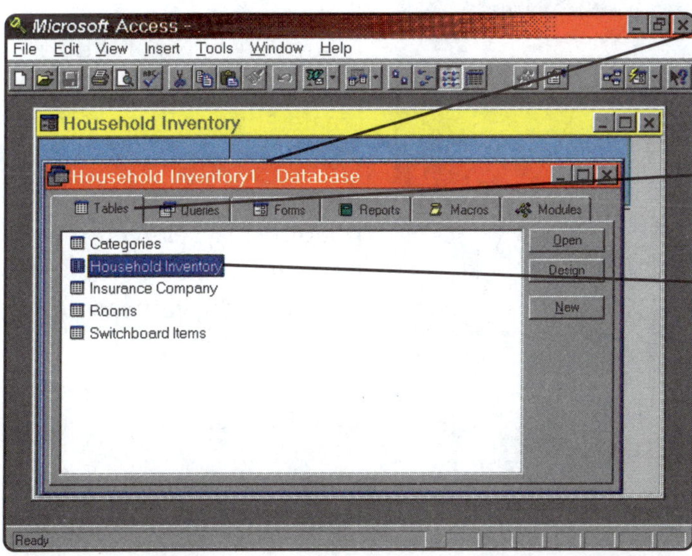

1. **Open** the **Household Inventory1: Database** if it is not already open.
2. **Click** on the **Tables tab** to bring it to the front.
3. **Click twice** on **Household Inventory** to open it.

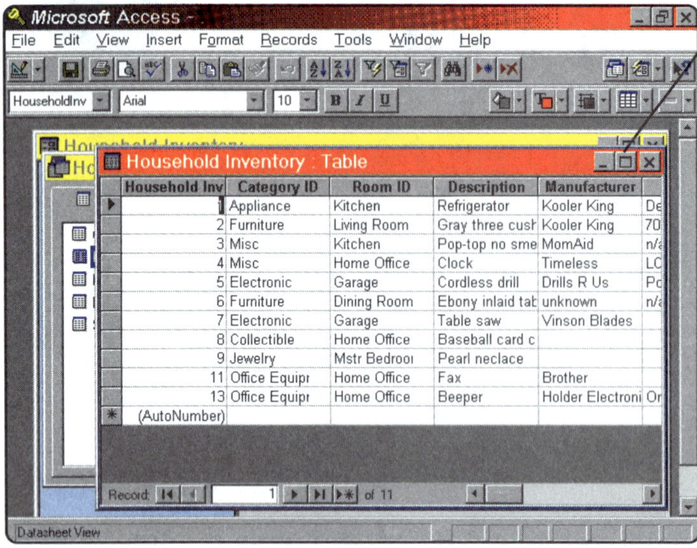

4. **Click** on the **Maximize button** (□) to enlarge the window.

RENAMING A COLUMN

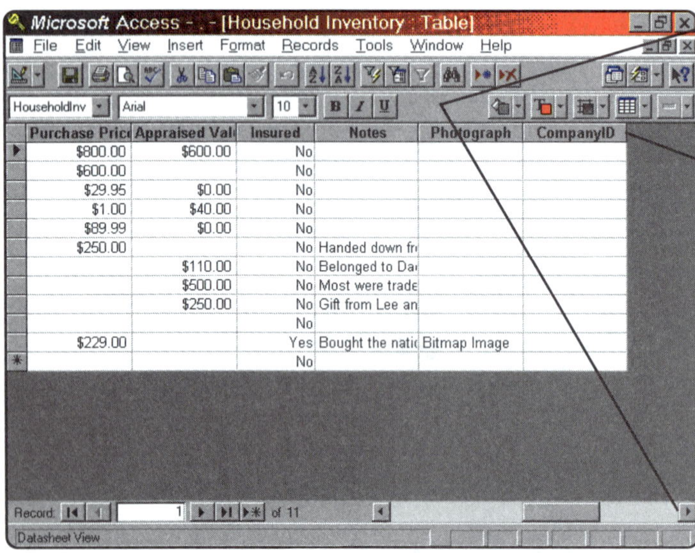

1. **Click repeatedly** on the ▸ to scroll to the right side of the table as shown here.

Notice the new column, "Company ID." This was created by the Wizard in Chapter 8 when you told the Wizard to create a relationship between the new "Insurance Company" table and the Household Inventory table. We'll deal with this column later in this chapter.

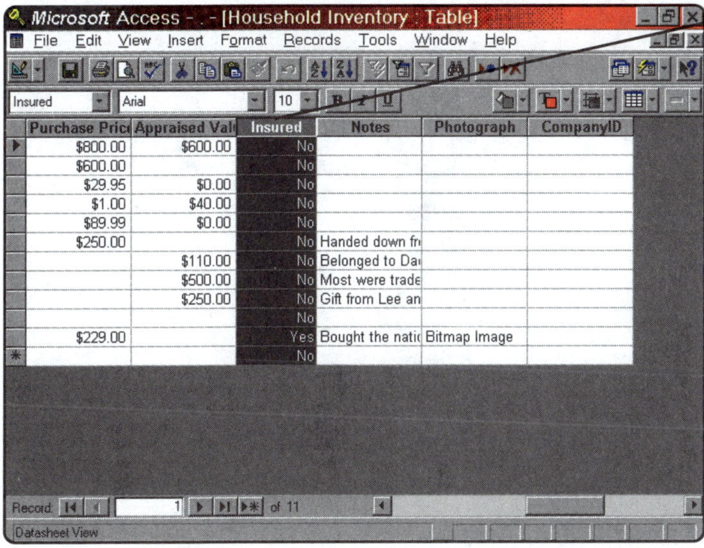

2. Click on **Insured** to highlight the column.

3. Click on **Format** in the menu bar. The Format menu will appear.

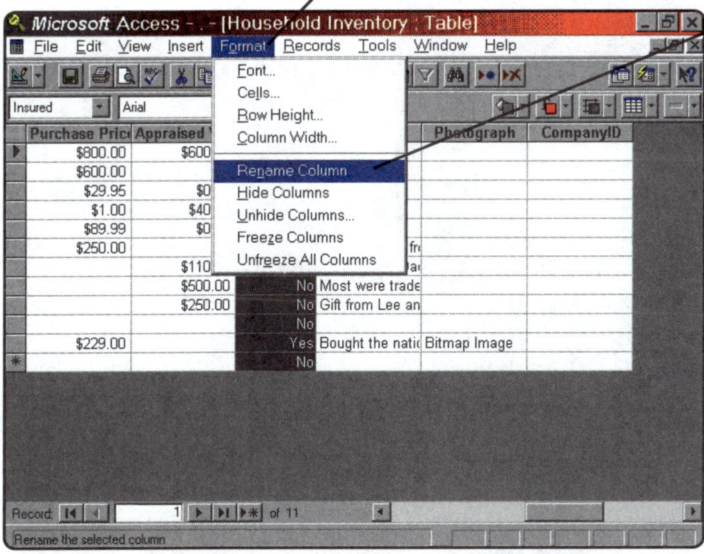

4. Click on **Rename Column**. The menu will close and "Insured" will be highlighted.

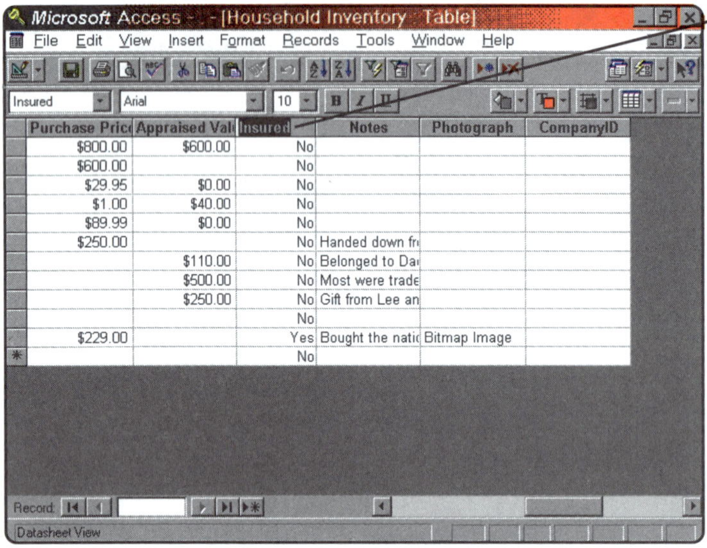

5. **Click** at the end of **Insured** to place the cursor.

6. **Type** a **?** to make the heading "Insured?".

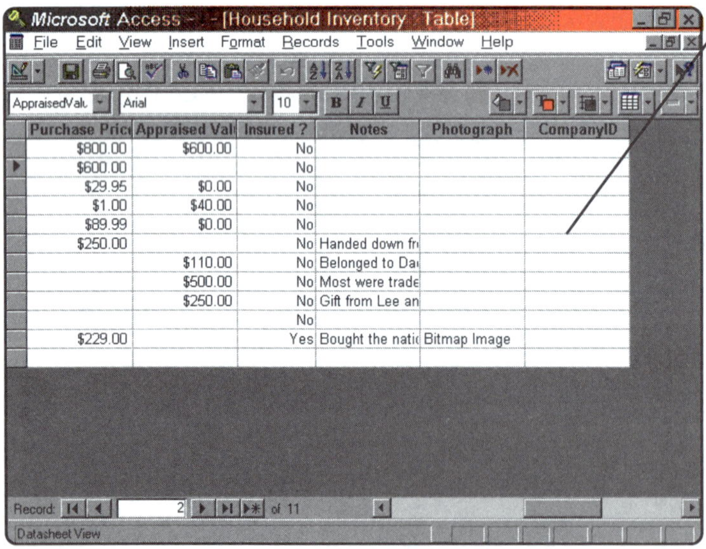

7. **Click anywhere** on the table *except* in that column, to complete the change.

CHANGING THE COLUMN WIDTH

In this example, you will change the width of the "Appraised Value" column so that the entire title will show.

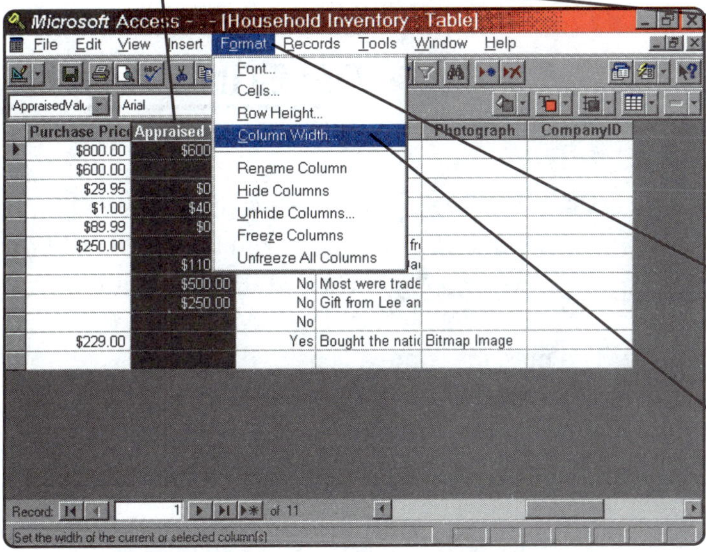

1. **Click** on the **heading of the column** you want to change. In this example, it is the Appraised Value column. The entire column will be highlighted.

2. **Click** on **Format** in the menu bar. The Format menu will appear.

3. **Click** on **Column Width**. The Column Width dialog box will appear.

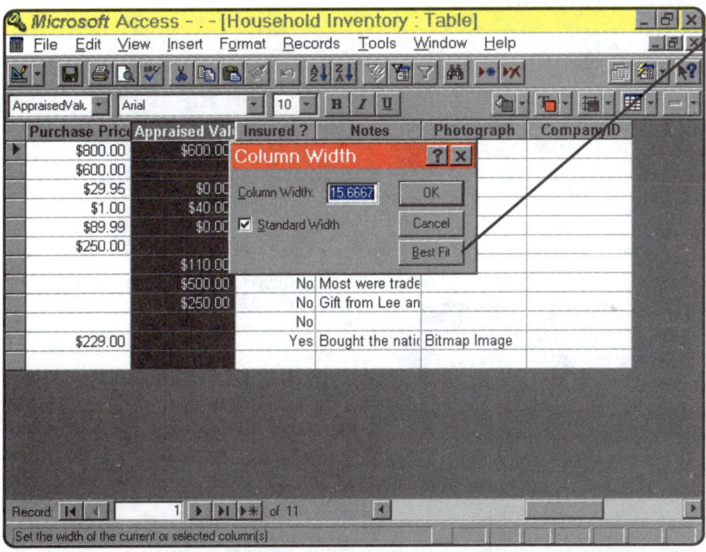

4. **Click** on **Best Fit**. The column will enlarge to include the longest entry.

If you're familiar with Excel, these tables work much the same way a spreadsheet works. To automatically expand a column in Excel you click twice in the heading on the line at the right edge of the column. You can do this in Access too.

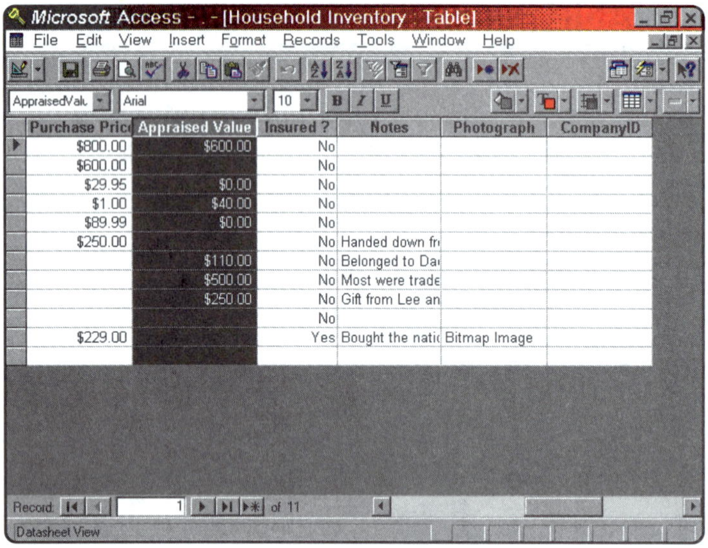

Notice that the column has expanded to show the entire phrase "Appraised Value."

DELETING A FIELD

In this example, you'll delete the field (column) for Photograph. You'll use the right mouse button to bring up a *context sensitive* pop-up menu. The menu is context sensitive because Access knows what action you performed prior to clicking the right mouse button and brings up a menu that contains only the choices that can follow the initial action. Pretty clever people these programmers!

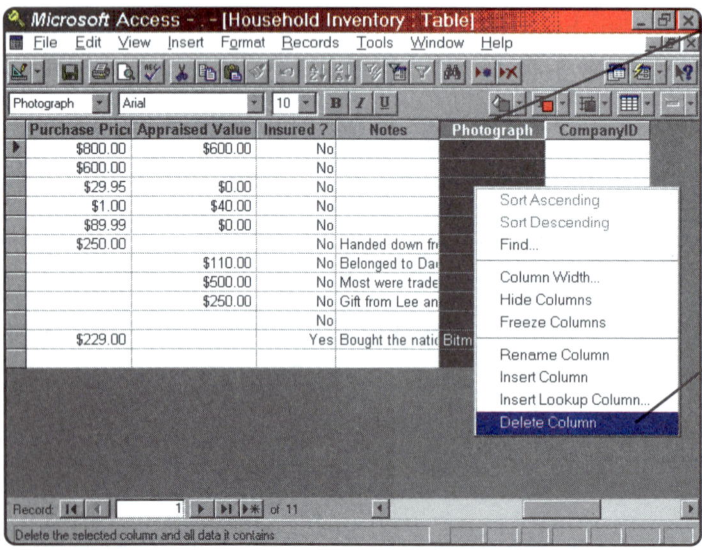

1. **Click** on the **heading** of the field you want to delete. The entire field will be highlighted.

2. **Click** on the ***right* mouse button**. A pop-up menu will appear.

3. **Click** on **Delete Column**. A message box will appear.

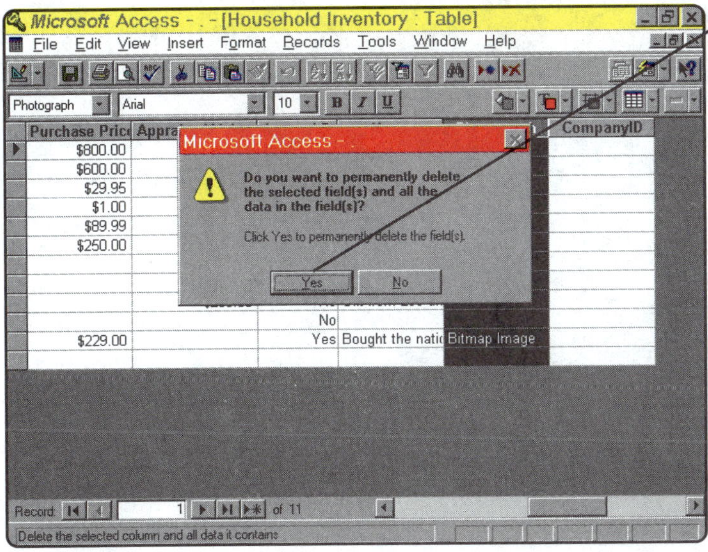

4. Click on **Yes**. The dialog box will close and the column will disappear from your table.

MOVING A COLUMN

In this section, you'll move the new column labeled "Company ID" next to the Insured? column.

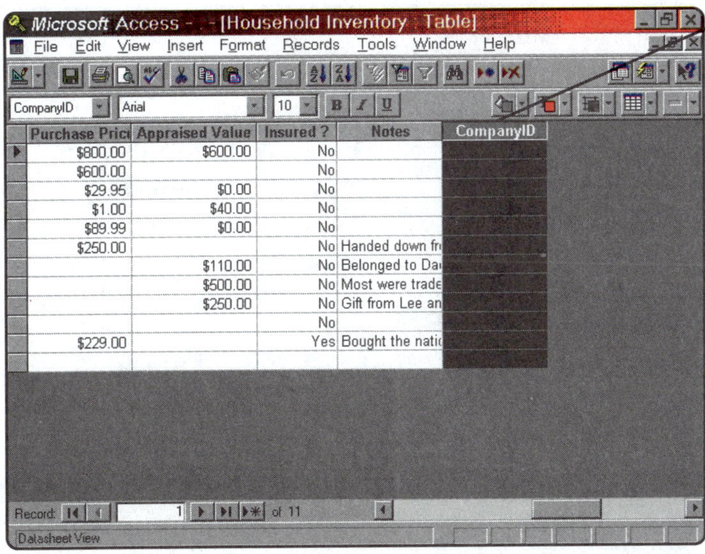

1. Click on the **heading** of the column you want to move. The entire column will be highlighted.

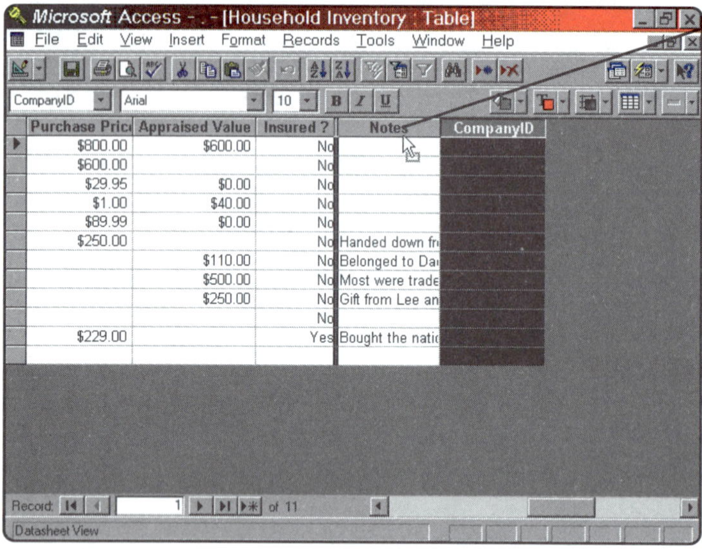

2. **Press and hold** the **mouse button** as you **drag** the column to the new position. In this example, place it to the right of the Insured? field.

3. **Release** the **mouse button** when the column is in place.

Notice that the column is in the new position on the table.

HIDING A COLUMN

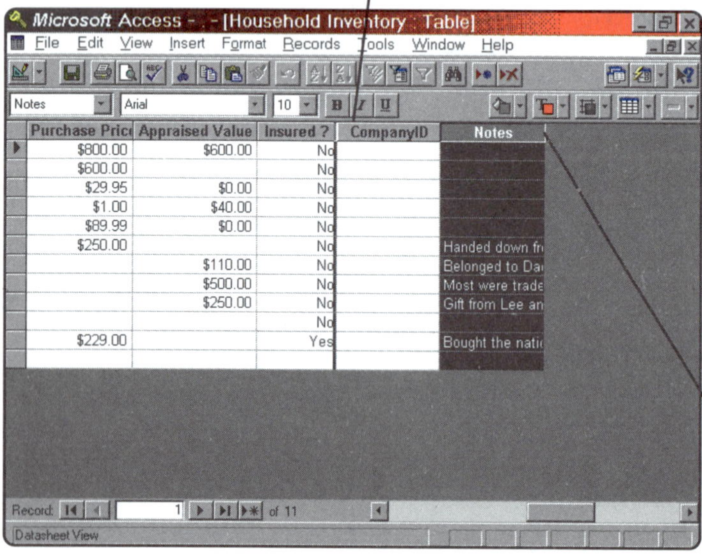

Access tables can contain a tremendous amount of data. You may not want to look or scroll through all of it during a particular work session. Or, you may not want other people to see a particular field. In this section you'll hide the Notes column.

1. **Click** on the **heading** of the column you want to hide to highlight it.

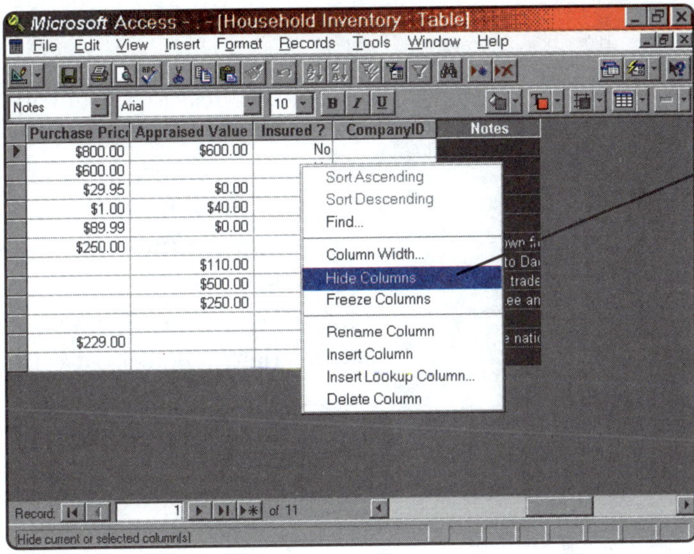

2. **Click** the ***right* mouse button**. A pop-up menu will appear.

3. **Click** on **Hide Columns**. The column will disappear.

UNHIDING A COLUMN

In this section, you'll unhide the Notes column that you just hid in the section above. It doesn't matter where your cursor is placed for this section.

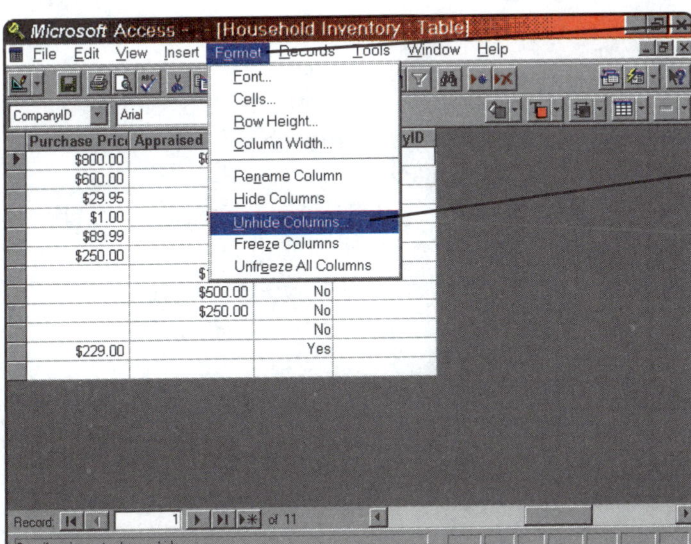

1. **Click** on **Format** in the menu bar. The Format menu will appear.

2. **Click** on **Unhide Columns**. The Unhide Columns dialog box will appear.

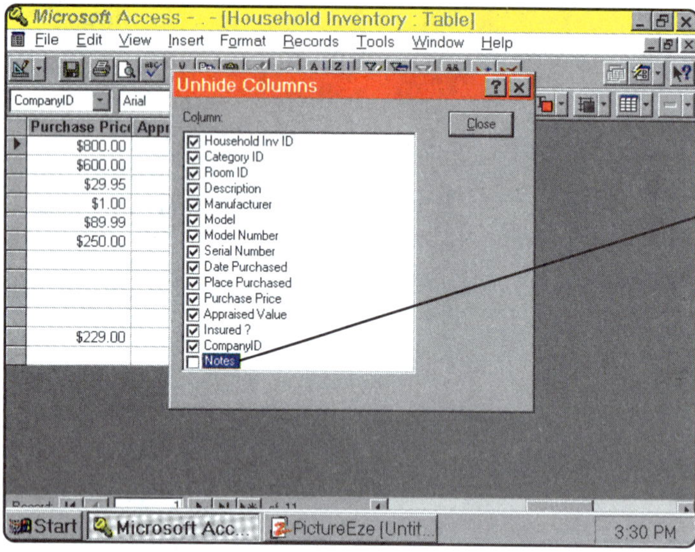

Notice that the Notes column is on the list, but the check box beside it is empty to show that it is hidden.

3. **Click** on **Notes** to put a check mark in the box.

4. **Click** on **Close**. The Notes field will appear once again.

SAVING CHANGES

Because you've made a number of changes to the Household Inventory table, you may want to save these changes before you go to the next section.

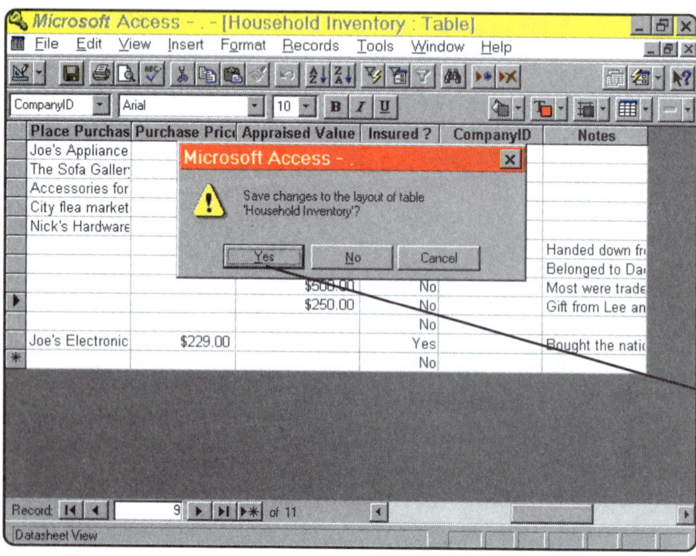

1. **Click** on the **Close button** (☒) on the right of the menu bar to close the Household Inventory table.

The message box you see here will appear asking if you want to save the changes.

2. **Click** on **Yes** to save the changes you made.

CREATING A RELATIONSHIP BETWEEN TWO TABLES

In Chapter 8, you used the Wizard to create a new table called, "Insurance Company." If you followed along with the directions, you told the Wizard to create a relationship between the new table and the Household Inventory table. That was half the job. In this chapter, you'll finish the job and formalize the relationship between the Company ID column in the Household Inventory table and the new Insurance Company table. First, you must open the Household Inventory table in Design view.

1. **Click** on the **Tables tab** to bring it to the front of the Database window. The window appears here in its maximized form.

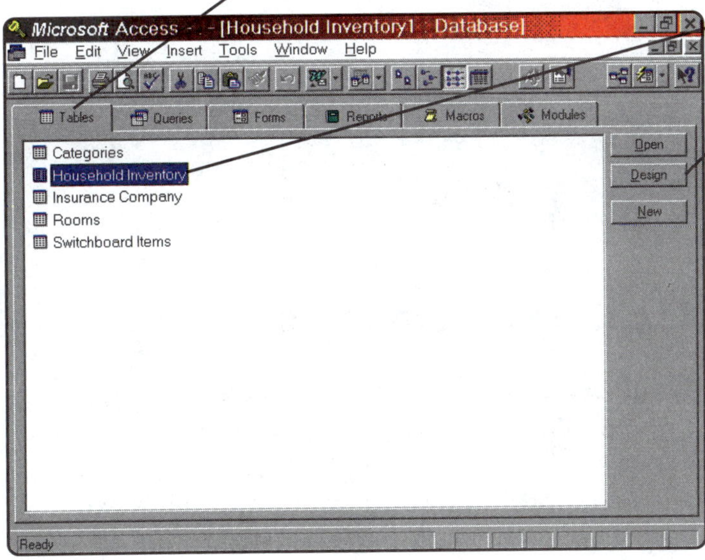

2. **Click** on **Household Inventory** to highlight it.
3. **Click** on **Design** to open the table in Design view.

CHANGING FIELD PROPERTIES

Field properties control the appearance of the data in a column. You can set field properties to meet conditions such as: how data must be entered; how a number will be formatted; whether a field will accept text or numbers; and whether you can add any text or whether you must choose from a predetermined list. You can do all this when the table is in Design view.

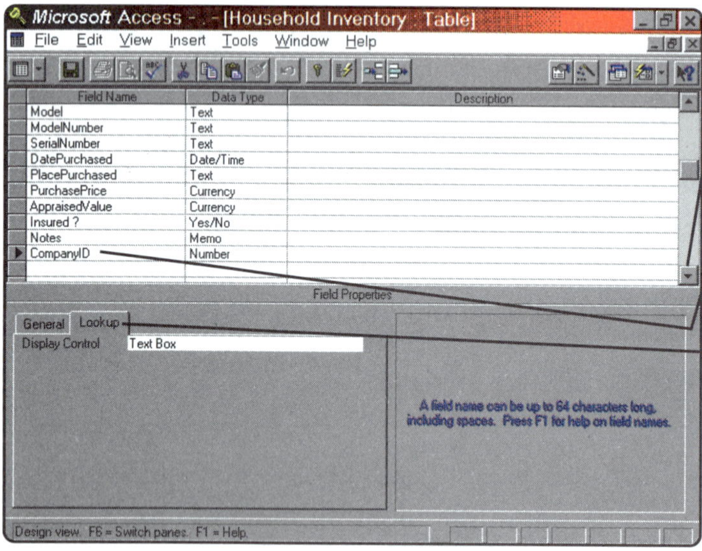

1. **Click** on the ▼ on the scroll bar to bring CompanyID into view as shown here.

2. **Click** on **CompanyID**. A ▸ will appear to the left of the name.

3. **Click** on the **Lookup tab** in the Field Properties portion of the window to bring it to the front.

Creating a Combo Box

It's often a good idea to limit the data that can be entered into a field to a specific list of choices. This allows you to do a meaningful sort on the field or to write a report based on the field. Access has two ways to make a list of choices: a list box and a combo box. In a list box the list is always displayed. In a combo box the list is hidden and appears only when you click on a button in the field. In this next section, you'll create a combo box in the CompanyID field.

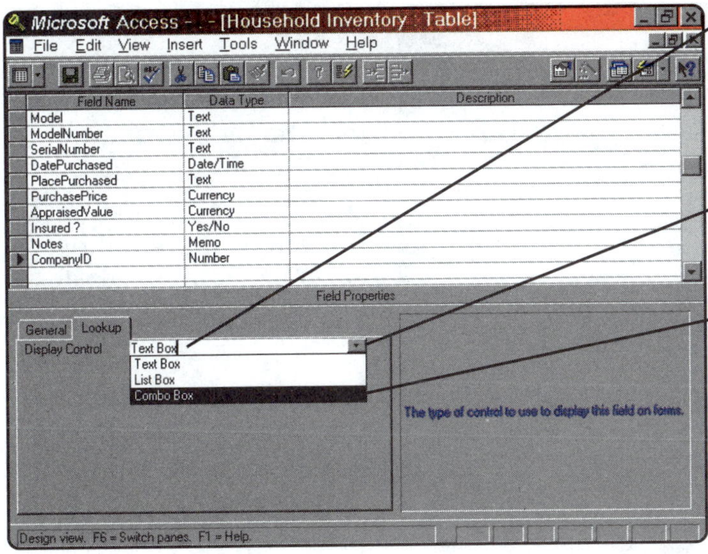

1. **Click** in the **box** to the right of Display Control. A ▼ will appear in the box as you see here.

2. **Click** on the ▼. A pull-down list will appear.

3. **Click** on **Combo Box**. The list will close.

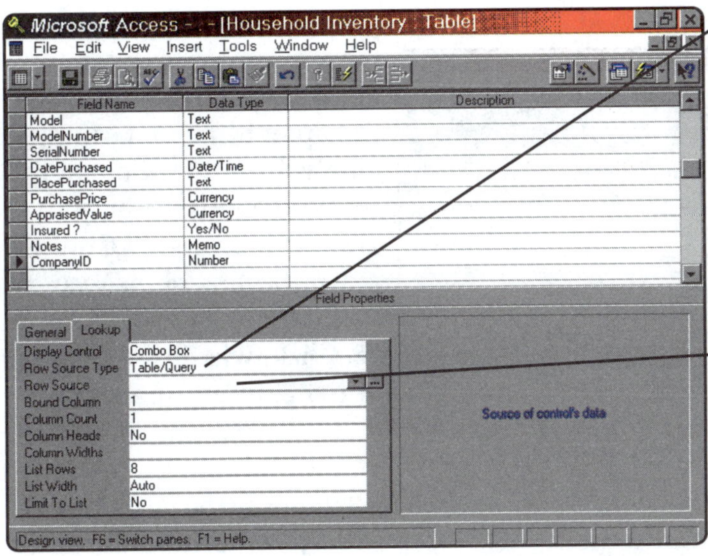

Notice that Table/Query appears in the Row Source Type box. Table/Query means that a table (or a query) is the source of the data for CompanyID. In our example, the source is a table.

4. **Click** on the **box** to the right of Row Source. On your screen it will be empty. When you click, two buttons will appear.

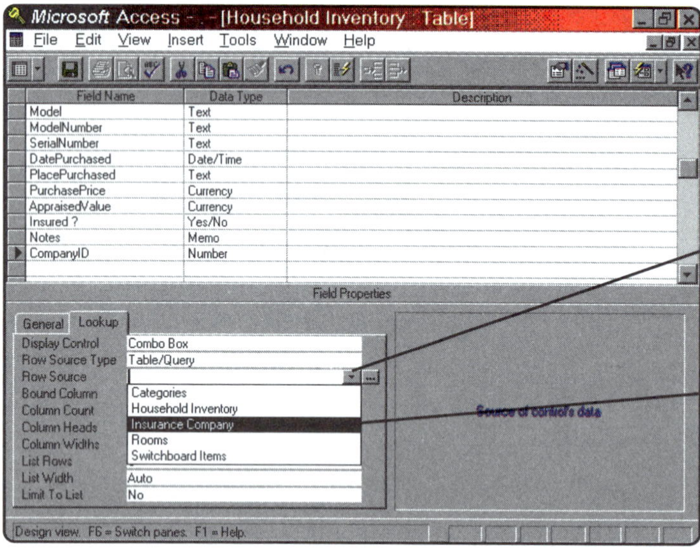

The Row Source provides Access with specific information about the source of the data for the combo box list.

5. **Click** on the ▼ button. A list of tables in the database will appear.

6. **Click** on **Insurance Company**, which is the table you created in Chapter 8.

7. **Confirm** that Bound Column shows a number 1. This means that the data in the list is *bound*, or connected, to the first column in the Insurance Company table. If you remember from Chapter 8, the first column in the Insurance Company table contains the primary key information (the unique identification of the record).

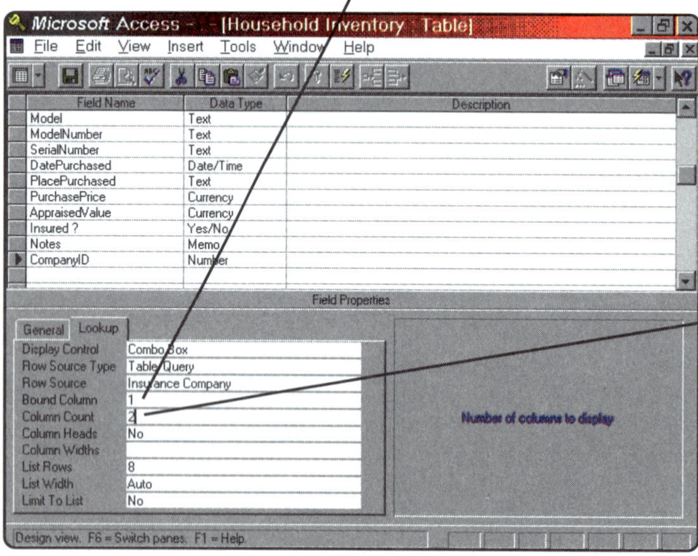

8. **Click twice** in the **Column Count box** and change the number to **2**. This means that we want to use the first two columns in the Insurance Company table for the data that will show in our list.

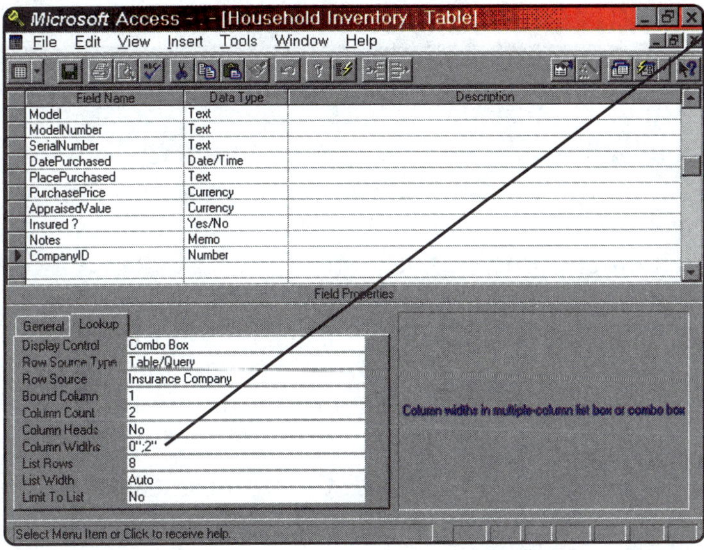

9. **Click** in the **Column Widths box** to place the cursor.

10. **Type 0";2"** (the number 0 with the inch symbol, then a semicolon, then the number 2 with the inch symbol). The explanation of this step is a little bit more complicated.

Back in step 7 you connected (or bound) this combo box list to the primary key in the Insurance Company table. If you remember, the Wizard set this up as an AutoNumber primary key and the AutoNumber function sets a unique number for each record. Numbers are not particularly helpful labels because everyone forgets exactly what the number stands for. In step 8 you told Access that you want to use the data in the first two columns of the Insurance Company table.

Typing a column width of 0" tells Access that you want to hide the information in column 1 of the Insurance Company table. Typing a column width of 2" tells Access to display the information in the second column of the Insurance Company in a 2" column in the Household Inventory Table. The 2" is completely arbitrary. You could pick 3" or 1.5". The point is to create a column wide enough to display recognizable information. The semicolon tells Access that 0" is for the first column width and 2" is for the second column width. If you had three columns in the table and the information you wanted to display was in column three, you would type 0";0";2".

SAVING THE COMBO BOX

You've made all the changes necessary to create the combo box. All you need to do now is save the work you've done. If you make changes in the design of a table, Access won't let you leave the Design view without deciding if you want to save the changes.

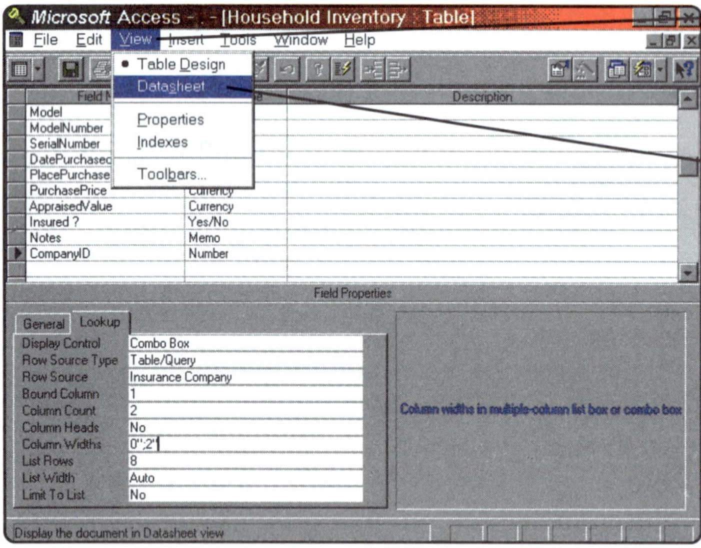

1. **Click** on **View** in the menu bar. The View menu will appear.
2. **Click** on **Datasheet** to return to the Datasheet view. A message box will say that you have to save the table.

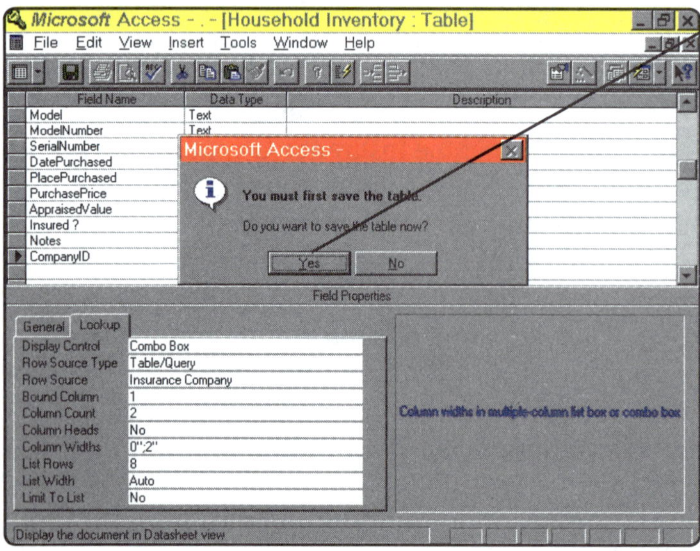

3. **Click** on **Yes** to save the changes you made.

ENTERING DATA USING THE COMBO BOX

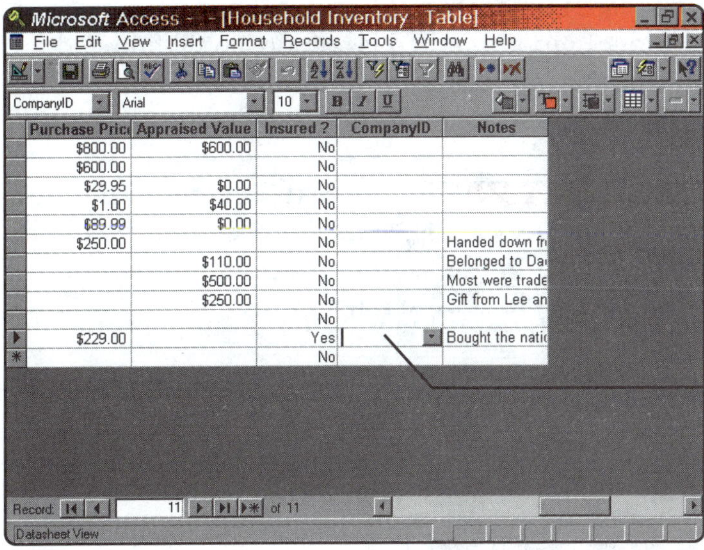

In this section, you'll use the combo box to enter the name of an insurance company for an insured item.

1. **Scroll** through the columns until you see the CompanyID column.

2. **Click** on the **row** where you want to add an insurance company name. The combo box button (▼) will appear.

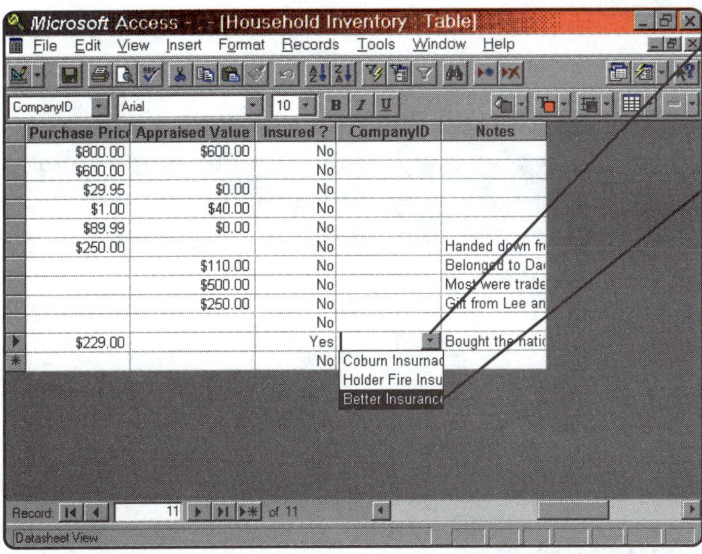

3. **Click** on the ▼ button. A list of insurance companies will appear.

4. **Click** on the **appropriate name**.

REPLACING TEXT IN A COLUMN

You've just been informed that Joe's Appliances, in the Place Purchased field, has changed its name to Holder Emporium. In this section, you'll find and replace the text, "Joe's Appliances" with the text, "Holder Emporium," in the Place Purchased column.

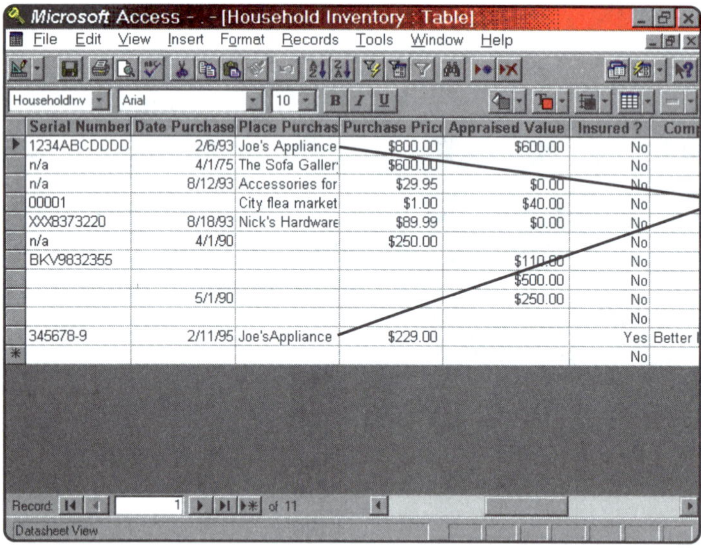

1. **Scroll** through the table until you can see the **Place Purch** column as shown here.

Notice the two instances of Joe's Appliances.

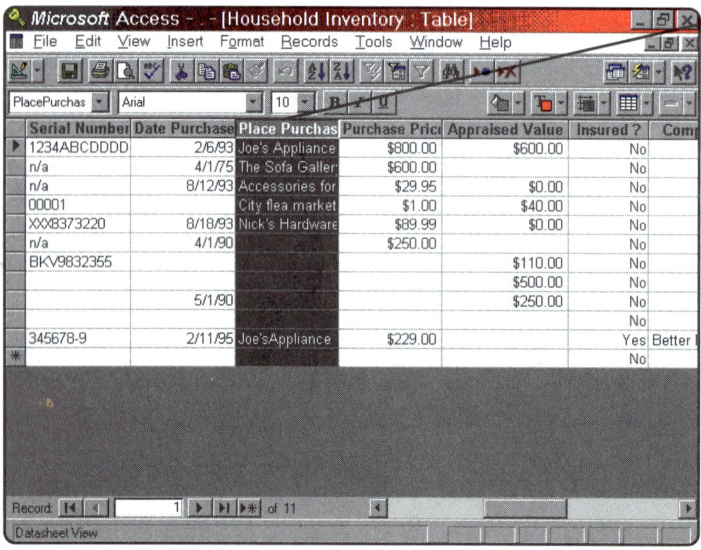

2. **Click** on the **heading** of the Place Purchased column to highlight the entire column.

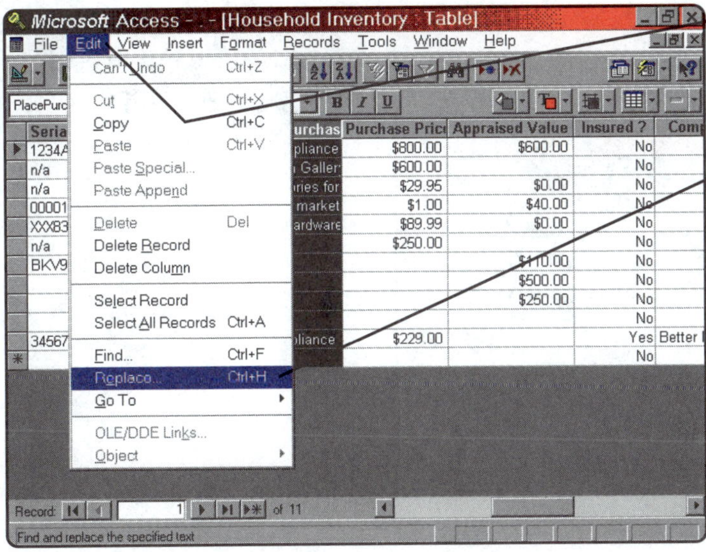

3. **Click** on **Edit** in the menu bar. The Edit menu will appear.

4. **Click** on **Replace**. The Replace in field: Place Purchased dialog box will appear.

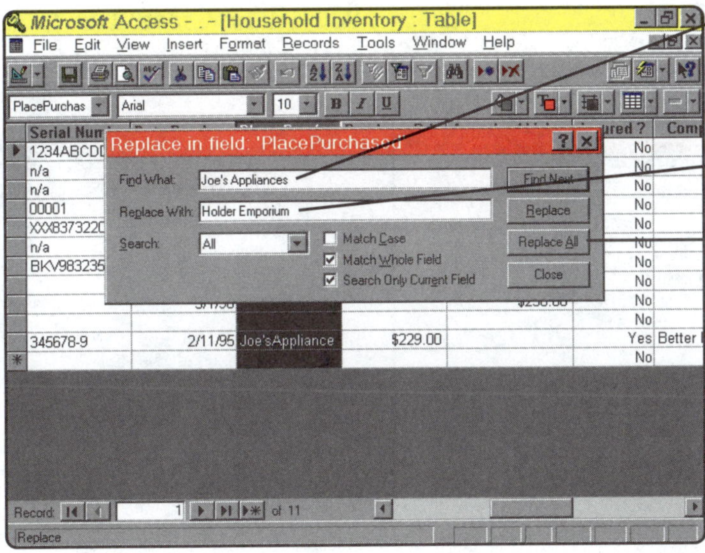

5. **Type Joe's Appliances** then **press** the **Tab key** on your keyboard.

6. **Type Holder Emporium.**

7. **Click** on **Replace All**. A Microsoft Access dialog box will appear.

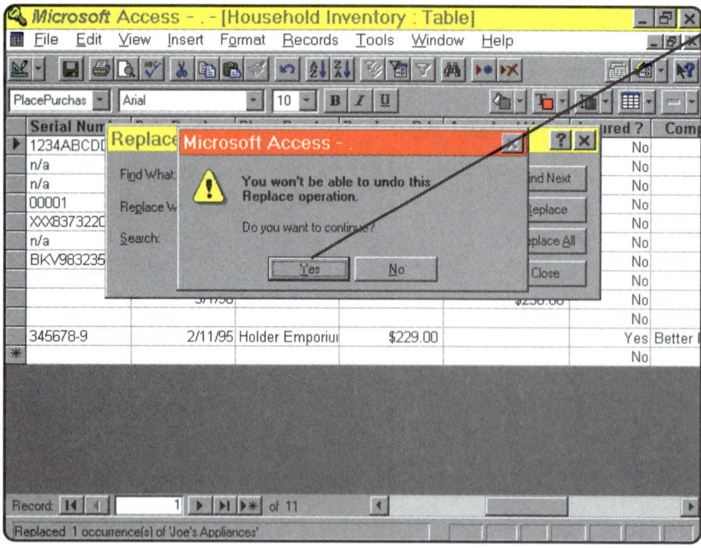

8. **Click** on **Yes**. The Replace in field: Place Purchased dialog box will appear.

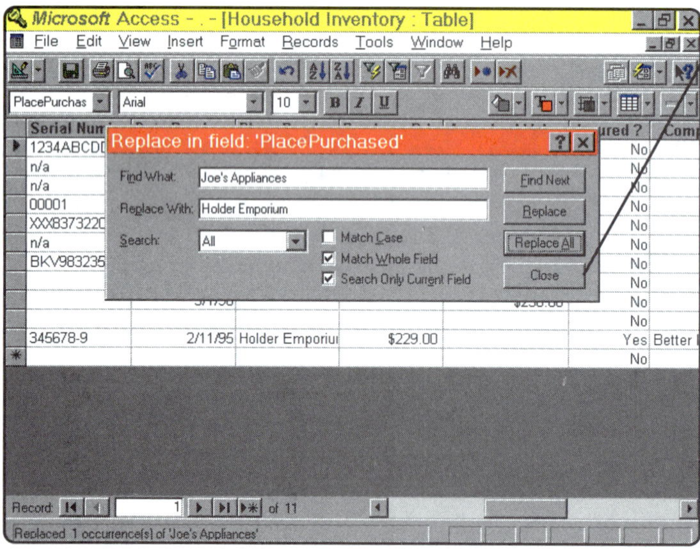

9. **Click** on **Close**. The dialog box will disappear.

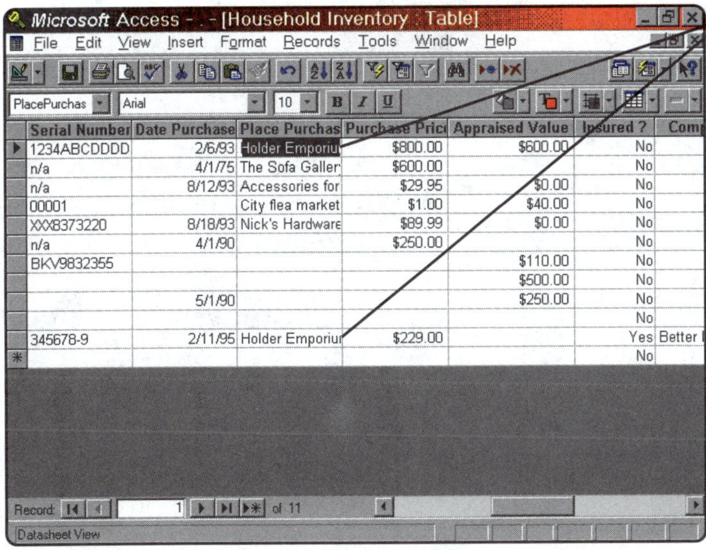

Notice that Holder Emporium has replaced all listings for Joe's Appliances.

FREEZING COLUMNS

If you have a lot of columns in a table, you can lose track of what a particular record (row) is about when the beginning columns have scrolled out of sight. You can freeze one or more columns on your screen so that they always show no matter how far to the right you have scrolled.

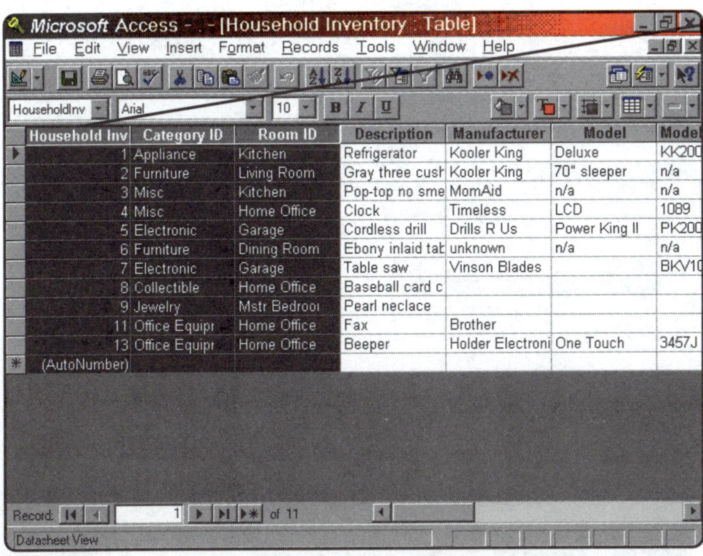

1. **Click** on the **heading** of column 1 to highlight the entire column.

2. **Press and hold** the **Shift key** and **click** on the **headings of columns 2 and 3**. Holding the Shift key allows you to select more than one column at the same time.

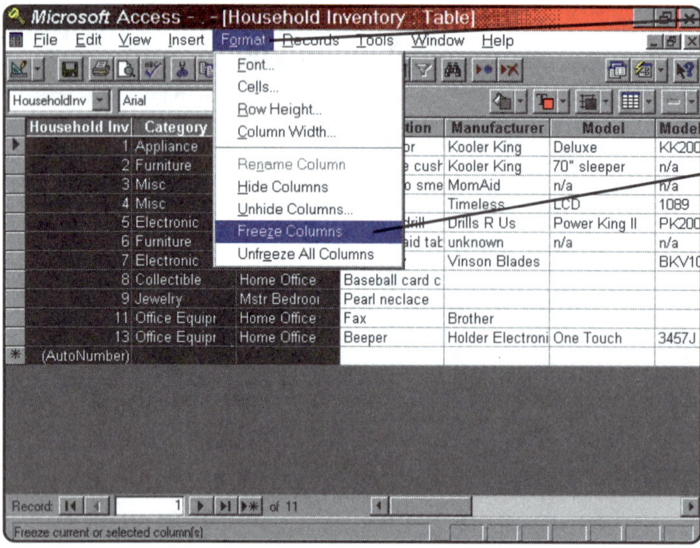

3. **Click** on **Format** in the menu bar. The Format menu will appear.

4. **Click** on **Freeze Columns**. The highlighted columns will be frozen.

5. **Click anywhere** on the table to remove the highlighting.

Notice the black "freeze mark" to the right of column three. Everything to the left of this mark is frozen.

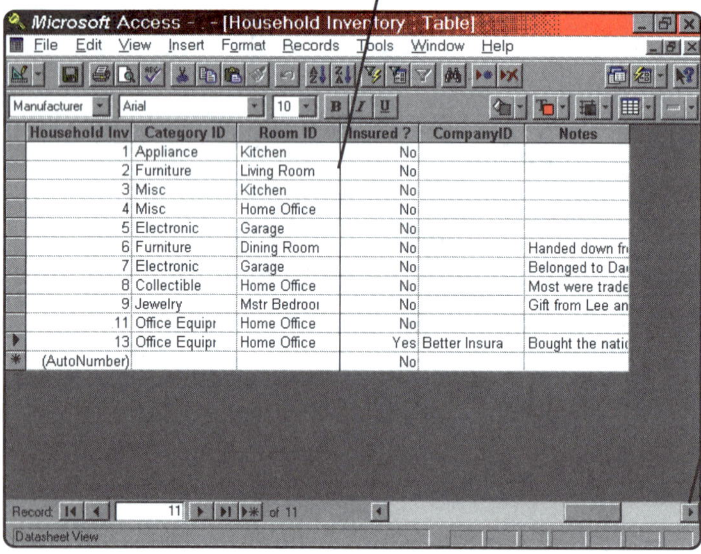

Note: If you chose to freeze only column 3, it would be moved to the first column position so that columns 1 and 2 can scroll out of sight. In this example, you froze the first three columns so all three will remain in sight.

6. **Click** on the ▸ on the scroll bar to scroll to the far right of your table. Notice that the first three columns remain in view.

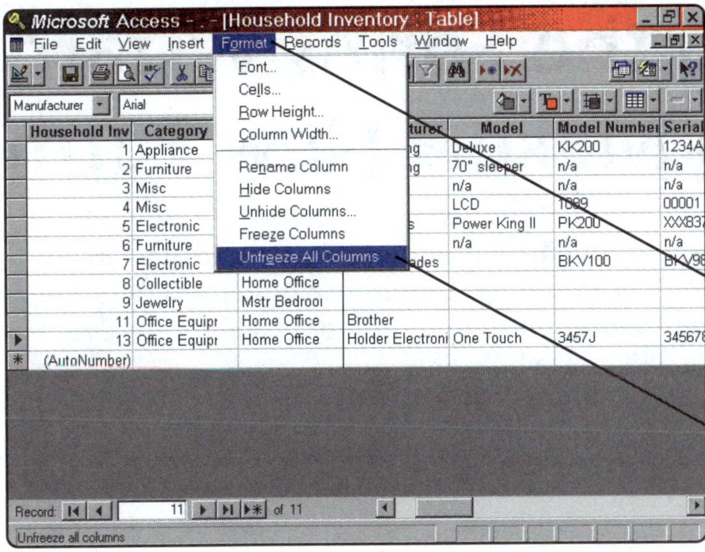

Unfreezing a Column

To unfreeze a column, or field, repeat the steps in the previous section.

1. **Click** on **Format** in the menu bar. The Format menu will appear.
2. **Click** on **Unfreeze All Columns**.

CLOSING THE DATABASE TABLE

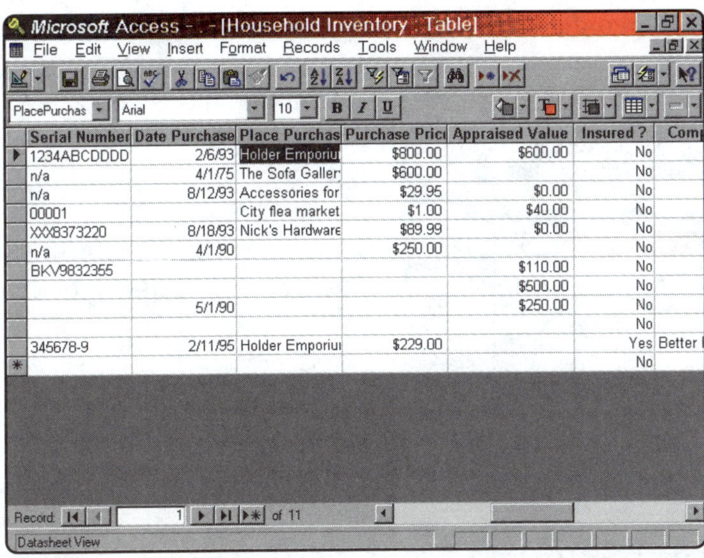

1. **Click** on the **Close button** (☒) on the right of the menu bar to close the Household Inventory table and return to the Database window.
2. When you see a message box (not shown here) asking if you want to save the changes, **click** on **Yes**.

CHAPTER 10

Using the Forms Wizard to Make a New Form

Access gives you a choice of entering data directly onto a table or making a form to use for your data entry. One of the advantages of using a form is that you can move through numerous records quickly to add new information or to make changes to your records. In this chapter, you will do the following:

- ✔ Make a form for an existing table

STARTING THE FORM WIZARD

1. **Open** the **database,** if it isn't already on your screen.

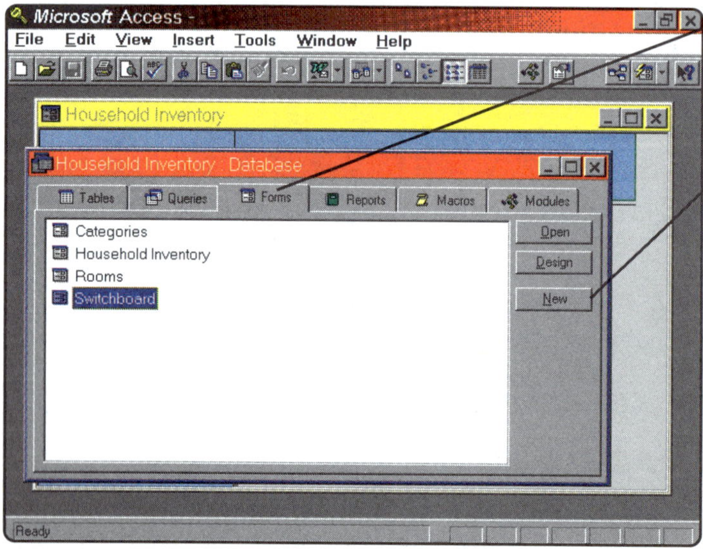

2. **Click** on the **Forms tab** to bring it to the front of the window.
3. **Click** on the **New button**. The New Form dialog box will appear.

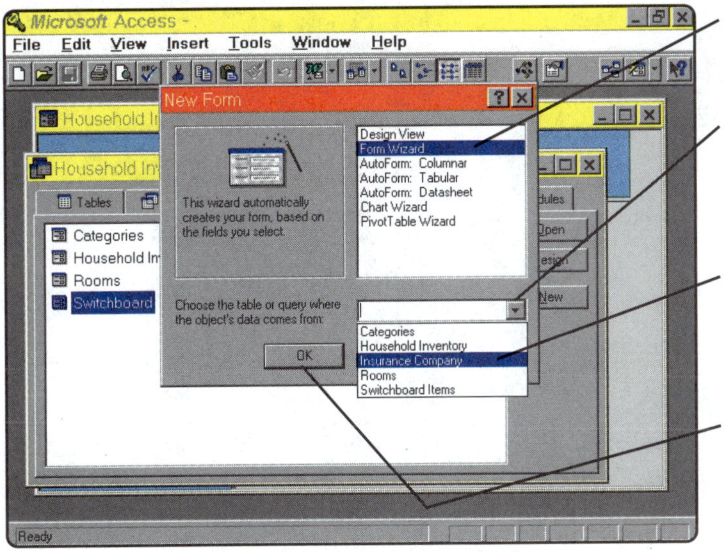

4. **Click** on **Form Wizard** to highlight it.

5. **Click** on ▼ in the Choose the table box. A pull-down list of tables will appear.

6. **Click** on **Insurance Company.** The list box will close.

7. **Click** on **OK**.

CHOOSING THE FIELDS

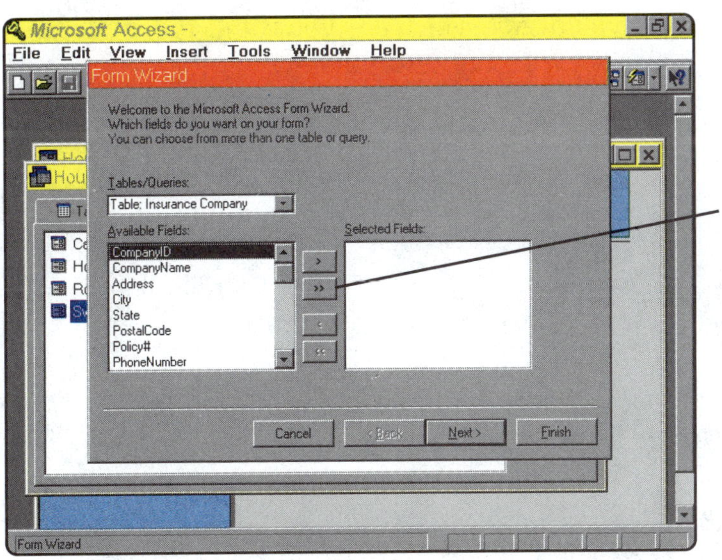

Notice that all of the fields associated with the Insurance Company table appear in the Available Fields box.

1. **Click** on the **>> button** to select all. The fields will appear in the Selected Fields box.

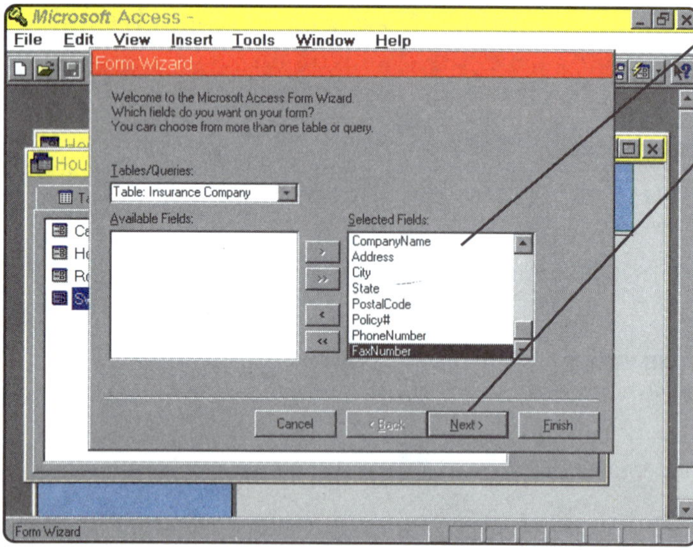

These are the fields that will appear on the new form.

2. **Click** on **Next >**. The Form Wizard dialog box will appear.

CHOOSING LAYOUT AND STYLE

Take a minute and click on the three layout types to help you decide which one you want. Your selection will appear in the view window.

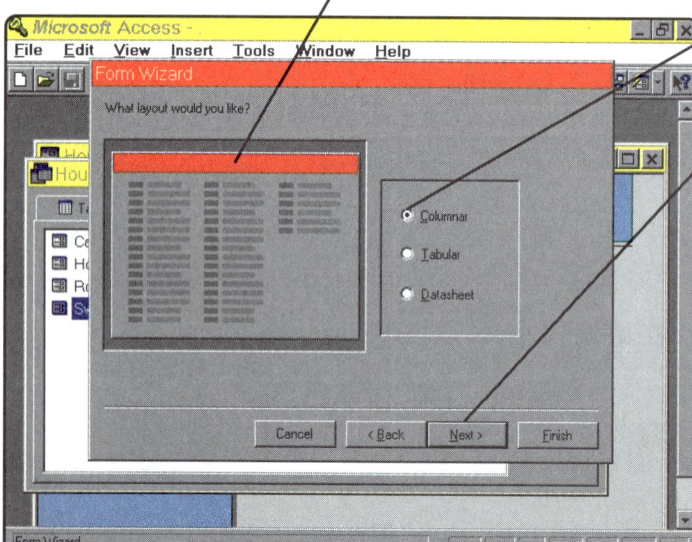

1. **Click** on the **Columnar** to put a dot in the circle.

2. **Click** on **Next >**. The Form Wizard dialog box will appear.

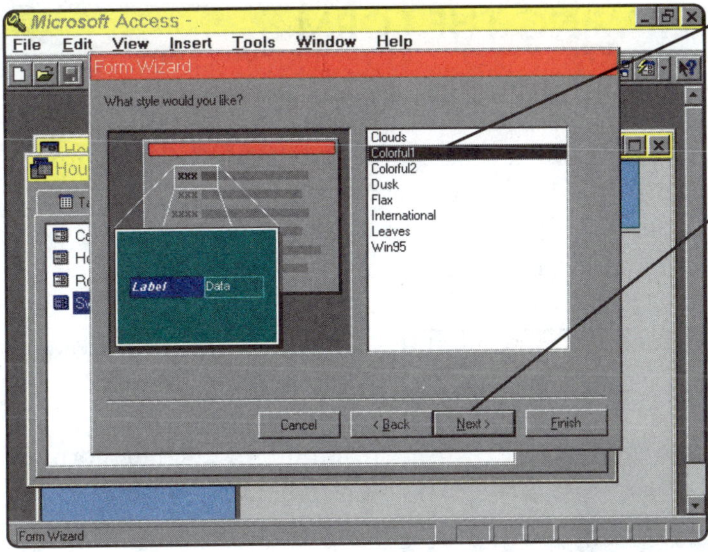

Notice that the style chosen in Chapter 1, "Creating a Database Using the Database Wizard" is selected.

3. **Click** on **Next >**. The Form Wizard dialog box will appear.

NAMING THE FORM

This is simple. The form has already been named. No reason to change it.

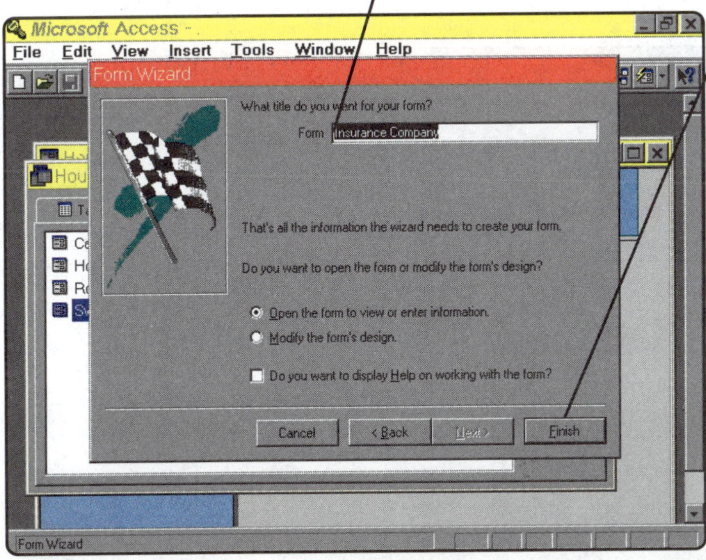

1. **Click** on **Finish**. The Insurance Company form will appear.

VIEWING THE FORM

Notice that in this example the form appears with three completed records as indicated by the record number at the bottom of the window. In Chapter 8, "Using the Table Wizard to Make a New Table", we entered three records directly onto the table.

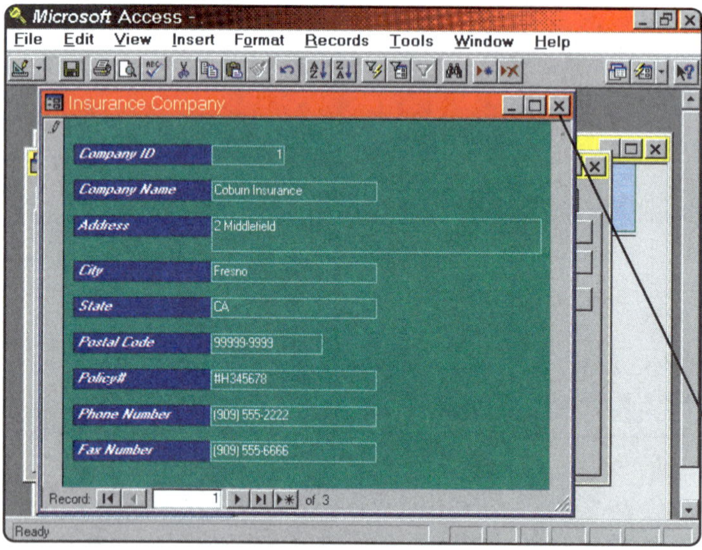

1. **Click** on the ▸✳ button at the bottom of the window to add a new record. See Chapter 4, "Using a Form to Change Data", if you need help. In this example, we will not add another record.

CLOSING THE FORM

1. **Click** on the **Close button** (☒) in the title bar. The Database window will appear.

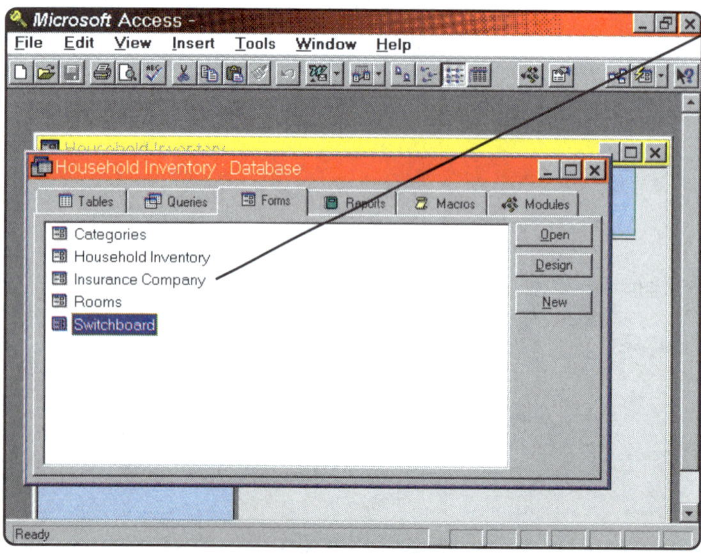

Notice that Insurance Company has been added to the list of forms.

CHAPTER 11

Customizing the Switchboard and Other Forms

If you followed along in Chapter 9 and customized a table, the easiest way to update the form that goes with the table is to delete the old form and have the Form Wizard make a new one for you. However, it's also easy to customize an existing form without the Wizard's help. In fact, when the Database Wizard creates your database, it includes the means to update the Switchboard form that you see when you start the database. In this chapter, you will do the following:

- ✔ Modify the Switchboard form
- ✔ Customize a form

MAKING THE SWITCHBOARD TEXT EASIER TO READ

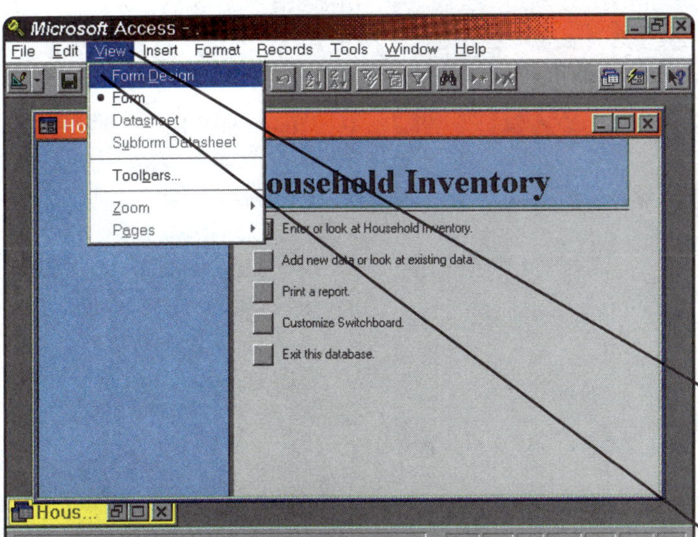

First we'll make a couple of changes to the text on the Switchboard form.

1. **Open Access and the database** if you have not already done so. Go to the main Switchboard form if you are not alredy there.

2. **Click** on **View** in the menu bar. The View menu will appear.

3. **Click** on **Form Design**. The form will appear in Form Design mode.

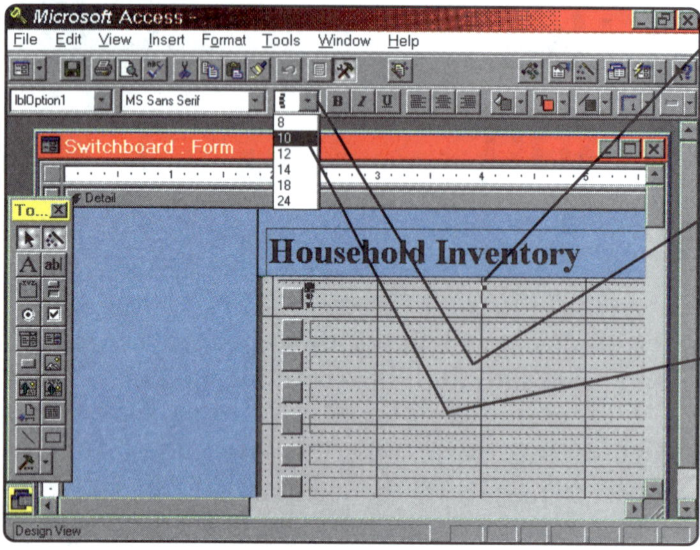

4. **Click** on the **top text box**. Little squares, called "handles," will appear on its edges.

5. **Click** on the ▼ next to the Font Size list box. A list will appear.

6. **Click** on **10**. The list will close. Any text that appears in the box on the form will now be a bit larger and easier to read.

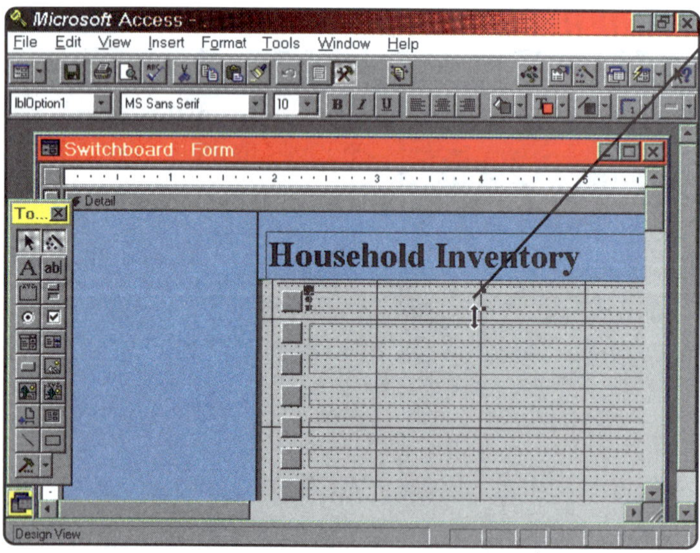

7. **Place** your **mouse pointer** over the handle in the middle of the lower edge of the text box. As you do, it will turn into a two-headed arrow pointing up and down.

8. **Press and hold** the **mouse button** and **drag** the **lower edge** of the text box down to enlarge the text box slightly for the larger size font.

9. **Repeat steps 4 to 8** for the other text boxes on the form.

Saving the Changes

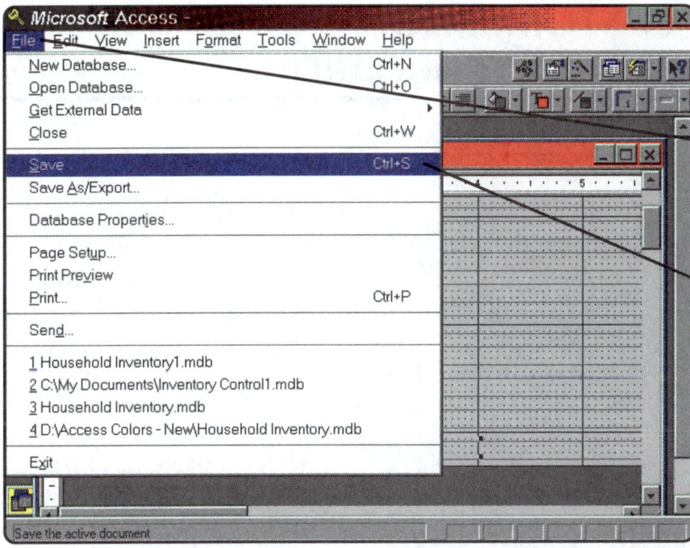

1. **Click** on **File** in the menu bar. The File menu will appear.

2. **Click** on **Save**. The menu will close, and your changes to the form will be saved.

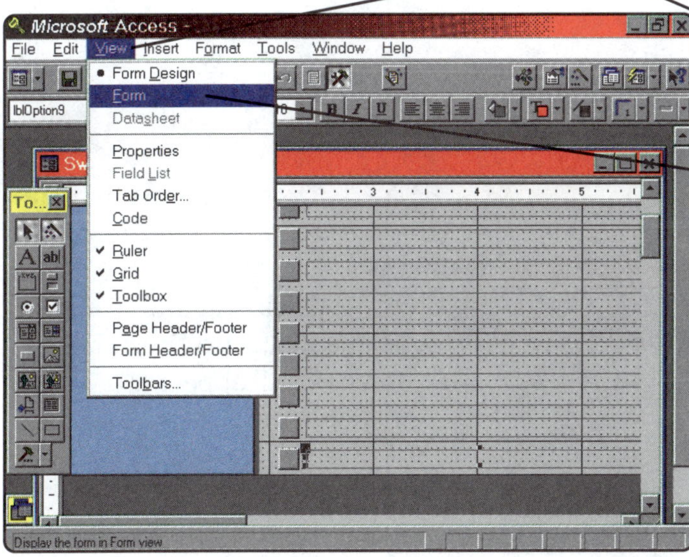

3. **Click** on **View** in the menu bar. The View menu will appear.

4. **Click** on **Form**. The Switchboard form will appear in Form mode, with the text larger and easier to read.

CUSTOMIZING THE SWITCHBOARD

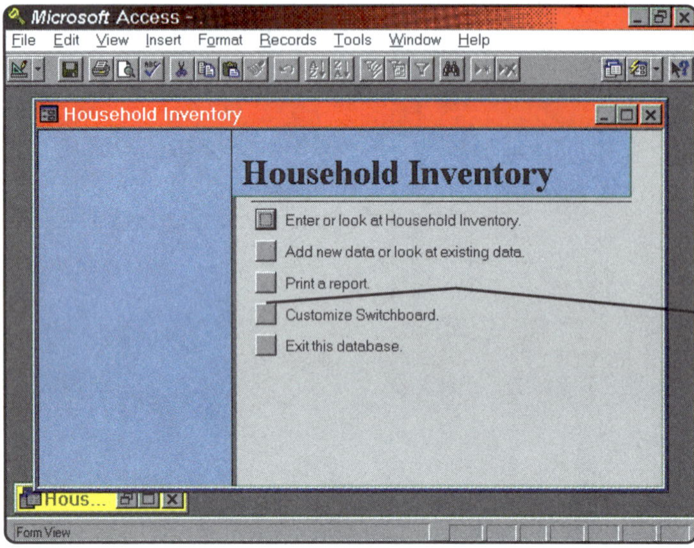

The Database Wizard that we used to create this database made it easy for us to add, delete, or rename Switchboard options. For our example, we'll add a button for opening a form.

1. **Click** on the **Customize Switchboard button**. The Switchboard Manager dialog box will appear.

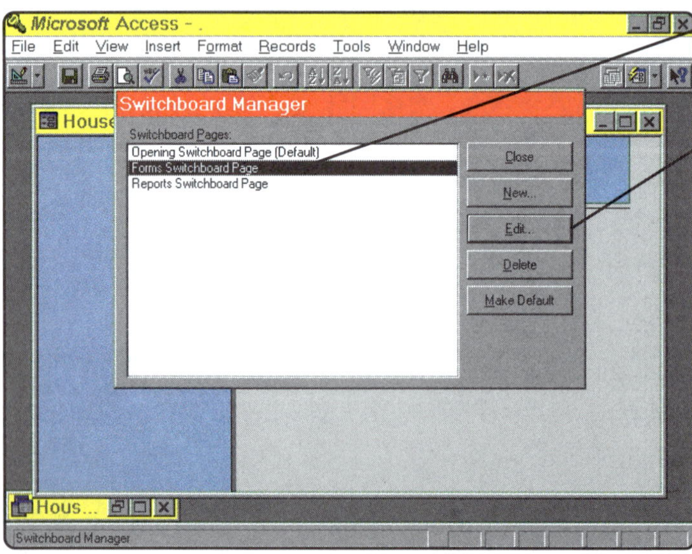

2. **Click** on **Forms Switchboard Page** to highlight it.

3. **Click** on **Edit**. The Edit Switchboard Page dialog box will appear.

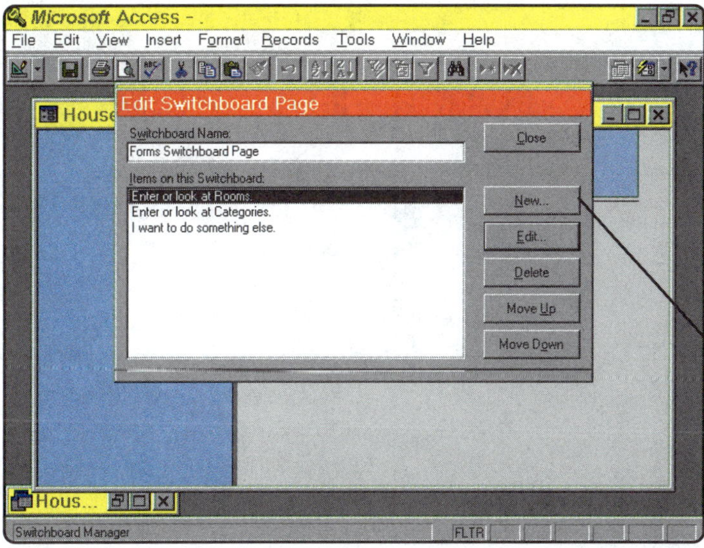

Adding a New Option

We'll add an option for editing or looking at the form for insurance companies that was added in the last chapter.

1. **Click** on **New**. The Edit Switchboard Item dialog box will appear.

You can edit the text next to an existing option, or delete an option by clicking on the option to select it in this dialog box, then clicking on the Edit button or the Delete button.

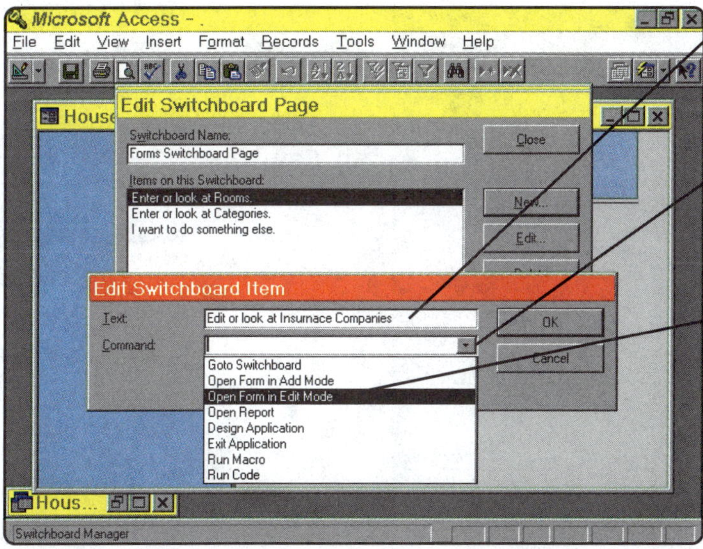

2. **Type Edit or look at Insurance Companies** in the text box.

3. **Click** on the ▼ next to the Command list box. A list will appear.

4. **Click** on **Open Form in Edit Mode**. The list will close.

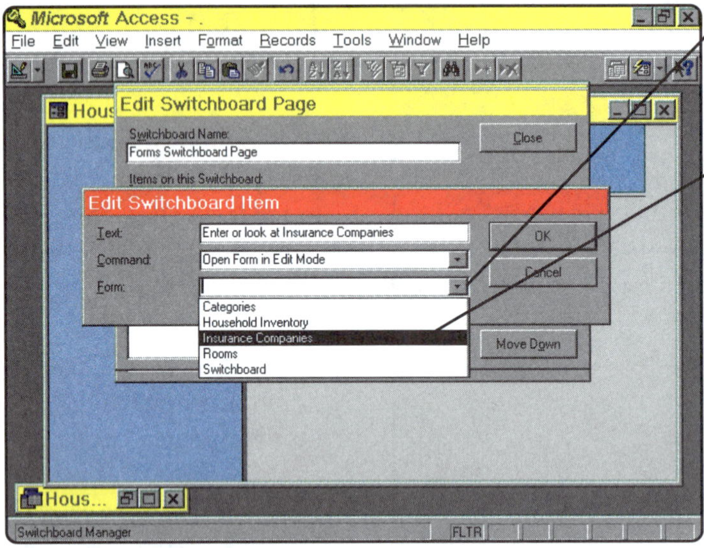

5. **Click** on the ▼ next to the Form list box. A list will appear.

6. **Click** on **Insurance Company**. The list will close.

Note: Your list of forms will vary depending on the database you are using and whether you have followed along with the examples in this book.

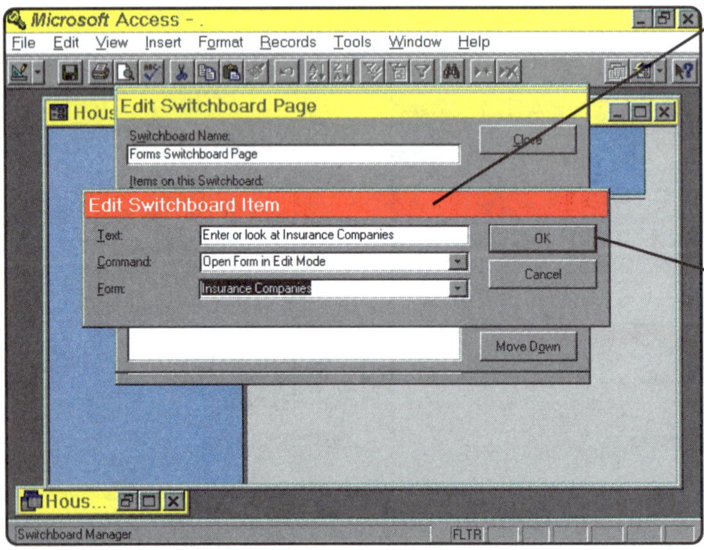

The dialog box now shows the form we want to get to, how we want it opened, and the text we want to appear next to the button that will open it.

7. **Click** on **OK**. The dialog box will close.

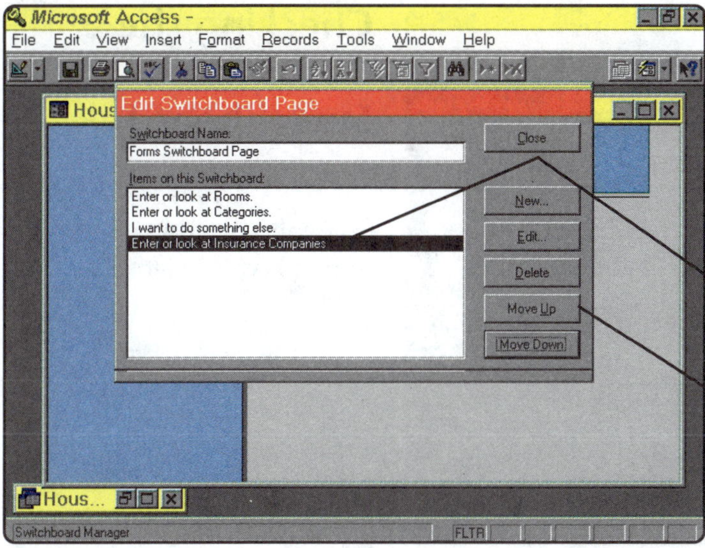

Changing the Options Position

You can change the order in which the options on a Switchboard page appear.

1. **Click** on the **option** you want to move to select it.
2. **Click** on **Move Up** (or Move Down). The option's position in the dialog box will change.

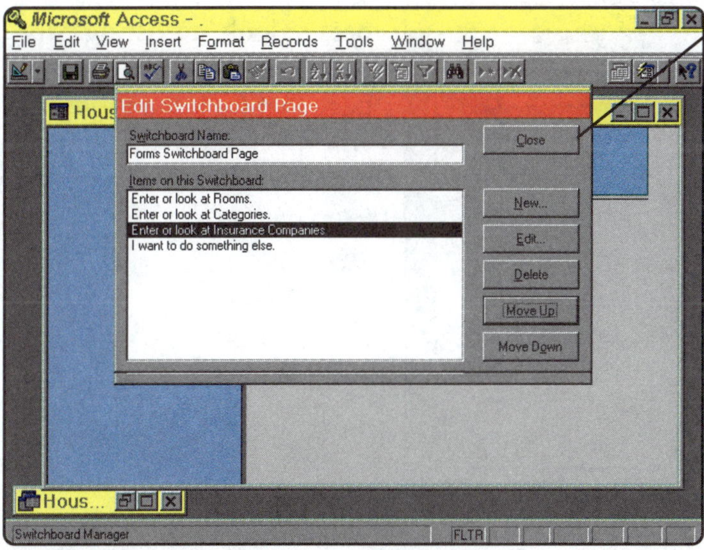

3. **Click** on **Close**. The dialog box will close.

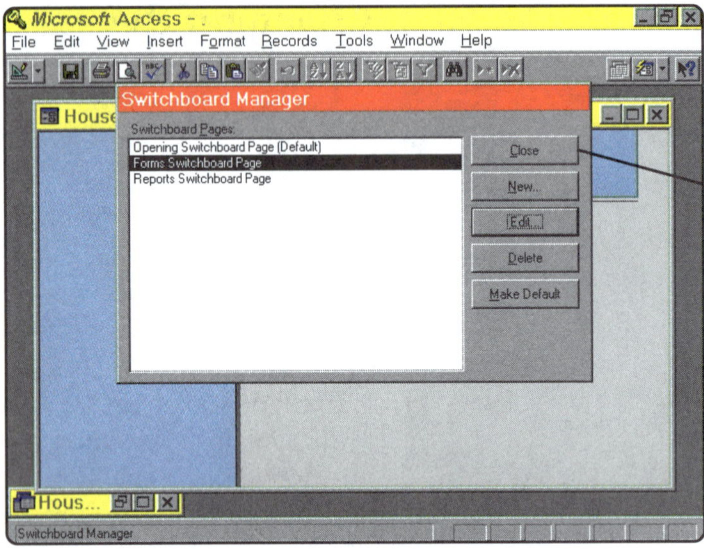

Checking the Customized Switchboard

1. **Click** on **Close**. The Switchboard Manager dialog box will close.

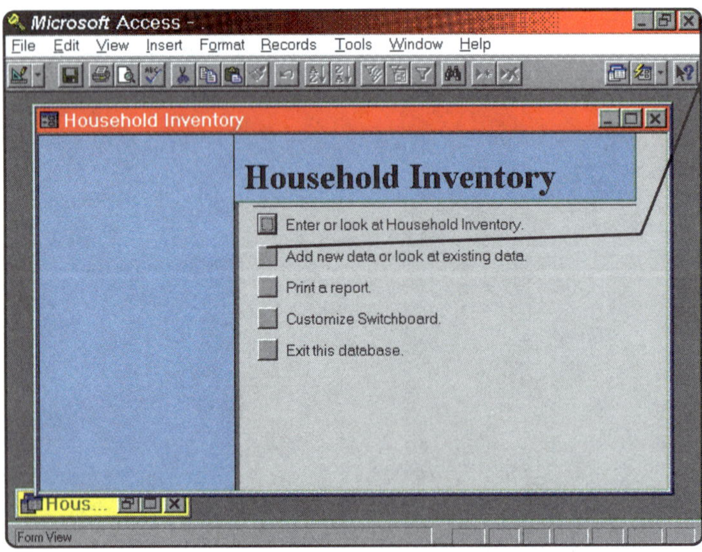

2. **Click** on the **Add new data or look at existing data button**. The Switchboard page that we just customized will appear, with our new button and the text we typed to go with it.

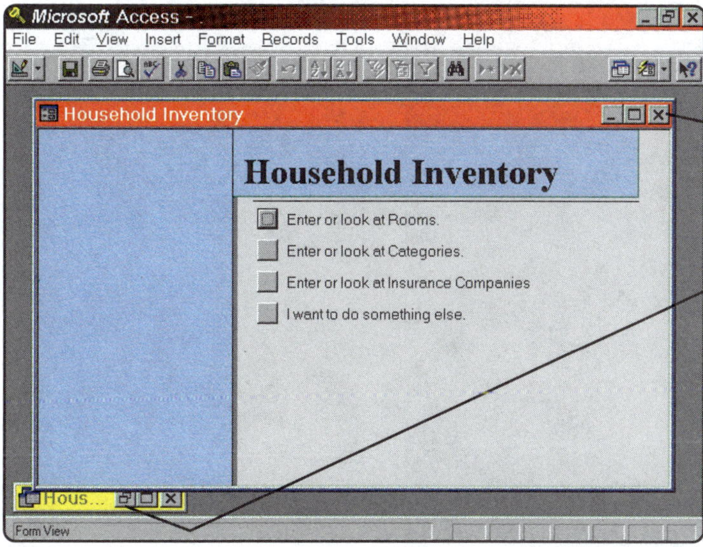

Now we'll move on to customizing other forms.

3. **Click** on the **Close button** (☒). The Switchboard will close.

4. **Click** on the **Restore button** (🗗) on the minimized database. The Database dialog box will appear.

Note: In the next section we delete a form and have the Form Wizard make a new one to take its place. We're doing this because we customized the Household Inventory table in Chapter 9. In such a case, it's much easier to have the Form Wizard create a new form that includes the custom changes to the table it's based on than to go through the steps involved in changing the old form. If you're worried about losing a form in this exercise, you can close your database, open a copy of it or one of the sample databases that come with Access, and practice using the sample or copy.

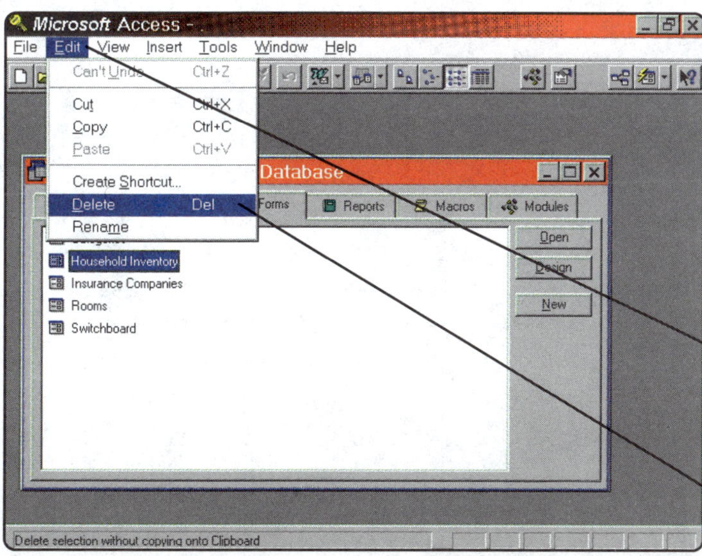

CUSTOMIZING FORMS

1. **Click** on **Household Inventory** to highlight it.

2. **Click** on **Edit** in the menu bar. The Edit menu will appear.

3. **Click** on **Delete**. A message box will appear.

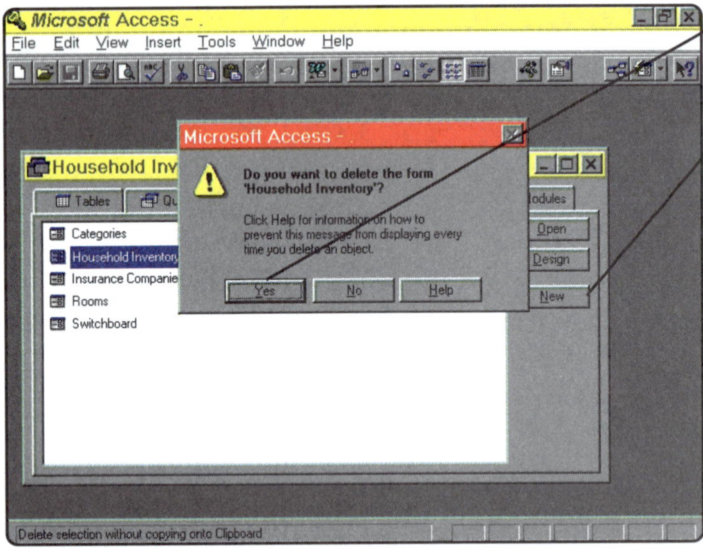

4. **Click** on **Yes**. The form will be deleted.

5. **Click** on **New**. The New Form dialog box will appear.

Making a New Form

The Form Wizard is covered in more detail in the previous chapter. Here we'll just show you the first steps that are needed to make the form we'll be customizing later in this chapter.

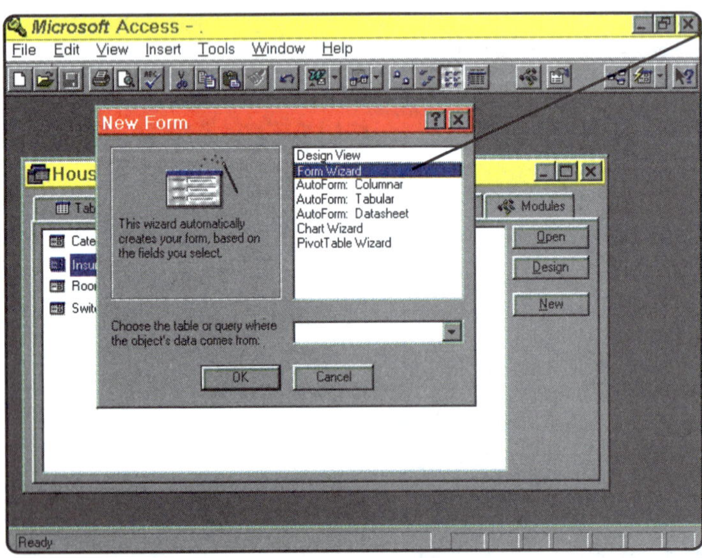

1. **Click** on **Form Wizard** to highlight it.

2. **Follow the rest of the steps** shown in the previous chapter to complete the process of making a new Household Inventory form with the Wizard's assistance. The completed form will appear. The form on your screen may not be exactly like the one shown here.

Moving Several Fields

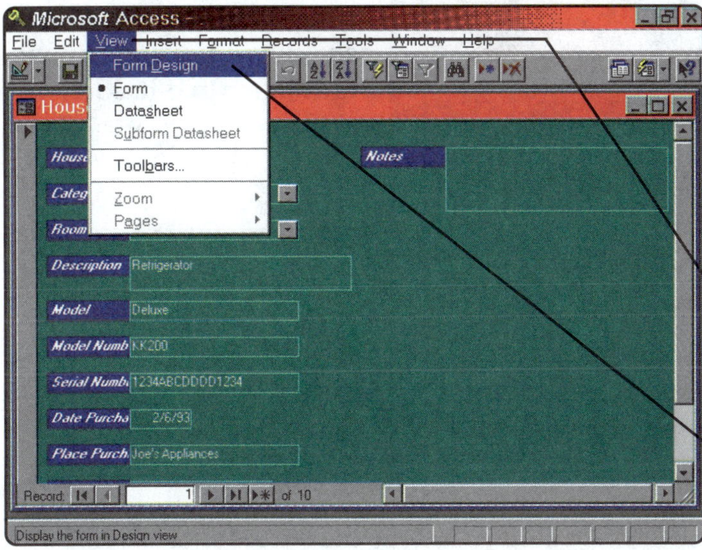

The new Household Inventory form appears with the default colors given to it by the Wizard. The fields and labels on the form are too close together, so we'll adjust their sizes.

1. **Click** on **View** in the menu bar. The View menu will appear.

2. **Click** on **Form Design**. The form will appear in Form Design mode.

3. **Place** your **mouse pointer** just above the point where the fields and labels meet.

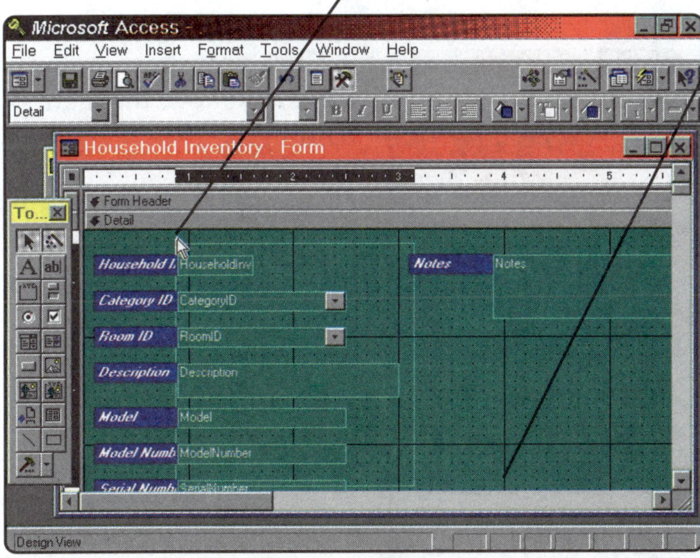

4. **Press and hold** the **mouse button** and slowly **drag** the highlight line that appears to the right and down until it surrounds all of the fields. As you drag the line down, the form will move down to let you see the rest of the fields.

5. **Release** the **mouse button**. The fields will be highlighted by handles. If you don't get this right the first time, press the Escape key to remove the highlighting and try again.

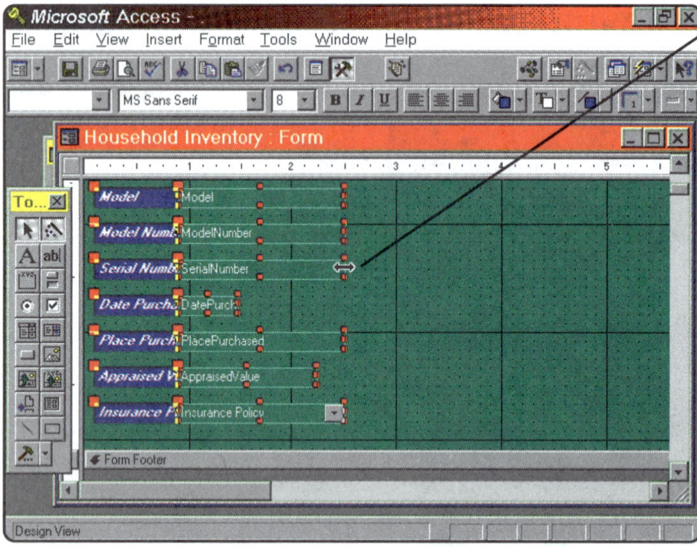

6. **Move** your **mouse pointer** over the middle handle on the right side of any field. As you do, it will turn into a two-headed arrow pointing left and right.

7. **Press and hold** the **mouse button** as you **drag** the right sides of the fields about one inch to the right. The fields will all expand to the right.

8. **Repeat step 7** to move the left sides of the fields about three-fourths of an inch to the right, so that they are away from the field labels.

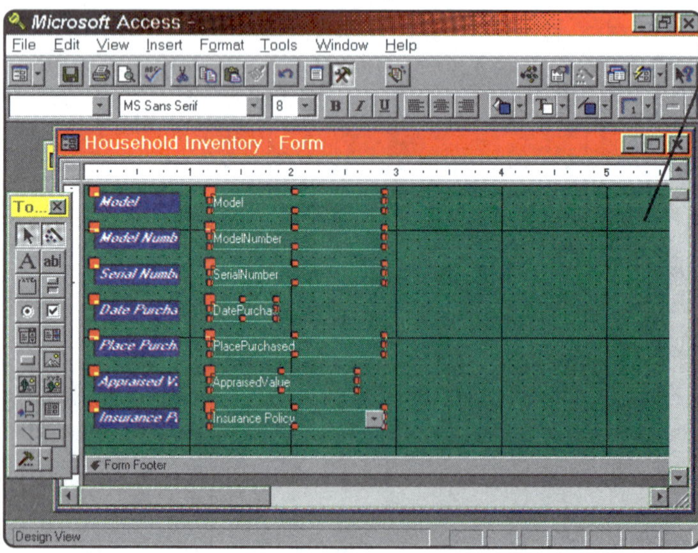

9. **Click anywhere** on the form to remove the highlighting.

10. **Repeat steps 3 to 7**, highlighting the labels instead of the fields, to move the right side of the labels to the right, so that the words in them show, but the labels are still separated from the fields.

ADDING A COMMAND BUTTON

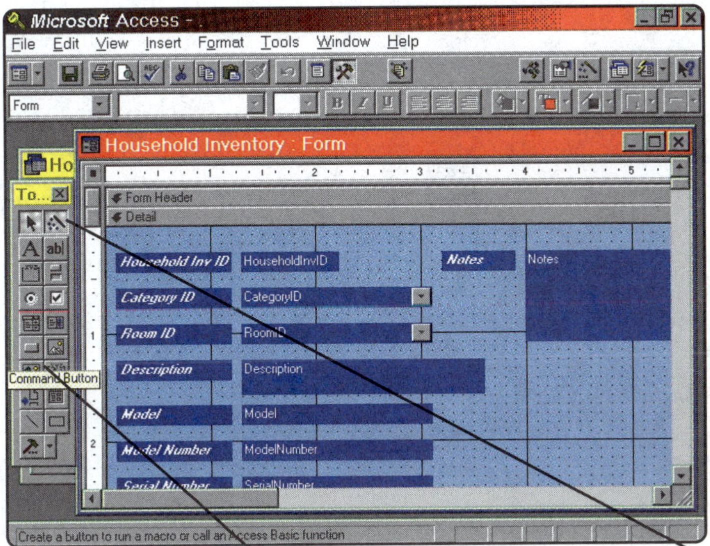

A command button, like the buttons on the Switchboard form, lets you issue commands to Access with a click of your mouse. In this example, you'll add a button that you can use to close the Household Inventory form. The color of the form in these examples is based on changes made with the "magic wand" in Chapter 7, "Changing the Look of Your Forms."

1. **Click** on the **Wizard button.**
2. **Click** on the **Command button icon** on the toolbar.

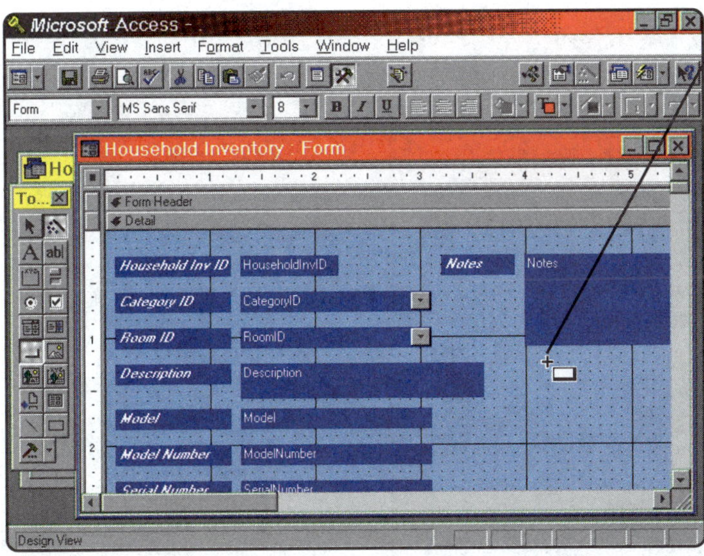

3. **Move** your **mouse pointer** over the form. As you do, it becomes a plus sign with a box. You'll want to position the center of the plus sign on the spot where you want the upper left corner of your new command button to be.
4. **Click** the **mouse button** when the plus sign is where you want it. Some handles for the new button will appear for a moment, then the Command Button Wizard dialog box will appear.

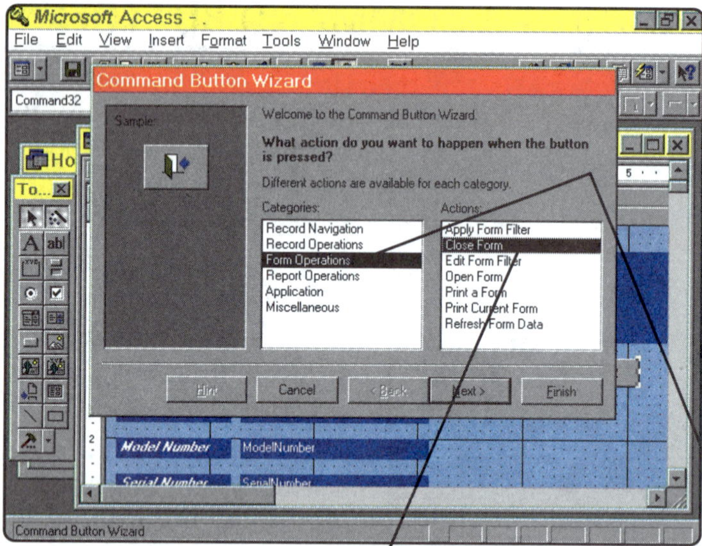

The Command Button Wizard lists several different types of actions (commands) that are available for each of several different categories. Click on each category in turn to see the actions that are available for it. For our example, we're using the Close Form action from the Form Operations category.

5. **Click** on **Form Operations** to highlight it.

6. **Click** on **Close Form** to highlight it.

7. **Click** on **Next >**. Another Command Button Wizard dialog box will appear.

This dialog box lets us customize the button.

8. **Click** on **Picture** to place a dot in the circle.

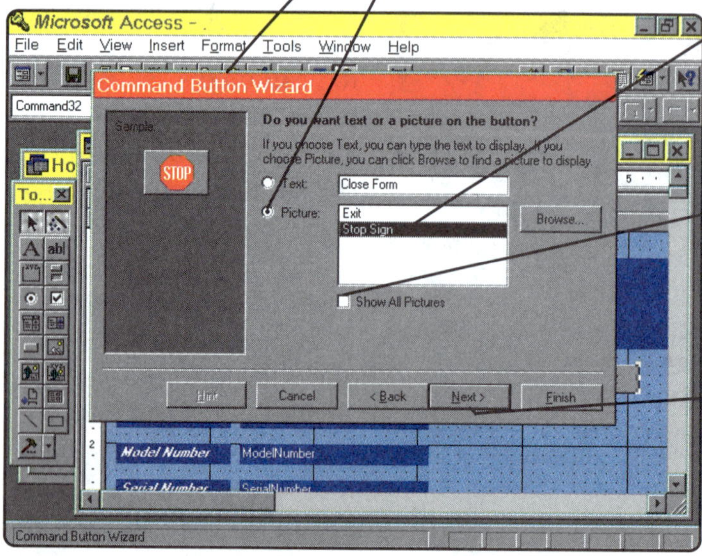

9. **Click** on **Stop Sign** to highlight it. A picture of the Stop Sign button will appear in the Sample box on the left.

You can click in the Show All Pictures box to see a list of all of the pictures available for the button.

10. While Stop Sign is highlighted, **click** on **Next >** and another Command Button Wizard dialog box will appear.

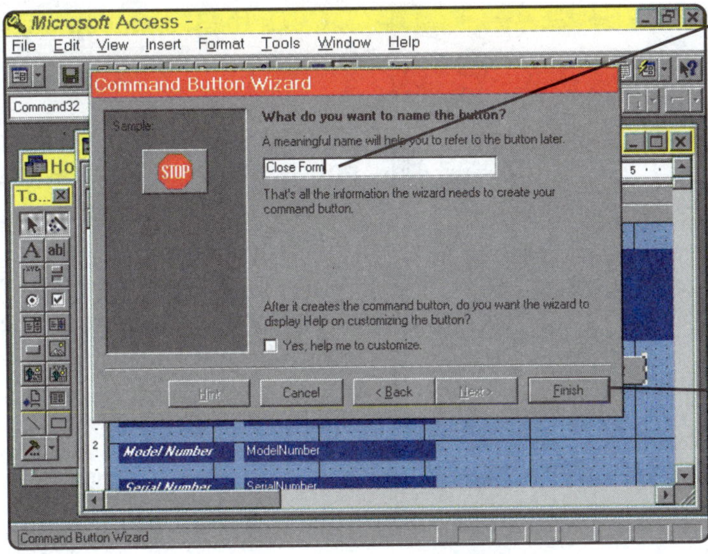

11. **Type Close Form** (or any other name you want to use) in the text box. This name will not appear on the button. It is only to give the button a unique name to distinguish it from all of the other elements, or "objects" that make up the database.

12. **Click** on **Finish**. The Wizard will create the button on the form.

ADDING A LABEL

Now that we have a new button on our form, we should label it so that its function is clear. The new button has handles around it so that we can move it around if we choose to.

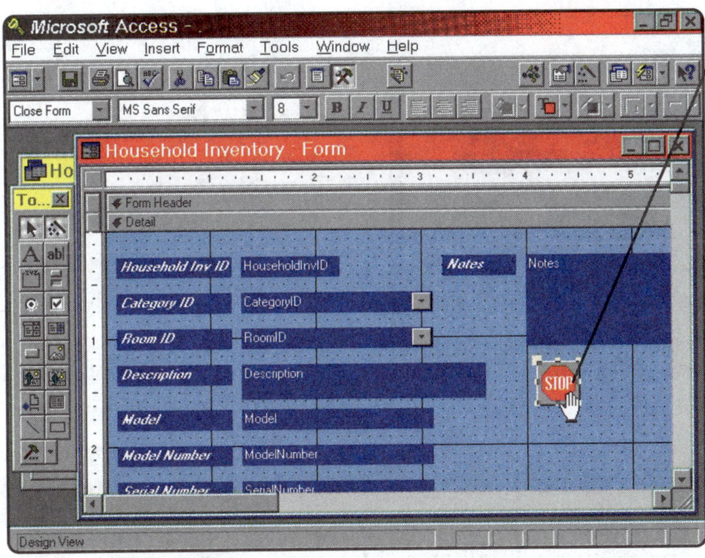

1. **Place** your **mouse pointer** over the button. As it moves over the button it will turn into a hand.

2. **Press and hold** the **mouse button** as you **drag** the button to the spot where you want it to be. We're leaving a little space to its left for a label in our example.

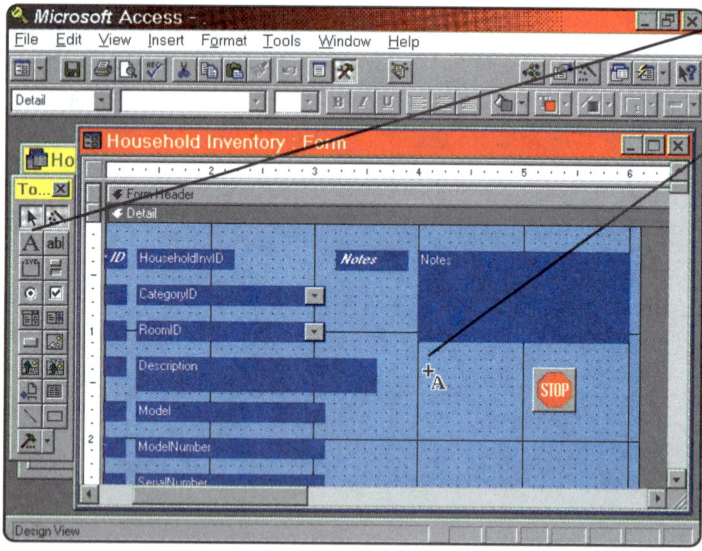

3. **Click** the **Label icon** on the toolbar.

4. **Move** your **mouse pointer** over the form. As you do, it will turn into a plus sign and letter "A." We'll want to position the center of the plus sign at the spot where we want the upper left corner of our label to be located.

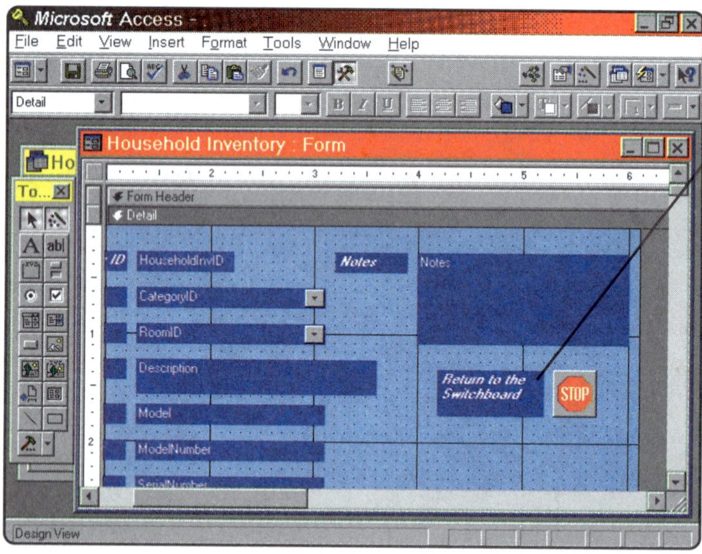

5. **Click** the **mouse button** to place the label.

6. **Type Return to the**.

7. **Press** the **Shift and Enter keys** at the same time to start a new line.

8. **Type Switchboard**.

9. **Press** the **Enter key**. The label will be complete.

You can click on the label to highlight it, and then click on it again to place the cursor and edit the label if you want to change it. You can also click on it to highlight it, then press the Delete key (Del) on your keyboard to delete the label and start over.

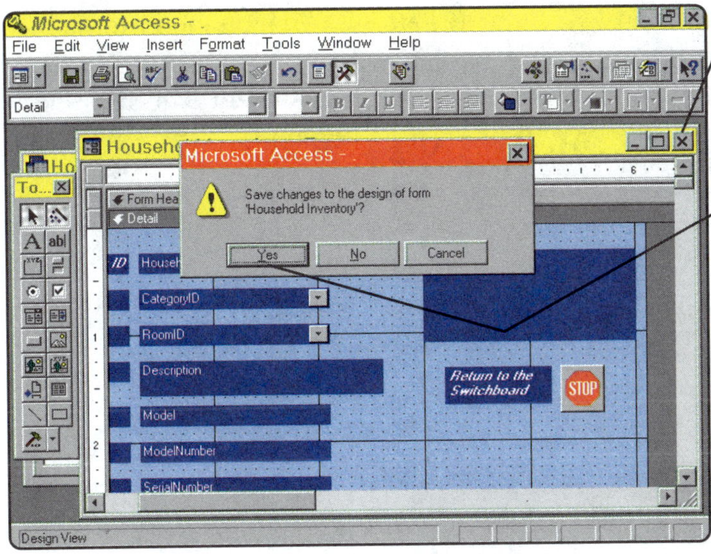

10. Click on the **Close button** (☒) to close the form. A message box will appear.

11. Click on **Yes**. The changes will be saved, and the form will close.

Checking on the Changes

Now we can open our customized form and see the results of all this effort.

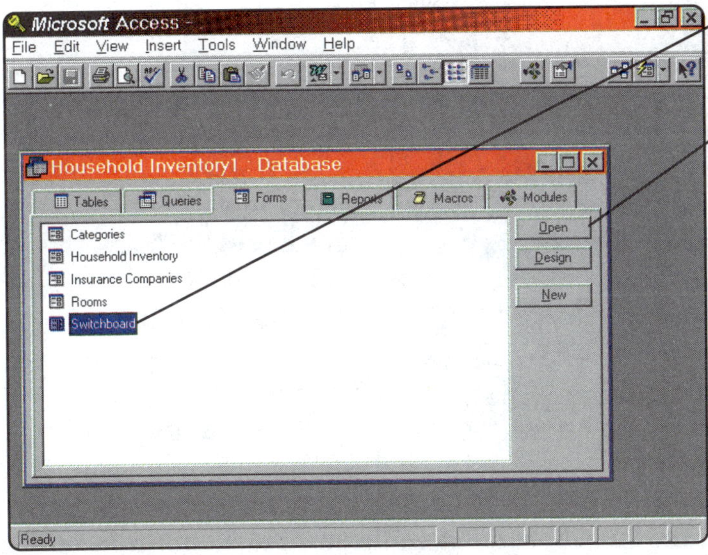

1. Click on **Switchboard** to highlight it.

2. Click on **Open**. The Switchboard will appear.

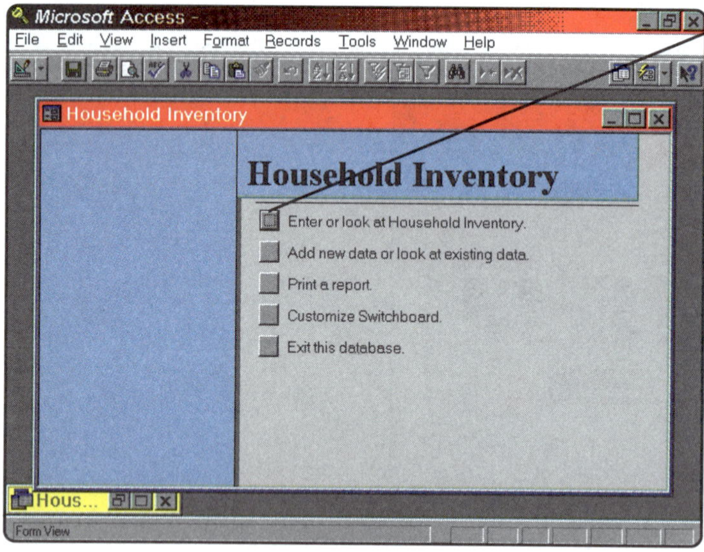

3. **Click** on the **Enter or look at Household Inventory button**. The Household Inventory form will appear.

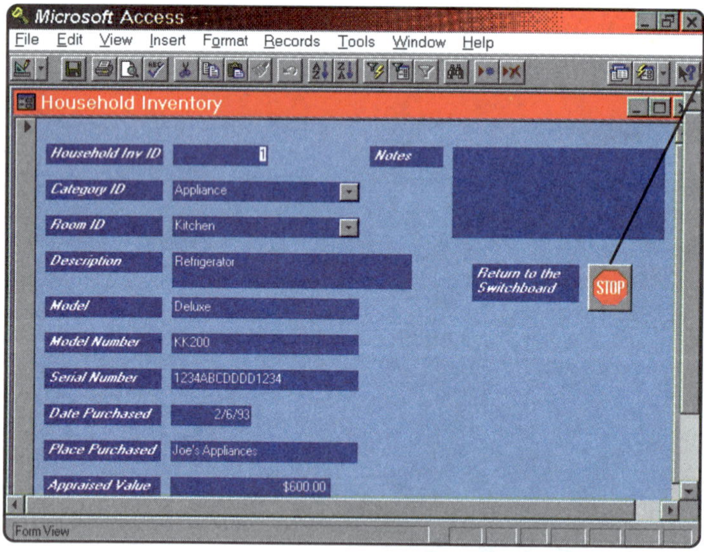

And there's our new button! In Chapter 20 we'll show you how to add a button that's linked to a "Macro." Macros are another way to use your database more efficiently.

Remember that the button only closes the form. When you use the Switchboard to go to the Household Inventory form, closing the form will return you to the Switchboard. If you open the Household Inventory form from the database dialog box, you won't go to the Switchboard when the form is closed. You could say that the label we made is a little misleading, but it was set up this way assuming that the database will be used through the Switchboard.

CHAPTER 12

Using the Report Wizard to Make a New Report

You can use the Wizard feature to make a report in a matter of minutes. Your finished product is guaranteed to look professional. In this chapter, you will do the following:

✔ Make a report for an existing table

STARTING THE REPORT WIZARD

1. **Open** to the **Database window** you see here, if it isn't already on your screen.

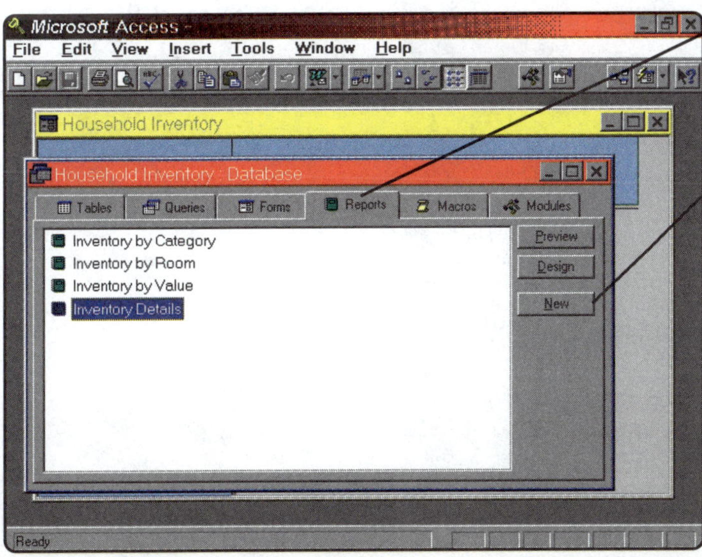

2. **Click** on the **Reports tab** to bring it to the front of the window.

3. **Click** on the **New button**. The New Report dialog box will appear.

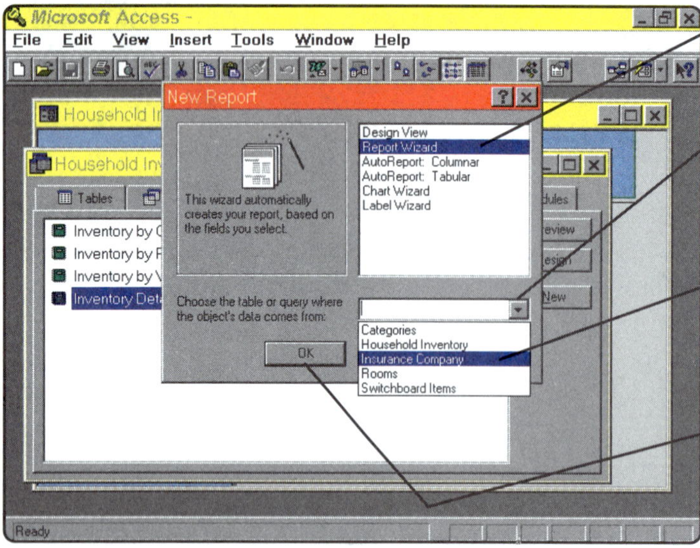

4. **Click** on **Report Wizard** to highlight it.

5. **Click** on ▼ in the Choose the table box. A pull-down list of tables will appear.

6. **Click** on **Insurance Company.** The list box will close.

7. **Click** on **OK**.

CHOOSING THE FIELDS

Notice that all of the fields associated with the Insurance Company table appear in the Available Fields box.

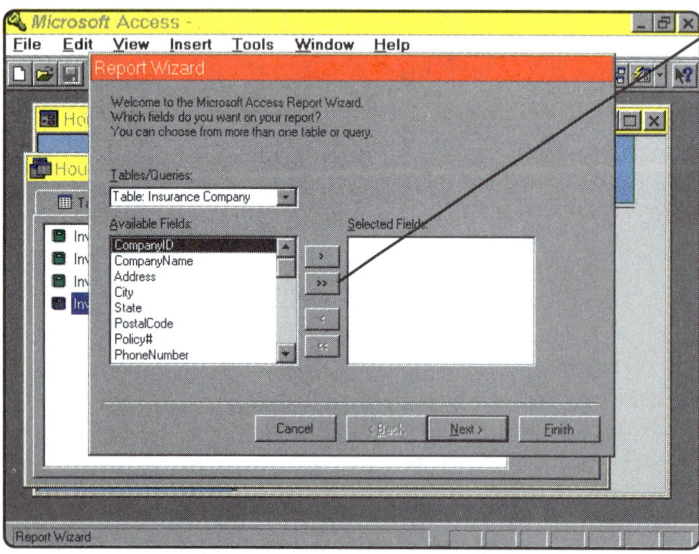

1. **Click** on the **>> button** to select all. The fields will appear in the Selected Fields box.

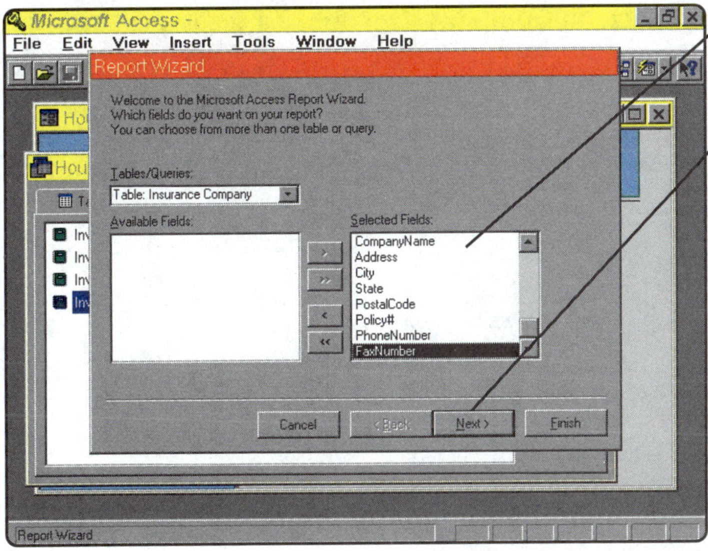

These are the fields that will appear on the new report.

2. **Click** on **Next >**. Another Report Wizard dialog box will appear.

CHOOSING GROUPS

Notice that in this view you see a list of all the fields that will appear on the report. In this section, you will select two of those fields to be grouped separately at the top of each record.

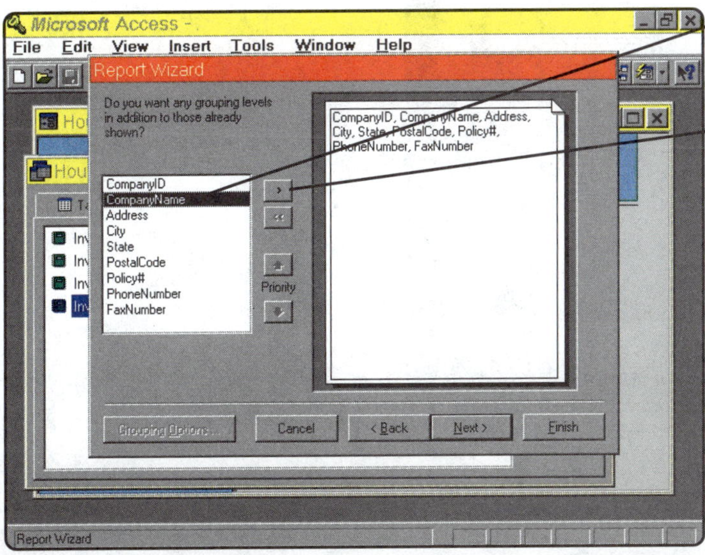

1. **Click** on **CompanyName** to highlight it.

2. **Click** on the ▸ **button**. The CompanyName field will appear in a separate box above the other fields.

3. **Click** on **CompanyID** to make a second group.

4. **Click** on the ▸ **button.** The CompanyID field will appear in a separate box below the newly created CompanyName box.

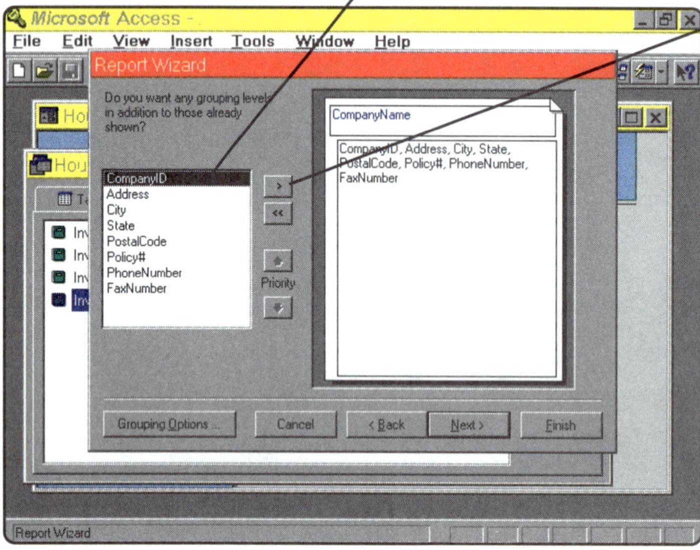

Notice the new grouping on the report.

5. **Click** on **Next >**. Another Report Wizard dialog box will appear.

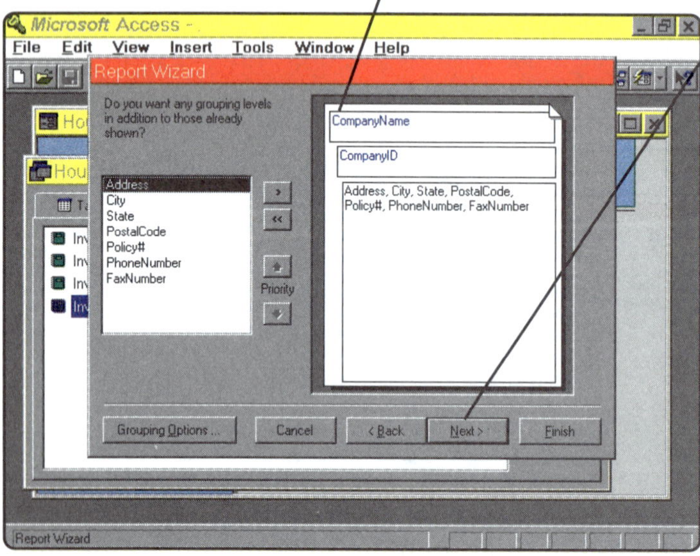

SORTING DETAILS

You can sort up to four fields in your records alphabetically. In this example, we will sort the report by the State field.

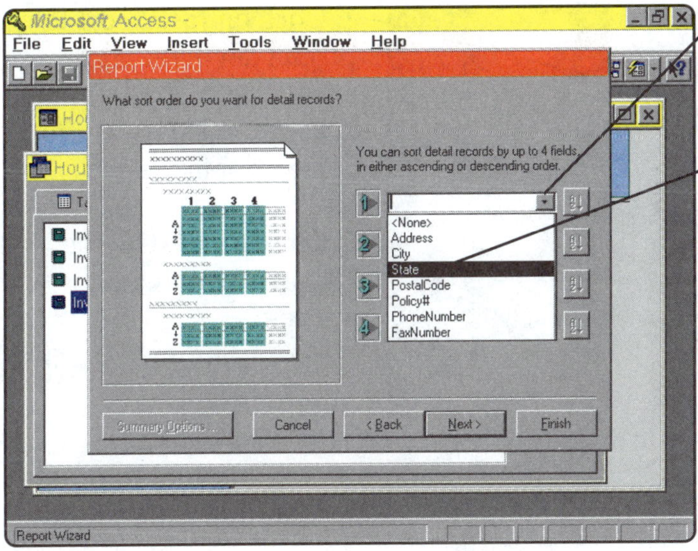

1. **Click** on the ▼ in the 1 text box. A pull-down list of fields will appear.
2. **Click** on **State** to highlight it. The box will close, and State will appear in the 1 text box.

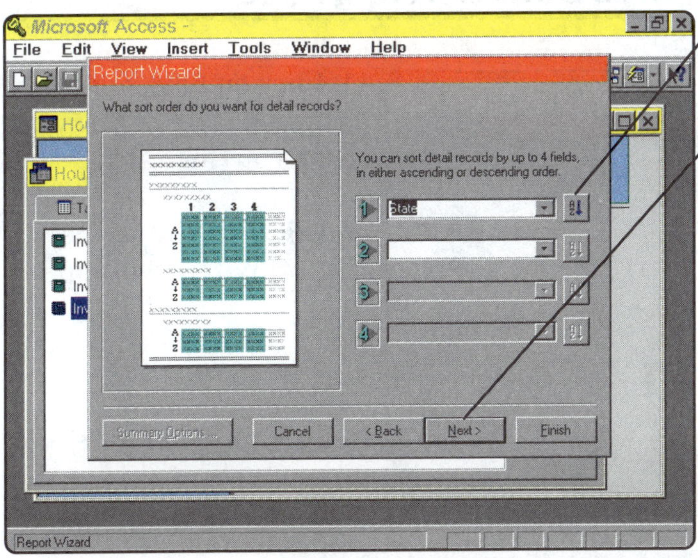

Notice that the field will be sorted from A to Z.

3. **Click** on **Next >**. The Wizard Report dialog box will appear.

CHOOSING THE LAYOUT VIEW

Access gives you several choices of layouts. Click on the different selections to see each layout in the view window.

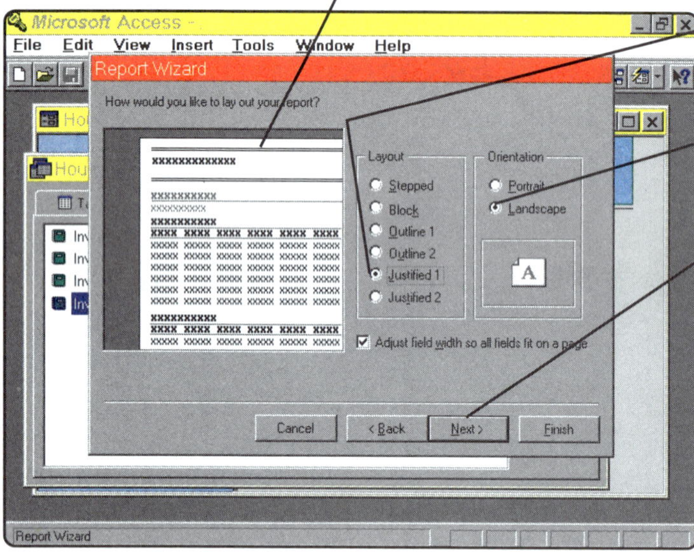

1. **Click** on **Justified 1** to place a dot in the circle.
2. **Click** on **Landscape** to place a dot in the circle.
3. **Click** on **Next >.** The Report Wizard window will appear.

CHOOSING THE STYLE

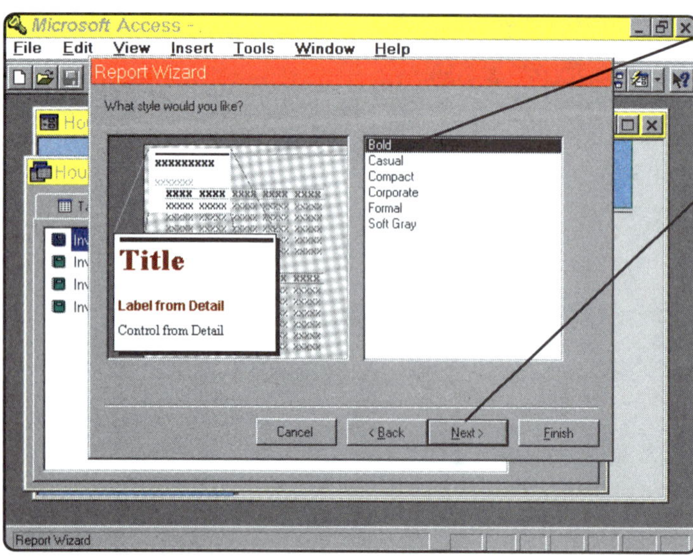

1. **Click** on **Bold** if you want to match the style that was chosen in Chapter 1.
2. **Click** on **Next >**. The Report Wizard will appear.

NAMING THE REPORT

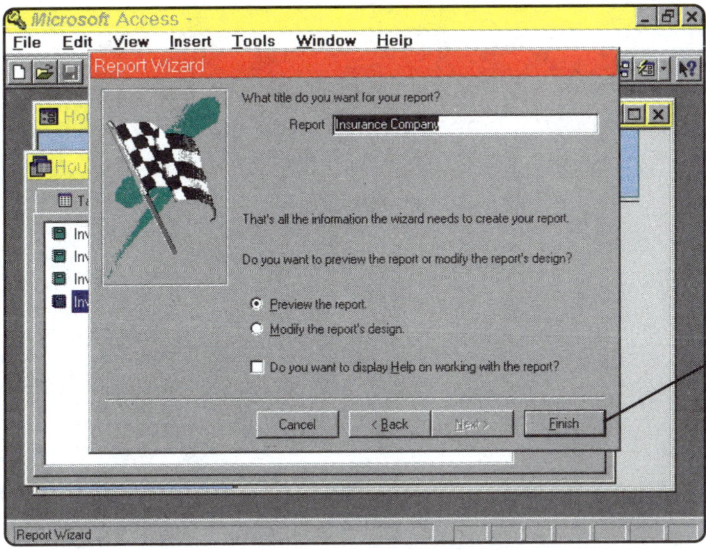

Access has already named the report for you. Type a new name in the Report text box if you want to change the name. Otherwise, the checkered flag is flying, and you are ready to cross the finish line.

1. **Click** on **Finish**. The Insurance Company report will appear.

VIEWING THE REPORT

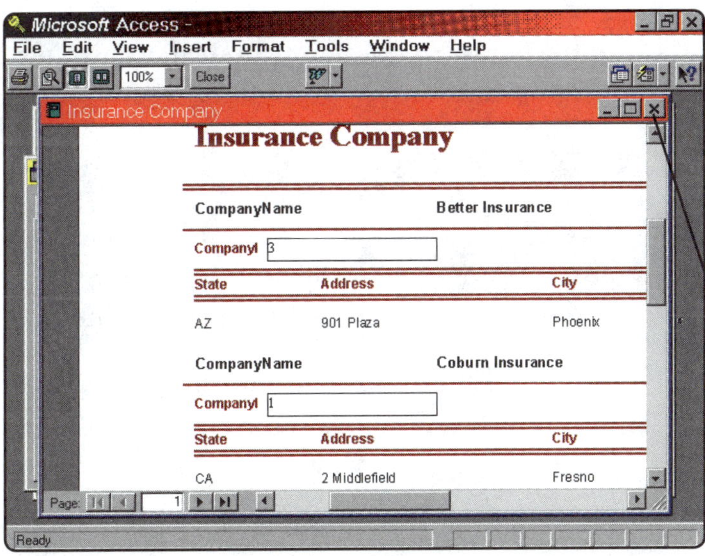

In this example, you will notice that the company names have been sorted alphabetically by state.

CLOSING THE REPORT

1. **Click** on the **Close button** (☒) in the title bar. The Report will close.

CHAPTER 13

Customizing a Report

You can customize existing reports very easily. However, it's a good idea to save the report under a different name, so that if you change your mind or make a major error, you still have your original report intact. In this chapter, you will do the following:

- ✔ Rename a report
- ✔ Change the report header
- ✔ Delete fields
- ✔ Move fields
- ✔ Resize a report layout

RENAMING THE REPORT

In this section, you'll rename the "Insurance Company" report to "Insurance Company Fax" before you customize or redesign the report.

1. **Open** the **Household Inventory1: Database** if it is not already open.

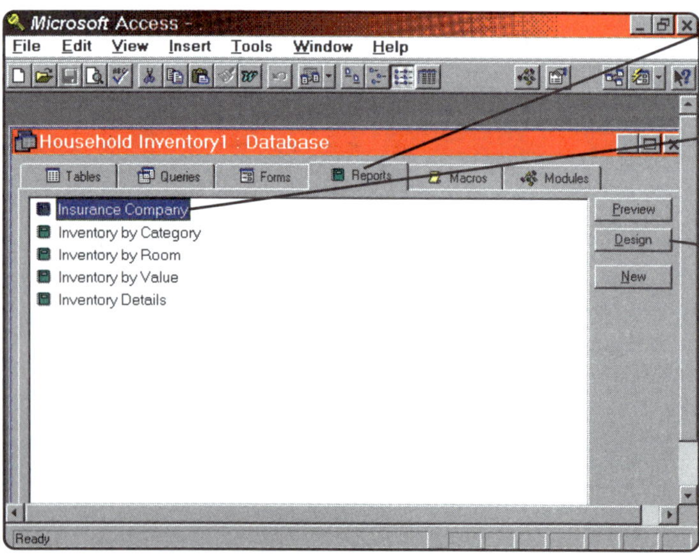

2. **Click** on the **Reports tab** to bring it to the front.

3. **Click** on **Insurance Company** to highlight it.

4. **Click** on **Design. The** Insurance Company Design view will appear.

5. **Click** on the **Maximize button** (□) on the title bar, if necessary, to make your screen look like this one.

6. **Click** on **File** in the menu bar. The File menu will appear.

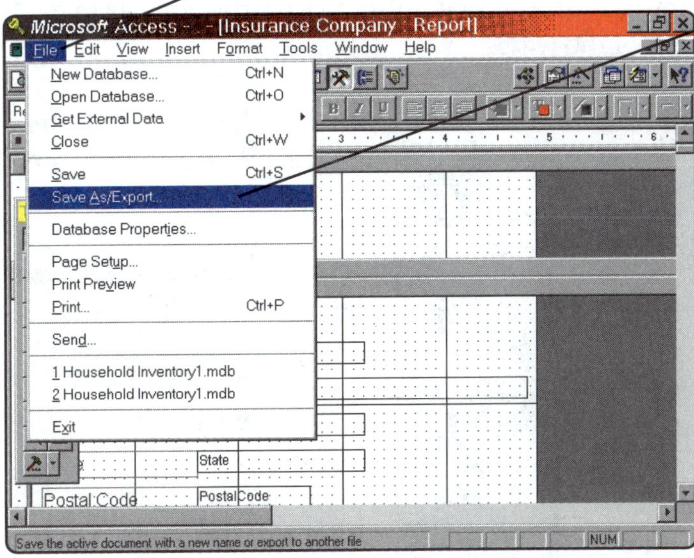

7. **Click** on **Save As/Export**. The Save As dialog box will appear.

8. **Type** the **new name** for the file. It will replace the highlighted text.

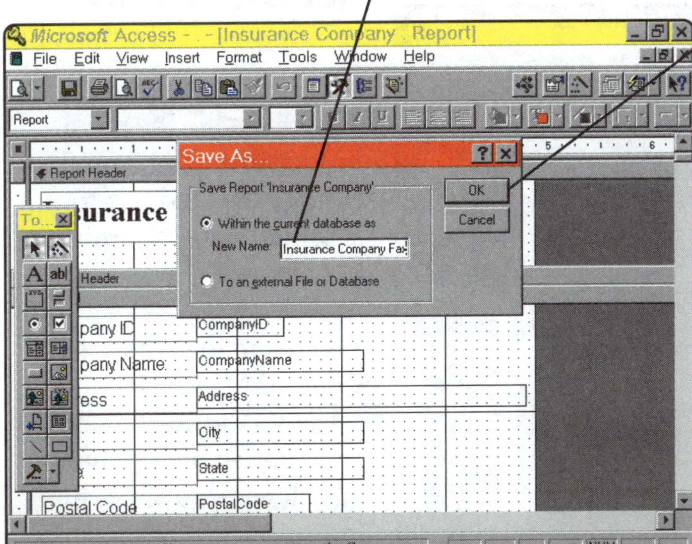

9. **Click** on **OK**. The dialog box will close, and the new file name will appear in the title bar.

"DOCKING" A TOOLBAR

You can move a toolbar around anywhere on your screen . You can "dock" it so it's in a horizontal format like the other toolbars under the menu bar. In this example, you'll dock the Controls toolbar to get it out of the way.

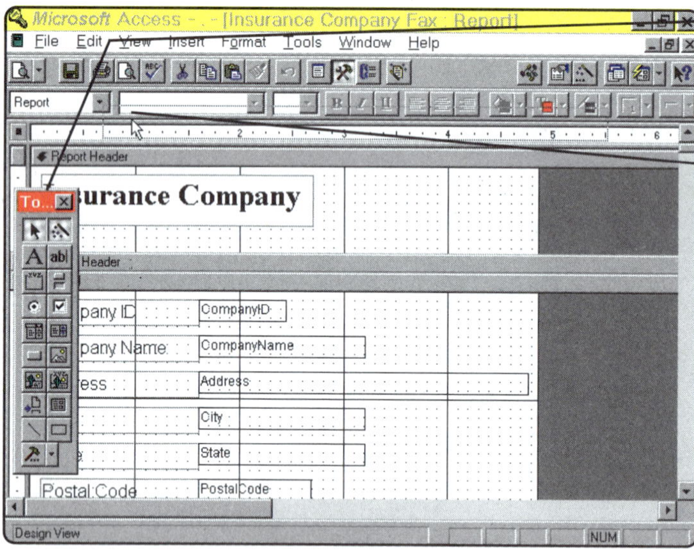

1. **Place** the **mouse pointer** on the **title bar** of the Controls toolbar.
2. **Press and hold** the **mouse button** as you **drag** the toolbar up above the ruler.
3. **Release** the **mouse button**. The toolbar will snap into place between the ruler and the Report Design toolbar.

CHANGING THE REPORT HEADER

In this example, you'll add "Numbers" to the report header title. First, you'll enlarge the field box to accommodate the additional word.

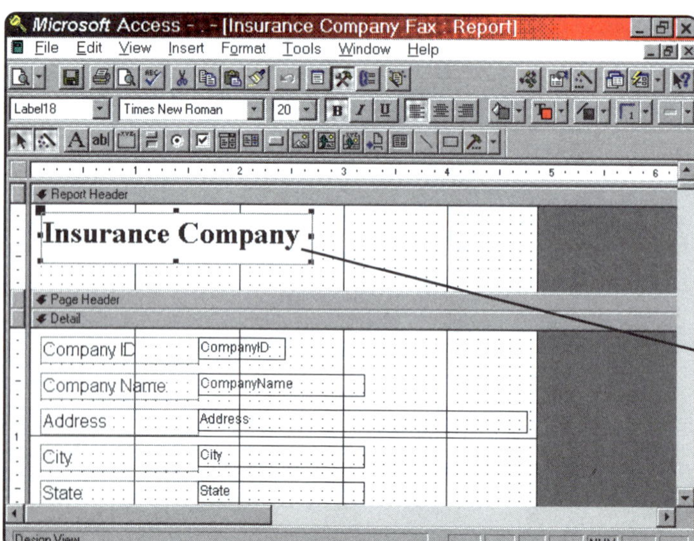

1. **Click** in the **"Insurance Company" field box** to select it. The box will be surrounded by square handles as you see in this example.

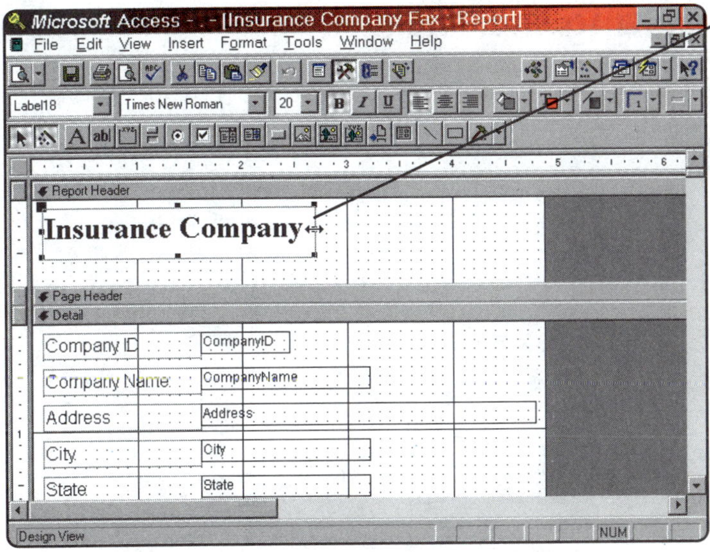

2. **Place** the **mouse pointer** on **top** of the **middle handle** on the right of the field border. The cursor will change to a two-headed arrow.

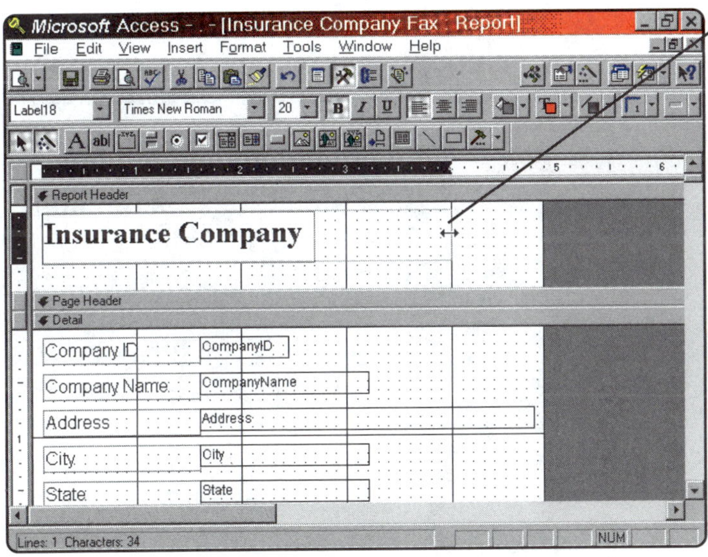

3. **Press and hold** the **mouse button** as you **drag** the border to the right to enlarge it.

Notice that the ruler indicates the size of the field as you drag.

4. **Release** the **mouse button**. The "Insurance Company" field box will be enlarged.

Editing the Title

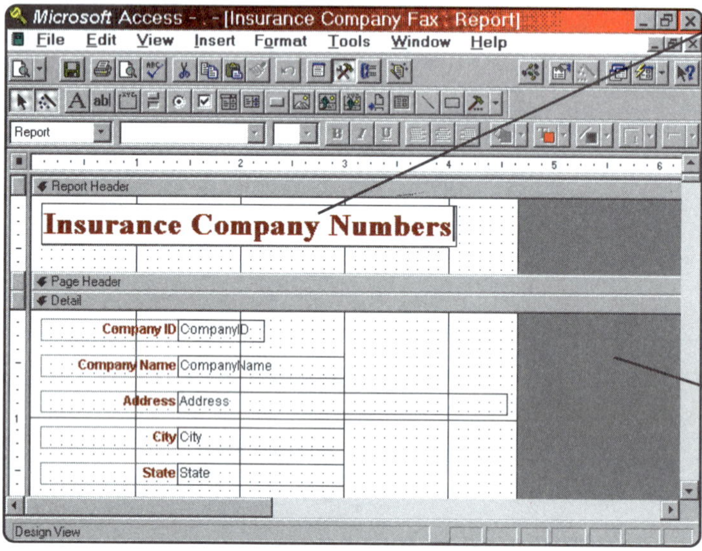

1. **Click** at the end of **"Company"** to place the cursor. The cursor will be in the shape of an I-beam.

2. **Press** the **Spacebar** once to insert a space.

3. **Type Numbers**.

4. **Click anywhere** on the dark gray background to remove the selection handles.

DELETING FIELDS

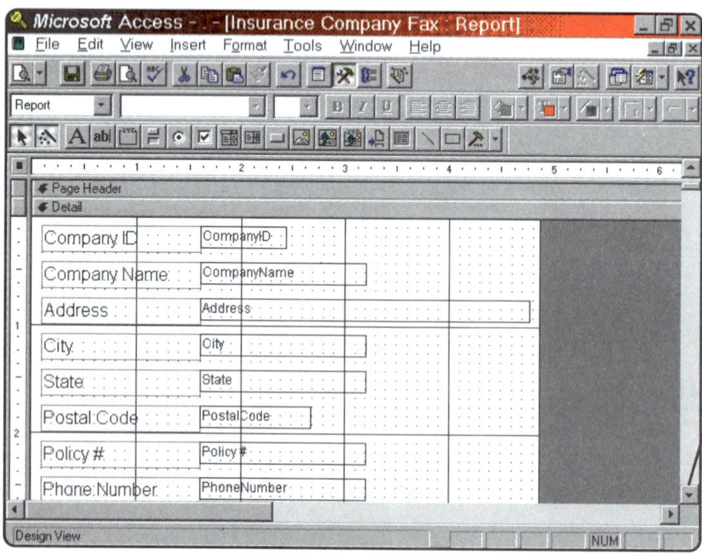

Because the report we're customizing in this example will contain only the company name, the policy #, and the phone and fax numbers, you'll delete the other fields from the report.

1. **Click** on the ▼ on the scroll bar to scroll "Insurance Company Numbers" up out of the way as you see in this example.

Deleting Multiple Fields

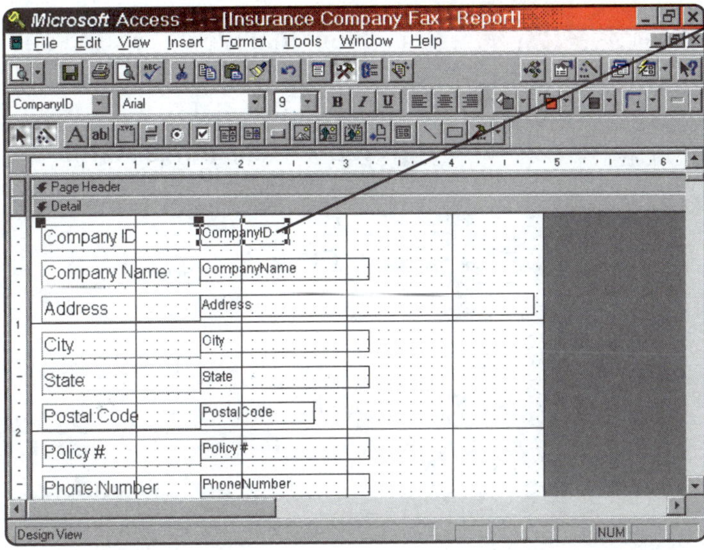

1. **Press and hold** the **Shift key** as you click on the "Company ID" field. The Company ID field and the Company ID label on the left will both be selected.

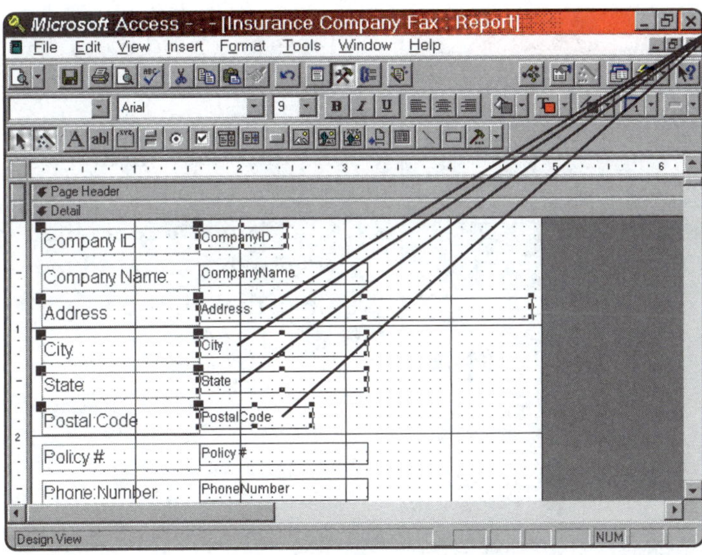

2. **Continue** to **hold** the **Shift key** as you click on each of the fields you want to delete. In this example, we'll delete the **Address, City, State, and Postal Code fields**.

3. **Press** the **Delete key**. All of the selected fields will be deleted.

MOVING FIELDS

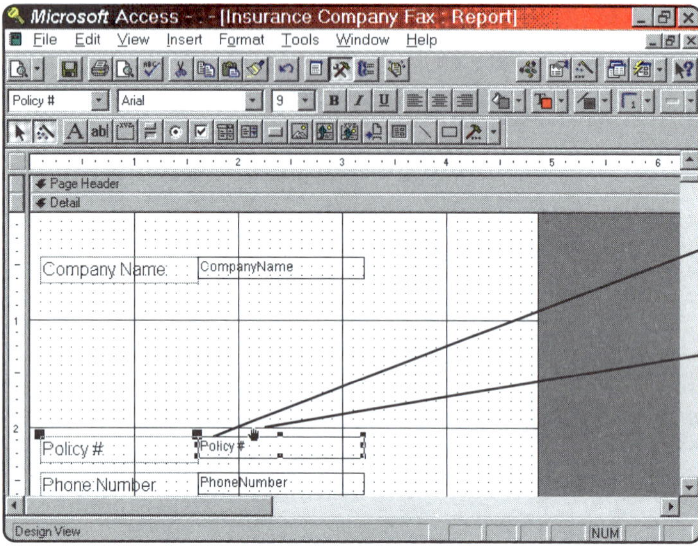

Now that we've created all the space by deleting the unwanted fields from the report, let's move all the fields up and realign them.

1. **Click** on the **Policy # field** to select it.
2. **Place** the **cursor** on the **border** of the field. The cursor will become a hand as you see in this example. Be careful *not* to place the cursor on a square handle.

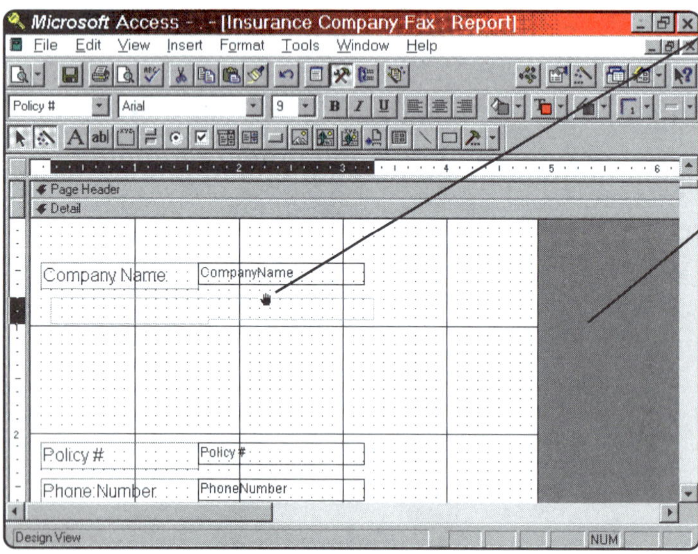

3. **Press and hold** the **mouse button** as you **drag** the field box up, below the Company Name field.
4. **Click anywhere** on the dark gray background to remove the selection handles.

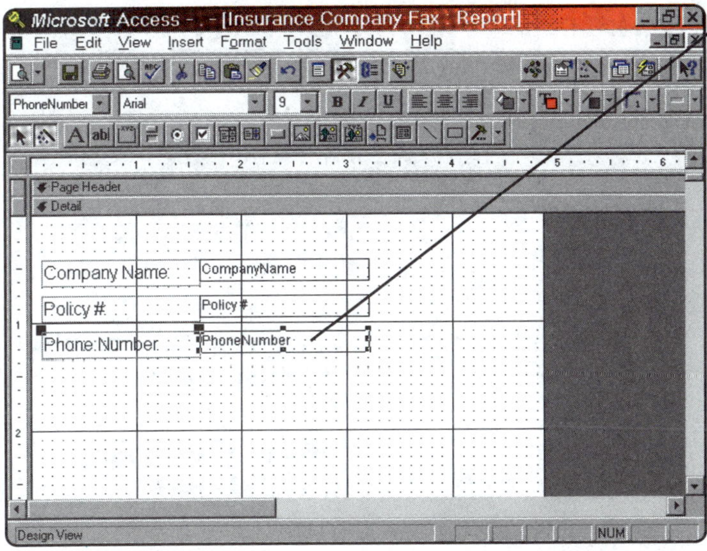

5. **Repeat steps 1 to 4** to move the **Phone Number field** as you see in this example.

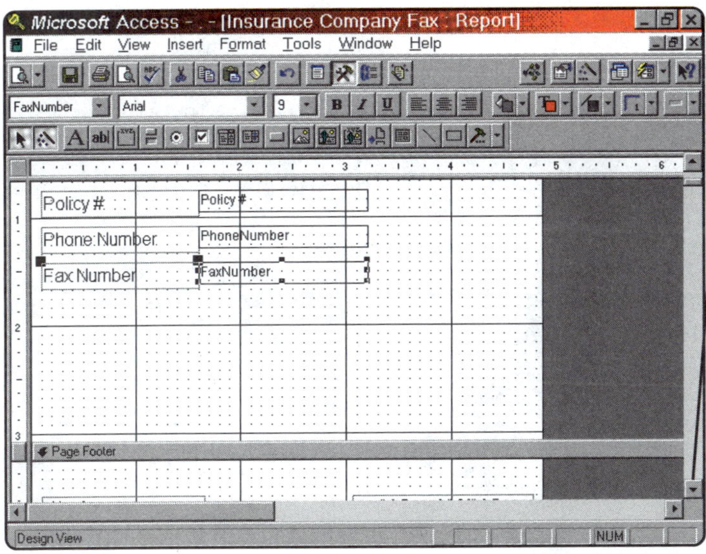

6. **Click** on the ▼ on the scroll bar to see the Fax Field.

7. **Repeat steps 1 to 4** to move the **Fax Number field** as you see in this example.

RESIZING THE REPORT LAYOUT

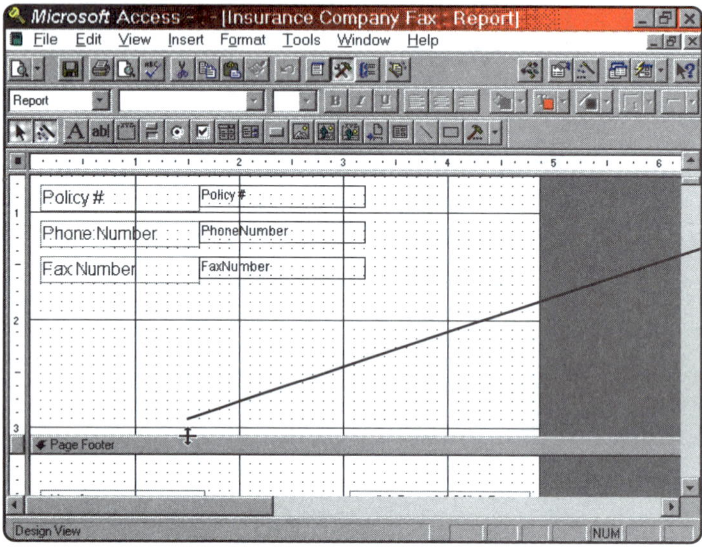

Now that we've moved all of the remaining fields into close formation, let's eliminate the space at the bottom of the report layout.

1. **Place** the **mouse pointer** at the **top edge** of the **Page Footer bar.** The cursor will change to a heavy line with a two-headed arrow.

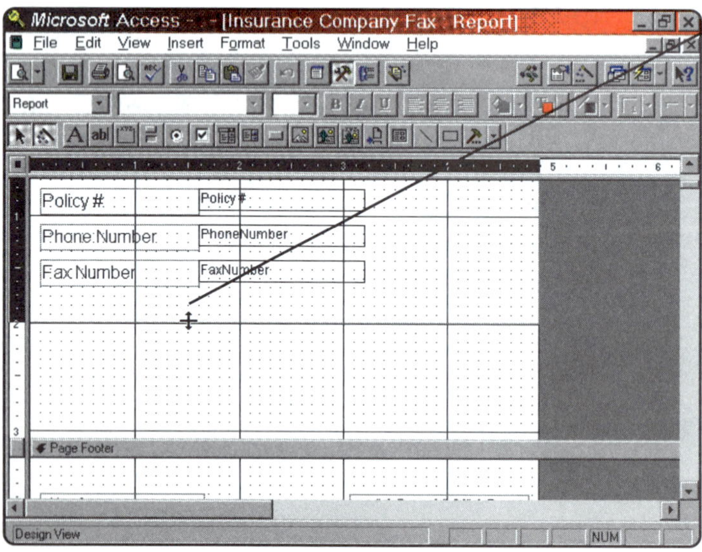

2. **Press and hold** the **mouse button** as you **drag** the border up to shorten it.

Notice that the ruler indicates the size of the field as you drag.

3. **Release** the **mouse button**. The report layout will be shortened.

PREVIEWING THE REPORT

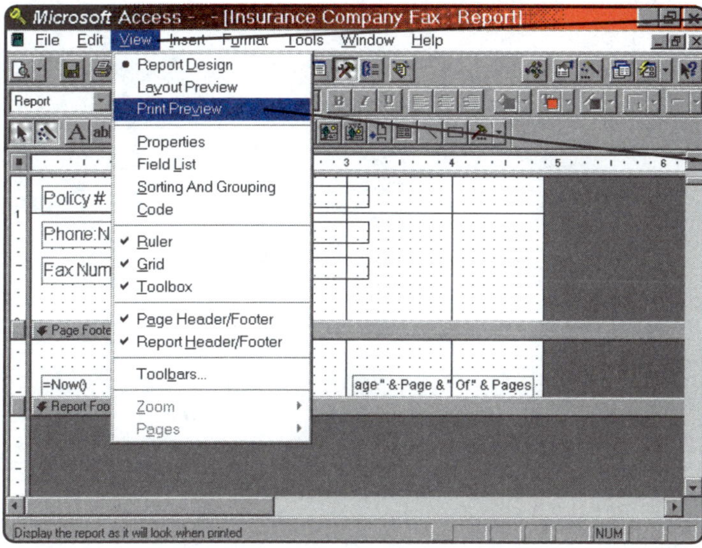

1. **Click** on **View** in the menu bar. The View menu will appear.

2. **Click** on **Print Preview.** The Preview screen will appear.

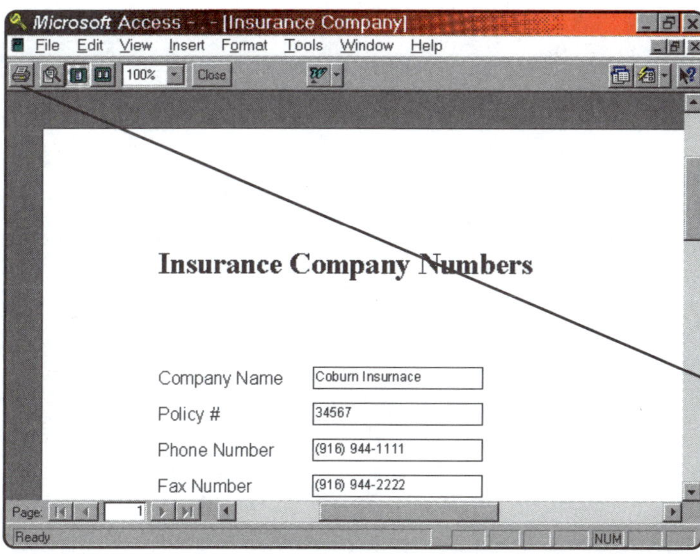

SAVING AND PRINTING

1. **Press and hold the Ctrl key** on your keyboard as you press the **"s" key (Ctrl+s)**. This is another way to save your work.

2. **Click** on the **Print button.** The Insurance Company Numbers Report will print.

ACCESS FOR WINDOWS 95

Part III: Importing and Exporting Data

CHAPTER 14

Importing a File into Access

Importing a database file from another program into Access is as easy as can be. In this chapter, you will do the following:

✔ Open and name a new database

✔ Import a file from another program

OPENING A BLANK DATABASE FILE

In this section, you will open and name a blank database file. In the section that follows you will import a table from another database program.

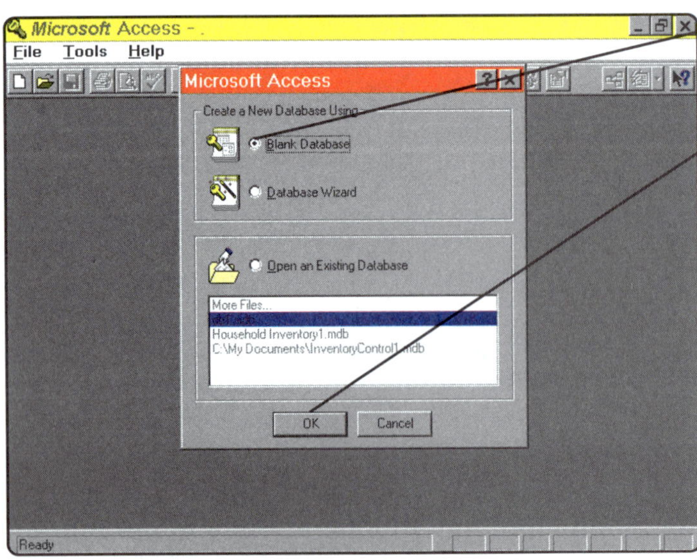

1. **Click** on **Blank Database** to put a dot in the circle.

2. **Click** on **OK**. The File New Database dialog box will appear.

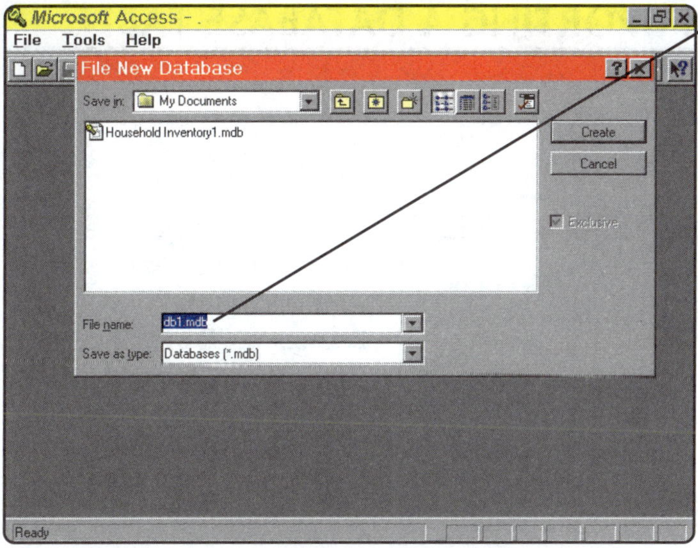

Note: Access automatically assigns a name. It is highlighted so that you can easily rename it. Your screen may not show the file extensions.

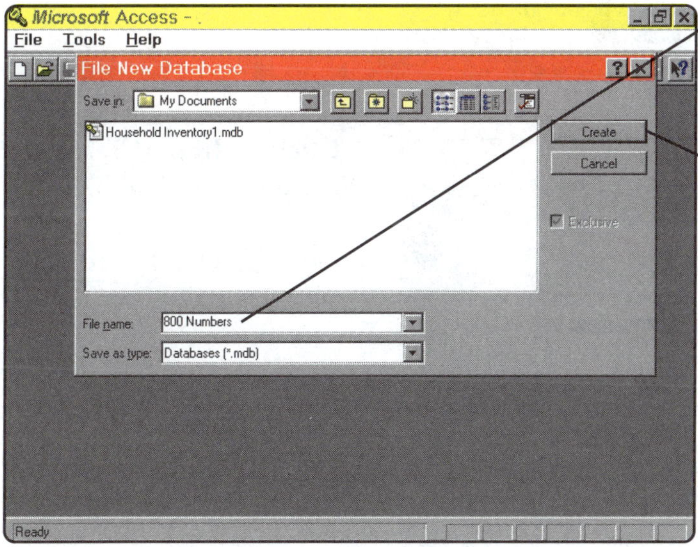

3. **Type** a **name** for the new database. In this example, it is 800 Numbers.

4. **Click** on **Create**. A dialog box with your file name will appear.

IMPORTING A DATABASE TABLE

In this section, you will import a database (dbf) table into Access.

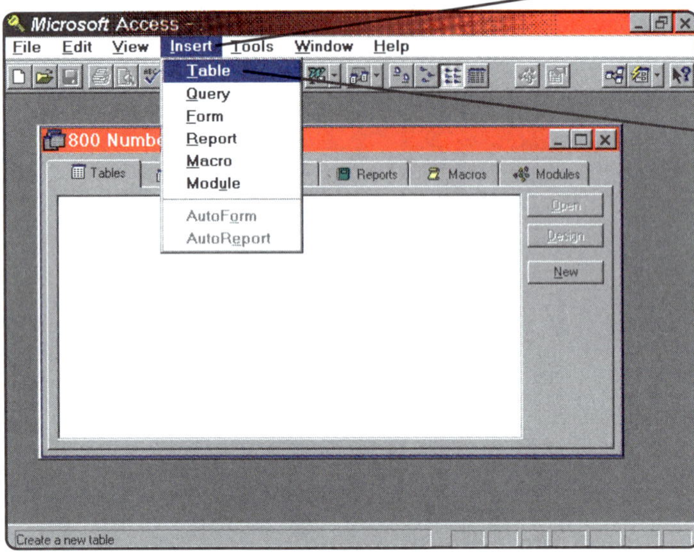

1. Click on **Insert**. The Insert menu will appear.
2. Click on **Table.** The New Table dialog box will appear.

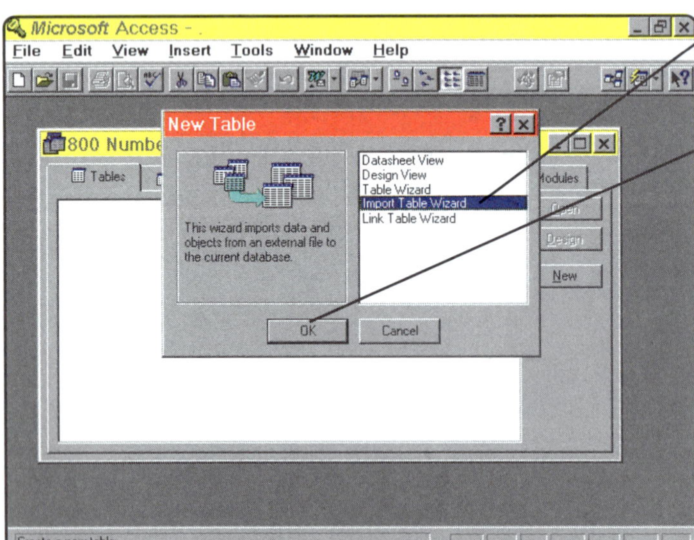

3. Click on **Import Table Wizard** to highlight it.
4. Click on **OK**. The Import dialog box will appear.

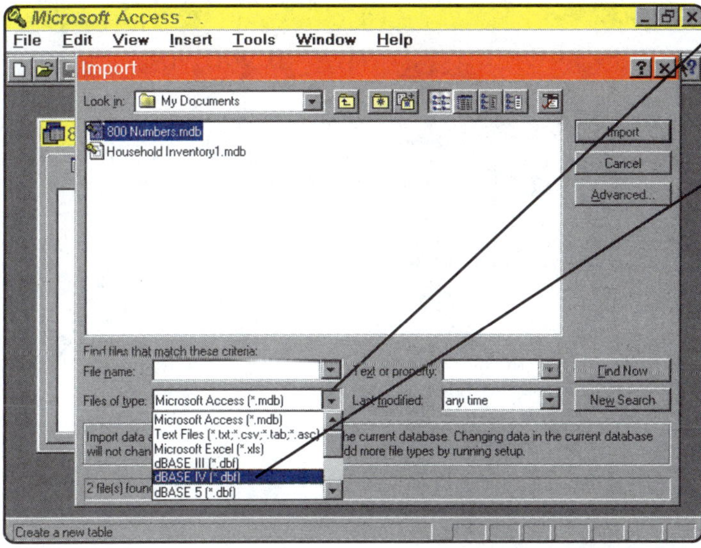

5. **Click** on the ▼ on the Files of type dialog box. A pull-down list will appear.

6. **Click** on the **file type**.

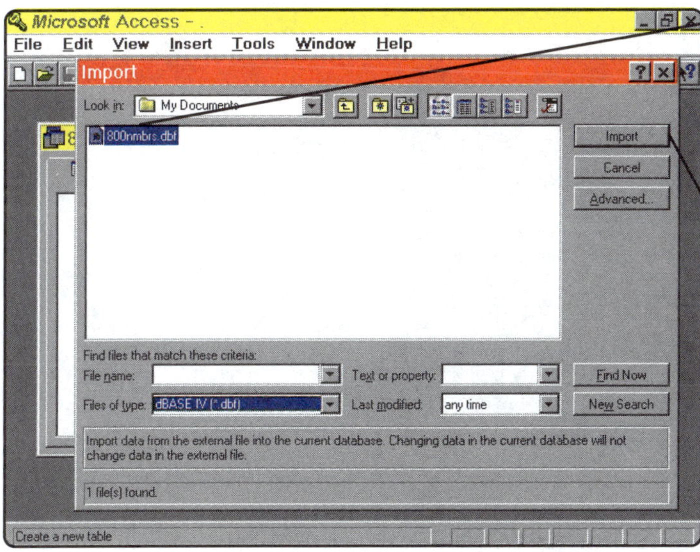

Note: We put a dBase IV (*.dbf) file here to illustrate.

7. **Click** on the **name** of the file.

8. **Click** on **Import**. An Access message box will appear.

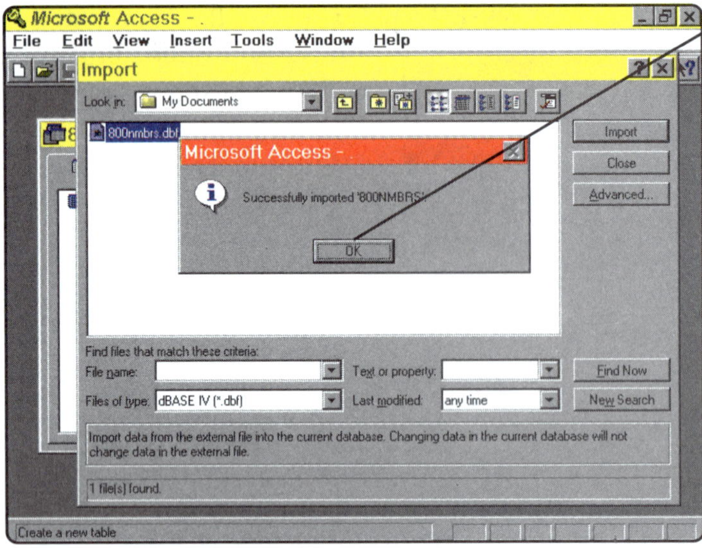

9. **Click** on **OK**. The message box will close.

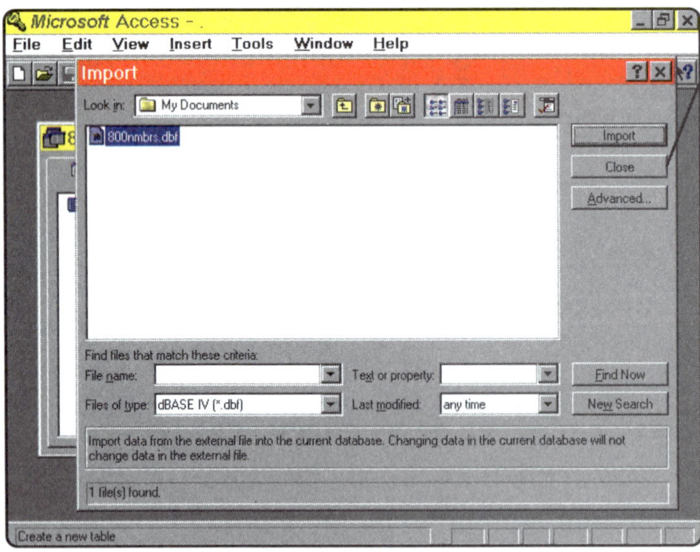

10. **Click** on **Close.** The Import dialog box will close.

VIEWING THE IMPORTED FILE

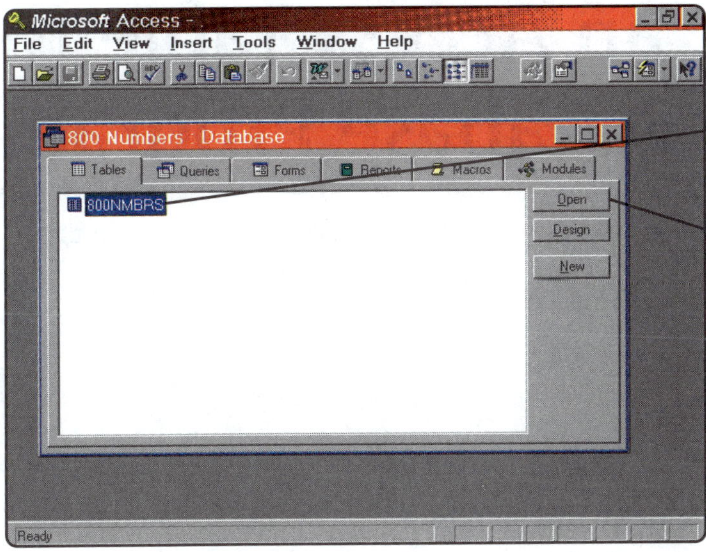

In this section, you will open your file.

1. **Click** on the **File** to highlight it.

2. **Click** on **Open**. Like magic your file will appear.

Voilà.

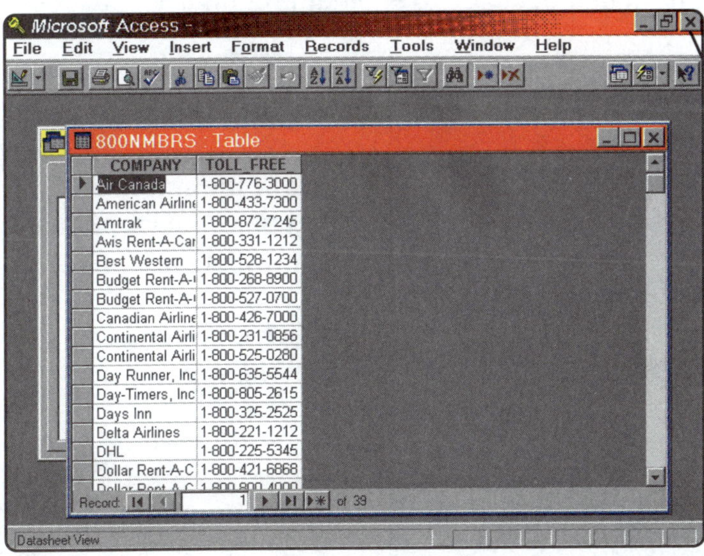

CLOSING ACCESS

1. **Click** on the **Close button** ([X]). The program will close.

CHAPTER 15

Exporting an Access Table to Another Database Program

Exporting an Access database table to another program is as easy as can be. In this chapter, you will do the following:

- ✔ Open an Access database
- ✔ Export an Access table to another program

OPENING AN ACCESS DATABASE FILE

In this section you will open an Access database file. In the section that follows you will export a table from that database to another program.

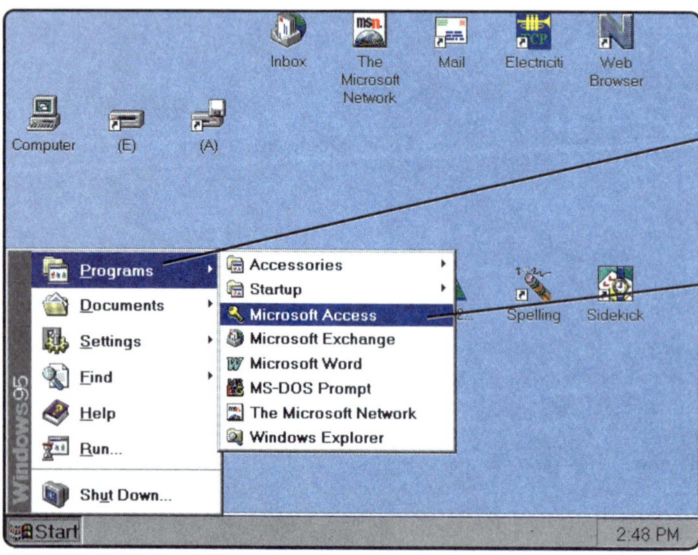

1. **Click** on the **Start button**. The Start Menu will appear.
2. **Move** the **cursor** over **Programs.** The Programs menu will appear.
3. **Click** on **Microsoft Access.** The program will open.

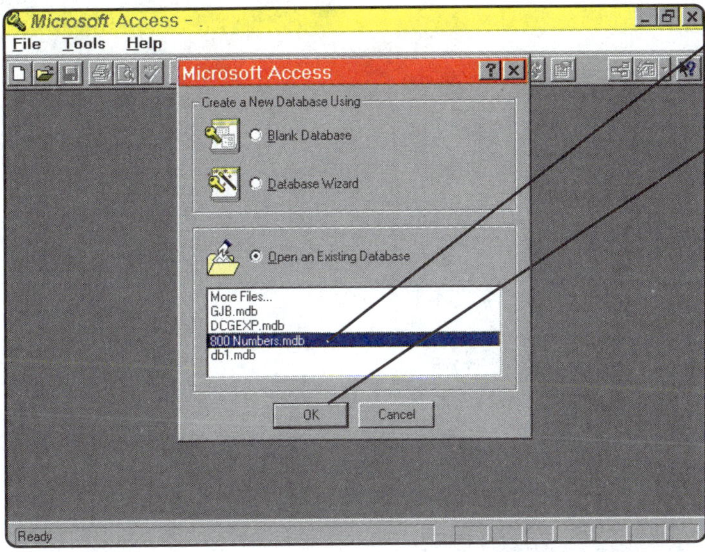

4. **Click** on the **file** you want to open.

5. **Click** on **OK**.

EXPORTING A TABLE

In this section, you will export an Access table to Excel 7. Access will automatically convert the table into an Excel table.

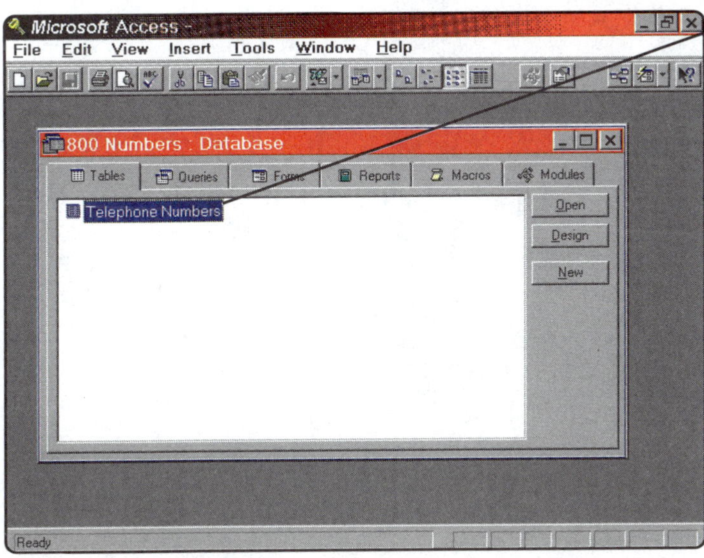

1. **Click** on the **table** that you want to export to highlight it.

2. **Click** on **File** in the menu bar. The File menu will appear.

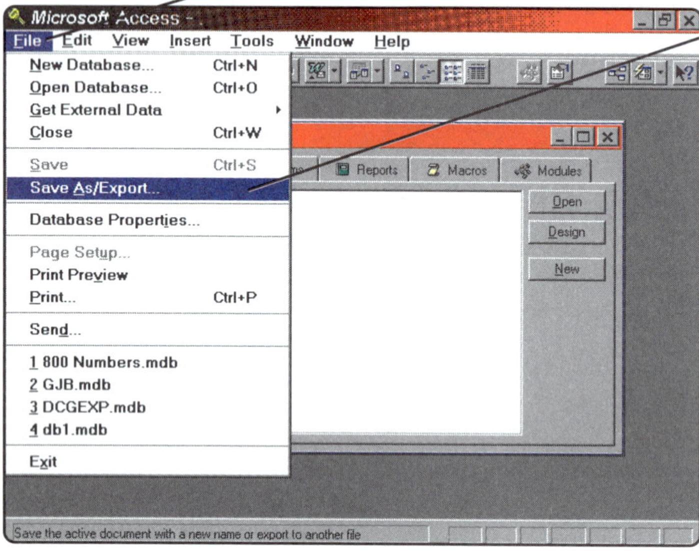

3. **Click** on **Save As/Export**. The Save As dialog box will appear.

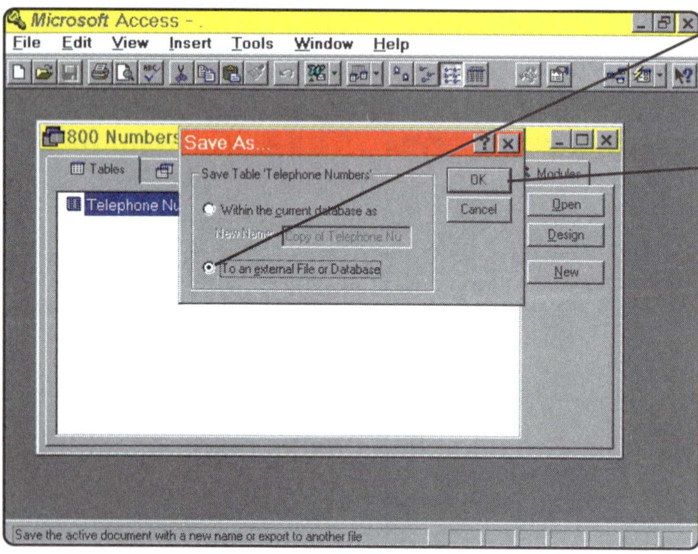

4. **Click** on **To an external File or Database** to put a dot in the circle.

5. **Click** on **OK**. The Save Tables dialog box will appear.

Selecting the Type of Database File

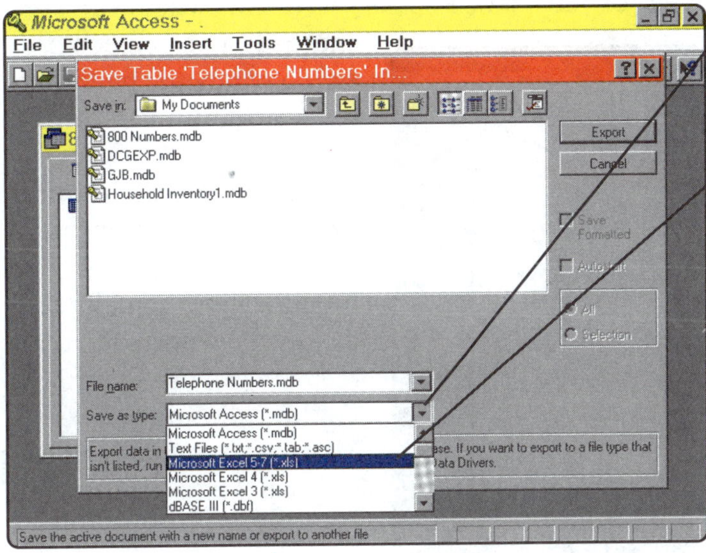

1. **Click** on the ▼ on the Save as type dialog box. A pull-down list will appear.
2. **Click** on the **file type**. In this example, it is Excel 5-7 {*.xls}. Again, depending on the View/Options Settings you have in Windows Explorer, you may not see file extensions.

Exporting the File

Notice that the file name now has an Excel .xls extension.

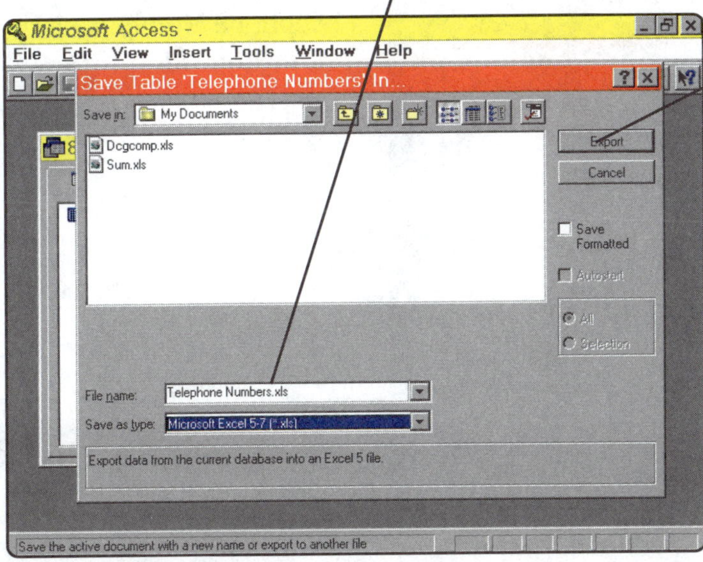

1. **Click** on **Export**. The dialog box will close.

Viewing the Results

For some unknown reason, Access did not tell us that the "export" process was successful. When we checked My Documents, sure enough, the new Excel file was there.

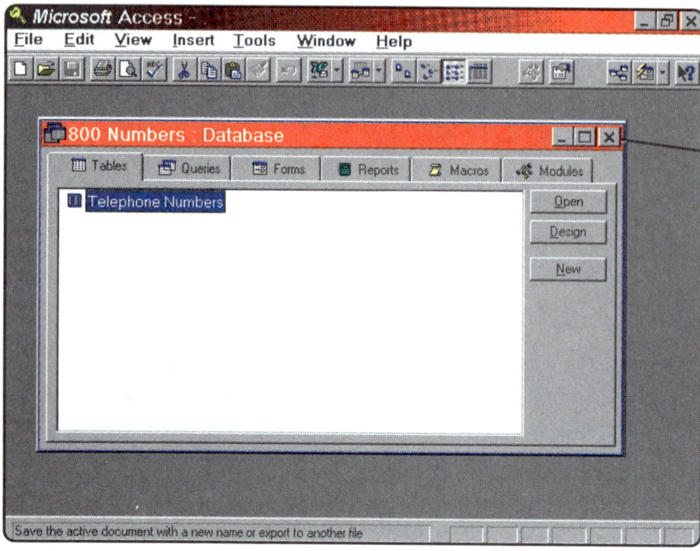

1. **Click** on the **Close button** (☒) to close the database.

If you want to actually see the newly exported Excel file, you can use Windows Explorer, Windows File Manager, or actually open it in Excel. You can also follow the importing steps in the previous chapter to arrive at the screen shown below.

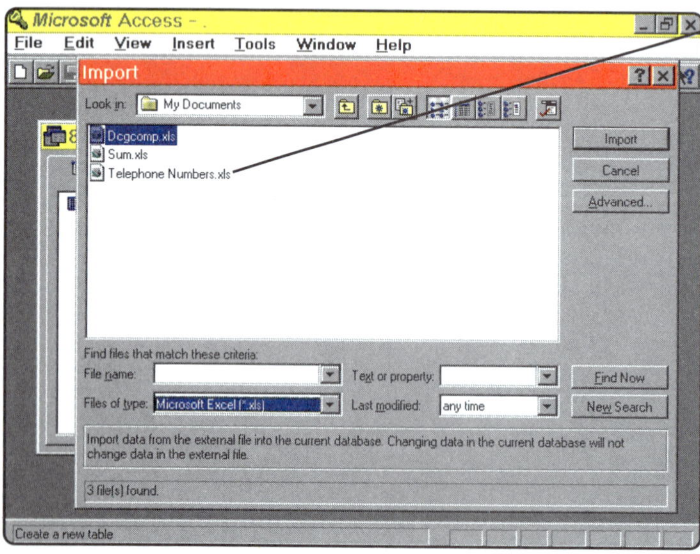

Notice the new Excel file (Telephone Numbers.xls). You've done it!

ACCESS FOR WINDOWS 95

Part IV: Using Special Features

CHAPTER 16

Customizing Access

In Access, there are lots of ways to customize the program to make it more enjoyable to use. For example, you can enlarge the toolbar buttons so that the buttons are easier to see. You can also choose different views to display the way your database files look. In this chapter, you will do the following:

- ✔ Enlarge the toolbar buttons
- ✔ Explore the database views
- ✔ Customize the startup view
- ✔ Remove a toolbar button
- ✔ Add a button to the toolbar
- ✔ Move a toolbar button

ENLARGING THE TOOLBAR BUTTONS

In this section, you'll make the toolbar buttons larger.

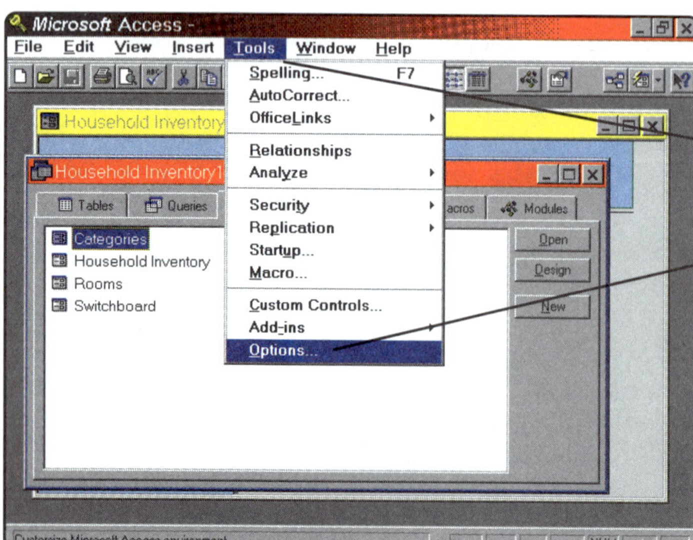

1. **Open** a **database** if one is not already open.
2. **Click** on **Tools.** The Tools menu will appear.
3. **Click** on **Options**. The Options dialog box will appear.

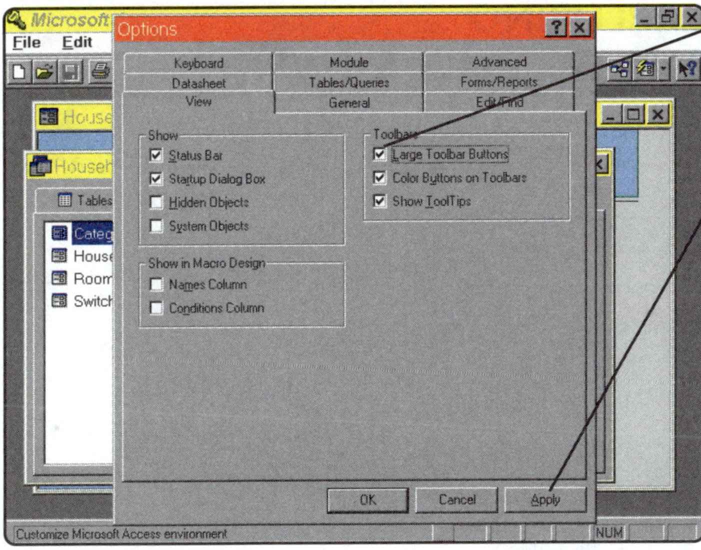

4. **Click** on **Large Toolbar Buttons** to put a ✔ in the box.

5. **Click** on **Apply**. There will be a short hourglass intermission.

Notice that the buttons are larger.

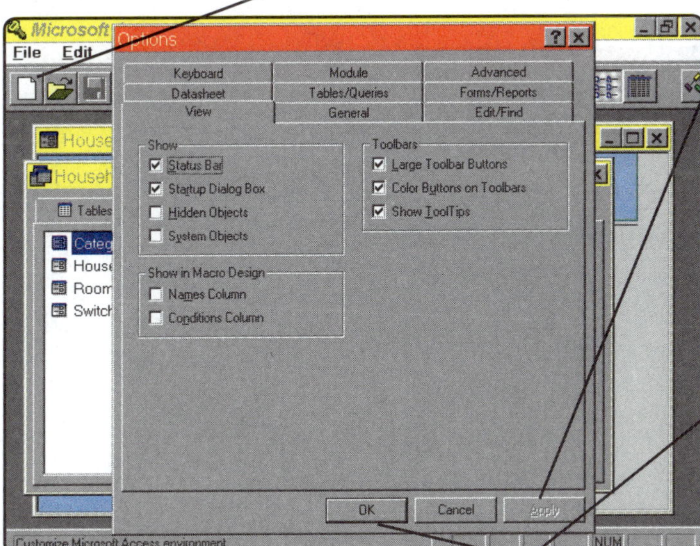

Notice also that "Apply" is now grayed out.

6. **Click** on **OK**. The dialog box will close.

EXPLORING THE DATABASE VIEWS

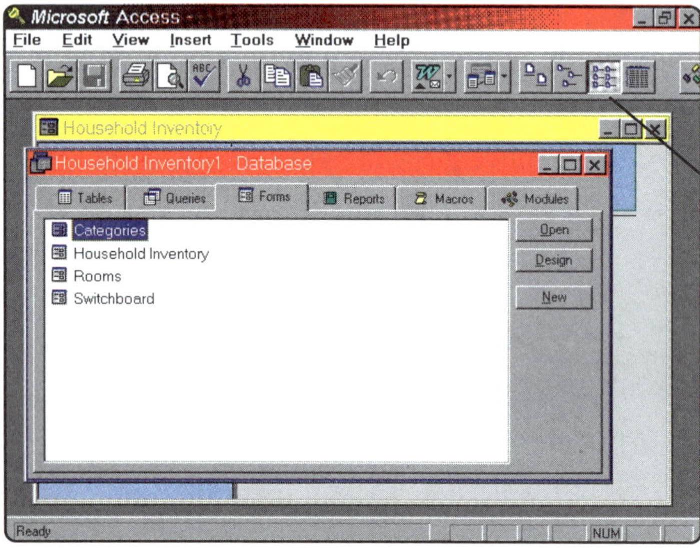

In this section, you'll check out some of the different ways your database files can be set up. Let's explore.

When this button is pressed, the database is in List view.

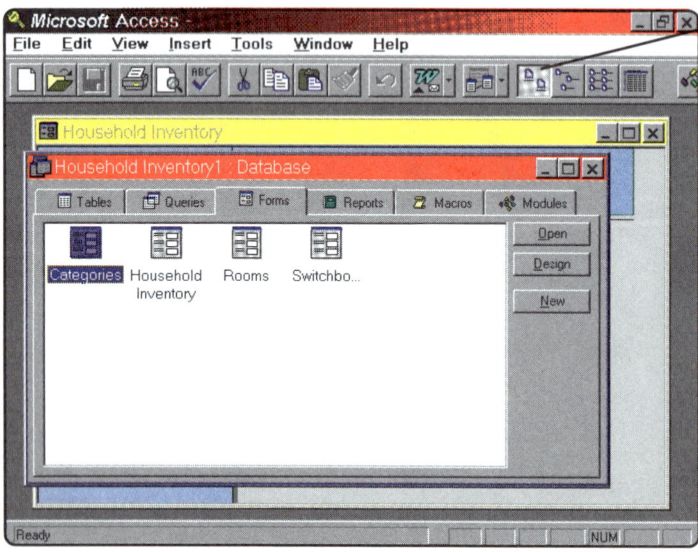

1. **Click** on the **Large icons button** on the toolbar. Icons will be added to each file name.

2. Click on the **Tables tab.**

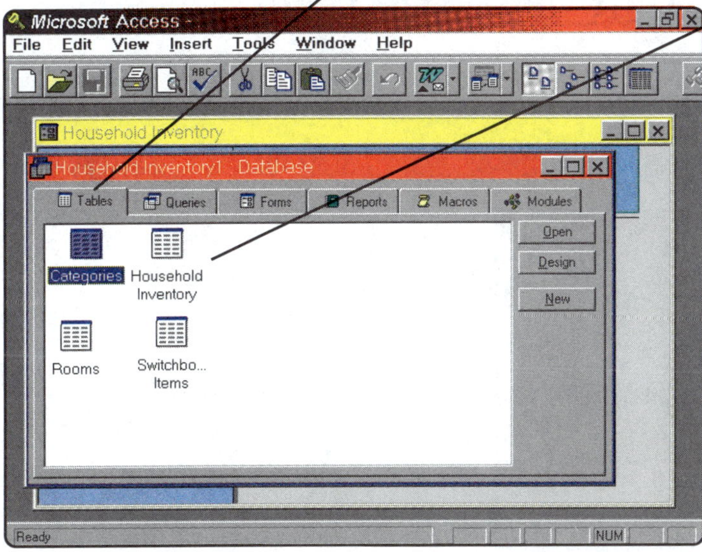

Notice that the icons have changed their appearance. Your icons may be lined up differently.

3. Take a moment and **click** on the **tabs** and watch the icons change.

Want details? Go on to the next step.

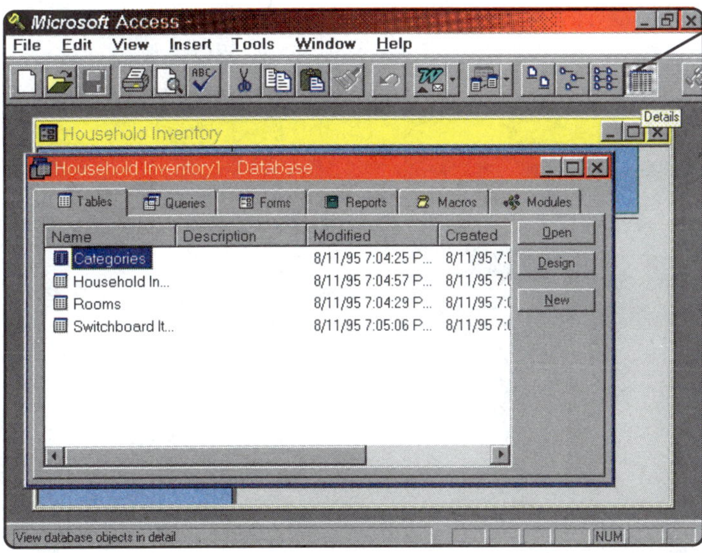

4. Click on the **Details button** in the toolbar to get this view.

CHANGING THE TABLES FONT SIZE

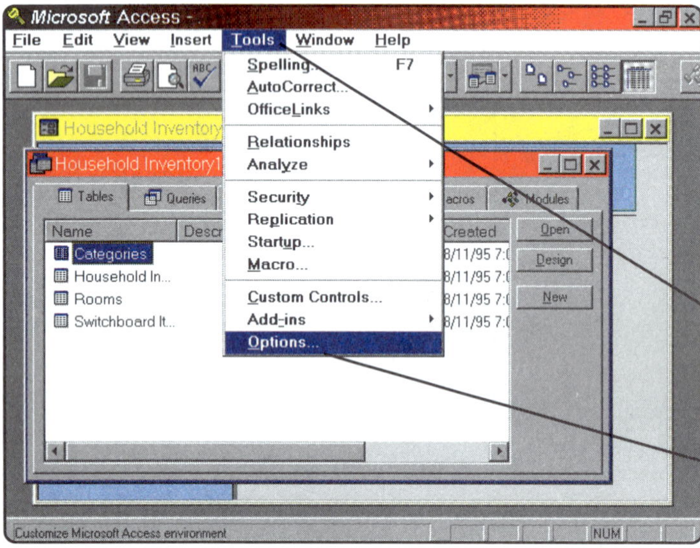

Changing the font style, color, and size for all of your tables is as easy as can be. In this example, you'll change the size of your table font from 10 points to 12 points.

1. **Click** on **Tools** in the menu bar. The Tools menu will appear.

2. **Click** on **Options.** The Options dialog box will appear.

3. **Click** on the **Datasheet tab**. The Datasheet tab will move to the front of the dialog box.

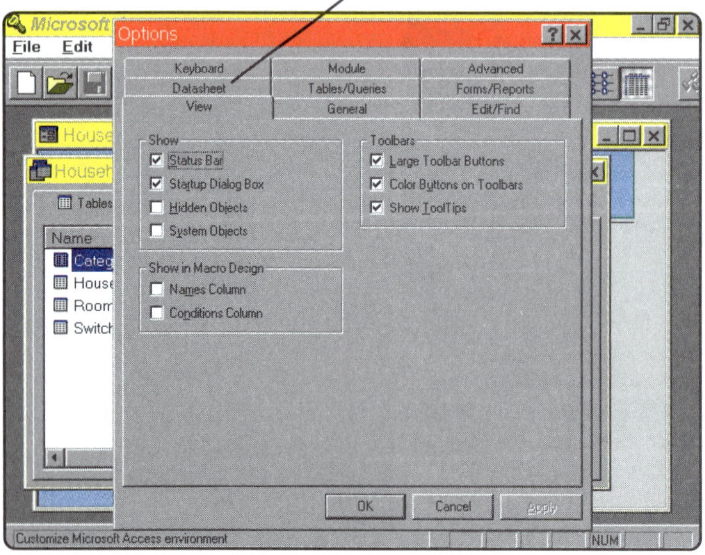

4. **Click** on the ▼ on the (font) size text box. A list box with font sizes will open.

5. **Click** on **12** (pts). The list box will close.

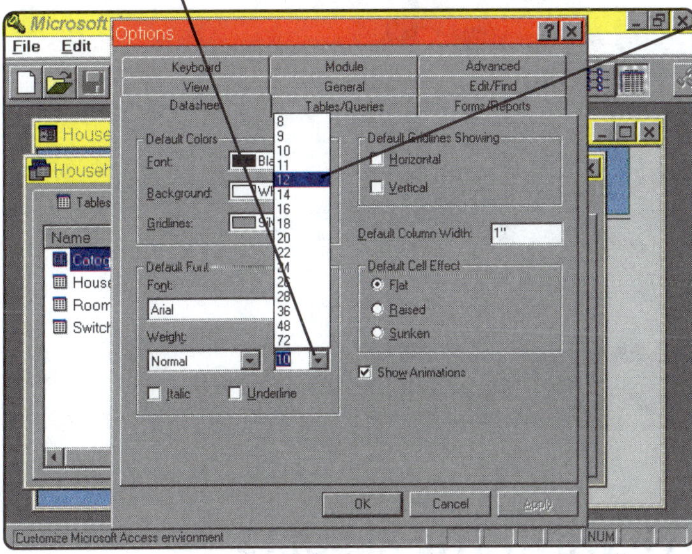

6. **Click** on **Apply.**

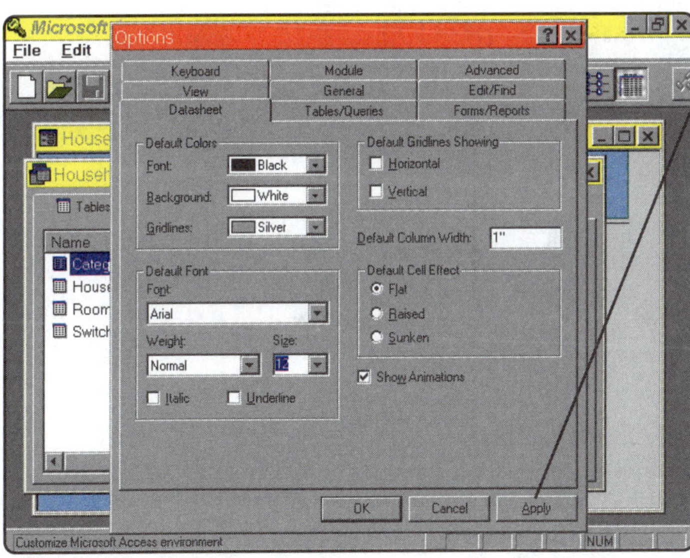

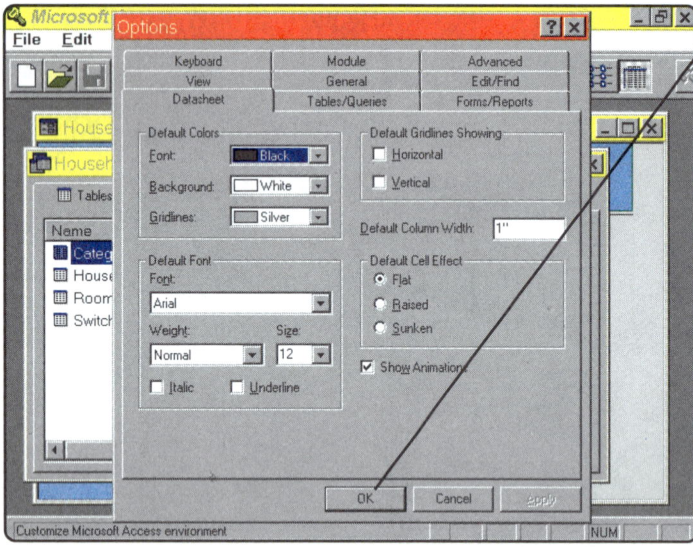

7. **Click** on **OK**. The dialog box will close.

VIEWING THE RESULTS

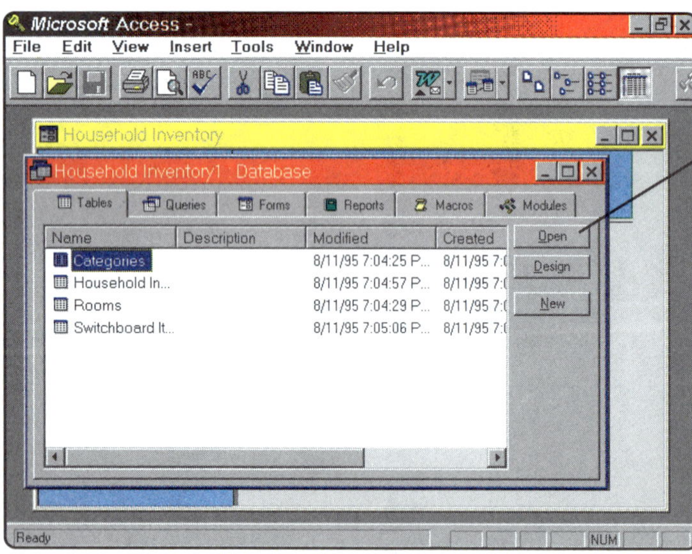

Now let's check out what we've done.

1. **Click** on **Open**.

Notice that the font size in this table is larger and easier to read (12 points) than the standard font.

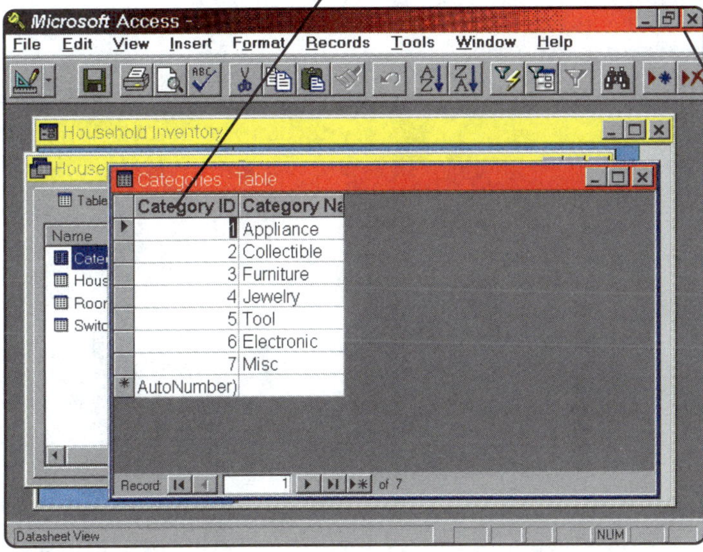

CLOSING ACCESS

1. **Click** on the **Close box** (☒) on the Access title bar to close the program.

SWITCHING OFF THE SWITCHBOARD ON STARTUP

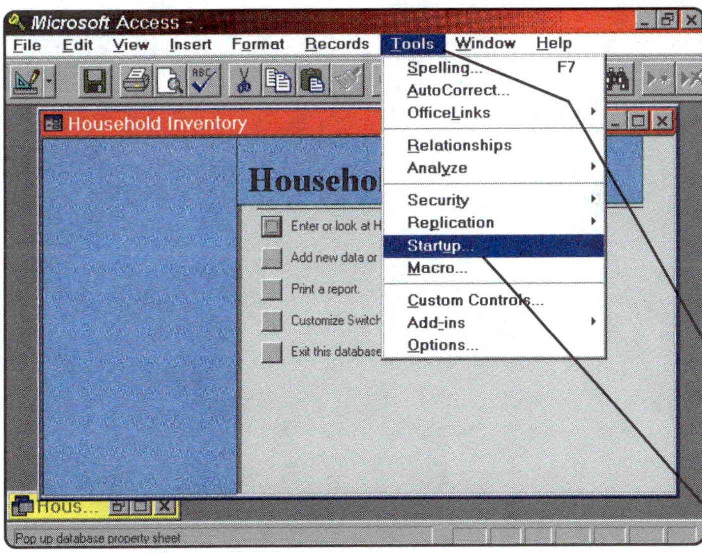

If you're tired of seeing the Switchboard view every-time you boot up and want to go directly to the Data-base tables, here's how:

1. **Open Access** and the **Household Inventory** as you see in this example.

2. **Click** on **Tools** in the menu bar. The Tools menu will appear.

3. **Click** on **Startup**. The Startup dialog box will appear.

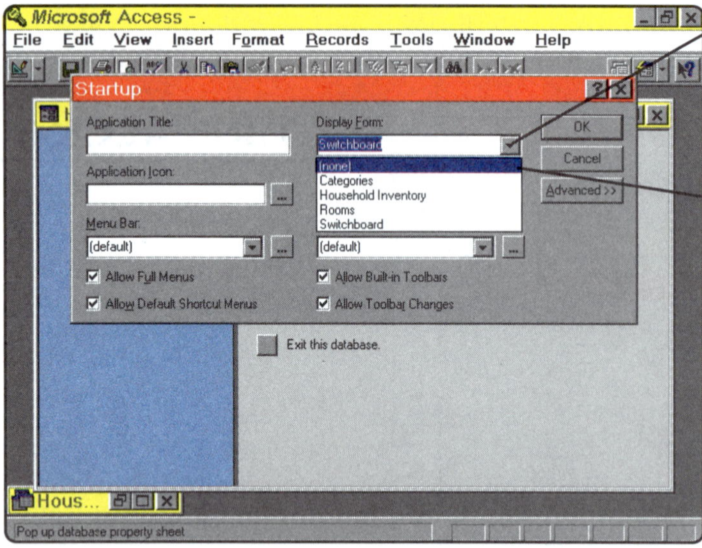

4. **Click** on the ▼ to the right of the Display Form text box. A pull-down list will appear.

5. **Click** on **(None)**. The list will disappear, and None will appear in the text box.

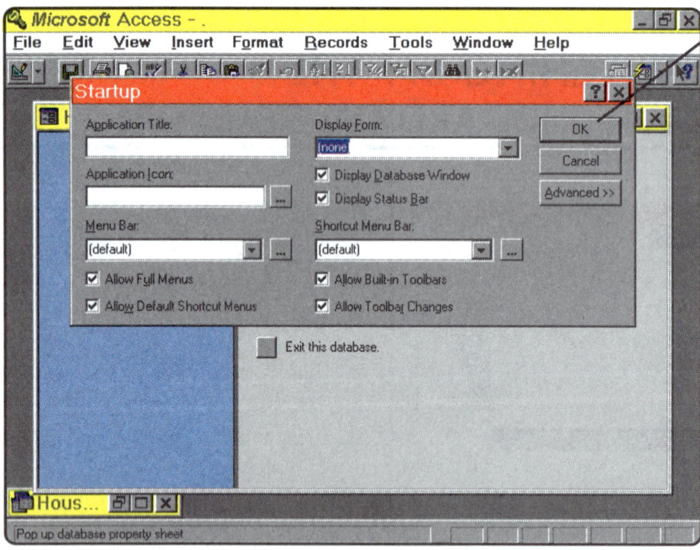

6. **Click** on **OK**. The dialog box will close.

You need to close Access before the change will take effect.

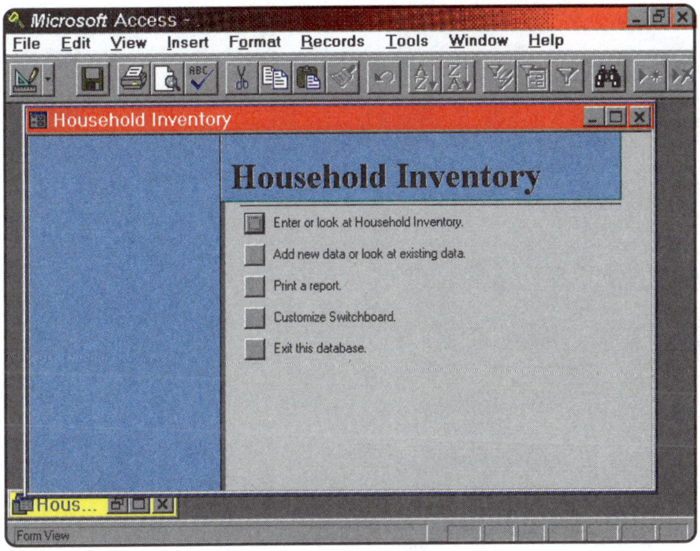

The next time you open Access, this screen will not appear.

REMOVING A TOOLBAR BUTTON

1. **Place** the **mouse pointer anywhere** on the **toolbar**.

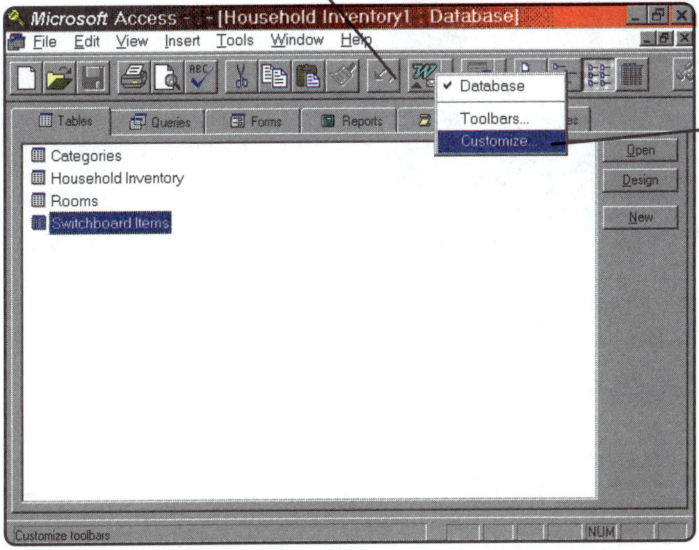

2. **Click** the ***right*** **mouse button**. A menu will appear.

3. **Click** on **Customize**. The Customize Toolbars dialog box will appear.

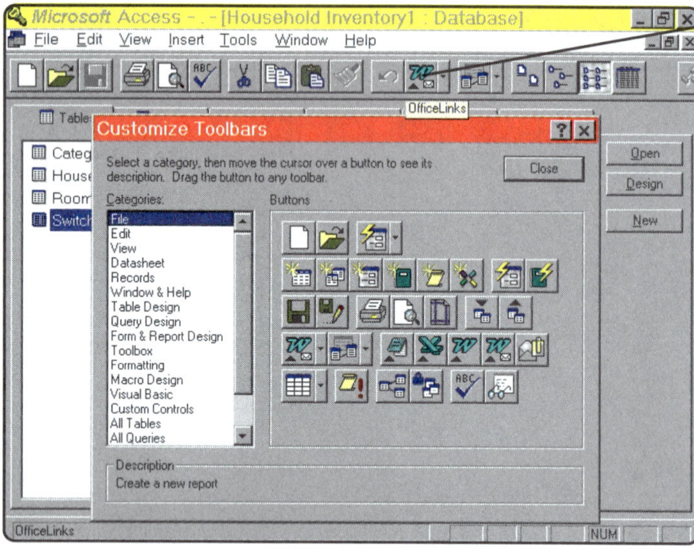

4. Place the **mouse pointer** on the **button** you want to **remove**. In this example, it's OfficeLinks.

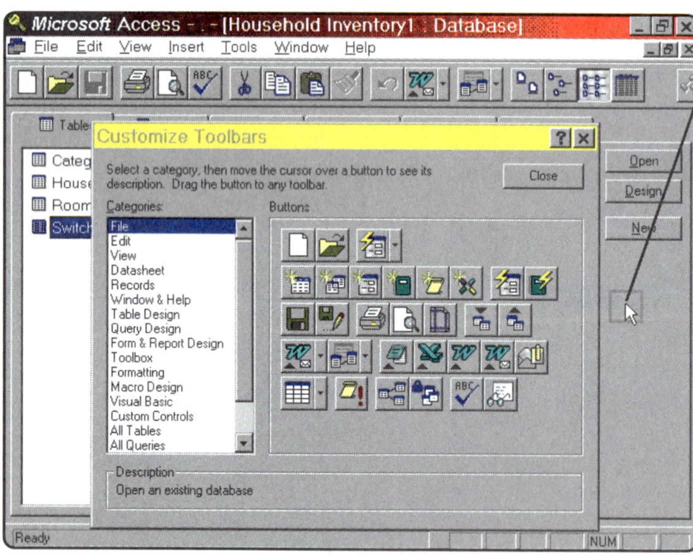

5. Press and hold the **mouse button** as you **drag** the button down and to the right.

6. Release the **mouse button**. The OfficeLinks button will disappear.

ADDING A BUTTON TO THE TOOLBAR

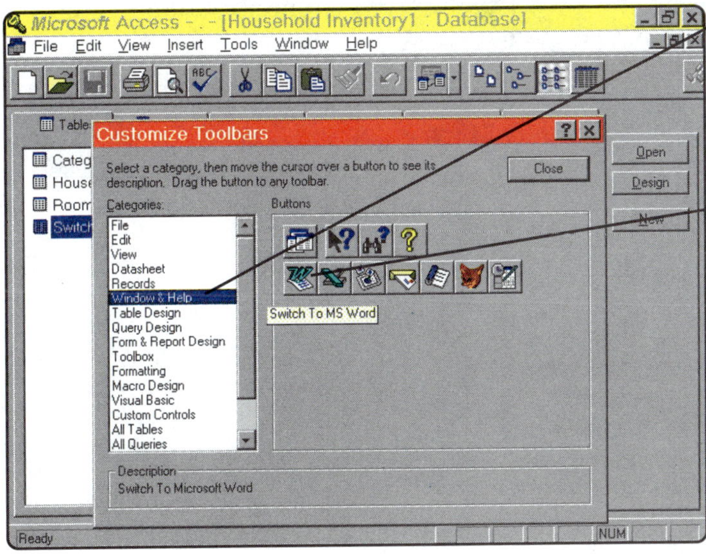

1. **Click** on the **category** of the type of button you want to add. In this example, it's Window & Help.

2. **Place** the **mouse pointer** on the **button** you want to add to your toolbar. Notice that a description of the button's function appears.

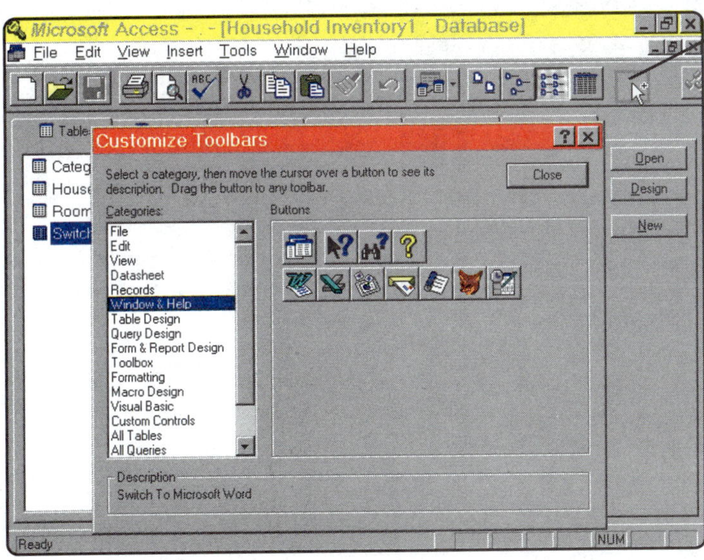

3. **Press and hold** the **button** as you **drag** it to the toolbar.

4. **Release** the **mouse button**. Voilà! You did it.

MOVING A TOOLBAR BUTTON

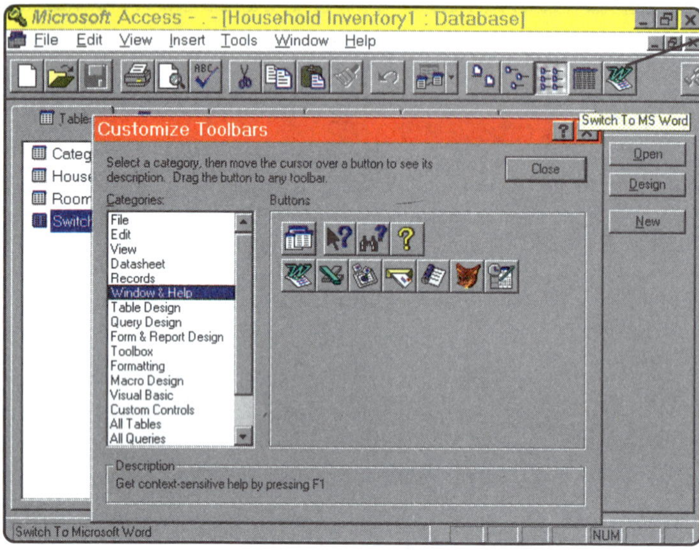

1. **Place** the **mouse pointer** on the **button** you want to move.

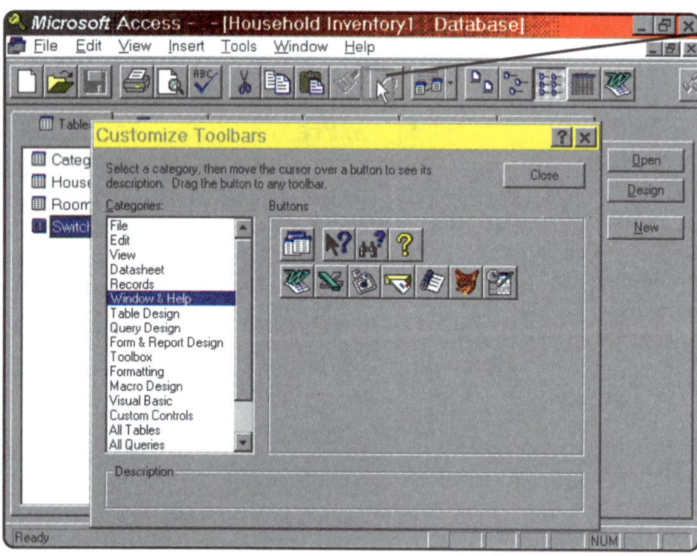

2. **Press and hold** the **button** as you **drag** it to a new position on the toolbar.

3. **Release** the **mouse button**. The button will move to its new location.

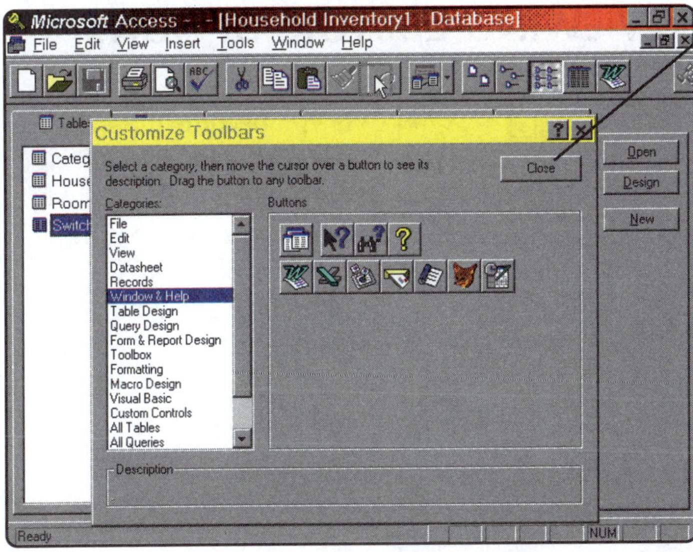

4. Click on **Close**. The Customize Toolbars dialog box will close.

CLOSING ACCESS

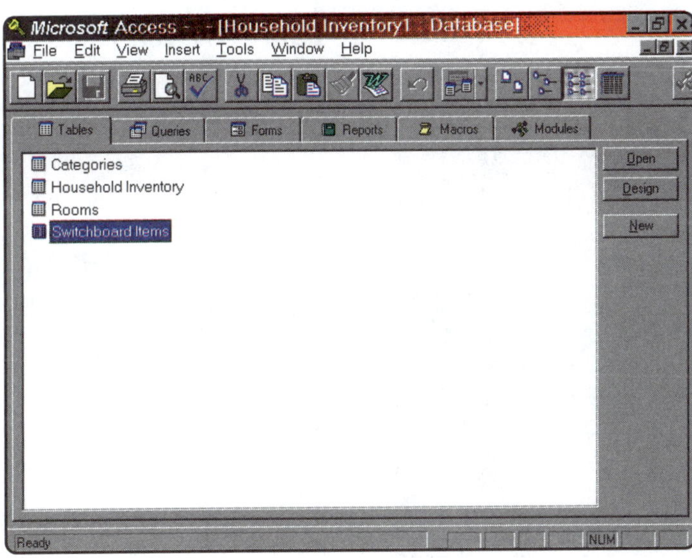

1. Click on the **Close box** (☒) in the Access title bar to close the program.

REVIEWING CUSTOM OPTIONS

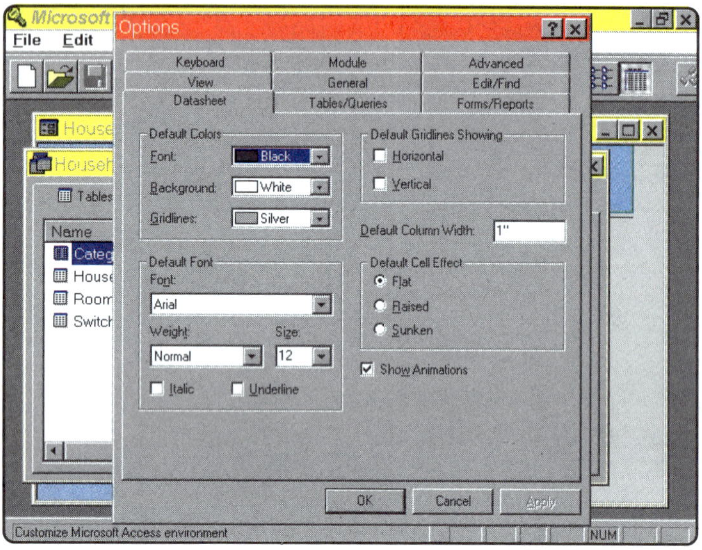

As you become more sophisticated in designing your Access databases, you may want to explore the other "tabs" in the Options dialog box. See your owner's manual for details.

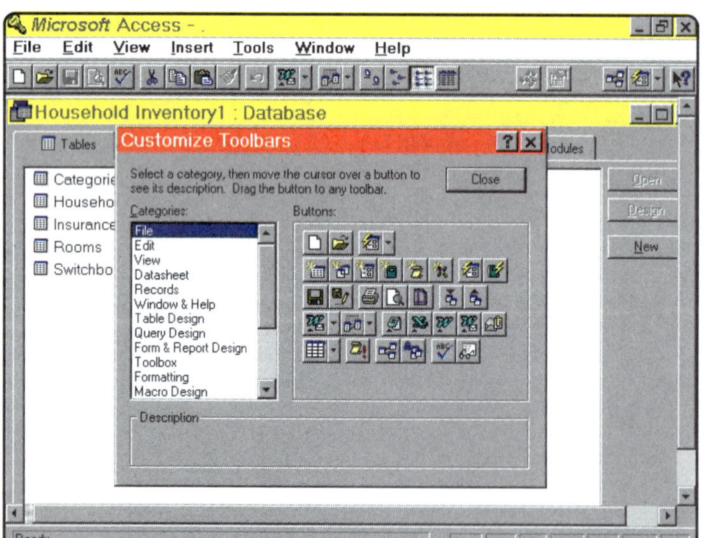

You can also create custom toolbars easily by dragging buttons to the desktop.

CHAPTER 17

Using Passwords

Microsoft Access lets you set a password for your database so that no one can open it without the password. This kind of password is called a "database password." If you are part of a workgroup, there are several more password options available. They won't be discussed in this chapter. **Be warned**: If you forget or lose your "database password," it can't be recovered, and you will loose your database! In this chapter, you will do the following:

- ✔ Set a database password for a specific database
- ✔ Remove a database password

SETTING A PASSWORD

In order to set a password, you must first close the database, then reopen it in the "Exclusive mode."

Exiting the Database

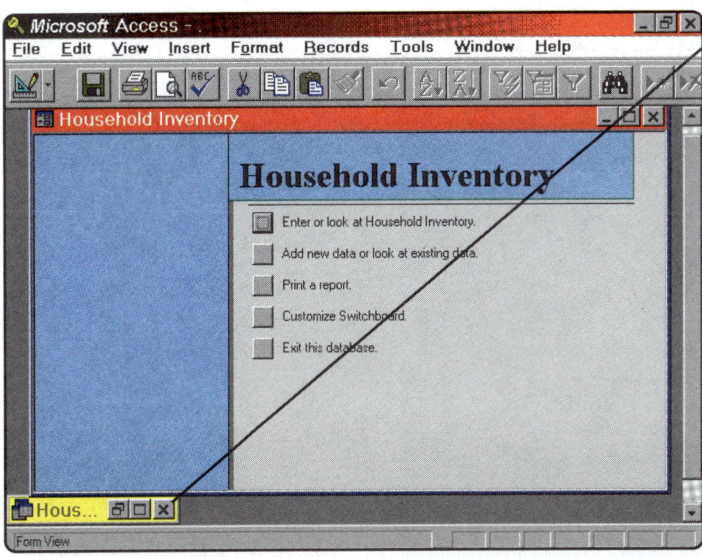

1. **Click** on the **Close box** (☒) on the title bar of the minimized database. The database windows will disappear.

Note: The toolbar buttons are "large size" in this chapter. If you want to make them small, go to step 4 in the first section of Chapter 16 and remove the ✔ from the Large button option.

Opening the Database in Exclusive Mode

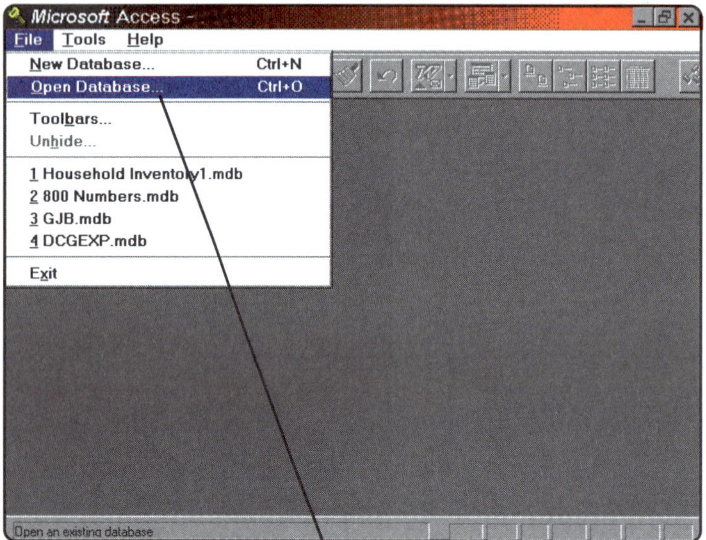

In this book, we aren't covering the network version of Access. However, if you are on a network, you can prevent others from opening your database while you're using it by clicking on Exclusive at the time you open the database.

If you're not on a network, you still have to open the database in "Exclusive" mode in order to set a password.

1. **Click** on **File** in the menu bar. The File menu will appear.

2. **Click** on **Open Database**. The Open dialog box will appear.

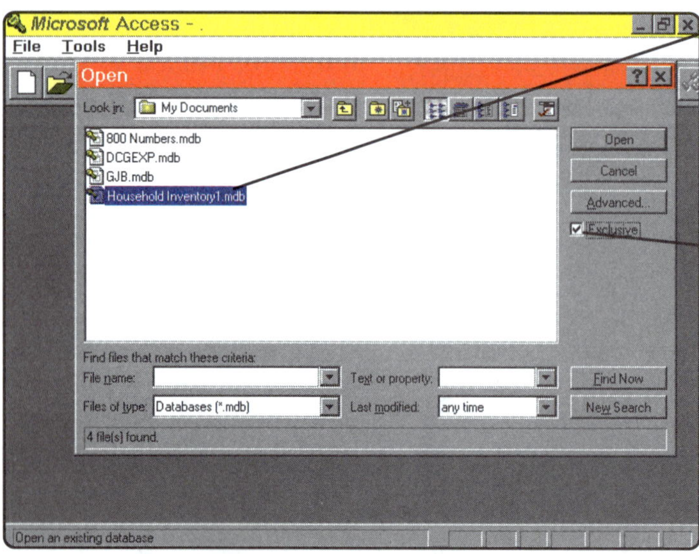

3. **Click** on the **database** to which you want to assign a password to highlight it. In this example, it's Household Inventory.

4. **Click** on **Exclusive** to place a ✔ in the box.

5. **Click** on **Open**. The database will open.

Assigning the Password

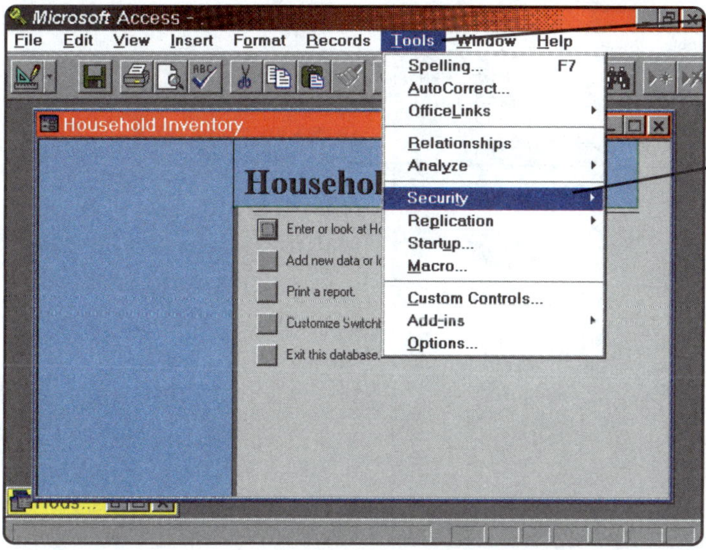

1. **Click** on **Tools** in the Menu bar. The Tools menu will appear.
2. **Click** on **Security**. A second menu will appear.

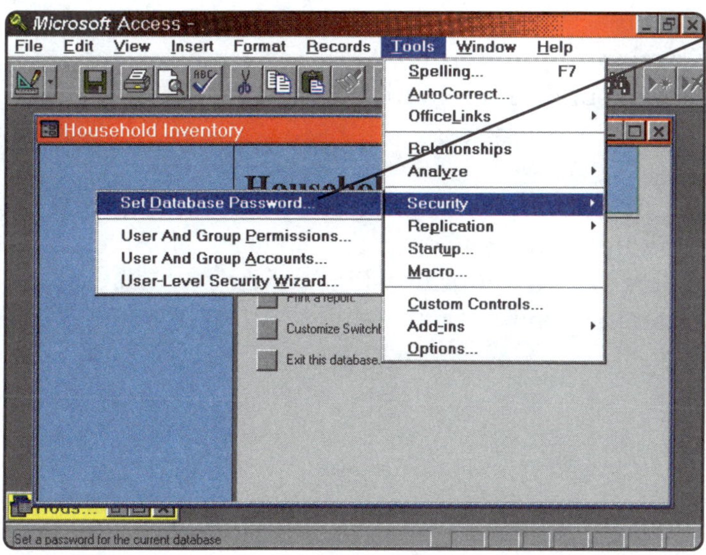

3. **Click** on **Set Database Password**. The Set Database Password dialog box will appear.

4. **Click** in the **top text box** to place the cursor.

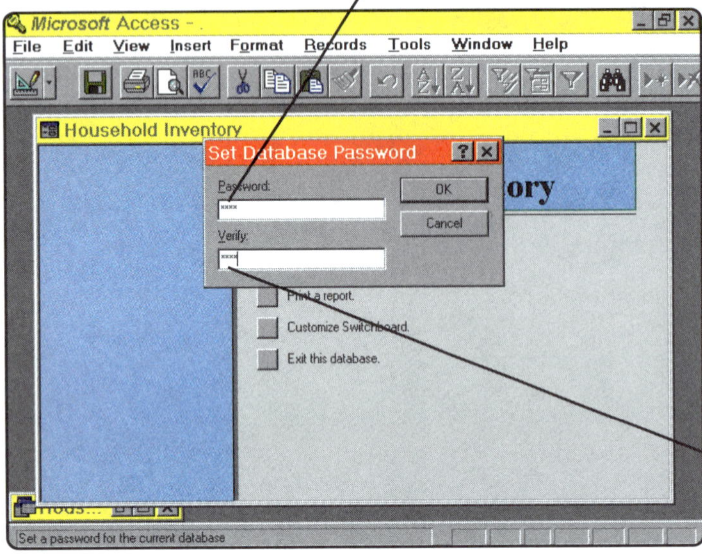

5. **Type** the **password**. Each letter or number you type will show as an asterisk (*). A password can include up to 15 characters in any combination. The password feature is case-sensitive, so if you use a combination of uppercase and lowercase letters, you must remember the exact combination.

6. **Click** in the **bottom text box**.

7. **Type** the **password** again to verify it.

Caution: If you forget or loose this password, you will loose your database! Write your password down and put it in a safe place.

8. **Click** on **OK**. The dialog box will close. The next time anyone tries to open the database, an Access dialog box will appear, asking for the password in order to open the database.

REMOVING A PASSWORD

Note: Unless you have opened the database with "Exclusive" checked, you can't remove the password.

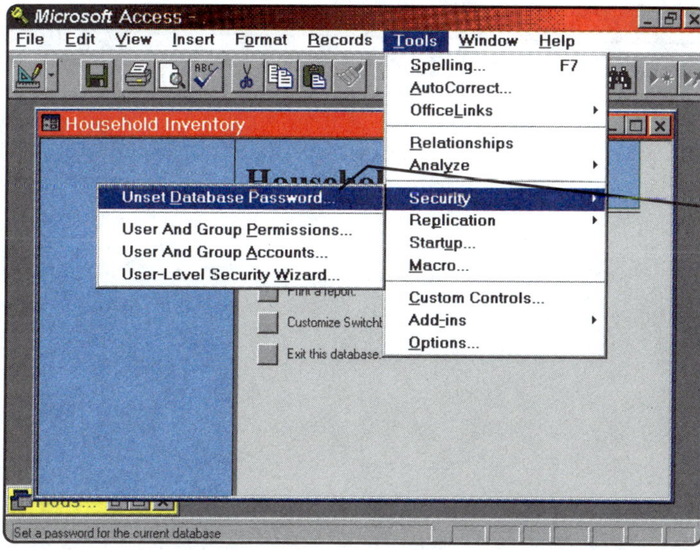

1. **Repeat all** of the **steps** from the beginning of this chapter until you see the menu in this example.
2. **Click on Unset Database Password**. The Unset Database Password dialog box will appear.

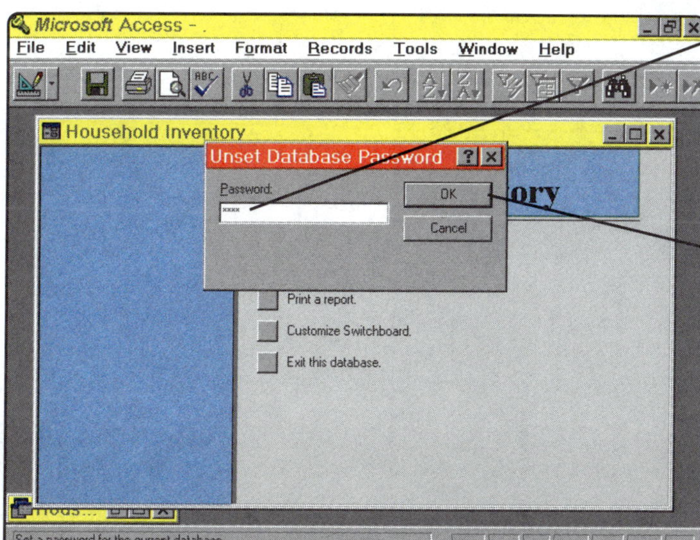

3. **Click** in the **text box** to place the cursor.
4. **Type** the **password** you want to remove.
5. **Click** on **OK**. The dialog box will close, and the password will be deleted.

CHAPTER 18

Making a Shortcut Icon to Open a Database

If you use your database frequently, you can put an icon on your desktop that will open the database. In this chapter you will do the following:

- ✔ Make a shortcut icon for your database
- ✔ Put the shortcut icon on your desktop
- ✔ Delete the shortcut icon

MAKING A SHORTCUT ICON

You don't have to close the database in order to make a shortcut icon.

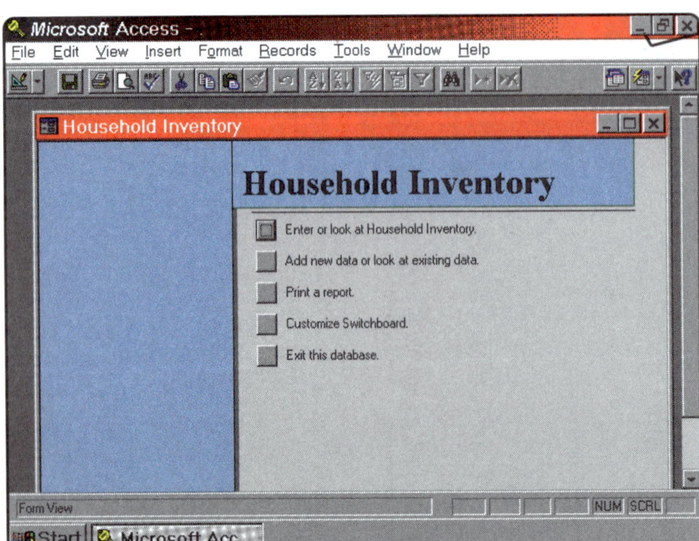

1. **Click** on the **Minimize button** (▁) on the right side of the Access title bar. It will disappear into the Taskbar at the bottom of your screen.

2. **Click twice** on **My Computer**. The My Computer dialog box you see here will appear.

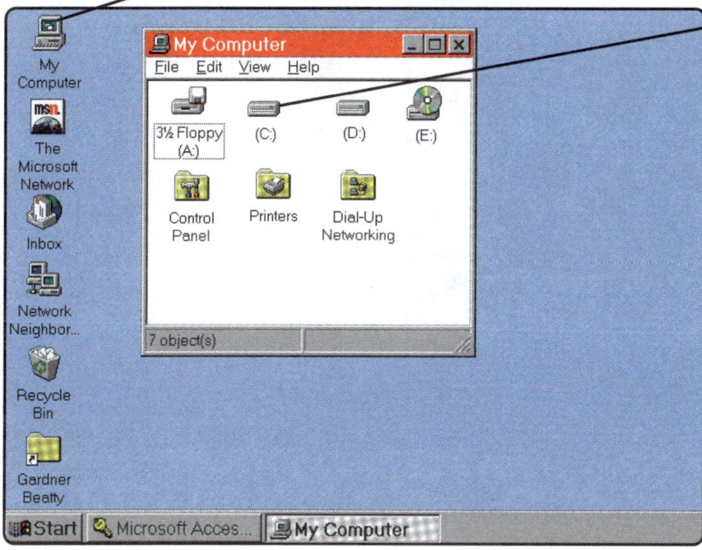

3. **Click twice** on the **(C:)** drive icon. The C:\ drive dialog box will appear.

If your view doesn't look like the one you see here, you can change to this view.

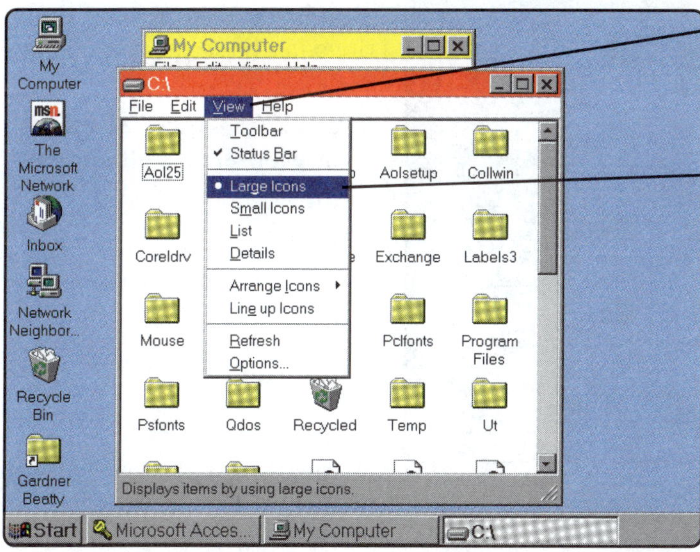

4. **Click** on **View** in the menu bar. The View menu will appear.

5. **Click** on **Large Icons**. The view will change to large icons.

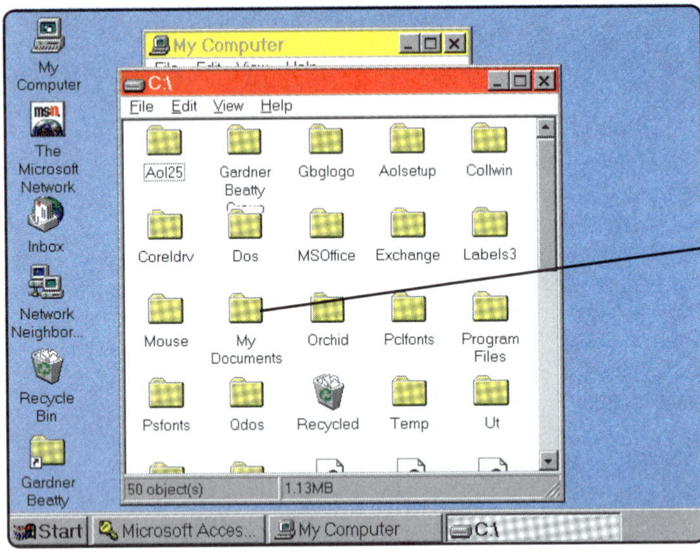

6. **Click** on the ▼ on the scroll bar until you see the My Documents folder (or the folder in which you saved the database.)

7. **Click twice** on the **My Documents folder**. The My Documents window will open.

8. **Click** the ***right*** **mouse button** on the Household Inventory icon. A pop-up menu will appear.

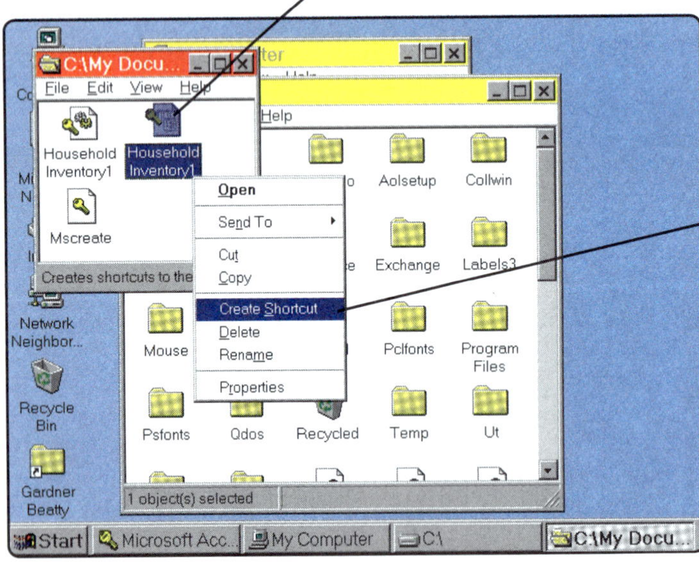

Note: There will be two icons for each database. Be sure to choose the icon that does *not* have the two gears.

9. **Click** on **Create Shortcut**. A shortcut icon will appear in the My Documents window.

MOVING THE SHORTCUT ICON TO THE DESKTOP

Once you have created the shortcut icon, it's a simple process to drag it to the desktop.

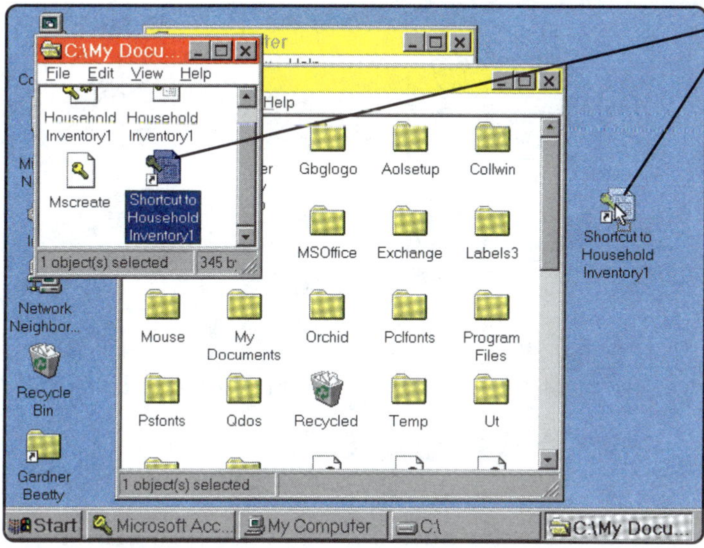

1. **Press and hold** on the **shortcut icon** and **drag** it to the desktop. You'll see a "ghost" icon as you drag.

2. **Release** the **mouse button** when the icon is on the desktop.

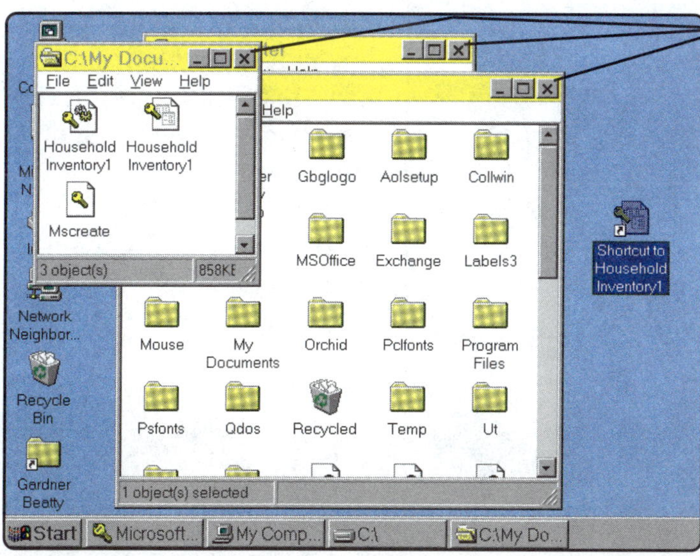

3. **Click** on the **Close buttons** (☒s) on the My Documents, C:\, and My Computer windows to close them.

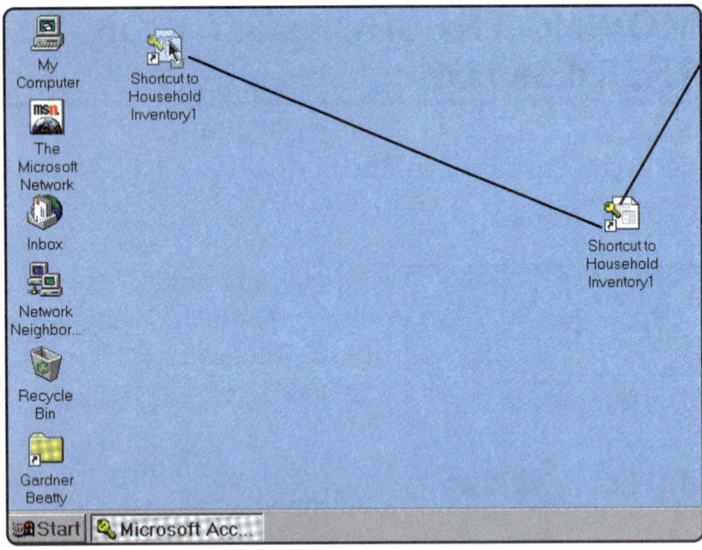

4. **Press and hold** on the **shortcut icon** as you **drag** it to whatever location on your desktop you find most convenient.

The next time you want to open the database, click twice on the shortcut icon. Access will open directly to your database.

DELETING A SHORTCUT ICON FROM THE DESKTOP

1. **Click** the ***right*** **mouse button** on the shortcut icon. A pop-up menu will appear.

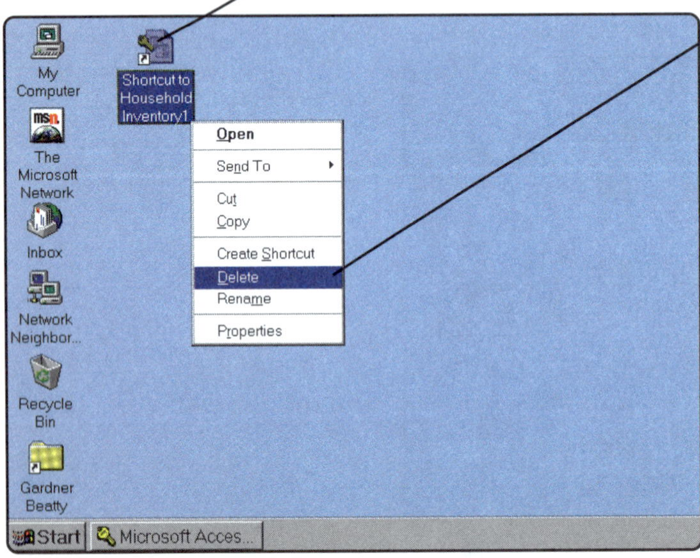

2. **Click** on **Delete**. The Confirm File Delete dialog box will appear (not shown here) to ask if you're sure you want to send the shortcut icon to the recycle bin.

3. **Click** on **Yes**. The dialog box will close, and the shortcut icon will disappear.

CHAPTER 19

Using Online Help

Access for Windows 95 is far easier to use than any of its earlier versions, yet it is still an exceptionally powerful and complex database program. But just as it has Wizards to help you perform tasks, it has a Wizard to help you find answers: the Answer Wizard. The Wizard is one of several ways you can find help online; each aims to satisfy different ways of searching. In this chapter, you will do the following:

- ✔ Explore Access's online help
- ✔ Get answers from the Answer Wizard

OPENING HELP

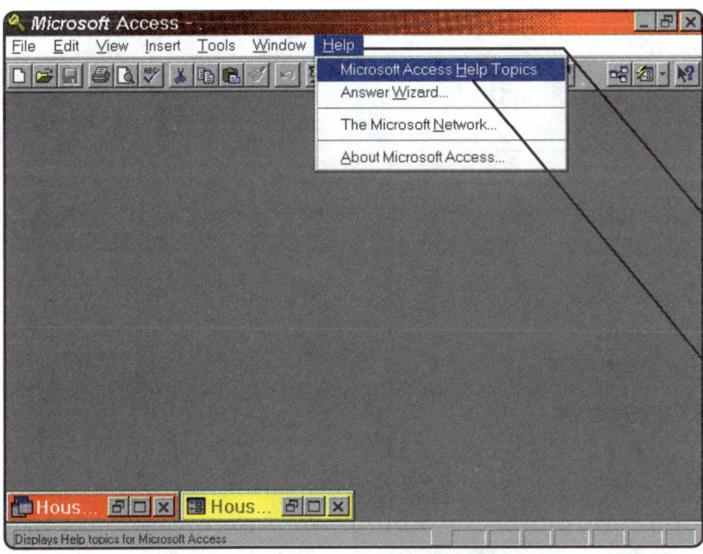

For our example, we've minimized the database at the bottom of the screen to make things easier to see. We'll start by opening Help.

1. **Click on Help** in the menu bar. A menu will appear.

2. Click on **Microsoft Access Help Topics**. After a pause, the Help Topics dialog box will appear.

At the top of the dialog box are four tabs for the different functions within Help:

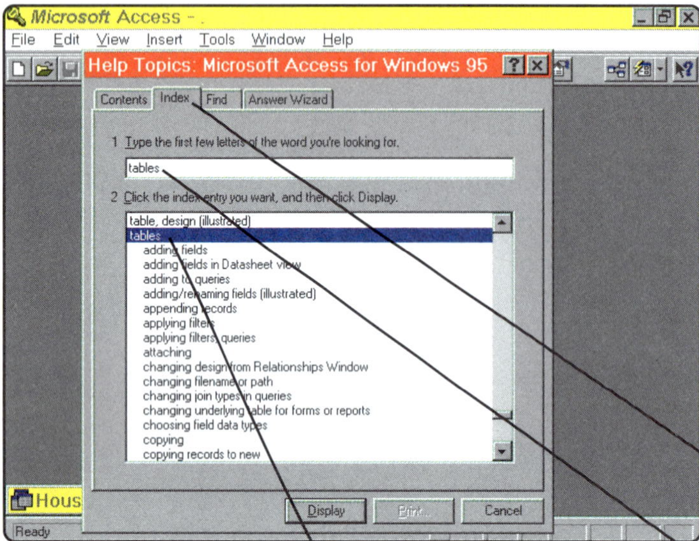

- Contents—similar to the table of contents in a book.
- Index—similar to the index in a book.
- Find—where you can search for words.
- Answer Wizard—more about the Wizard later.

3. **Click** on the **Index tab** to bring it to the front.

4. **Type tables** into the index text box. Index entries that have to do with tables will appear in the lower box.

5. **Click twice** on **tables**. A Topics Found dialog box will appear with topics.

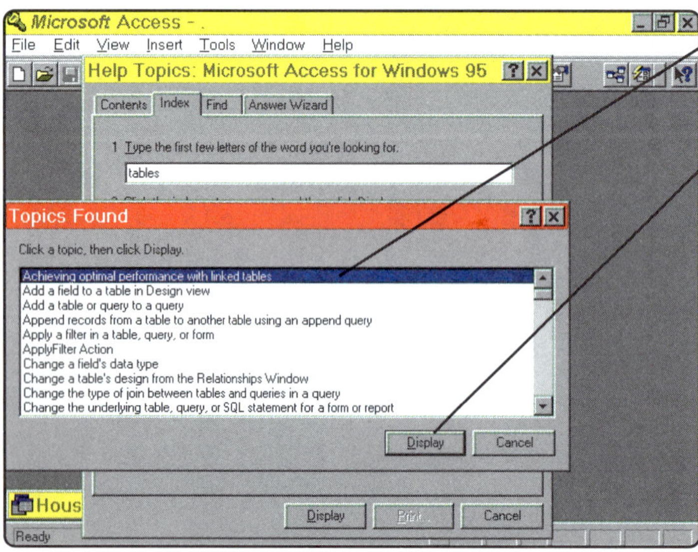

6. **Click** on a **topic** that interests you to highlight it.

7. **Click** on **Display**. A Microsoft Access for Windows 95 dialog box will appear containing help on the topic.

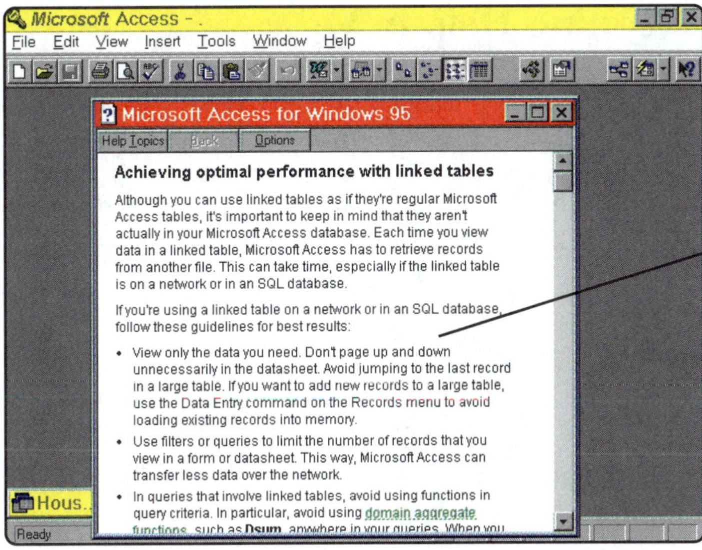

Printing a Topic

Once you've reached the topic's dialog box, you can print it.

1. **Place** your **mouse pointer** anywhere on the window.

2. **Click** your ***right*** **mouse button**. A pop-up menu will appear.

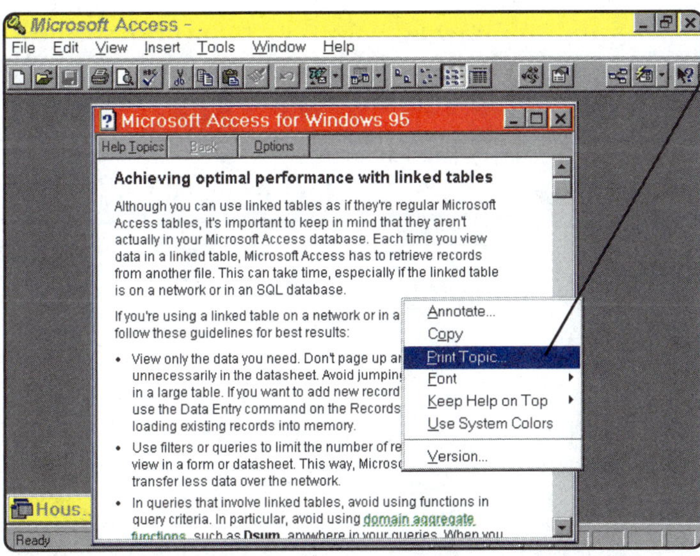

3. **Click** on **Print Topic**. A Print dialog box will appear (not shown here). **Click** on **Yes** to print the topic.

Note: You can also print by clicking on Options in the menu bar of the Help window then clicking on Print Topic in the Options menu.

Keeping Help in View

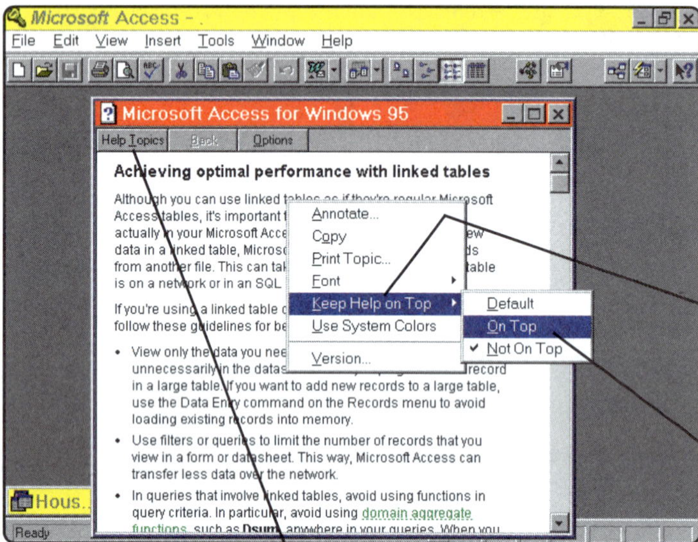

You can keep a Help window from disappearing behind other windows.

1. **Click** the **right mouse button**. A pop-up menu will appear.
2. **Move** the **mouse pointer** down to **Keep Help on Top**. Another menu will appear.
3. **Click** on **On Top**.

If you find that you don't like Help always on top of other windows, repeat steps 1 and 2 then click on Not on Top.

4. **Click** on the **Help Topics Button** to return to the index and continue your search. If you click on the Close button (☒), you'll have to start over.

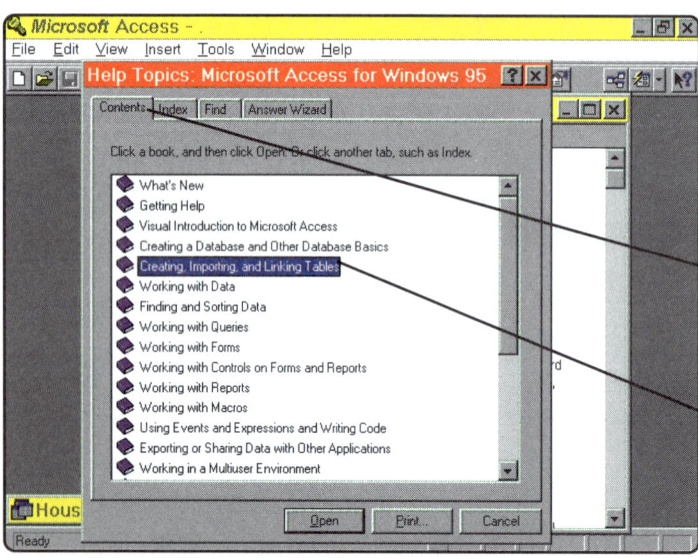

BROWSING "CONTENTS"

Contents is like the table of contents in a book.

1. **Click** the **Contents tab**. The Contents list will appear.
2. **Click** twice on a **topic** to open additional subtopics.

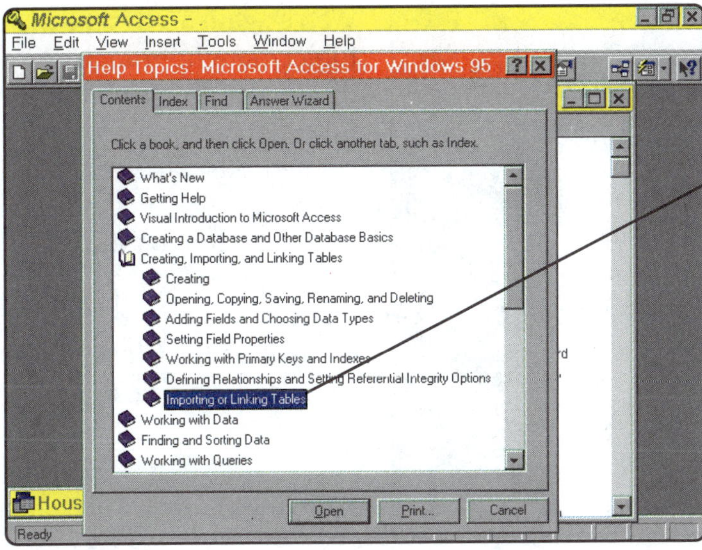

The lists open to other lists that narrow your topic down further.

4. **Click twice** on a **listing**. Another list will appear. The items in the list have question marks in front of them, indicating that they lead to a topic dialog box.

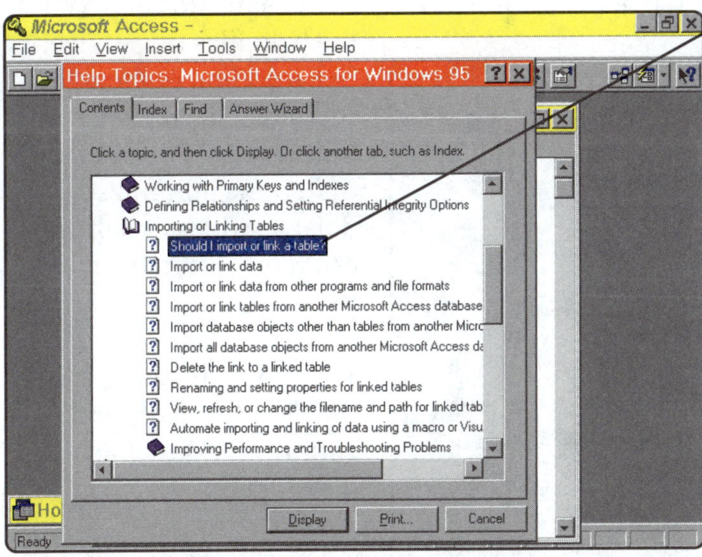

5. **Click twice** on a **topic**. A Microsoft Access for Windows 95 dialog box will appear.

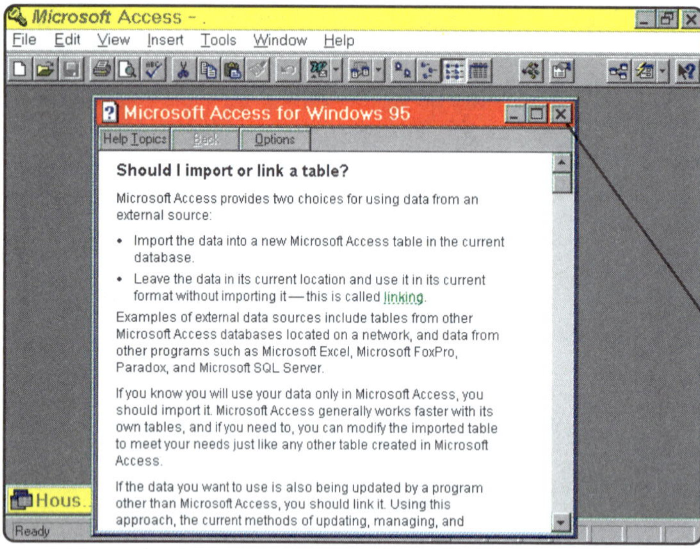

We've again arrived at a topic, though through a different search technique. Like before, the topic can be printed. Also like before, you must click on the Help Topics button to return to your search.

6. **Click** on the **Close button** (☒). Help will close.

SEEKING WITH "FIND"

The first time you use Find, a Setup Wizard creates a database made up of words that occur in the text of the help topics. The database can include all words in the help files (maximized), or a selection of them (minimized). Try the minimized setting (the default) first. If the minimized database doesn't help, you can rebuild it in the maximized form.

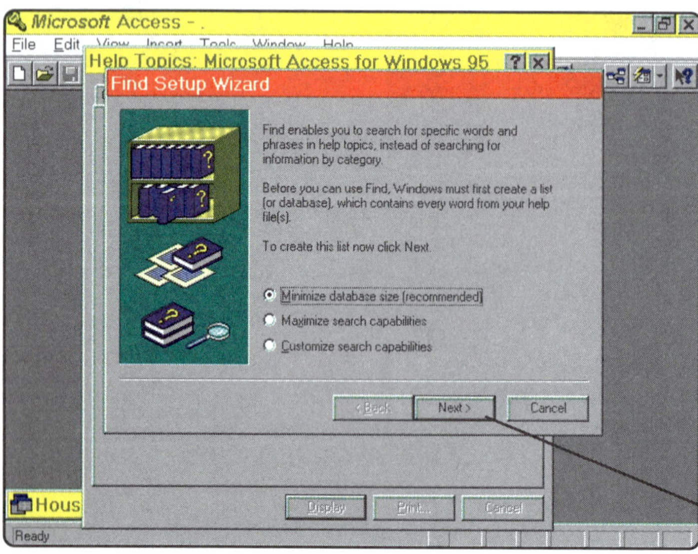

1. **Open Help** and **click** on the **Find tab**. The Find Setup Wizard dialog box will appear.

2. **Click** on **Next >**. The Wizard will begin to assemble the database.

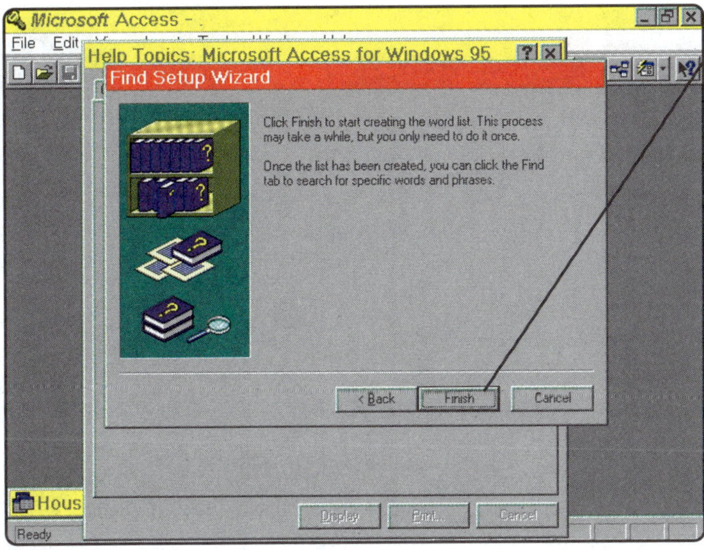

3. Click on **Finish**. The Wizard will start to do its magic.

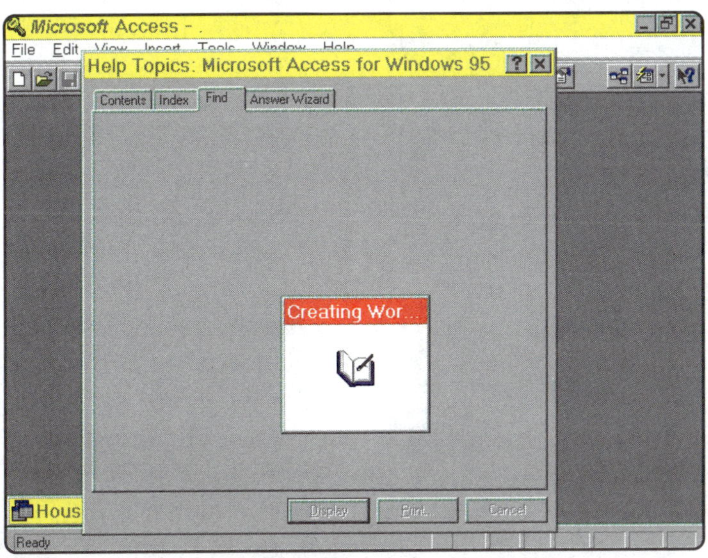

It takes a while to create the database. During the process an animated icon of a pen writing in a book appears.

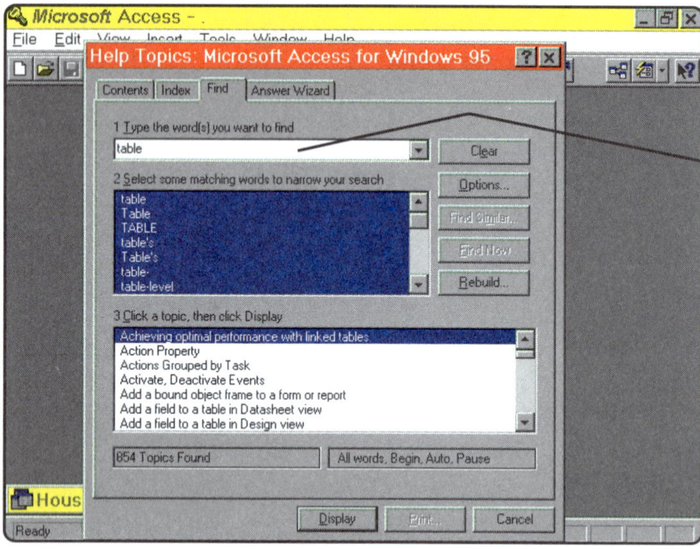

The completed database is searched in much the same way you search the Index.

4. **Type** a **word** in the text box. As you do, words and phrases in the database that match what you type will appear in the middle box, and relevant help topics will appear in the lower box.

All of the lines in the middle box will be highlighted. You can highlight selected lines by holding down the Control key while you click on the lines. The topics that appear in the lower box will change according to which lines in the middle box, and how many, are highlighted.

Getting Help in Context

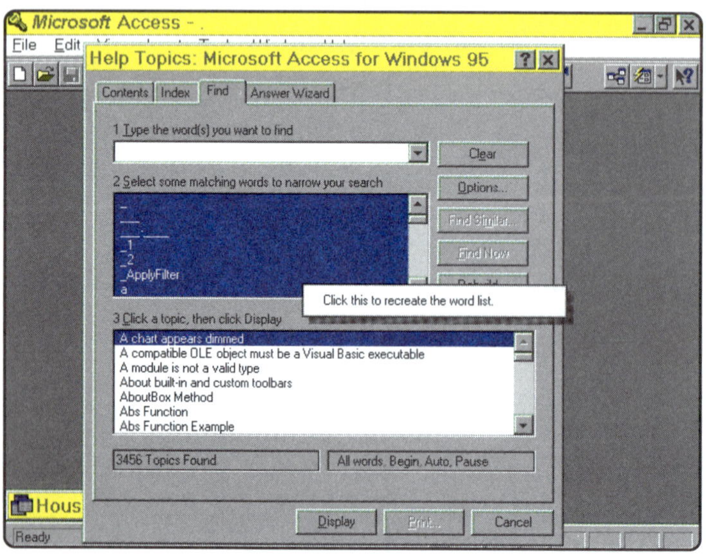

Screens in Windows 95 and programs written for it often display a button with a question mark on it. If you click on this button, your mouse pointer changes to a pointer with a question mark attached to it. If you then click on an element on the screen, any help that's available for the button, box, or other item that you clicked on will appear. In this screen, we clicked on the question mark, then on the Rebuild button.

Finding a Topic

If you make several searches for different words, each will be "remembered" in this box. You can click on the ▼ to recall them.

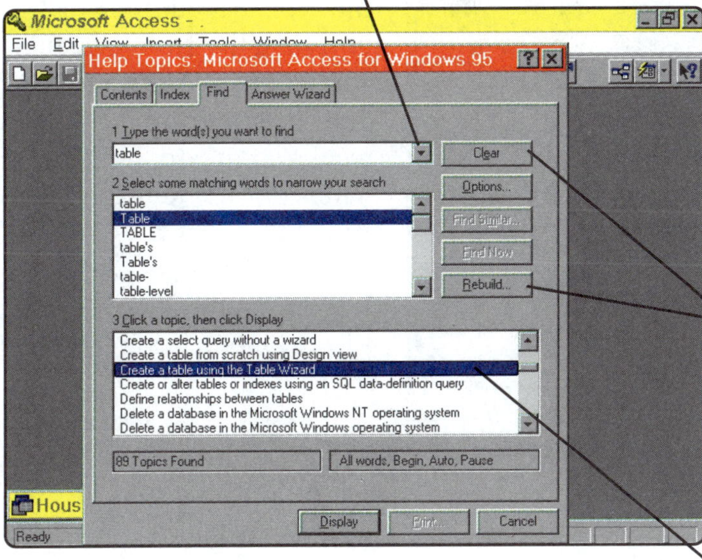

1. **Click** on one of the **lines** in the middle box to highlight it. The help topics related to the highlighted line in the middle box will appear in the lower box.

To rebuild the database in maximized form, click on the Rebuild button. To search for another topic, click the Clear button and type in a new word.

2. **Click twice** on a **topic**. A Microsoft Access for Windows 95 dialog box will appear.

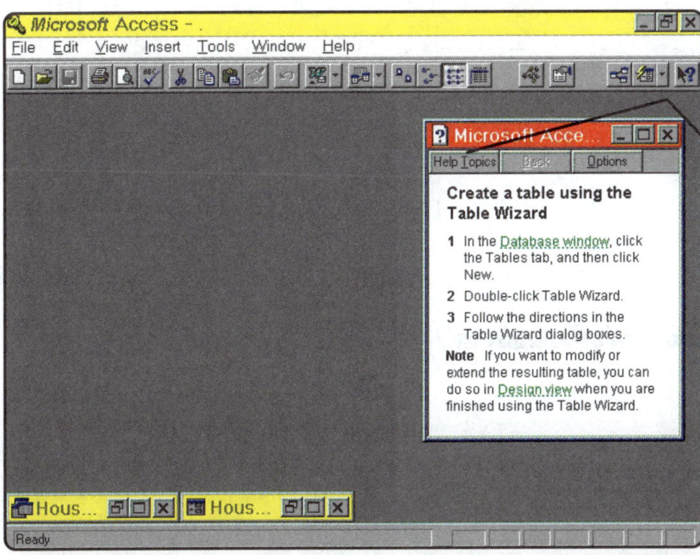

The topic dialog box in this case is "sized" to fit the topic.

3. **Click** on the **Help Topics button**. The Help Topics dialog box will reappear.

USING THE ANSWER WIZARD

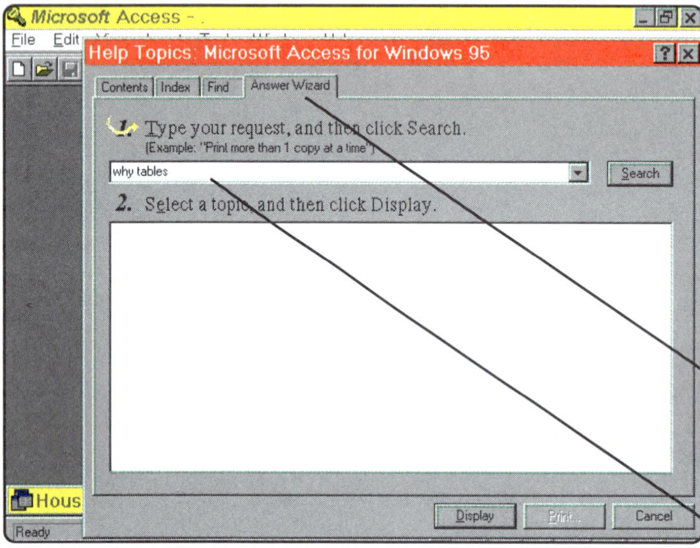

The Answer Wizard uses "artificial intelligence." You can type in a question or phrase in the same way that you would say it to another person. If some of the results seem odd, remember that artificial intelligence is still in its infancy.

1. **Click** on the **Answer Wizard tab** to bring it to the front.

2. **Type** a **phrase** in the text box. In this example we used "why tables."

3. **Click** on **Search**. After a moment, the search results will appear in the lower box.

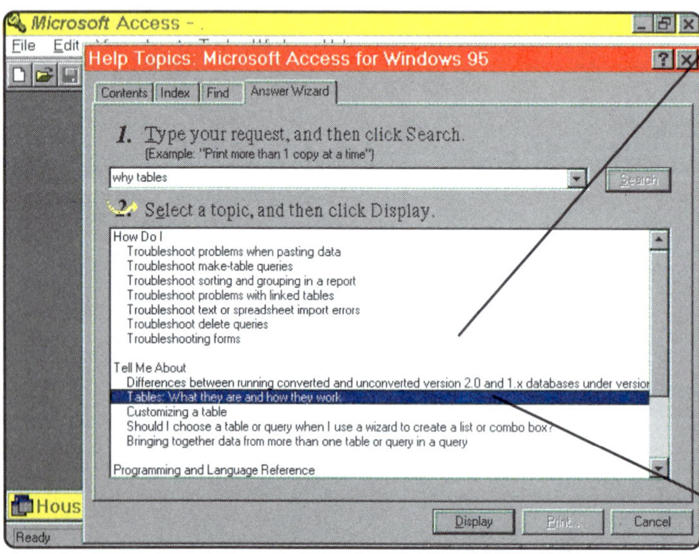

The results are divided into different areas: "How To" for help with a specific task, "Tell Me About" for general understanding of a topic, and "Programming and Language Reference" for detailed information.

"Tell Me About" leads to visual answers that illustrate topics in Access.

4. **Click twice** on **Tables: What they are and how they work**. A card will appear.

Using Visual Answers

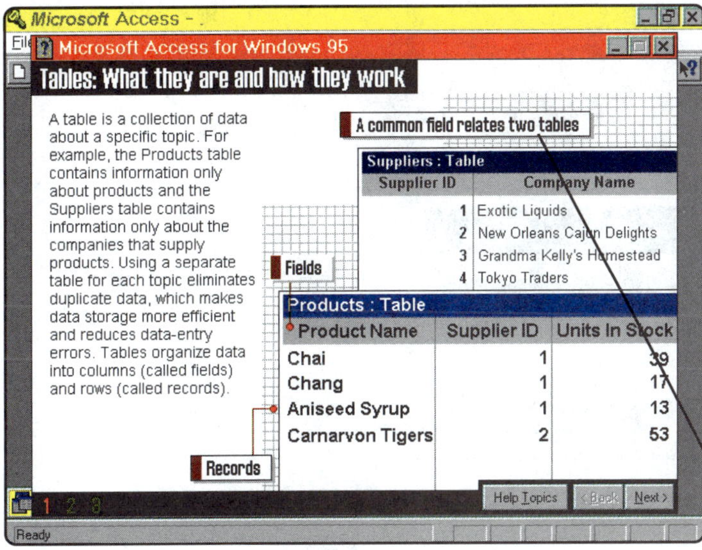

This part of Help explains aspects of the program using what were called *cue cards* in previous versions of Access. (The old cue cards, however, weren't illustrated like these.) A paragraph of text information discusses the illustrated topic. Labels point to items being covered, and lead to more information on the items.

1. **Click** on **A common field relates two tables**. A box with more information will appear.

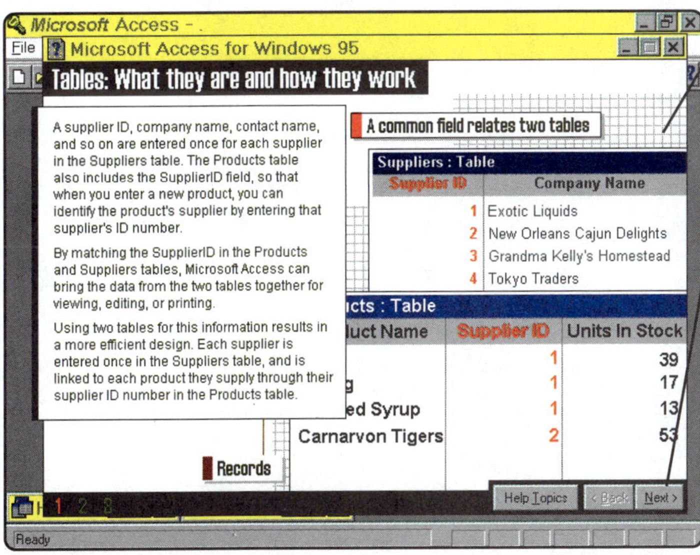

2. **Click away** from the box to close it.

3. **Click** on **Next >** to see the next illustration on the topic.

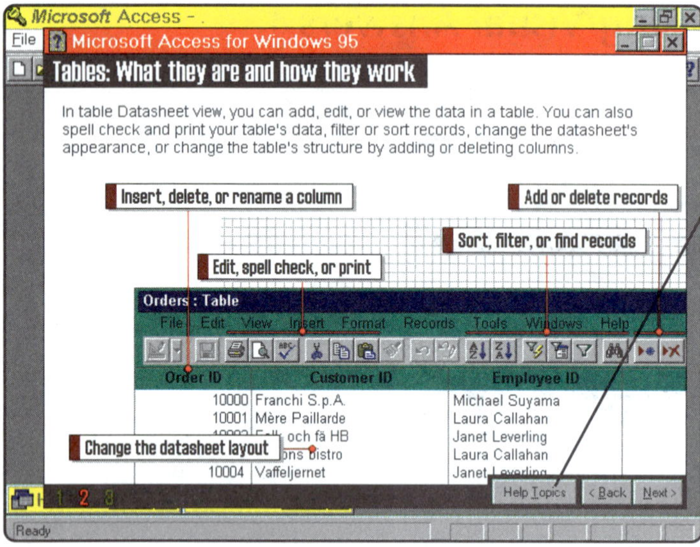

If the Next button is grayed out, you're at the last illustration for the topic.

4. **Click** on **Help Topics** to return to Help.

OR

5. **Click** on the **Close button** (☒) to quit.

CHAPTER 20

Making and Using Macros

Macros are shortcuts that help you automate repetitious tasks. If there are several steps you take repeatedly while using Access, or a phrase you type into a form over and over again, you can make a macro to do this work for you. Then, every time you want to perform the tedious task, you simply run the macro instead. Macros can be linked to buttons on forms, run from a menu, or linked to keys on your keyboard. For our example, you'll make a simple macro that prints a record, and link the macro to a button on the Household Inventory form. In this chapter, you will do the following:

- ✔ Make a macro
- ✔ Link a macro to a button

MAKING A MACRO

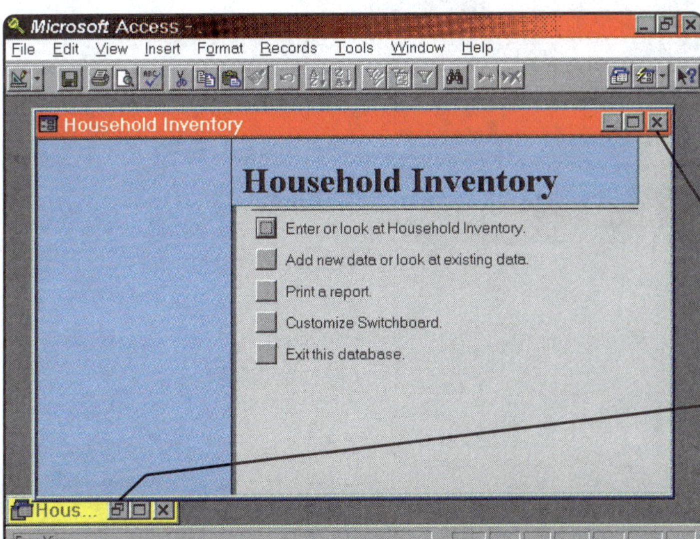

1. **Open Access and the database** if you have not already done so. This example starts at the main Switchboard.

2. **Click** on the **Close button** (☒). The Switchboard will close.

3. **Click** on the **Restore button** (🗗) on the minimized object. The Household Inventory1: Database dialog box will appear.

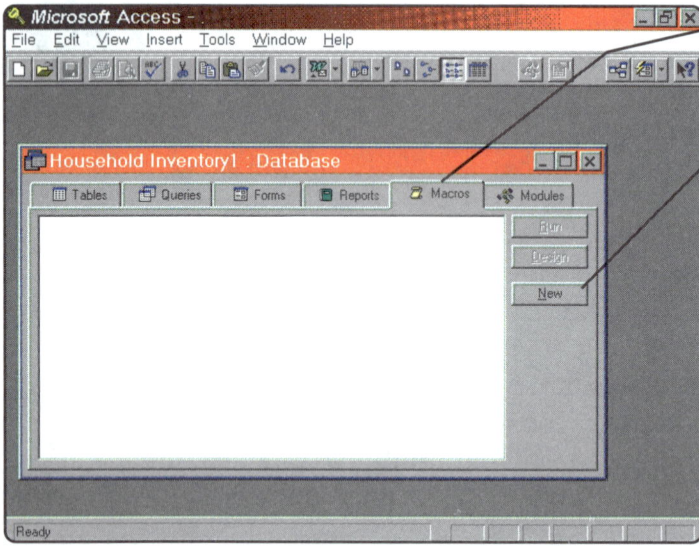

4. **Click** on the **Macros tab**. The Macro box will appear.

5. **Click** on **New**. The Macro1: Macro dialog box will appear.

Selecting an Action

Macros combine several "actions" (steps). These actions can be menu commands, basic functions like printing, or entering strings of text. Before you make a macro, you have to think about the steps that are involved in whatever it is that you want the macro to do for you. For this example of printing a record, there are actually two steps: 1) selecting the record you want to print, and 2) issuing the print command.

First, you tell the macro to select a record using a command on the Edit menu.

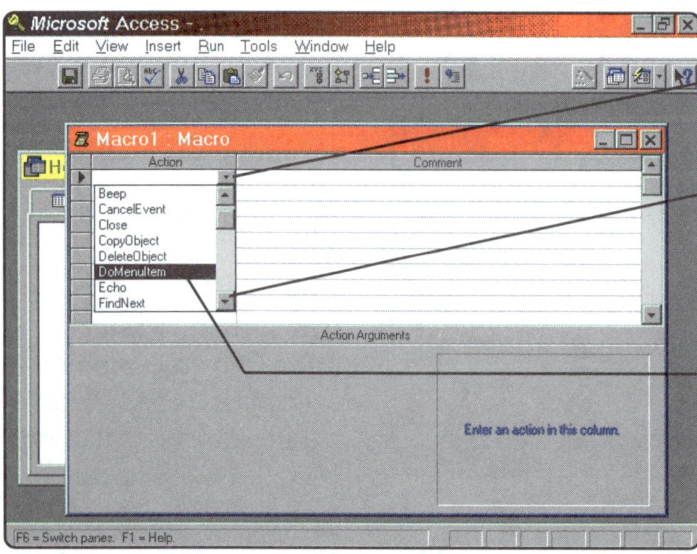

1. **Click** on ▼ to see a list of choices.

2. **Click repeatedly** on the ▼ to scroll down the **Actions list** until you see DoMenuItem.

3. **Click** on **DoMenuItem** to select it. A number of boxes will appear under Action Arguments.

The macro isn't trying to start a fight. The word "argument" is used here to refer to the specific thing that the action we selected does. Since there are dozens of "MenuItems" it can "Do," you have to supply an argument to tell the macro which "DoMenuItem" we want it to perform.

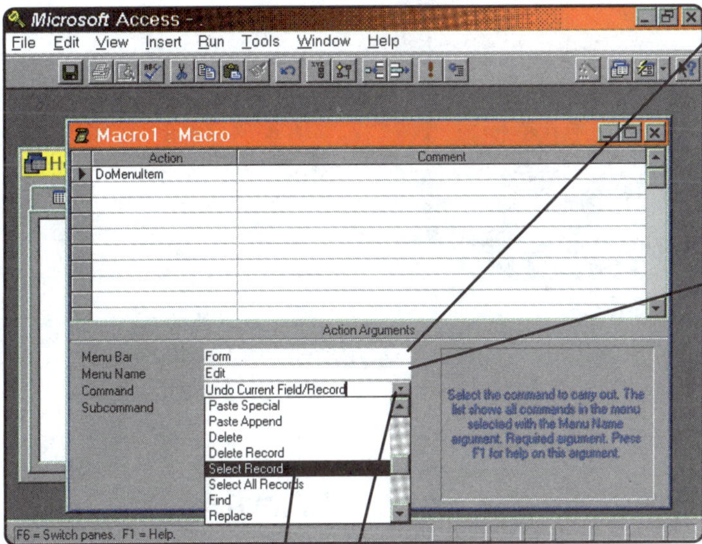

The first box shows the menu bar you want the macro to use. In this example, it's the one that appears when we're using a form.

The second box shows the menu that has the command you want performed. In this example, it's the Edit menu. These two boxes are actually list boxes. They can be changed in the same way we'll change the third box.

4. **Click** in the **Command box** (the third box) to place the cursor. A ▼ button will appear on the right.

5. **Click** on the ▼ at the right end of the Command box. A list will appear.

6. **Click** on **Select Record**. The list will close, and Select Record will appear in the Command box.

Note: The menu bar you select has to be appropriate to what you're doing in Access at the time you want the macro to run. For example, you have to be using a form to have access to the Form menu bar available.

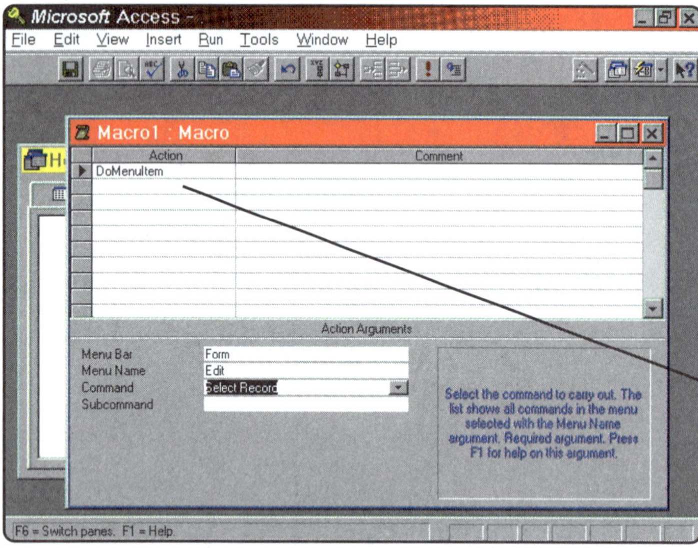

The first part of what you want the macro to do is complete. If you recall, you want it to select a record, then print it. The action and arguments you specified will get the macro to select the record. Now you have to get it to print the record.

7. **Click** in the **second Action box**. A ▼ will appear at the end of the box.

Notice that hints about the actions and arguments appear in the lower right corner of the dialog box.

Selecting a Second Action

1. **Click** on the ▼. The list of actions will appear.

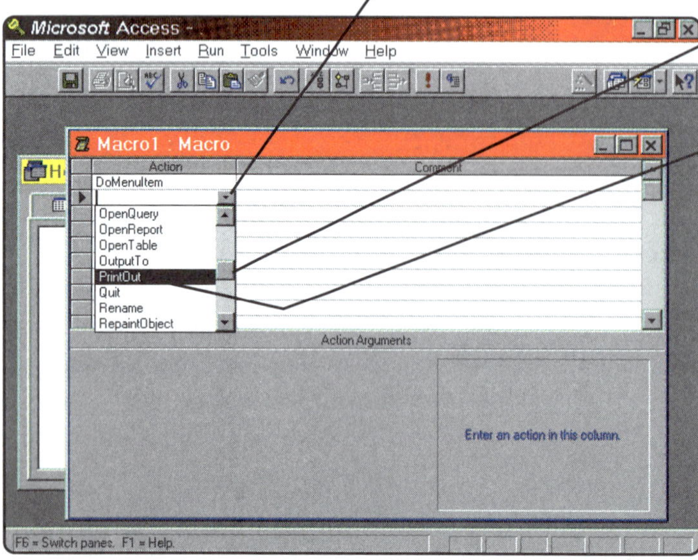

2. **Scroll down** the **list** until you see PrintOut.

3. **Click** on **PrintOut**. Several boxes for possible arguments will appear in the Action Arguments area of the dialog box.

Notice that the boxes aren't the same as the ones that appeared when you selected "DoMenuItem." Different "actions" will have different "arguments."

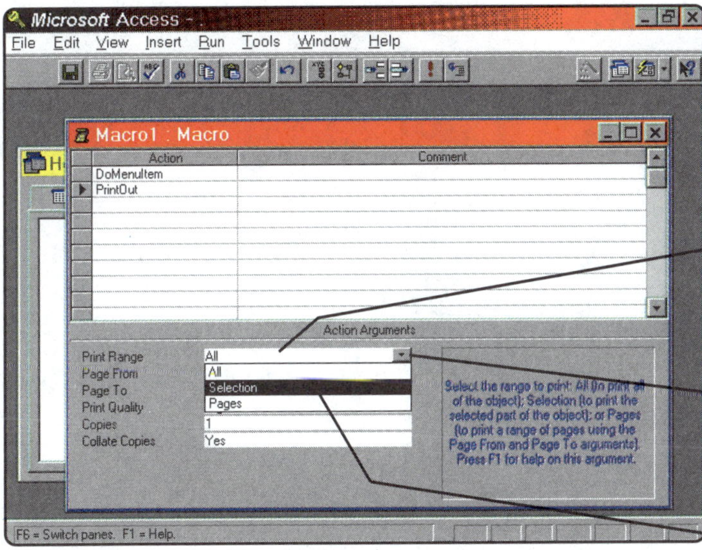

The first Action Argument box, Print Range, is the only one you have to deal with for printing the selected record.

4. **Click** in the **Print Range box** to place the cursor. A ▼ will appear at the right.

5. **Click** on the ▼ at the right end of the Print Range box. A list will appear.

6. **Click** on **Selection**. The list will close, and "Selection" will appear in the box.

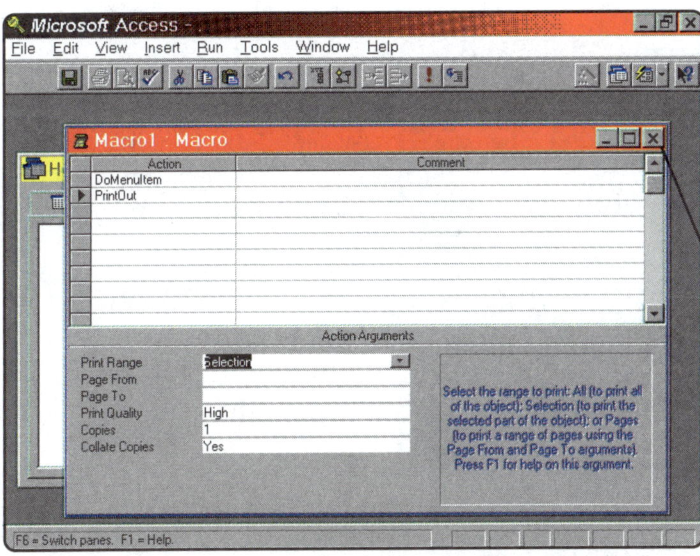

The macro is now set to select a record, and print the "selection." If you use the macro in Form view, the record that appears in the form will be the one that gets selected and printed.

7. **Click** on the **Close button** (☒). A message box will appear.

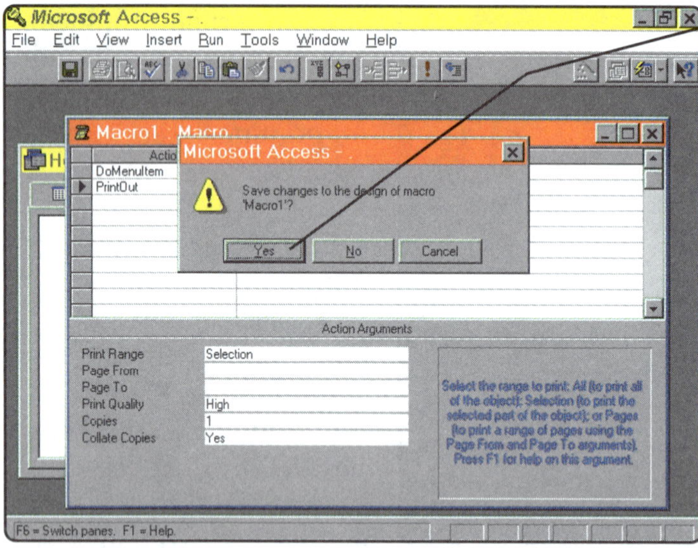

8. **Click** on **Yes**. A Save As dialog box will appear.

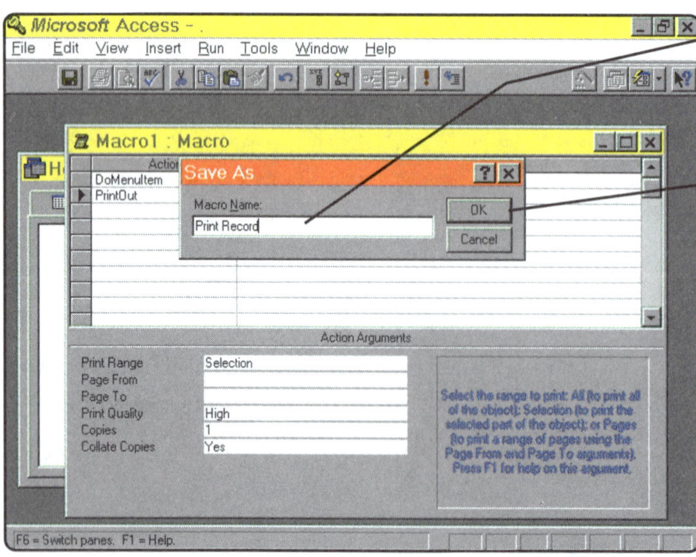

9. **Type a name** for the macro. In this example we used Print Record.

10. **Click** on **OK**. The Save As box and Macro1: Macro dialog box will close.

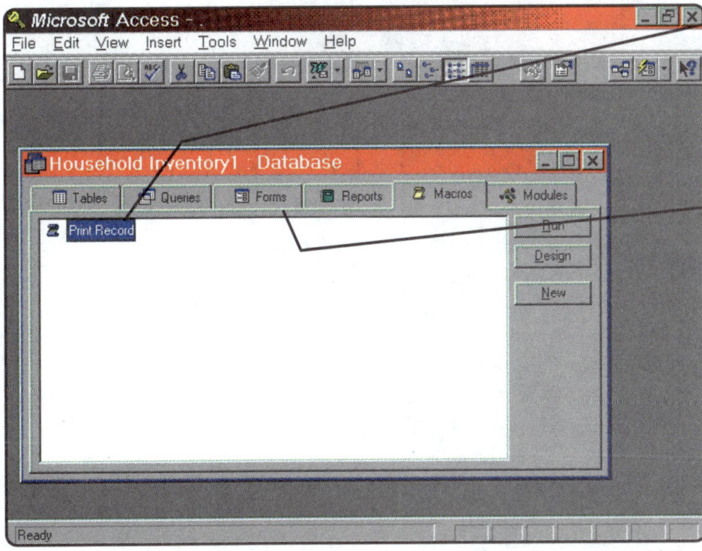

Your completed macro shows up here, in the Macros list. Now you'll see how macros are run.

11. **Click** on the **Forms tab**. The Forms list will appear.

RUNNING A MACRO

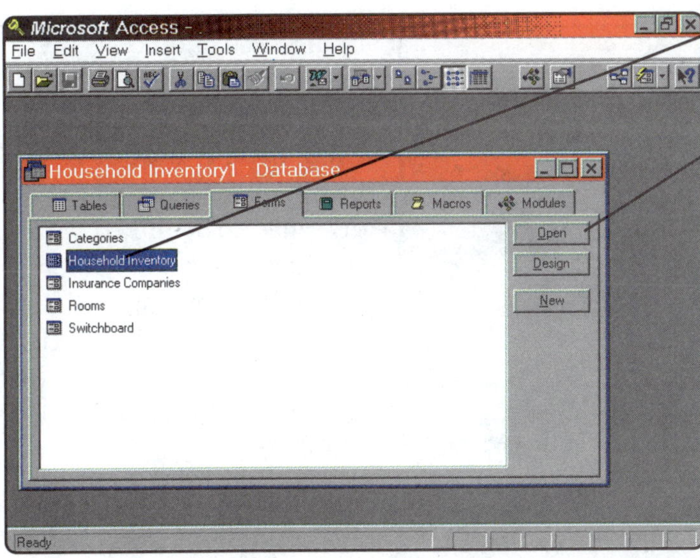

1. **Click** on **Household Inventory** to highlight it.

2. **Click** on **Open**. The Household Inventory form will appear.

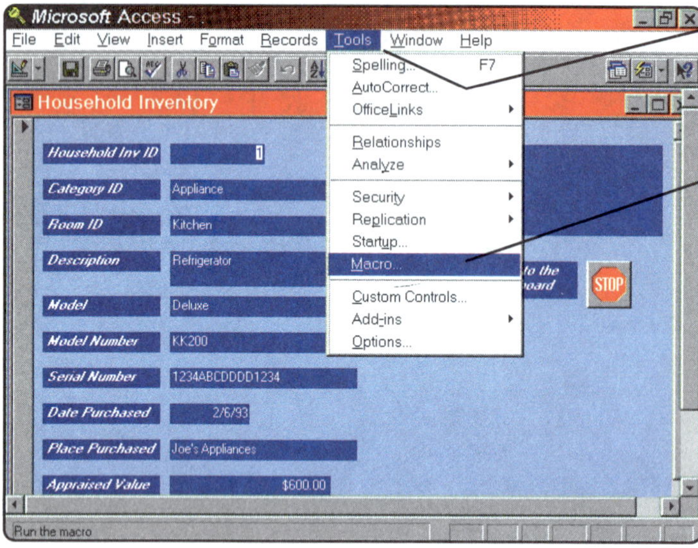

3. **Click** on **Tools** in the menu bar. The Tools menu will appear.

4. **Click** on **Macro**. The Run Macro dialog box will appear.

The Run Macro dialog box contains a list box that lets you select a macro to run. To run the macro, you'd click on it, then click on OK. You've only made one macro, so that's all that you can see in our example below.

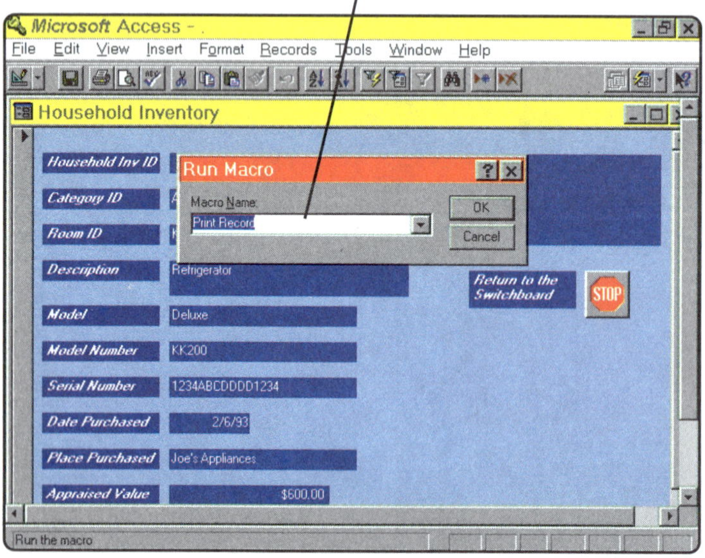

In this case, it takes as many steps to run the macro as it does to print the record using the menus. But your Print Record macro was designed to be linked to a command button on a form. It is only an example of the much more complex, and timesaving macros that you can write following the steps that have been shown.

LINKING A MACRO TO A COMMAND BUTTON

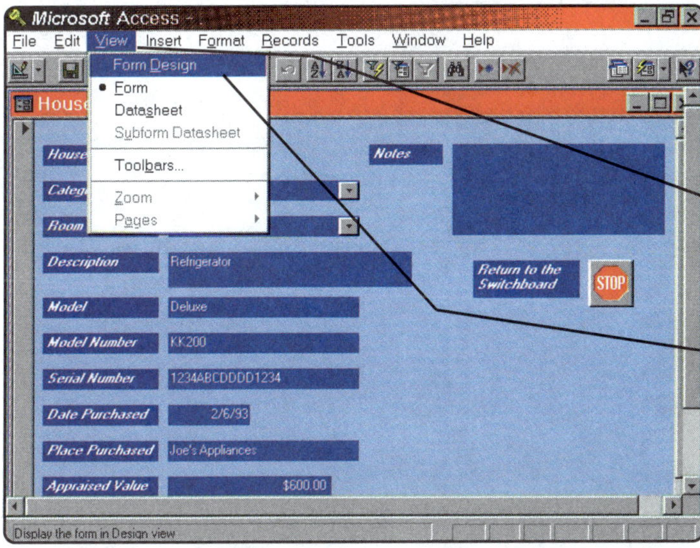

In this section, you'll install a command button in a form, much like you did in Chapter 11.

1. **Click** on **View** in the menu bar. The View menu will appear.

2. **Click** on **Form Design**. The form will switch to Design view.

3. **Click** on the **Command Button icon** on the toolbar. Your toolbar may be docked above the form if you followed the steps in Chapter 13.

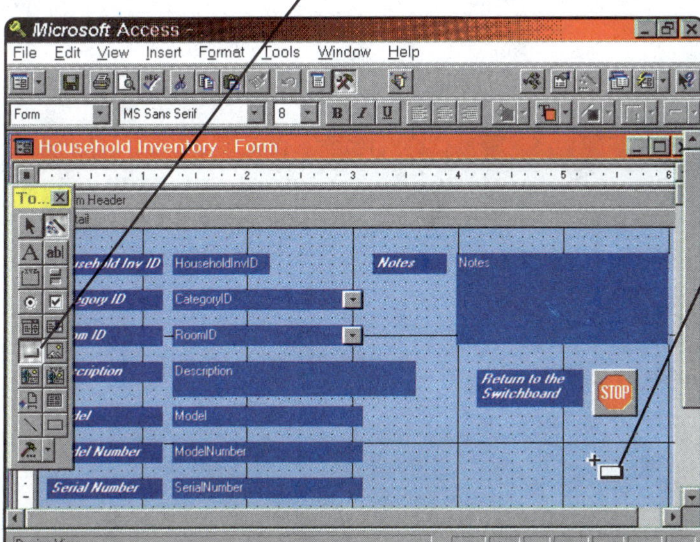

4. **Move** your **mouse pointer** over the form. As you do it will become a plus sign with a box.

5. **Move** the **plus sign** to the spot where you want the upper left corner of the command button to be located.

6. **Click** the **mouse button**. The command button will be placed, and the Command Button Wizard will appear.

Setting Up the Button

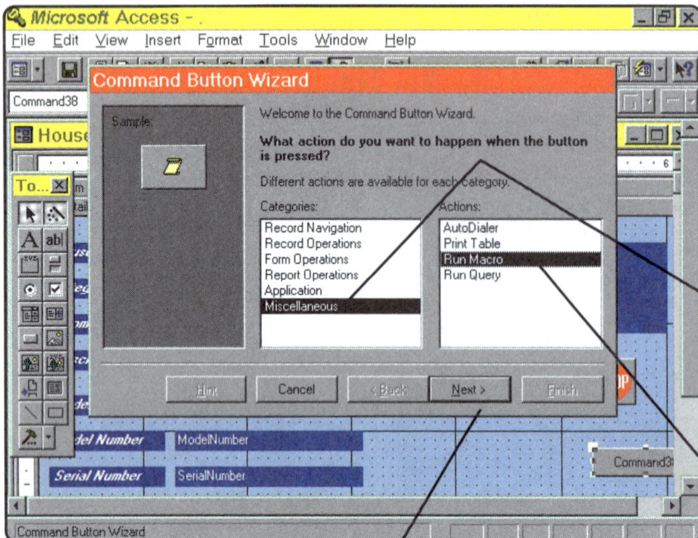

You have to tell the Wizard what you want the command button on our form to do. Several types of "actions" are listed on the right for each of the "categories" listed on the left.

1. **Click** on **Miscellaneous** in the Categories box. The list of miscellaneous actions will appear.

2. **Click** on **Run Macro** in the Actions box.

3. **Click** on **Next >**. Another Command Button Wizard dialog box will appear.

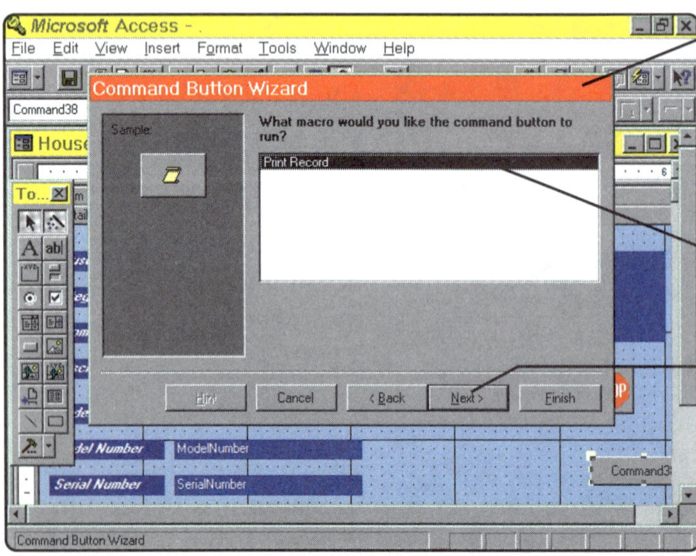

This dialog box lets you choose the macro you want to run. Since you've only made one, that's all you have to choose from in the list.

4. **Click** on the **macro** you want to run to highlight it.

5. **Click** on **Next >**. Another Command Button Wizard dialog box will appear.

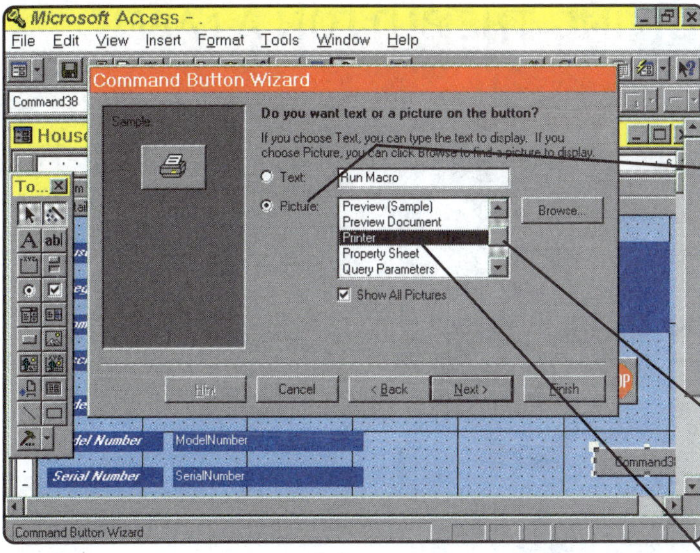

This dialog box lets us choose text or a picture to appear on the button.

6. **Click** on **Picture** to place a dot in the circle.

7. **Click** on **Show All Pictures** to place a ✔ in the square.

8. **Scroll down** the **list** of pictures until you see "Printer."

9. **Click** on **Printer**. A picture of the Printer button will appear in the Sample box on the left.

10. **Click** on **Next >**. Another Command Button Wizard dialog box will appear.

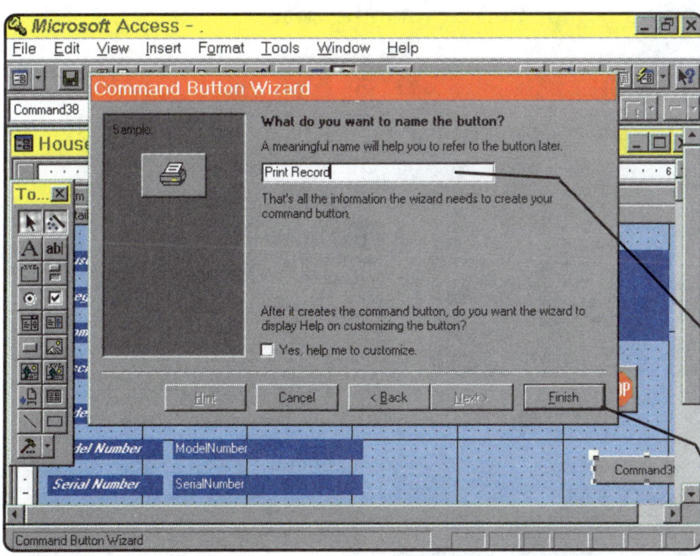

This dialog box asks for a name for the button. The name won't appear on or near the button. It's only to give it a unique name to differentiate it from all the other objects, or elements that make up the database.

11. **Type a name** for the button. In this example, it is Print Record.

12. **Click** on **Finish**. The button will be created and placed on the form.

GIVING THE BUTTON A LABEL

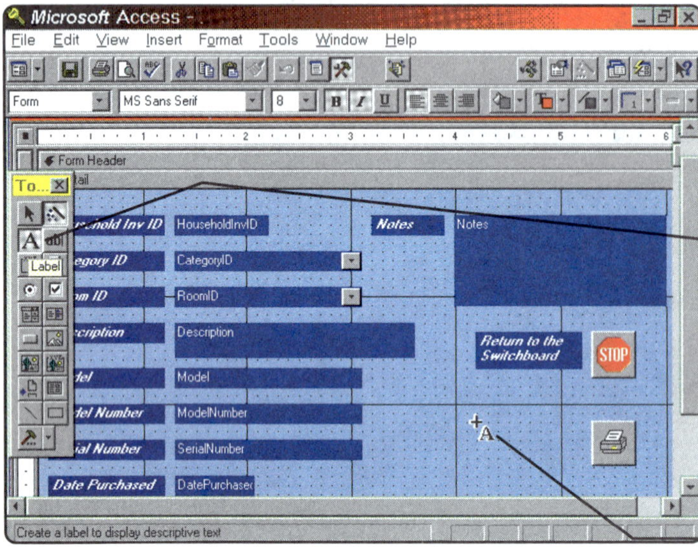

Now that you have the new button, you should label it so that its purpose is clear to anyone who uses the database.

1. **Click** on the **Label icon** on the toolbar.

2. **Move** your **mouse pointer** over the form. As you do, it will turn into a plus sign with a letter "A."

3. **Move** the **plus sign** to the spot where you want the upper left corner of the label to be located.

4. **Click** the **mouse button**. The label will be placed, and a cursor will be flashing in it.

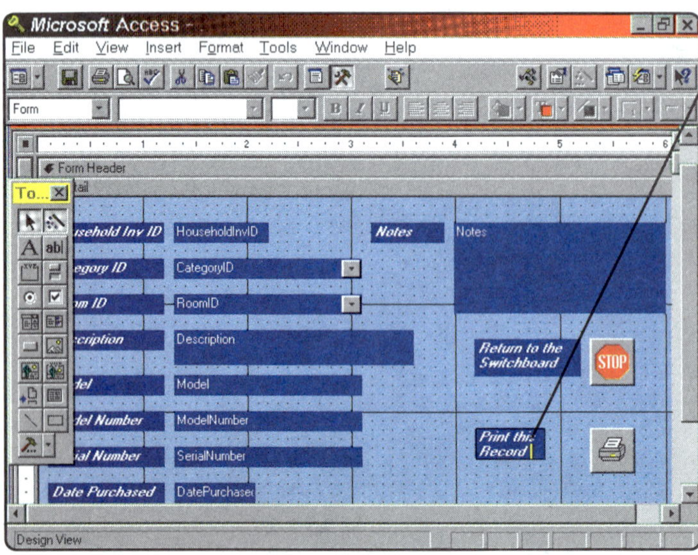

5. **Type Print this** (the first line in the example you see here).

6. **Press** the **Shift and Enter keys** at the same time to start a new line in the label.

7. **Type Record**.

8. **Press Enter**. The label will be completed.

TRYING OUT THE NEW COMMAND BUTTON

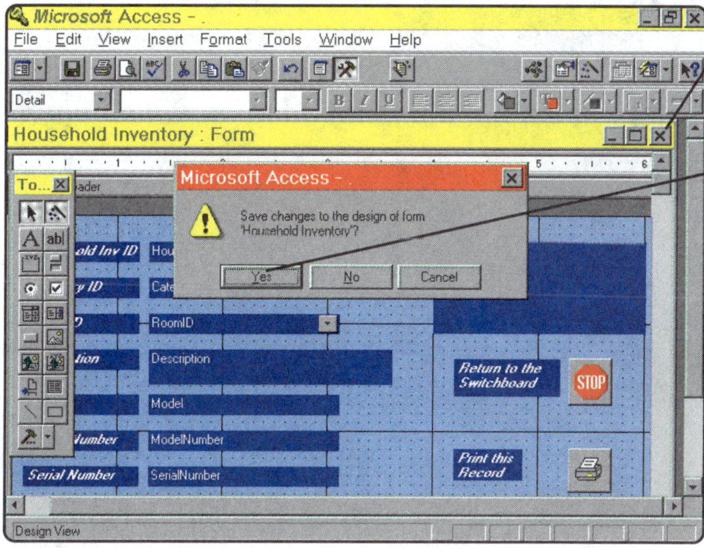

1. **Click** on the **Close button** (☒). A message box will appear.
2. **Click** on **Yes**. The changes will be saved, and the form will close.

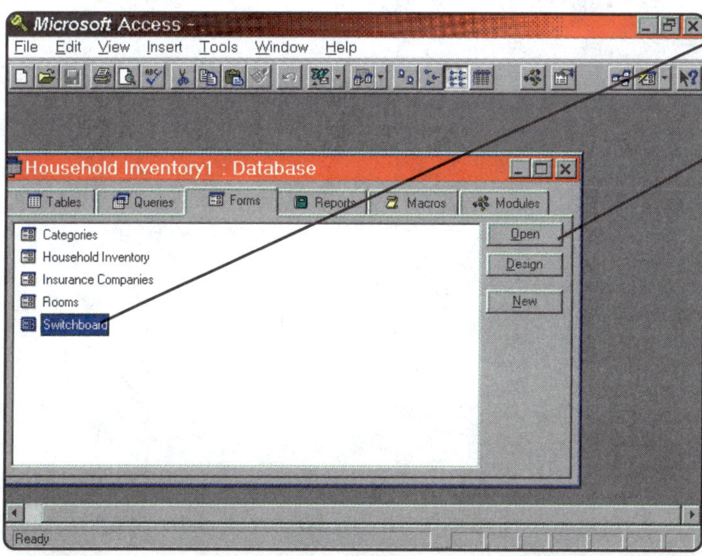

3. **Click** on **Switchboard** to highlight it.
4. **Click** on **Open**. The Switchboard will open.

Printing a Record

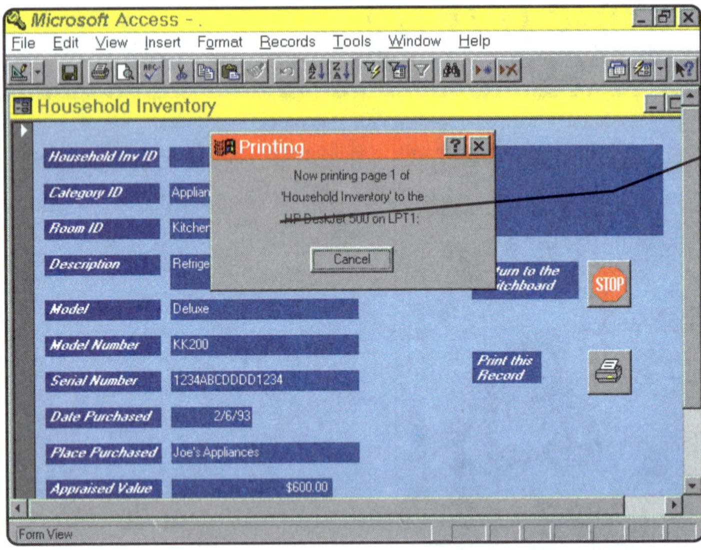

1. **Click** on the **Enter or look at Household Inventory button**. The Household Inventory form will appear.

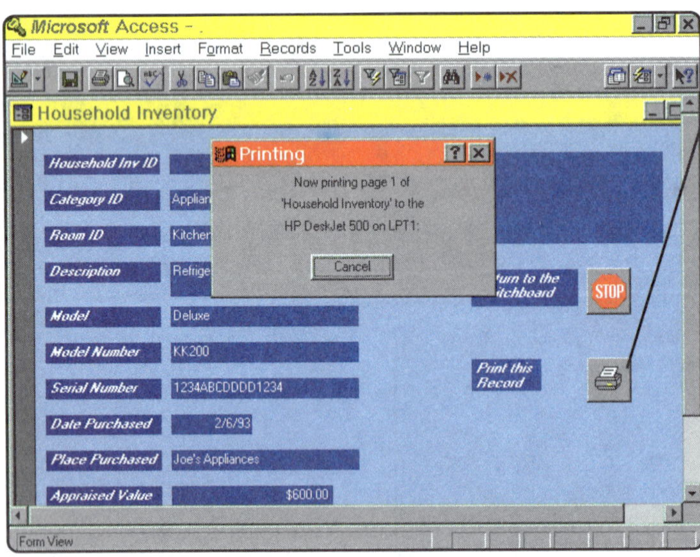

2. **Click** on the **Print this Record button**. A message box will appear briefly, and the record on your screen will print.

CHAPTER 21

Using the Performance Analyzer and Table Analyzer Wizard

Access not only provides you with Wizards to build and customize your database, it gives you the means to refine your database using analyzers. The "Performance Analyzer" checks such things as forms, reports, and macros, and suggests ways you can improve them. The "Table Analyzer Wizard" can go through your database and track down instances where your tables contain duplicate data that could be eliminated by using new, separate tables. It'll even offer to build the new tables for you! In this chapter, you will do the following:

- ✔ Check a macro and a table using the Performance Analyzer
- ✔ Take a quick look at the Table Analyzer Wizard

OPENING THE ANALYZER

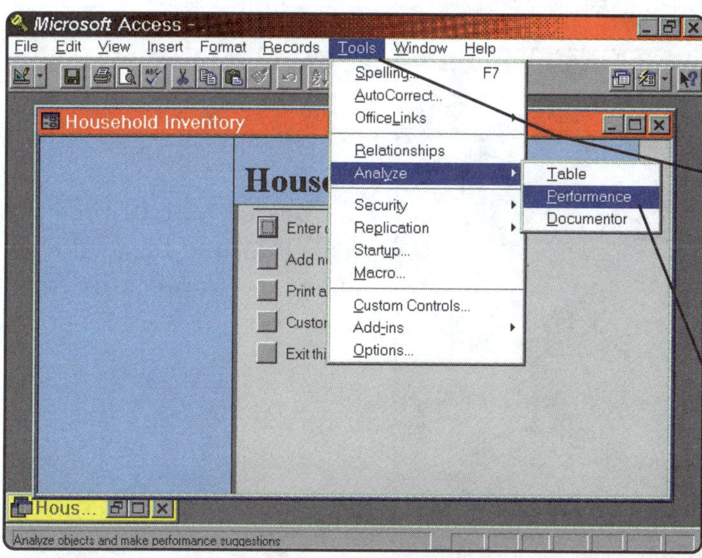

1. **Open Access and the database** if you have not already done so.
2. **Click** on **Tools** in the menu bar. The Tools menu will appear.
3. **Click** on **Analyze.** Another menu will appear.
4. **Click** on **Performance.** The Performance Analyzer dialog box will appear.

SELECTING OBJECTS TO ANALYZE

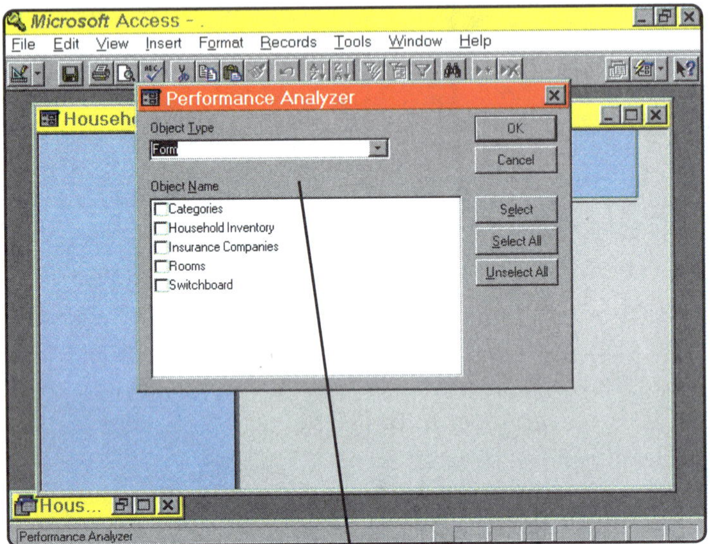

Many of the elements that make up Access are referred to as "objects." This has to do with the programming behind them and makes sense if you're discussing computer programs. But to most people, they're reports, forms, tables, etc. Once you've assembled a database, you may benefit from having the Performance Analyzer test the objects and offer suggestions for improving them.

The Performance Analyzer dialog box lists types of objects in the upper box, and the specific objects that are available for each type in the lower box.

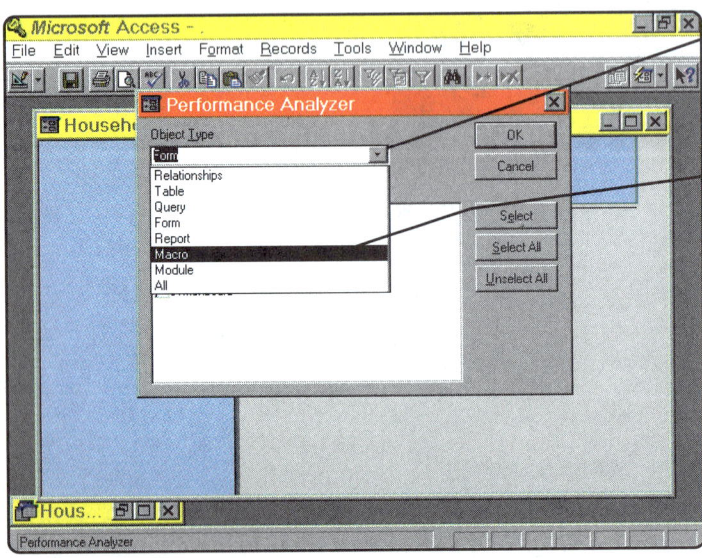

1. **Click** on the ▼ at the end of the Object Type box. A list will appear.
2. **Click** on **Macro**. The list will close, and the available macros will appear in the lower box.

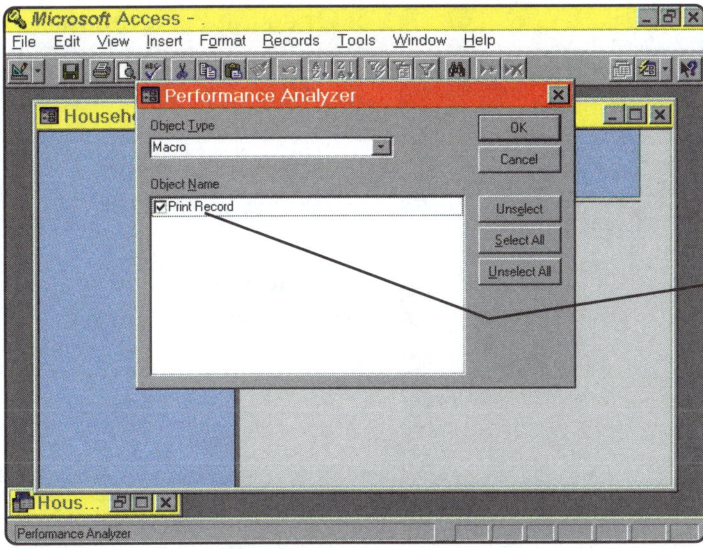

The only macro listed is the one we made in Chapter 20 to print a record. If there were several, we could select more than one for analysis.

3. **Click** on the **object(s)** you want to analyze to place a check in the squares.

4. **Click** on **OK**. A message box will appear briefly, followed by another Performance Analyzer dialog box.

This dialog box lists the suggestions for improvements that the Analyzer came up with. If it has several, click each in turn to see more information on each in the lower box. If you want to carry out the suggestion, click on it to select it, then click on the Optimize button. We suggest that you quit the Analyzer and make a backup copy of your database first, so that you can compare the original and improved versions without risk.

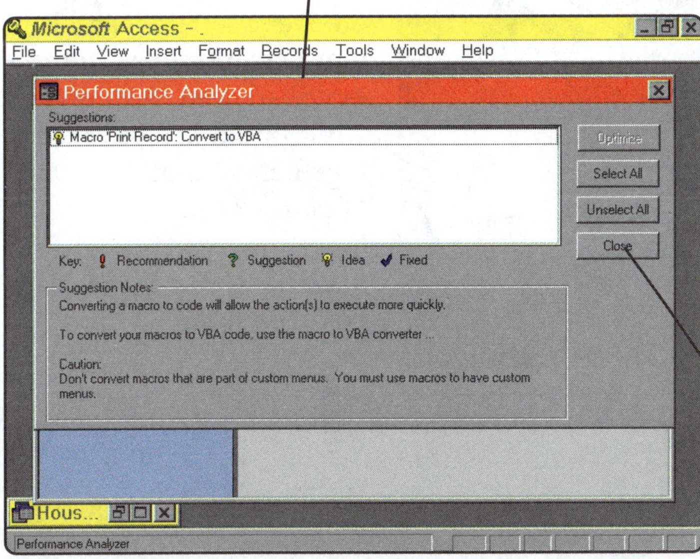

In this case, the suggestion is to translate our little macro into VBA code (Visual Basic for Access). The macro is so tiny that the speed improvement would be in terms of nanoseconds, so we'll pass on this suggestion.

5. **Click** on **Close**. The Performance Analyzer will close.

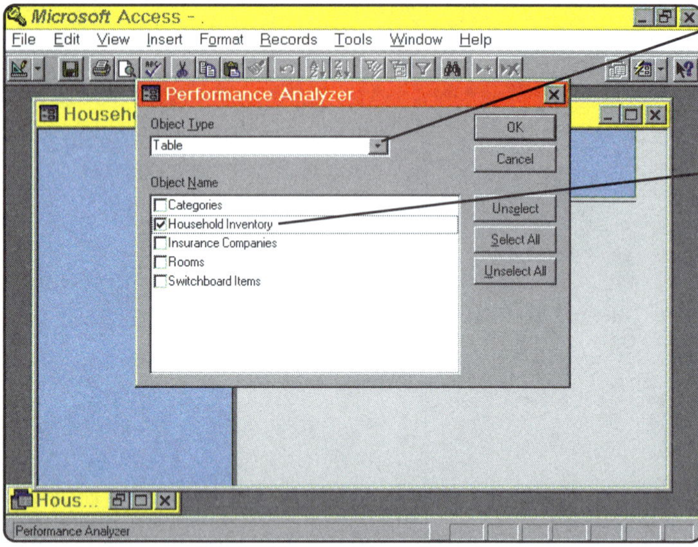

6. **Open** the **Performance Analyzer** again, and **repeat steps 1 to 2** to select Table.

7. **Click** on **Household Inventory** to select it.

8. **Click** on **OK**. The suggestions, if any, will appear.

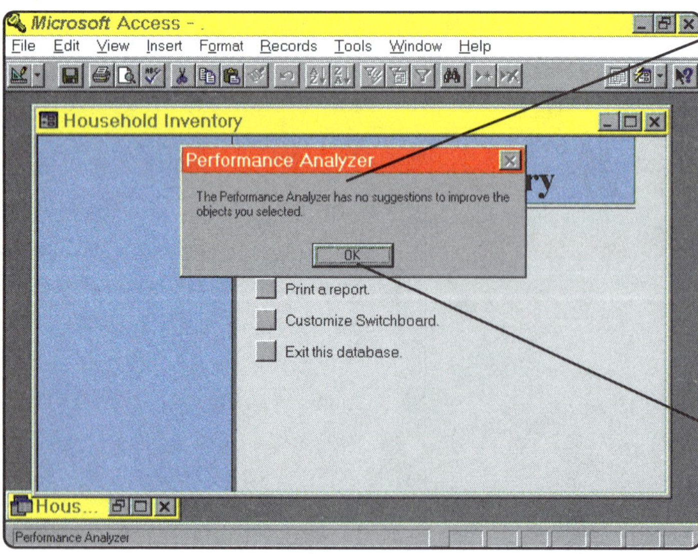

What a surprise! The table, created by the Database Wizard at the beginning of the book, can't be improved on. We're certain that this wouldn't be the case if the table had been used for a while or if it had been put together without the Wizard's help.

9. **Click** on **OK**. The message box will close.

ANALYZING TABLES

The Table Analyzer Wizard looks into your tables and tries to detect duplicated data. If there are many duplicates, it will suggest that the data that's being duplicated be separated to form two new tables from the old table. This can improve the database's efficiency. Even with the Wizard's help, this isn't a procedure to undertake lightly, or without backing up your database first. It's most helpful for large, complex databases that have been in use for a while.

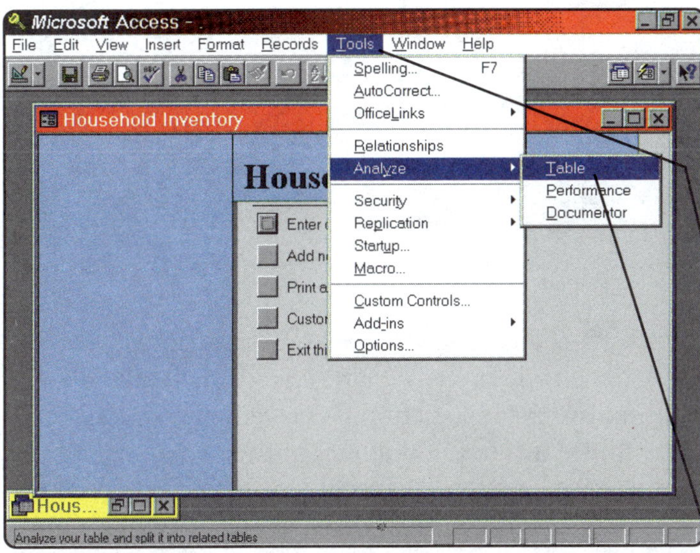

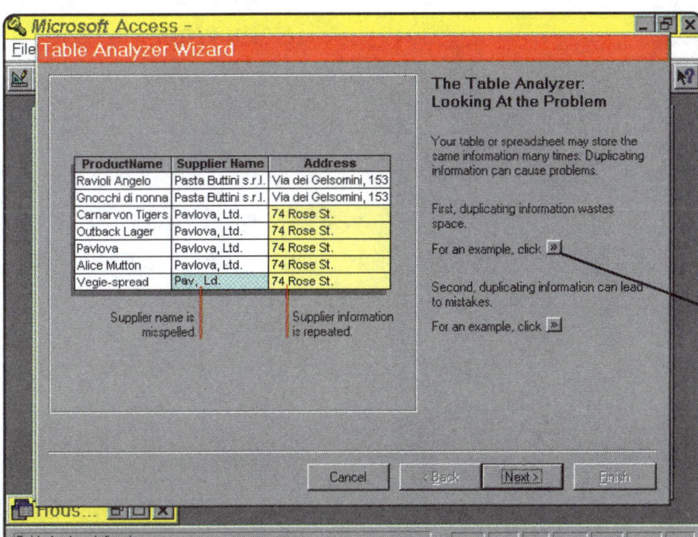

1. **Click** on **Tools** in the menu bar. The Tools menu will appear.

2. **Click** on **Analyze**. Another menu will appear.

3. **Click** on **Table**. The Table Analyzer Wizard dialog box will appear.

First, the Wizard explains, with some examples, what it's proposing to do.

4. **Click** on the upper **>> button**. An example of how duplicates waste space will appear.

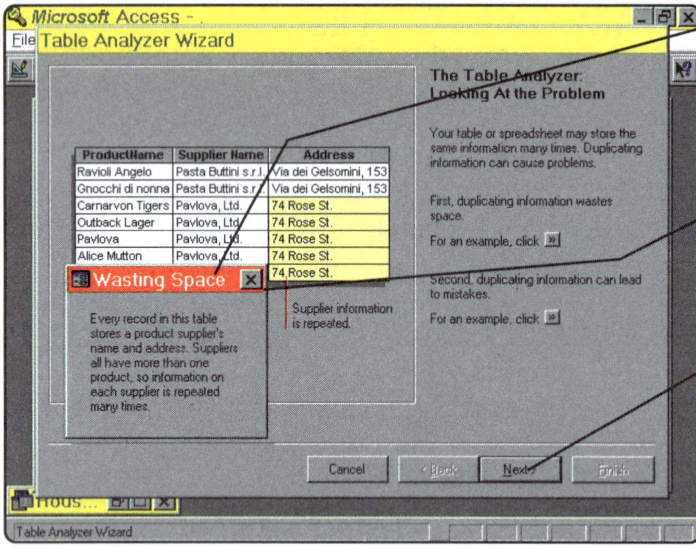

We moved the example dialog box to the side to show it and the screen it refers to better.

5. **Click** on the **Close button** ([X]). The example dialog box will close.

6. **Click** on **Next >**. Another screen of information about the Table Analyzer Wizard will appear.

If you have a large database and believe that you may benefit from the Wizard's help, click on Next and follow the instructions. The Wizard will create new tables out of the old one, but won't damage the old one in the process. The old table will be saved so that you can compare its performance with the new ones. But back up everything first just in case.

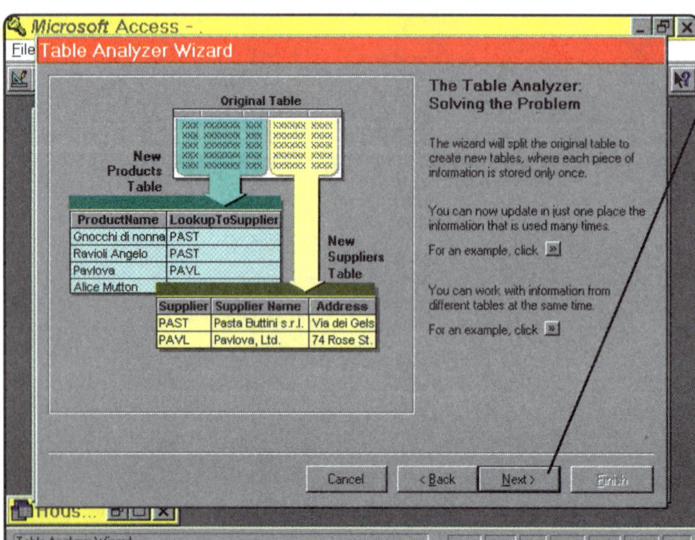

7. **Click** on **Next >** to continue the analysis.

OR

8. **Click** on **Cancel** to quit the Table Analyzer Wizard.

ACCESS FOR WINDOWS 95

Appendices

APPENDIX A

Installing Access for Windows 95

Windows 95 has simplified the way you install programs. In fact, if your computer has a CD-ROM drive, the process is not only simple, it is very FAST. Our example shows installing Access as a stand-alone program. If you are installing it as part of Microsoft Office, your steps will be nearly identical to the ones shown here (we'll point out where they are not). In this chapter, you will do the following:

- ✔ Install Access 7 for Windows 95

OPENING THE CONTROL PANEL

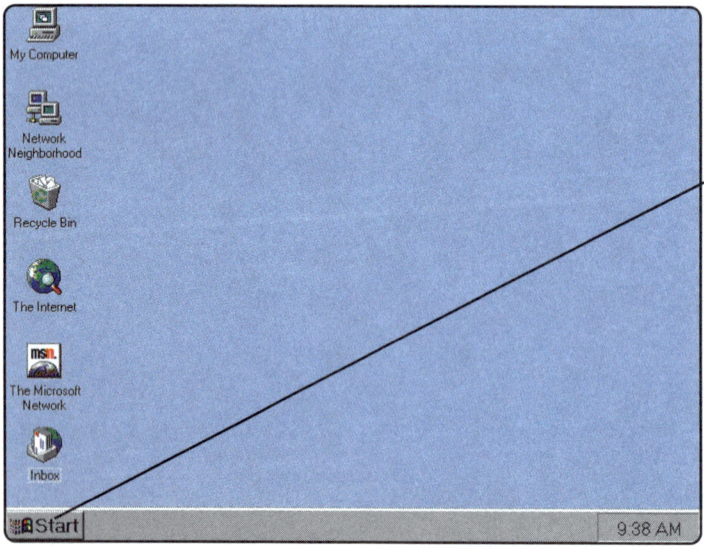

To begin the installation, you must open the Control Panel.

1. **Click** on the **Start button** in the taskbar. A menu will appear.

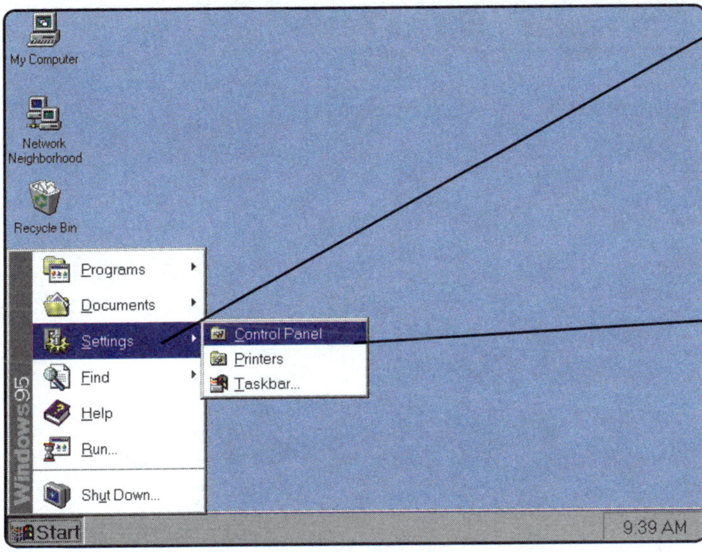

2. **Move** the **mouse arrow** up the menu to Settings. A second menu will appear.

3. **Move** the **mouse arrow** over to highlight Control Panel.

4. **Click** on **Control Panel**. The Control Panel dialog box will appear.

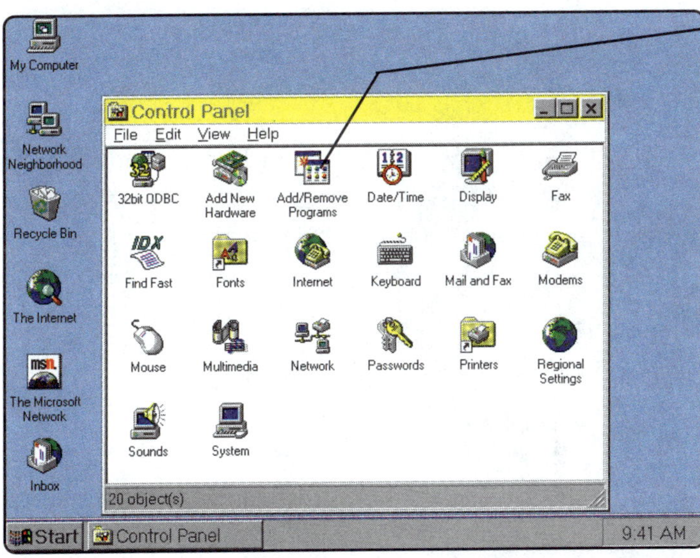

5. **Click twice** on **Add/Remove Programs**. The Add/Remove Programs Properties dialog box will appear.

INSTALLING A PROGRAM

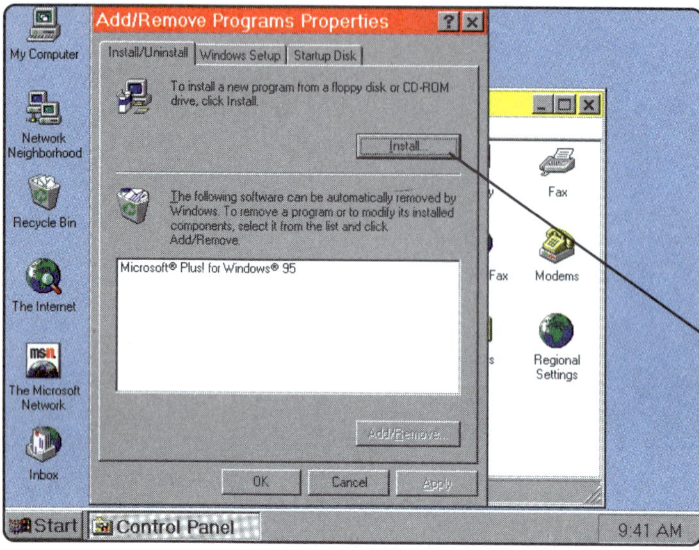

The following sections illustrate an installation using a CD-ROM disk. However, if you are using floppy disks for your installation, your screens will vary slightly from these examples.

1. **Click** on the **Install button**. The Install Program From Floppy Disk or CD-ROM dialog box will appear.

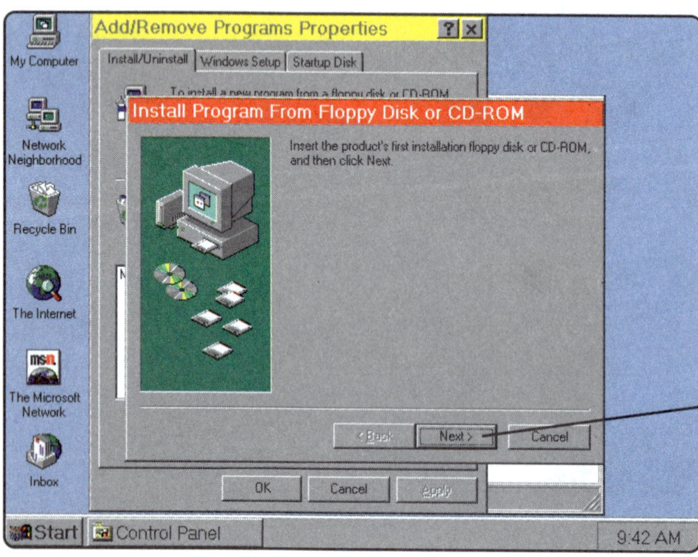

2. **Insert** your **CD-ROM disk** into your CD-ROM drive, or insert Installation diskette 1 into drive A (or drive B). Remember that for some CD drives you have to place the CD-ROM disk into a carrier before you insert it into the drive.

3. **Click** on **Next >**. Once Windows 95 finds the installation program disk, the Run Installation Program message box will appear.

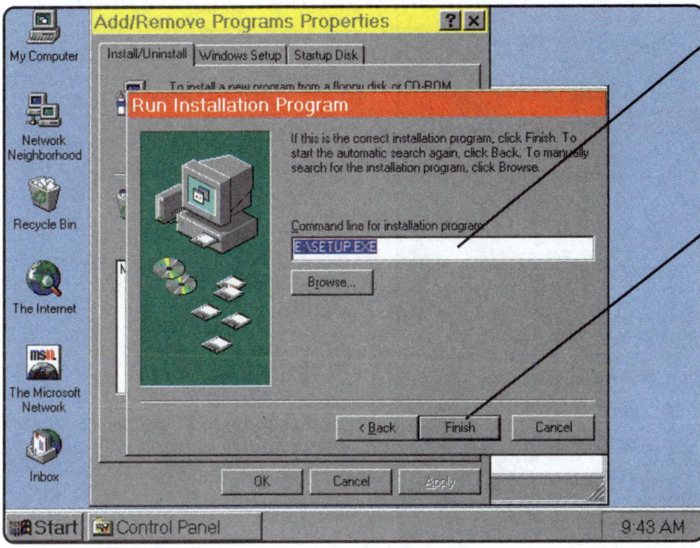

Notice that the command line for the installation automatically appears in the text box.

4. **Click** on **Finish**. The Setup Message box will appear.

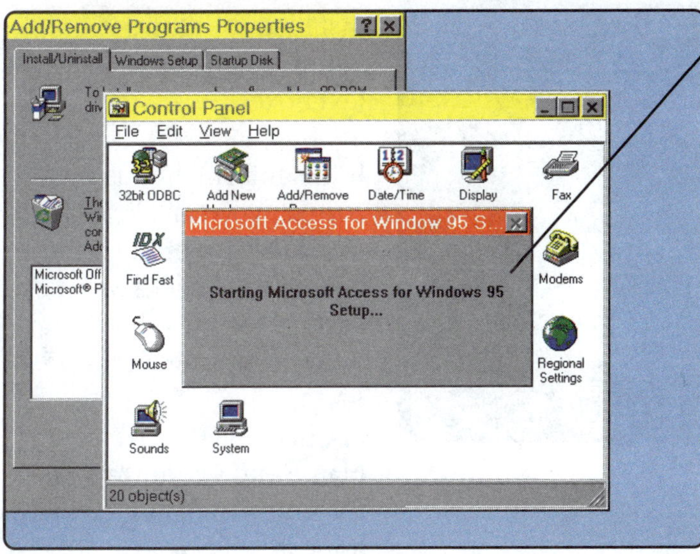

After a few moments, the Microsoft Access for Windows 95 Setup dialog box will appear.

Next, a Microsoft Access for Windows 95 welcome message screen will appear.

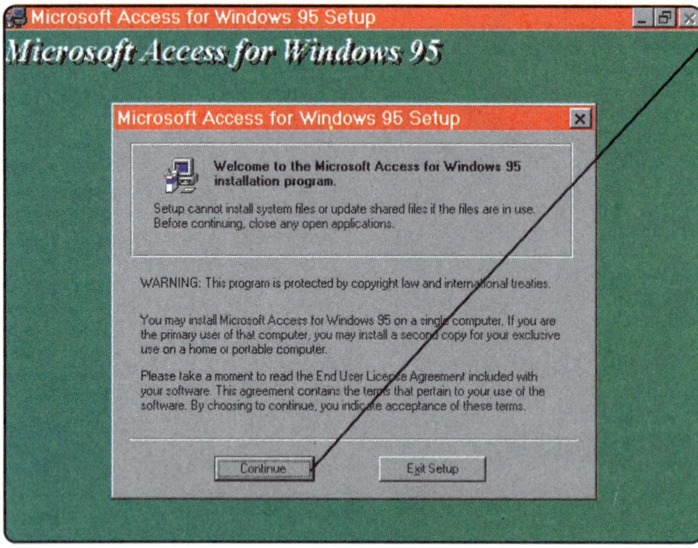

5. **Click** on **Continue**. The Name and Organization Information dialog box will appear.

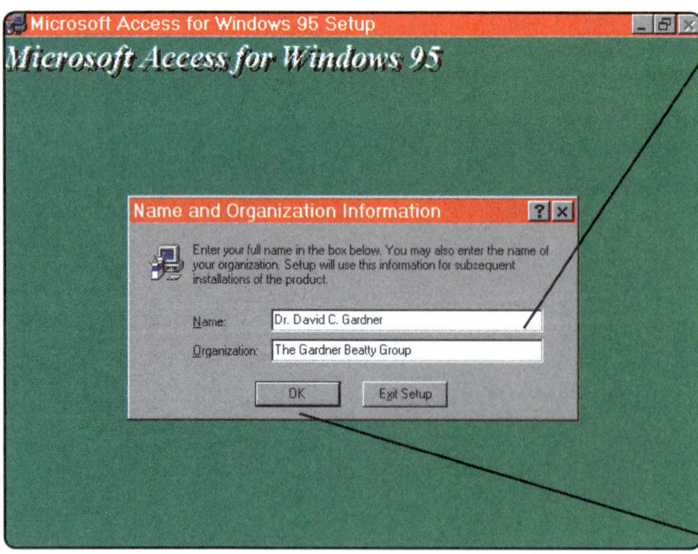

Notice that the name and organization information that you used when you installed Windows 95 automatically appears in the text boxes.

If this information is not correct, you can click to place the cursor in either box, use the Backspace key to delete what's there, and type something else.

6. **Click** on **OK**. The Confirm Name and Organization Information dialog box will appear.

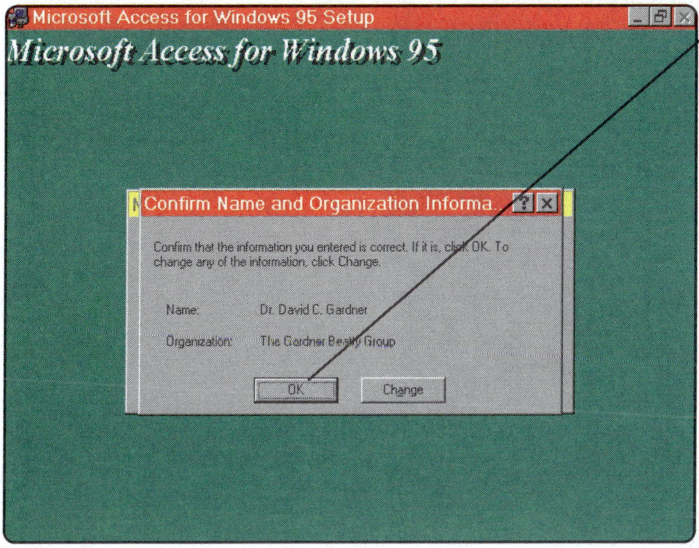

7. **Click** on **OK** if the information is correct. The Microsoft Access for Windows 95 Setup dialog box will appear.

If the information is not correct, **click** on **Change**. The previous dialog box will appear. After making your corrections, **click** on **OK** to return to this dialog box.

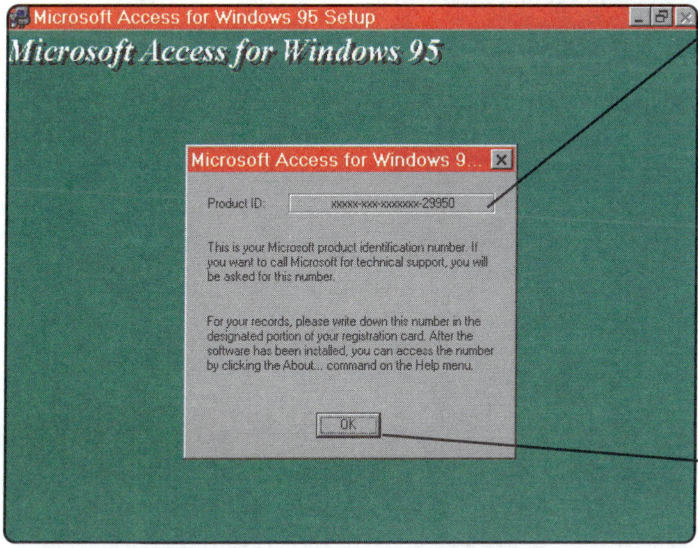

Notice that your registration number appears on this screen. It is important that you make a note of the number and keep it handy. Write it down inside the front cover of your Access Users Manual. If you call Microsoft for technical support, you will need to tell them this number.

8. **Click** on **OK**. A small message box will appear.

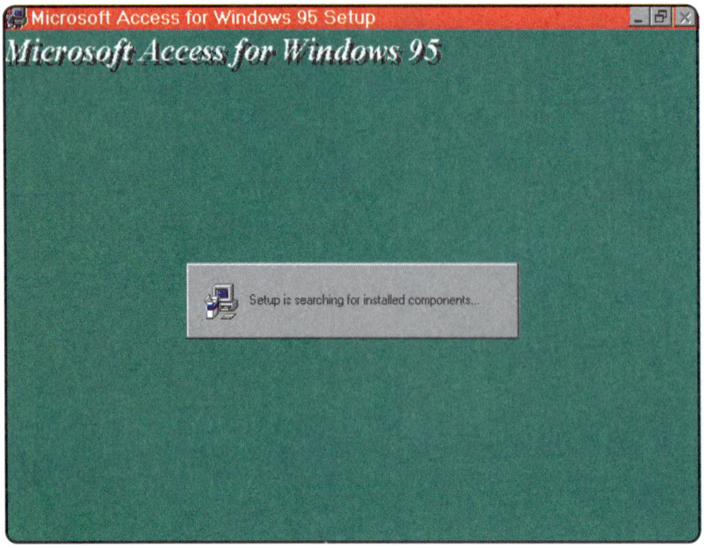

The hourglass will appear briefly along with the message box that says "Setup is searching for installed components."

Selecting a Folder

Access will automatically be installed to a new folder (directory) called MSOffice\Access on your computer's C drive.

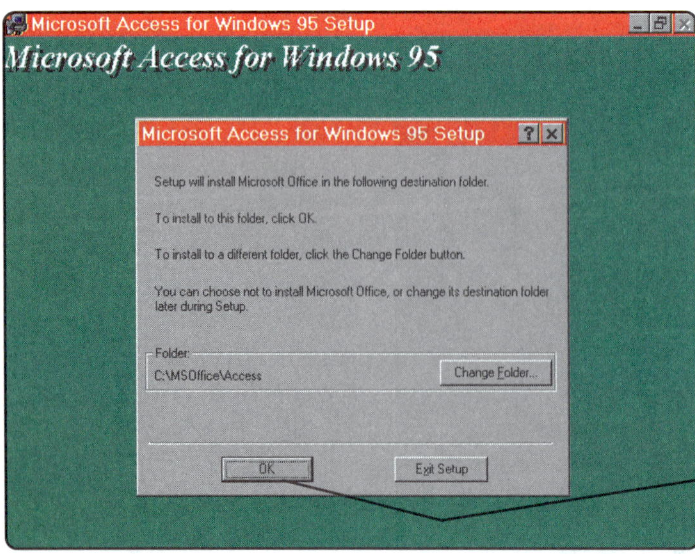

If you wish to install it in another directory (folder) or on another drive, click on the Change Directory button. A Change Directory dialog box will appear. Type in the new folder name and path, and click on OK. A confirmation destination message box will appear. Click on Yes to confirm.

1. **Click** on **OK**. After a few moments, the Microsoft Access for Windows 95 dialog box will appear.

SELECTING FEATURES TO INSTALL

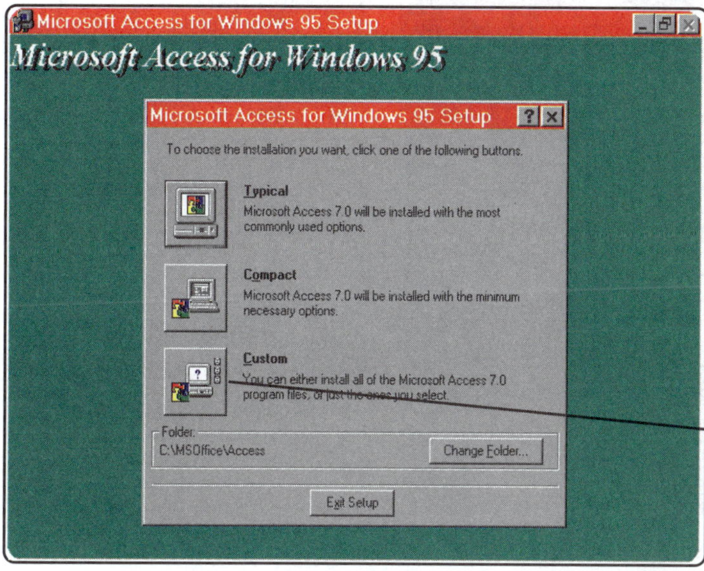

If you are installing Microsoft Office, you will be asked which programs you wish to install. We recommend the Custom installation. This lets you select the components that you want to install now; you can add or remove components later as well.

1. **Click** on **Custom**. The Microsoft Access for Windows 95 - Custom dialog box will appear. All of the components of Access will be selected (there will be a ✔ in the box next to each).

2. **Click** on any **component** you DO NOT want to install, to remove the ✔ from the box next to it.

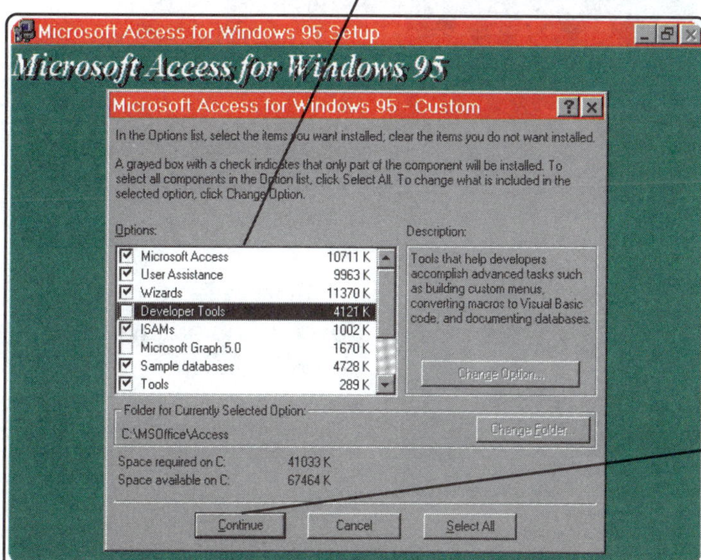

Unless you will be doing advanced programming, you will not need "Developer Tools." If you have already installed Microsoft Excel, you will probably have installed Microsoft Graph as well. Most of the rest of the components are likely to come in handy.

3. **Click** on **Continue**. A "Setup is checking for necessary disk space" message will appear.

Watching and Waiting

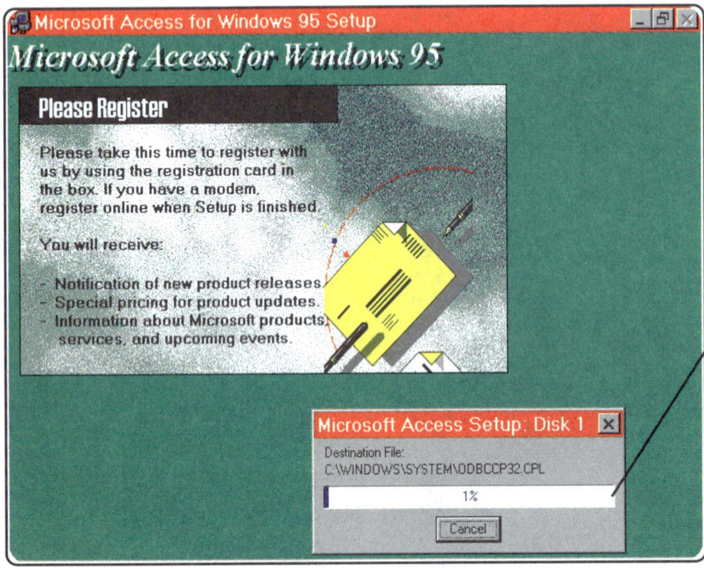

At this point sit back and relax for a few moments. If you're using diskettes, you will occasionally be prompted to insert the next one that is needed into your disk drive.

The Microsoft Access Setup: Disk 1 dialog box will show you the progress of the installation.

Completing the Installation

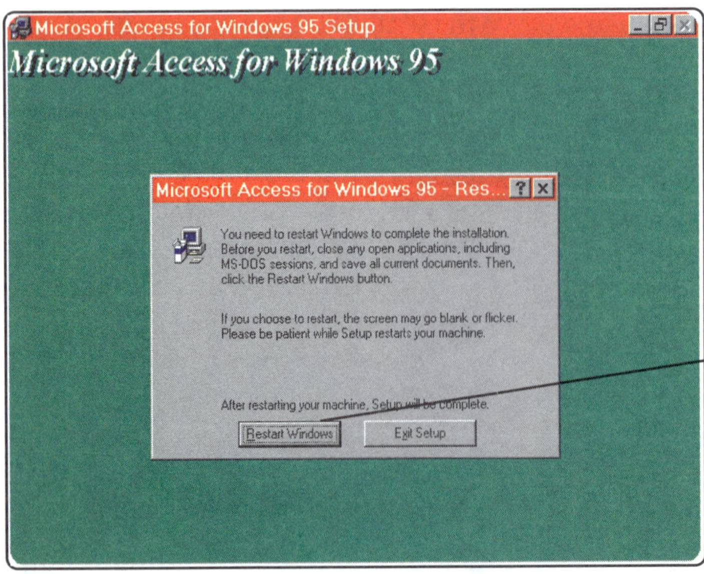

Looks like everything is complete, and you are nearly finished. The Setup program just needs to restart your computer so that the changes it has made to your system can go into effect.

1. **Click** on **Restart Windows.** Windows will shut down, then start up again.

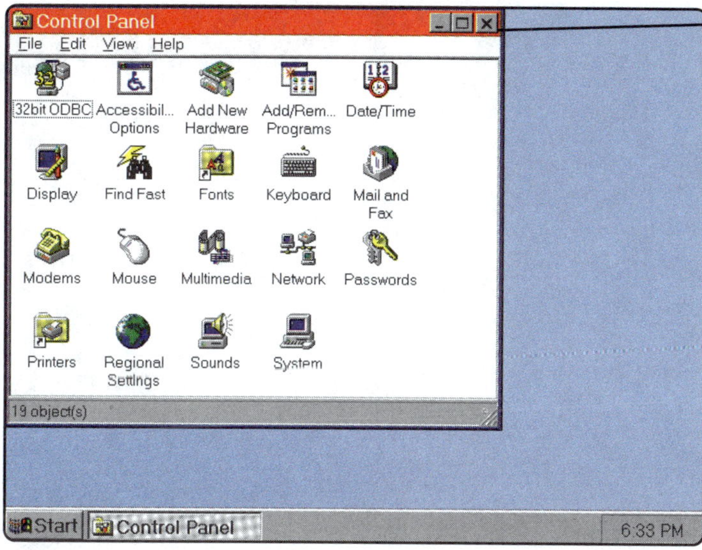

2. **Click** on the **Close button** (☒) on the right side of the program group title bar. The Control Panel window will close.

VIEWING MICROSOFT ACCESS

Now you can explore your new program.

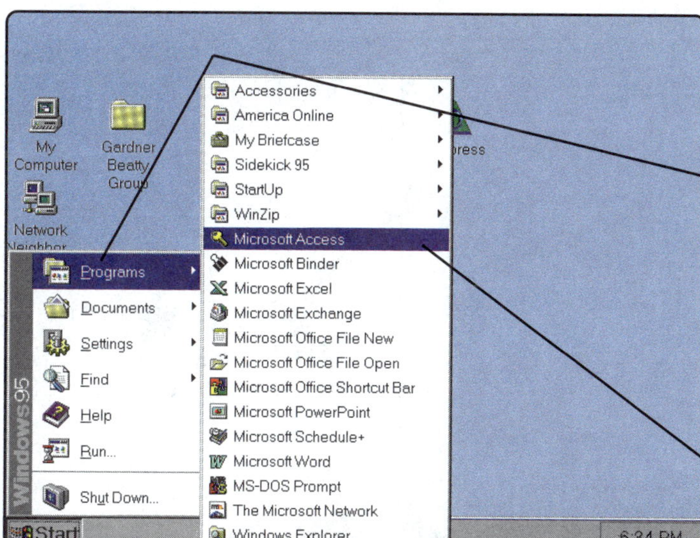

1. **Click** on the **Start button** on the taskbar. A menu will appear.

2. **Move** the **mouse arrow** up the menu to Programs. The Programs menu will appear.

3. **Move** the **mouse arrow** to Microsoft Access.

4. **Click** on **Access** and you will be on your way!

APPENDIX B

Hiding the Taskbar

If you do not want the taskbar showing on your screen all the time, you can hide it from view. This also gives you a little extra screen space for the programs you're using. You can get it back anytime you need it with a simple mouse movement. In this chapter, you will do the following:

- ✔ Hide the taskbar
- ✔ Get the hidden taskbar back

REMOVING THE TASKBAR FROM VIEW

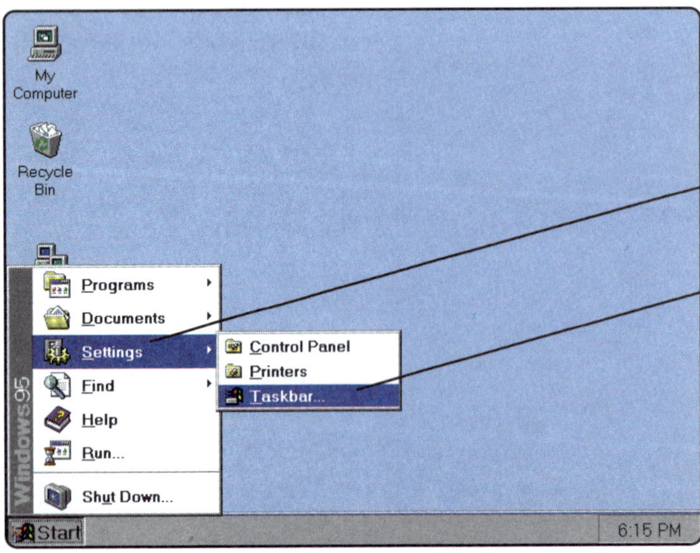

1. **Click** on **Start** in the left corner of the taskbar. A menu will appear.

2. **Click** on **Settings.** Another menu will appear.

3. **Click** on **Taskbar**. The Taskbar Properties dialog box will appear.

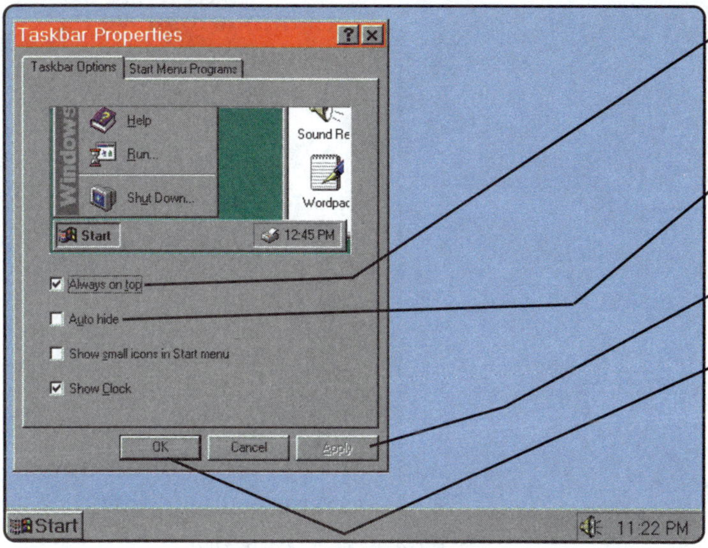

4. **Click** on **Always on top** to put a ✔ in the box if one isn't there already.

5. **Click** on **Auto hide** to put a ✔ in the box.

6. **Click** on **Apply**.

7. **Click on OK**. The dialog box will close. The taskbar will disappear in a moment.

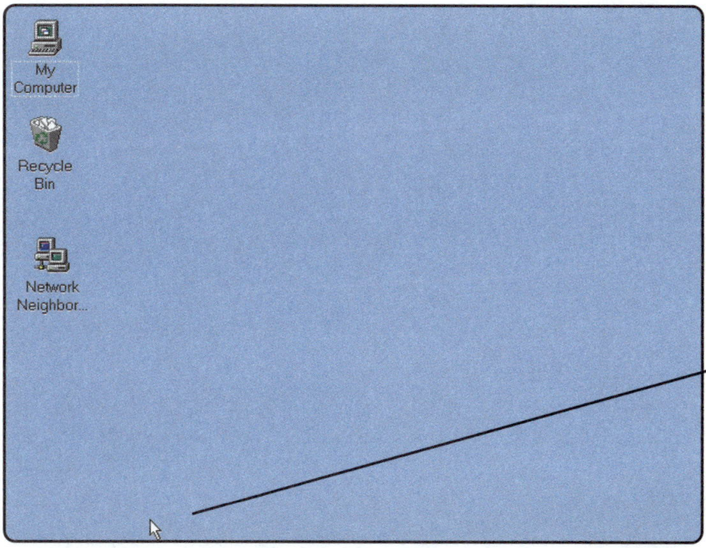

Getting It Back

You can get the taskbar back anytime you want to by a simple mouse movement. You can do this at any time, whether you're running a program or not.

1. **Move** the **mouse arrow** toward the bottom of the desktop.

2. **Continue** to **move** the **mouse arrow** until the taskbar reappears.

Note: To hide the taskbar, simply move the mouse arrow up on the desktop again.

Note: If you want to get the taskbar back permanently, repeat steps 1 to 6 in the first section of this chapter to remove the ✔ from the Auto hide box.

Index

D

E

F

G

H

I

L

M

N

O

P

Q

R

S

T

U

V

W

NOTES

NOTES

NOTES

NOTES

NOTES